A HISTORY OF KABBALAH

This volume offers a narrative history of modern Kabbalah, from the sixteenth century to the present. Covering all subperiods, schools and figures, Jonathan Garb demonstrates how Kabbalah expanded over the last few centuries, and how it became an important player, first in the European then subsequently in global cultural and intellectual domains. Indeed, study of Kabbalah can be found on virtually every continent and in many languages, despite the destruction of many centers in the mid-twentieth century. Garb explores the sociological, psychological, scholastic and ritual dimensions of kabbalistic ways of life in their geographical and cultural contexts. Focusing on several important mystical and literary figures, he shows how modern Kabbalah is deeply embedded in modern Jewish life, yet has become an independent, professionalized subworld. He also traces how Kabbalah was influenced by and contributed to the process of modernization.

Jonathan Garb is the Gershom Scholem Professor of Kabbalah at the Hebrew University of Jerusalem. In 2014, he received the Israel Academy of Sciences and Humanities' Gershom Scholem Prize for Kabbalah Research. His latest books include *Shamanic Trance in Modern Kabbalah* (2011) and *Yearnings of the Soul: Psychological Thought in Modern Kabbalah* (2015).

A History of Kabbalah

From the Early Modern Period to the Present Day

JONATHAN GARB

The Hebrew University of Jerusalem

CAMBRIDGE
UNIVERSITY PRESS

CAMBRIDGE
UNIVERSITY PRESS

Shaftesbury Road, Cambridge CB2 8EA, United Kingdom

One Liberty Plaza, 20th Floor, New York, NY 10006, USA

477 Williamstown Road, Port Melbourne, VIC 3207, Australia

314–321, 3rd Floor, Plot 3, Splendor Forum, Jasola District Centre, New Delhi – 110025, India

103 Penang Road, #05–06/07, Visioncrest Commercial, Singapore 238467

Cambridge University Press is part of Cambridge University Press & Assessment, a department of the University of Cambridge.

We share the University's mission to contribute to society through the pursuit of education, learning and research at the highest international levels of excellence.

www.cambridge.org
Information on this title: www.cambridge.org/9781316607022

DOI: 10.1017/9781316597071

First published 2020
First paperback edition 2023

A catalogue record for this publication is available from the British Library

Library of Congress Cataloging-in-Publication data
NAMES: Garb, Jonathan, author.
TITLE: A history of Kabbalah : from the early modern period to the present day / Jonathan Garb, The Hebrew University of Jerusalem.
DESCRIPTION: Cambridge, United Kingdom ; New York, NY, USA : Cambridge University Press, 2020. | Includes bibliographical references and index.
IDENTIFIERS: LCCN 2020009217 (print) | LCCN 2020009218 (ebook) | ISBN 9781107153134 (hardback) | ISBN 9781316607022 (paperback) | ISBN 9781316607022 (epub)
SUBJECTS: LCSH: Cabala–History. | Hasidism–History.
CLASSIFICATION: LCC BM526 .G3727 2020 (print) | LCC BM526 (ebook) | DDC 296.1/609–dc23
LC record available at https://lccn.loc.gov/2020009217
LC ebook record available at https://lccn.loc.gov/2020009218

ISBN 978-1-107-15313-4 Hardback
ISBN 978-1-316-60702-2 Paperback

For Ronna, who helped me modernize, with old-fashioned love

Contents

Figures

Acknowledgments

My profound thanks to my friends and colleagues, Avishai Bar-Asher, Jeremy Brown, Patrick B. Koch and Judith Weiss, for their learned and helpful comments on drafts of various chapters. My collaboration with Itzhak Melamed toward a history of pantheism offered valuable perspective on this more general history. I gave the book its finishing touches during a highly enjoyable fellowship at the Maimonides Centre for Advanced Studies (Jewish Scepticism) at the University of Hamburg. I am also grateful for the bibliographical assistance provided by Levana Chajes, Noam Lev-El, Tom Parnas and Elhanan Shilo. The vision and openness of Laura Morris in proposing the volume, Beatrice Rehl's dedication to following it through, Eilidh Burrett's gracious support, the attentiveness of Penny Harper and Divya Arjunan to the final crafting of the mansucript and the thoughtful and supportive comments of the outside readers all rendered my work with Cambridge University Press enjoyable and generative.

Introduction

This volume represents the first attempt to provide modern Kabbalah with a comprehensive and autonomous history. It is a good idea to stress at the outset that while Gershom Scholem, a founder of academic research in Jewish mysticism, began his own account of modern Kabbalah with the 1492 expulsion of the Jews from Spain, here we commence (for reasons to be explained in Chapter 1) with the spiritual revolution that took place in the Galilean town of Safed around the mid-sixteenth century. Since this time and even somewhat earlier, Kabbalah has been an important player not only in Jewish history, but also in the cultural and intellectual life of Europe.

It was only in the modern age of print and other forms of rapid communication that Kabbalah became a major factor in Jewish textual, liturgical and ritual life, engendered mass social movements (Sabbateanism, Hasidism and the Zionist school of R. Avraham Itzhak Kook) and also significantly impacted European intellectual life (mostly notably in the case of Baruch Spinoza). Fueled by print and lately digital technology, modern Kabbalah is quantitatively vast (and constantly expanding): the literature composed in various kabbalistic worlds in this period is staggeringly voluminous (rendering any attempt to summarize it in one volume a true challenge). For example, the *Otzar Ha-Hokhma* database (created in recent years in traditional Yeshiva circles in Jerusalem), one of several, contains approximately 10,000 Hasidic books (all modern) and printed works of Kabbalah (almost all modern). On the qualitative level, we are dealing with a highly diverse array of complex theosophical systems, intricate techniques, radical ecstatic and revelatory experiences and intense conflicts (also in scholarship…). All these spread not only throughout Kabbalah's continents of origin, Europe and the Middle East (especially impacting the sociopolitical development of the state of Israel) but also, later, to the Americas (as well as other global locations such as South Africa and India). All of the above processes greatly accelerated in the late modern period and hence my stress on the last two centuries.

Yet surprisingly, there is no scholarly (or even popular or traditional) book on the history of modern Kabbalah. Actually, there is no English-language work on the history of Kabbalah as such.[1] Scholem's canonical *Major Trends in Jewish Mysticism* is explicitly confined to what he himself regarded as the central schools of kabbalistic and pre-kabbalistic Jewish mysticism, mostly premodern (thus, there is virtually no discussion of the nineteenth and twentieth centuries in this 1941 book). Scholem's focus on the late antique, medieval (and at most early modern) periods is in tension with his above-noted emphasis on the very early modern event of the expulsion of the Jews from Spain, as well as his obvious fascination with the seventeenth-century Sabbatean movement and its offshoots.[2] Furthermore, the next generation of phenomenological overviews of prominent kabbalistic themes was also focused mainly on premodern periods (as in the works of Moshe Idel, Elliot Wolfson and Charles Mopsik).[3] This is obviously true of what is perhaps the most successful publishing project in the field, Stanford University Press' multivolume translation of the thirteenth-century classic, the *Zohar*. It is only in recent years that the autonomy of modern Kabbalah and its discontinuities with premodern forms have been increasingly recognized, due mainly to the work of Shaul Magid, Boaz Huss, myself and the new generation of scholars. As a result, we have seen a marked increase in specific studies devoted to modern figures and developments, yet without any attempt at organizing these in an unbroken and comprehensive narrative, which would also include the numerous unresearched (or entirely unstudied, even in traditional circles) centers, figures, texts and trends.

Actually, there are two schools that have captured the popular imagination from the early twentieth century, due to the writing of Scholem and his

[1] The Hebrew-language series on the history of Kabbalah, currently being composed by Joseph Dan, not yet reaching the modern period, frankly has had a very mixed academic reception. One should also note the undergraduate introduction to premodern Kabbalah, soon to be published by the Open University of Israel, and the user-friendly popular introductory work: Giller, *Kabbalah – A Guide for the Perplexed* (focused on the medieval period). One should praise Darmon, *L'Esprit de la Kabbale*, whose brief, mostly thematic history has a strong modern emphasis, addressing less-known corpora. See also Hallamish, *An Introduction to the Kabbalah*.

[2] As recent archival research by Jonatan Meir has revealed, Scholem himself drew up an outline for a project similar to the present one.

[3] See especially the monumental triad: Idel, *Kabbalah – New Perspectives* (later translated into Hebrew); Wolfson, *Language, Eros, Being*; Mopsik, *Les grands textes.*

archrival Martin Buber: the radical Sabbatean movement and the highly colorful Hasidic worlds. More recently, these have been joined by the twentieth-century schools of Kook (due to his remarkable influence on the history of Israel) and R. Yehuda Leib Ashlag (due to his universalistic reading of Kabbalah, facilitating massive popular reception and reworking). However, all of these have been sequestered in discrete conversations, rather than being integrated within the panorama of modern Kabbalah or, more ambitiously, within that of modern intellectual history. In this sense, the present project is complemented by broad studies of modern Judaism, such as those penned by David Ruderman and Leora Batnitsky.

This volume will provide a detailed century-by-century description of the major developments, schools, figures, works and challenges of modern Kabbalah. This narrative format, utilizing the convenient centennial convention (which does not always work neatly in actual practice), facilitates contextualization and dialogue with other fields of research. Yet again, the focus here shall be on the role played by Kabbalah in the development of modern Judaism (with the history of Christian Kabbalah/kabbalistic Christianity and its tributaries assigned a supportive role). The five historical chapters (whose respective length will favor later periods, as indicated above), will be preceded by a chapter explaining the uniqueness of modern Kabbalah and detailing the themes that it carried over from premodern periods. The concluding chapter will trace recurrent topics over the entire modern period, summarizing the differences between subperiods, and briefly pointing at domains for further research. The purpose of this structure is to combine a focus on recent and contemporary developments with long-term historical perspective.

Major scholarly positions and disputes, both early and current, will be extensively addressed, yet interwoven into the discussion of the kabbalistic materials, in order to prioritize the texts themselves. This choice reflects the heavily exegetical nature of kabbalistic discourse (referring both to canonical Jewish sources and, increasingly, to the kabbalistic canons and subcanons), in which the text itself is seen as an embodiment of the divine, with its study being regarded as the quintessential form of world-maintenance and world-enhancement. It can be well argued that this dominance of the text sets Kabbalah apart from most other forms of mysticism (alongside other differences, to be discussed in Chapter 1). Of course, this is not to negate nontextual dimensions of kabbalistic life, whether we are dealing with oral transmission, mystical or magical forms of life and practice or ineffable inner experiences. Nonetheless, unless we are speaking of contemporary or very recent phenomena, we only have access to the para-textual through its recording and preservation in texts.

This text-centered approach is also expressed in numerous, yet concise quotes from striking passages, found in existing translations or first translated here (thus increasing the scope of key texts available to readers in English). While the emphasis shall be on studies available in English, one of the aims of this work is to acquaint readers with the best of scholarly writing in other languages (naturally mostly Hebrew), in all three generations of modern Kabbalah research (the history of which shall be described in its context in Chapter 6, while its present state shall be addressed in Chapter 7). Thus, readers shall be exposed to the current burgeoning of graduate and postgraduate work in the field, alongside a taste of the vast material yet to be researched. Social scientific approaches, particularly sociology and psychology, shall also be engaged in dialogue, in order to explore the nexus of intellectual, cultural and social history (as in the case of formation of elite circles and later of mass movements).

The overall implications of the book include the need to place modern Kabbalah in its own context, thus capturing its autonomy from (yet also continuity with) earlier periods, its dialogue with mystical traditions in other religions, its basic coherence over five centuries and its unique impact on modern culture. It shall be argued that the reflexive nature of modernity carried over into the self-awareness of modern kabbalists (calling for a different toolkit from that employed in the study of medieval Kabbalah). Recurrent themes to be encompassed, century by century and also in tandem, will include: forms of social organization; new genres of writing (especially autobiography and hagiography) and literary style; the impact of print culture; systems of psychological thought; emergent forms of self-cultivation and regimes of ritual and daily life; increased sophistication in the cultivation of meditative or trance states; transformations of discourse on gender and sexuality; the increase of nationalistic discourse; and new ways of interpreting canonical, nonkabbalistic works (such as the Bible and the Talmud), joined by modern Kabbalah's self-interpretation. In sum, the main contributions of the book will be the first-time (in English) comprehensive historical-chronological presentation of kabbalistic literature, combined with a manageable and justifiable focus on the modern period; pioneering exposure to central schools, figures and works; especial treatment of recent and contemporary developments; a coherent account of central recurring themes; placement of the subject in a broader Jewish and extra-Jewish historical context; dialogue with the social sciences; an updated, critical and hopefully nonpartisan history of scholarship in various languages, pointing toward areas for further research.

1

Premodern and Modern Kabbalah

Breaks and Continuities

INTRODUCTION

The premise behind a separate history of modern Kabbalah lies in its autonomy from premodern Kabbalah. This is evident first and foremost on the intrinsic level – the self-consciousness of modern kabbalists and their unique forms of social organization and new genres of writing. Yet this claim also rests on extrinsic factors – the impact of the dramatic changes heralded by Jewish and general modernity. At the same time, autonomy by no means entails independence or isolation, so that the chapter will take up the major themes continuing premodern kabbalistic approaches. These include exegesis of canonical texts (Bible and Talmud), gendered views of the divine world and perceptions of theurgical or magical impact of embodied human action on the supernal and, conversely, the demonic realms. In this context, we shall follow specific historical chains of continuity and examine the changing role of canonical premodern kabbalistic corpora, especially the thirteenth- and fourteenth-century Zoharic literature (composed in Castile, Spain). However, the excessive dominance of the influence of this corpus in existing studies of modern Kabbalah shall be critiqued.

It is well beyond the scope and goals of this work to examine in detail nonkabbalistic premodern influences on modern Kabbalah. These include general (Gnosticism and Neo-Platonism) and Jewish (*Heikhalot*, or chambers of the supernal realm, literature and magical writings) forms of mysticism in late antiquity. These were then joined by medieval phenomena: Jewish (*Hasidut Ashkenaz*, or German Pietism and Judeo-Sufi Pietism and Spanish mystical poetry) and general (Islamic and Christian mysticism). Some of these shall be alluded to throughout, yet strictly when the topic at hand calls for it. It is even less appropriate to do more than mention the complex and contested question of the interrelationship between mythical-mystical sources (Jewish or otherwise) dating to even earlier antiquity (e.g. the period of the Mishna, as in the second chapter of tractate *Hagiga*, Gnostic sources or the corpus of Philo) and the open manifestation of Kabbalah (literally reception of transmission), under that very name, in the Middle Ages.[1] Therefore, this chapter shall focus on modern Kabbalah's dialogue with its immediate predecessor, namely the tradition surfacing or developing, mainly in Southern Europe (Provence, Spain and Italy), between the twelfth and fifteenth centuries. Thus, it should be stressed, it does not purport to provide any history of medieval Kabbalah (though such a volume, placing this lore in its often-neglected historical-geographical context, would be greatly desirable).[2] Rather, it shall provide the modicum of detail necessary for appreciating the prelude to modern Kabbalah, a screenshot, as it were, of the state of affairs at its inception.

THE AUTONOMY OF MODERN KABBALAH

The writings of modern Kabbalah can be readily shown to reflect a strong awareness of its autonomy, on both intrinsic and extrinsic levels.[3] Firstly, kabbalists operating after the sixteenth century were often committed to autobiographical, biographical and hagiographical writing, producing a treasure of 'egodocuments', including diaries and letters.[4] In doing so, they stand in stark contrast to the dearth of personal testimonies in medieval Kabbalah. A major exception to this rule, that of the Spanish mystic R. Abraham Abulafia (1240–c.1291) and his followers, shall be discussed below. Actually, the historical study of premodern Kabbalah is troubled by the opposite tendency, toward pseudo-epigraphy (accompanied by writing in pseudo-Aramaic, imitating the lingua franca of late antiquity) and anonymity. The modern focus on the individual, clearly reflecting wider cultural trends (observable, for example, in sixteenth-century Spanish Christian mysticism), also lent itself to a discourse of much greater intricacy in psychological thought. Here one must mention the modern development

[1] See e.g. Stroumsa, 'A Zoroastrian Origin'; Scholem, *Major Trends*, 22–37; Wolfson, *Through a Speculum*, 33–51; Liebes, *Studies in Jewish Myth*, 1–64; Mopsik, *Les grands textes*, 52–65; Idel, *Ben*, 51–57, 160–164; Schäfer, *Origins of Jewish Mysticism*, esp. 20–25.

[2] For an example of such contextualization (discussing the earliest medieval center of Provence), see Ben-Shalom, *The Jews of Provence*, esp. 565–631.

[3] Garb, *Modern Kabbalah* (which contains a lengthy English abstract).

[4] Chajes, 'Early Modern Jewish Egodocuments'.

of the doctrine of reincarnation, not shared by all medieval kabbalists and in many cases highly esoteric.[5] Not coincidentally, it was in early modernity that the term 'interiority' came into its own.

Secondly, focused as they were on the charisma and mystical-psychological achievement of outstanding individuals (as well as the texts they composed), kabbalists from the sixteenth century onwards tended to cluster in fellowships or fraternities, again reflecting wider developments in the social structure of religion (especially apparent in the Catholic revival, aka Counter-Reformation, as well as the institutionalization of Sufi fraternities under the resurgent Ottoman Empire). While in the case of medieval Kabbalah we have often-vague scholarly discourse on circles and at best conjectures (based on literary analysis) as to interactions within alleged fellowships, in the case of modern kabbalists we have actual contracts enumerating the members of the fraternities and detailing their obligations and the goals and shared rites of the group.[6] Furthermore, the dominant medieval esoteric stance (in both mystical and philosophical circles), often extending to one-to-one oral transmission, mitigated against the development of larger groups.[7]

To wrap up our discussion of intrinsic factors, it should be stressed that modern kabbalists were keenly aware of both the innovative nature of their writing and practice and its divergence from earlier systems. Thus, they betray a strong sense of placement in specific generations. This self-perception joined an ideology of aggressive proliferation, often justified by that very generational situation. This combined set of beliefs powerfully breached the strong esotericist barriers erected by medieval kabbalists.[8] Although the new technology of print played an obvious role here, one should not ignore the even stronger effect of messianic hopes placed on the spread of Kabbalah (and underpinning the sense of the exceptional status of 'later generations'). It is no coincidence that it was only in the modern period that Kabbalah generated mass social movements, often of a messianic nature. It is also no coincidence at all that it was only in the Renaissance and in the modern period that Kabbalah significantly impacted the non-Jewish

[5] The most extensive development of this is in the writings of the radical R. Yosef ben Shalom Ashkenazi, who was loosely affiliated with R. David ben Yehuda he-Hasid (to be discussed below). Ashkenazi viewed reincarnation as a cosmic imperative, undergone by all beings, from the *sefirot* to the inanimate.

[6] Garb, *Modern Kabbalah*, 16, n. 15; Abrams, *Kabbalistic Manuscripts*, 409–415.

[7] Wolfson, 'Beyond the Spoken Word'; Wolfson, 'Circumcision'; Wolfson, 'Murmuring Secrets'.

[8] Halbertal, *Concealment and Revelation*, 140–141. Cf. Wolfson, 'Review'.

world. As we shall see, most of modernity also witnessed the almost unchallenged sway of Kabbalah over large areas of Jewish life, including Halakha, exegesis, liturgy and custom.[9] This process accompanied the gradual yet clear reduction in interest in philosophy, again in contradistinction from medieval Kabbalah (which engaged in a complex dialogue with this literature).[10]

As intimated just now, none of these processes can be detached from the powerful and constantly accelerating impact of European, Near Eastern and later global modernity on the Jewish world and its surroundings. The claim that modern Kabbalah constitutes an autonomous domain rests on the statements of many modern kabbalists (rather than being merely a scholarly conjecture). These writers responded in increasing detail to new technologies, geopolitical shifts, reformation and secularization and later to dramatic events such as the Chmielnicki massacres, the Holocaust and the formation of the state of Israel. Consequently, we shall not be surprised to encounter the explicit phrases 'us moderns', or 'modern kabbalists', usually coined in European languages. In this linguistic context one should note the importance of Jewish languages that largely developed in the modern period, most importantly Yiddish, yet also the Judaeo-Spanish or Ladino of the Spanish Diaspora, for the popular reach of Kabbalah. This vernacular development accompanied the decline in command of languages such as classical Arabic or Latin, both foundational for philosophical discourse in medieval Jewry. This shift also reflects a final extrinsic factor, the relocation of the Jewish and thus kabbalist center of gravity, from southwest Europe and northwest Africa eastwards and northwards, alongside with massive demographic expansion in these new regions. Cumulatively, geopolitical and individual (or micro-sociological) forms of awareness coupled in making modern kabbalists far more aware of their regional identities.

CONTINUITIES: EXEGESIS, GENDER, THEURGY AND MAGIC

Attempting to summarize the shared body of knowledge and practice that modern kabbalists inherited requires both massive simplification and a conscious avoidance of some scholarly schemata often used to describe premodern Kabbalah. The latter actually preserved its place of pride in writing and teaching, contributing to blanket assumptions of continuity with

9 For rare medieval critiques of Kabbalah, see Ravitzky, *Maimonidean Essays*, 181–204.

10 Huss, 'Mysticism versus Philosophy' (and the case study: Vajda, 'L'histoire du conflit entre la Kabbale et la Philosophie').

modern developments rather than examining it case by case. For instance, we shall not enter the knotty question of the validity of the Scholemian distinction (greatly developed by Idel) between the mainstream (often Zoharic) theosophical-theurgical and the ecstatic or prophetic Kabbalah associated with Abulafia.[11] Rather, this chapter will focus on four main themes that can be broadly claimed to encompass the various schools and concerns of medieval Kabbalah, all of which had continuous impact on its later forms. Some of these also markedly differentiate Kabbalah as a whole (to the extent that such an essentialist designation is viable) from the other major forms of Western mysticism.[12] Yet it is crucial to remember that even within these four centuries of medieval Kabbalah, one can discern various ruptures and divergences (also between geographical centers) which shall not concern us in this deliberately brief chapter.

The most obvious and enduring of continuous themes is the commitment to interpretation of sacral texts dating from antiquity. First and foremost amongst these we have the Hebrew Bible (which is of course a shared exegetical interest with Christian mysticism), especially the creation account in Genesis, the vision of the prophet Ezekiel (in the first chapter of the book of Ezekiel) and the Song of Songs. Kabbalistic exegetical concerns also gradually extended to Talmudic-Midrashic literature (mostly the *Mishna*, the cosmologically oriented Midrash Genesis Rabbah and the *Aggadic* portions of the Babylonian Talmud) and also encompassed the liturgy, as well as the enigmatic treatise (of debatable provenance), couched in cosmology, linguistic and anatomical terms, known as *Sefer Yetzira* (Book of Creation or Formation).[13] The assumption shared by virtually all kabbalists is that these texts contain a hidden, esoteric, sublime level, exposable by means of a host of new hermeneutical methods, including symbolism, inspiration gained in pneumatic or ecstatic states of consciousness, automatic writing and especially methods pertaining to the Hebrew language in which the great majority of the texts were composed.[14] The core belief here, again strongly consensual, is that this language is sacral, perhaps predating creation, rather than conventional.

[11] Scholem, *Major Trends*, 124, 145; Idel, *Kabbalah: New Perspectives*, xi–xix, 260–261; Wolfson, *Abraham Abulafia*, 94–134; Pedaya, *Vision and Speech*, esp. 135–136, 204–205.

[12] Cf. Wolfson, 'Structure, Innovation'; Huss, *The Existence of Jewish Mysticism*, 77–89, 93–95.

[13] Liebes, *Ars Poetica*, emphasizes continuity in reception of this treatise.

[14] Goldreich, *Automatic Writing*. Symbolism occupies a major place in the Scholemian interpretation of Kabbalah, yet this stress has been significantly modulated subsequently, esp. by Idel (see e.g. *Absorbing Perfections*, 272–313).

Prominent amongst the latter were techniques (also in the sense of aids for attaining mystical experiences), mostly originating in prekabbalistic German Pietism. These included recombinations of the letters, contemplation of their shape and composition (at times invoking parallels to the human form), as well as *gematria* (calculation of their numerical value). This linguistic speculation extended to discussions of the theosophical meaning of the vowels (which are separate from the letters in Hebrew) and the *te'amim*, or musical accents with which the Torah is ritually chanted in the synagogue.[15] Above all, kabbalists of various schools and periods shared the belief in the centrality of the divine names (a theme with clear Islamic parallels), especially the Tetragammaton.[16] Often, these linguistic concerns eclipsed the better-known visual imagery of the *sefirot* (to be described shortly), although much attention was given to parallels between the two systems. At the same time, numerous texts (especially within the above-mentioned Zoharic corpus but also reflecting Ashkenazic influences) assume that the key to penetrating the secret layer of the text lies in visionary experience:

> The Holy One blessed be He, enters all the hidden things that He has made into the Holy Torah . . . The Torah reveals that hidden thing and then it is immediately clothed in another garment, where it is hidden . . . and even though that thing is hidden in its garment, the sages, who are full of eyes, see it from within its garment. When that thing is revealed, before it enters into a garment, they cast an open eye on it, and even though [the thing] is immediately concealed, it does not depart from their eyes.[17]

The ongoing commitment to earlier corpora also entails the development of two themes central in virtually all of those.[18] The first of these is a linear historical narrative, blended (as is to be expected) with strong mythic images. Its span reaches from the creation and its nebulous origins, through the fall of Adam, the ancestral founders of Jewish nationhood and the Exodus, to the kingdom (especially that of David) and temple, through their destruction, and then through the Diaspora and its trials to the messianic

[15] See e.g. Abrams, 'From Germany to Spain'. For the complex question of the interrelationship between Ashkenazi mysticism, such as German Pietism, and Kabbalah, see e.g. Idel, 'Some Forlorn Writings', esp. 196.

[16] See Ben Sasson, *YHWH*, esp. 171–237.

[17] *Zohar*, vol. II, 98B, translated and discussed in Wolfson, *Through a Speculum*, 384–385 (see also 355).

[18] Though *Sefer Yetzira* is a seeming exception to this rule on both counts; see Meroz, 'Interreligious Polemics'.

redemption.[19] This historical, Bible-centered scheme should be contrasted to kabbalistic beliefs in large, recurring cosmic cycles of *shemitot* (sabbaticals) and *yovlim* (jubilees), of thousands and myriads of years. Although such views, relativizing both biblical history and its accompanying nomos, enjoyed some popularity (especially in the Byzantine areas in the fourteenth century), they were largely rejected in modern Kabbalah.[20] In this case of the cyclical macro-historical theory, one should note Islamic (in this case *Isma'ilic*) influence.[21]

The more common Bible-centered narrative of collective history joined a keen interest in personal soteriology (including the benefits of Kabbalah study itself for the afterlife). These sets of images focused on general themes of Jewish and indeed Western religiosity, including Paradise, Hell, the resurrection and 'the world to come' in general (on reincarnation, see above).[22] An associated concern, fueled by dialogue with Neo-Platonic and Aristotelian views, was with the origin, nature and destiny of the individual soul, at times conceived of as divine.[23] These deliberations were in turn part of wider concern with the self and self-knowledge, at times echoing contemporary philosophical argumentation.[24] The psychological and the hermeneutical impulses merged in the notion, most developed in the *Zohar*, that the Kabbalah represents the 'soul of the Torah', at times abrogating its plain sense, or *pshat*.[25] In other formulations, the *pshat* is the lowest rung of a quadruple hierarchy (known by its acronym *PARDES*), ascending through *drash*, or homily, *remez*, or hint (usually numerical) toward *sod*, or secret.[26]

The second and closely related concern is with the Law and its commandments (especially prayer), as well as the later overlay of Talmudic and indeed medieval decrees and customs.[27] Reflecting the keen interest in the temple extant in several kabbalistic circles, the kabbalistic rationales for the

[19] On Jewish myth and messianism (also in relation to theurgy), see e.g. Liebes, *Studies in the Zohar*, esp. 52–71; Dan, 'The Emergence of Messianic Mythology'; Fishbane, *Biblical Myth*, 256–305.

[20] Scholem, *On the Kabbalah*, 77–86; Pedaya, *Nahmanides*, esp. 233–273; Ogren, *The Beginning of the World* (as well as Chapter 2). On Byzantine Kabbalah, its sources and influence on early modern Kabbalah, see Idel, 'The Kabbalah in Byzantium', esp. 685–688, 694–701.

[21] Krinis, 'Cyclical Time'.

[22] See e.g. Bar-Asher, *Journeys of the Soul*; Weiss, 'Two Zoharic Versions'.

[23] See e.g. the commentary by Nahmanides on Genesis 2, 7.

[24] Altmann, *Studies in Religious Philosophy and Mysticism*, 1–40.

[25] Scholem, *On the Kabbalah*, 36, 63–64, and cf. Wolfson, *Luminous Darkness*, 56–96.

[26] On the *PARDES* method and its possible Christian sources, see Van der Heide, 'PARDES'. Based on a mystical tale found already in the Talmud, the term *Pardes* (translated as orchard) also refers to a realm of visionary experience.

[27] Matt, 'The Mystic and the Mitzvot'; Mottolese, *Bodily Rituals*.

commandments included the sacrificial rite (as well as other obsolete laws such as Levirate marriage). One can discern an especial effort to provide explanations for those commandments, such as the biblical laws of kosher nutrition, whose benefit is not self-evident. At times, the kosher diet was depicted as a regimen for facilitating mystical union with God (see anon on medical discourse in medieval Kabbalah):

> We have been commanded to seek union in Him . . . Now it is manifestly evident that the meaning here is not a corporeal joining but rather a joining of spirit. Furthermore, any thoughtful person understands that when the soul is united with the Creator all bodily sensations are eliminated such that it has no need for food nor drink nor any other bodily need. His limbs will be inactive and the food already in his stomach will be preserved so that he lose nothing because of the energy expended while he is united with Him to the extent that his intellect reaches in union with Him. And when his energy for union is expended, the soul awakens easily and quickly to bodily sensations like a slumbering individual awakened from his sleep . . . Therefore, when one is about to leave his senses, if he were to eat impure food – which, according to the medical experts, causes illness – there is no doubt that he would incur sickness.[28]

One of the most prominent junctures of these two themes of law and temporality was sacral time – the Sabbath (commemorating Creation, Exodus and Redemption) and the festivals (molded by the Talmud around sacral history).[29] However, at times the temporal discourses surrounding the messianic redemption at 'the end of time' created tensions with the Law, as utopian visions often slid into antinomian or hyper-nomian views (similarly to what we have just seen with regard to abrogation of the *pshat*).[30] A second juncture of history and law was that of sacral space, as in theosophical and mystical statements on the significance of the Land of Israel, Jerusalem and the Temple (and its sacrificial rites), as paralleling divine aspects.[31] In many cases, the performance of the Law was seen as ad-hoc sanctification of space by human action. An illustration of this theme can be seen in the Zoharic interpretation of the rite of the *sukka*, or week-long dwelling in a temporary

[28] Ya'akov ben Sheshet, *Meshiv Devraim Nekokhim*, translated in Dan (ed.), *The Early Kabbalah*, 143.

[29] On time in Kabbalah see Ogren (ed.), *Before and After*. On the Sabbath, see Ginsburg, *The Sabbath*.

[30] See Scholem, *The Messianic Idea*, 22–24, 40, 68–71; Wolfson, *Venturing Beyond*, 228–236, 266–277.

[31] Idel, 'On Jerusalem'; Mottolese, *Analogy in Midrash and Kabbalah*; Pedaya, *Name and Sanctuary*, esp. 34–35, 69–72, 154–177, 200–207.

booth during the Feast of Tabernacles. For the *Zohar*, the *sukka* becomes a receptacle for the *ushpizin* (guests), the invoked souls of the hallowed figures of the Jewish past (starting with the three forefathers, Abraham, Isaac and Jacob), who, as is often the case, parallel theosophical levels (to be described shortly).[32] Here nomian, spatial, psychological and historical discursive practices converged, and such convergences contributed to both the complexity and success of medieval Kabbalah.

The main tool for reinterpretation of the biblical narrative was theosophy, based on the core scheme of ten *sefirot*, taking the shape of a display of lights (often in color), a cosmic tree, the human body, an aquatic flow from fountains to wells or geometrical patterns, especially *mandala*-like circles.[33] This list should already indicate that the study of the *sefirot* (and other theosophical structures) was not merely theoretical lore, but rather often entailed practices of meditation, trance and contemplation, ascent, visualization, dream-work, etc.[34] At the same time, one must stress that the technical elaboration in medieval Kabbalah is often rudimentary compared to later developments (Abulafian Kabbalah again serving as the exception that proves the rule).

The nature of the *sefirot* (and thus the very meaning of the term) was debatable. Even within a single text, they could variously refer to divine attributes, potencies or emanations, nondivine vessels or tools for creation and maintenance of the world, or merely psychic attributes or traits.[35] The origin of the concept of the *sefirot* is also unclear: the term itself is found in *Sefer Yetzira*, but this short and cryptic text does not give us the list of their names (that are largely derived from the statement on the 'ten things with which the world was created' by the Talmudic sage Rav in Hagiga 12A), nor their interrelationships. The diachronic development of the doctrine of the *sefirot* (as in its evolution out of angelology or out of earlier and simpler binary views of the divine realm) shall not be addressed here, but rather the general form in which it reached modern Kabbalah. Though the exact structure of the *sefirotic* system was the subject of an entire genre of lists

[32] See e.g. *Zohar*, vol. III, 103B–104A.

[33] For representative texts, see Matt (ed.),*The Essential Kabbalah*, 38–39.

[34] On premodern kabbalistic dream-work, see Idel, *Les Kabbalistes de la nuit*, 12–28; Wolfson, *A Dream Interpreted*, esp. 159–168, 189–193, 244–257. For ascent, see Idel, *Ascensions on High*, esp. 41–45. On kabbalistic meditation, see Verman, *The History and Varieties of Jewish Meditation*, esp. 81–83, 187–188, 199–210. On contemplation, see Fishbane, *As Light before Dawn*, 178–247; Pedaya, *Vision and Speech*, esp. 137–171; Porat, 'A Peace without Interruption'.

[35] See Idel, *Kabbalah: New Perspectives*, 136–153.

and 'commentaries', containing numerous alternative forms of organization, modern kabbalists already largely worked with the scheme that shall now be presented. In terms of a single text, the *locus classicus* is the 'opening' to *Tikkunei Zohar* (see below on this fourteenth-century Spanish work), attributed to the prophet Elijah (and recited, mostly by Sephardim, before the daily afternoon prayer):[36]

> Elijah began to praise God saying: Lord of the universe! You are One but are not numbered . . . It is you who produced the Ten Perfections which we call the Ten *Sefirot*. With them you guide the secret worlds which have not been revealed and the worlds which have been revealed, and in them you conceal yourself from human beings . . . This is the order they follow: *Hesed* (Lovingkindness) is the right arm; *Gevurah* (Power) is the left arm; *Tiferet* (Beauty) the torso; *Netzah* (Victory) and *Hod* (Splendor) the two legs; *Yesod* (Foundation) the extremity of the body, the holy sign of the covenant [Circumcision]; *Malkhut* (Sovereignty) the mouth, which we call the Oral Law. The brain is *Hokhmah* (Wisdom), the inner thoughts. *Binah* (Understanding) is in the heart . . .The elevated *Keter* (Crown) is the Crown of Sovereignty . . . It is the skull upon which the *Tefilin* are placed. From within it is *yod, hé, vav, hé* [The Tetragammaton], which is the way of emanation. It provides the water for the tree, its arms and branches.[37]

However, in terms of a single volume, the doctrine of the *sefirot* is most succinctly, influentially and eloquently presented (mostly through creative exegesis of biblical verses and their Midrashic elaborations) in *Sh'arei Orah* (Gates of Light) by R. Yosef Gikatilla (1248–c.1325).[38] The *sefirot* are usually depicted as a set of three triads, with a somewhat separate lowest aspect paralleling the divine immanence in the lower world, *Shekhina* in rabbinical parlance. In some formulations, the *Shekhina* is identified with the totality of the Jewish people, or its supernal source.[39] Though the triads are sometimes pictured in sequential descending order, they are most often arranged in three horizontal lines, each consisting of three triads, with one placed on the left, one on the right and one in the center (as alluded to in the text just

[36] As we shall soon see again, recourse to the figure of the prophets, just like the very aspiration to prophetic inspiration, was not restricted to prophetic Kabbalah.

[37] Translated and annotated in Jacobs (ed.), *Jewish Ethics, Philosophy and Mysticism*, 115–118.

[38] On this foundational work, see Morlok, *Rabbi Joseph Gikatilla's Hermeneutics*. One should note the near-absence of the term *sefirot* itself in the bulk of Zoharic literature, a fact that should caution against a facile presentation of this corpus as the ultimate representation of medieval Kabbalah.

[39] Scholem, *On the Mystical Shape*, 140–196; Weiss, *Cutting the Shoots.*

quoted).[40] This highest set of *sefirot* almost invariably includes *Hokhma*, higher on the right (perhaps a residue of antique images of *Sophia*, with roots reaching back as far as Biblical Wisdom Literature) and *Binah*, lower on the left. This intellectual pair is balanced or crowned according to some systems by the higher aspect of the *Keter*. In resonance with contemporary developments in the Christian world, this aspect was often associated with volition (or will, with an affective overtone). Its depiction in many texts draws on earlier myths of the ascent or restoration of the divine crown. Thus, due to the circular nature often attributed to the *sefirotic* system, *Keter* as crown was often depicted (e.g. later in the source just quoted) as closely linked to *Malkhut* (translated here as kingship).[41] More philosophically oriented views identified *Keter* with nothingness (with *Hokhma* then referring to the beginnings of being), or in alternative, Aristotelian terms, with the 'cause of causes'.[42] Another option for counting ten *sefirot* (especially if *Keter*, as nothingness, was identified with *Ein-Sof*, or the infinite aspect usually seen as preceding the *sefirot*) was a lower aspect, known as *Da'at*, literally knowledge, yet at times with connotations of intuition or adherence (as in Genesis 4, 1).

The second triad is comprised of *Hesed* on the right, and a leftward aspect known variously as *Gevura*, *Din* (judgment), *Pahad* (fear). For this triad the balancing force is known as *Tiferet* (also translatable as splendor), yet often rendered as *Rahamim*, or mercy. While the first triad is intellectual or at least cognitive, the second one is obviously emotional. Frequently, kabbalistic exegetes anchored this set in the biblical narrative through a parallel to the three mythic ancestors of the Jewish people. While even *Hokhma* and *Bina*, and certainly *Hesed* and *Gevura* usually had some gendered associations (male and female respectively), *Tiferet* is most frequently associated with the male aspect of divinity.[43]

The final triad is somewhat less clear in its nature and structure. On the right and left we have two rather similar entities, known as *Netzah* (also translatable as eternity) and *Hod*. At times these are associated with the

[40] For the pictorial world of medieval Kabbalah, also in relationship to *Sefer Yetzira*, see Busi, *La Qabbalah Visiva*; Segol, *Word and Image*. A large volume on this topic by J. H. Chajes is currently in preparation.

[41] Green, *Keter*, 148–156.

[42] Matt, "Ayin'. At times (e.g. in *Tikkunei Zohar*), *Keter* is differentiated from 'the cause of causes', which presumably reflects an even higher level. This relates to the extensive medieval discussion of whether *Keter* and *Ein-Sof* are identical.

[43] On left/right and gender symbolism in premodern Kabbalah, see Wolfson, *Luminal Darkness*, 1–28.

biblical figures of the prophets. As we have just seen, the mediating aspect, *Yesod*, is clearly gendered in blatantly phallic terms, but is also frequently identified with the archetypal figure of the *tzaddik*, or righteous man (represented in the Bible by Joseph).[44] Indeed, the lowest set is often imagined in terms of pillars, providing a base for the entire structure. This architectonic imagery was conducive for parallels to the structure of the temple. Approaching the end of the medieval period, writers such as R. David ben Yehuda ha-Hassid (thirteenth-fourteenth century) developed hologramic notions, in which each *sefira* is further subdivided into ten *sefirot* (as well as expanding earlier images of 'the *sefirot* above the *sefirot*').[45] These diagrammatically depicted schemes joined his presentation of the supernal world in the form of *Mandala*-like circles.[46] Overall, the hierarchical, top-to-bottom structure of the *sefirot* was not merely a static set of forms. Rather, in a manner highly conducive to the theurgical discourse to be described soon, the *sefirot* were vividly portrayed (by Gikatilla and others), in terms of emanatory movement, from the creator or the infinite, toward increasingly tangible aspects in reality, reaching toward contact with the material realm. In this context, one should note the predilection of many medieval kabbalists for the spiritual over the material (to be somewhat mitigated amongst the moderns). In many cases (as in the possible interchangeability of *Keter* and *Malkhut*) there is also a theurgically beneficial returning direction upwards. In this sense, though this needs to be proven text by text, it is correct to say that medieval Kabbalah was influenced by Neo-Platonism (also in its Arabic forms) somewhat more than by Aristotelian thought.[47]

It must be said that the *sefirotic* system was far from the only theosophical or cosmological structure at large: as alluded to above, in numerous schemes, the *sefirot* are preceded by a formless and relatively monistic divine aspect known as *Ein-Sof*.[48] Other systems developed the structure of thirty-two paths of wisdom found in *Sefer Yetzira*, the system of supernal *Heikhalot* and exegesis of the Divine Chariot (as in Ezekiel 1), found in the earlier literatures bearing these names, hierarchies of angels found in these and other earlier literatures (especially German Pietism), or the Talmudic-Midrashic notion of fifty gates of *Binah* (understanding). Yet another rabbinic heritage that enjoyed substantial embellishment was that of the thirteen

44 Scholem, *On the Mystical Shape*, 88–139.

45 Idel, 'The Image of Man above the Sefirot'; Matt, 'David ben Yehudah Hehasid'.

46 For the comparison to the *Mandala* (popularized in the twentieth century by writers such as Carl Jung as a cross-cultural phenomenological-psychological symbol), see Idel, e.g. *Kabbalah: New Perspectives*, 105–110 (also discussing influences on modern Kabbalah).

47 Scholem, *Kabbalah*, 44–53.

48 Valabregue-Perry, *Concealed and Revealed.*

middot rahamim (measures or attributes of divine mercy). This system inspired discussions of the refinement of human *middot*, in the sense of emotional-behavioral traits. These texts joined the nascent kabbalistic branch of *Musar*, or self-improvement literature.[49] The system of four worlds (emanation or divine, creation or super-angelic, formation or angelic and action or material) acquired a substantial presence from the fourteenth century onwards, joining earlier speculations on the classical four material elements (earth, fire, water and wind), as well as more complex schemes assuming a plurality of worlds. At times, the quadruple system took an antinomian slant. This is obviously the case for the early fourteenth-century anonymous Castilian work *Tikunei Zohar* (Emendations of the Zohar) that claims that the messianic Torah of *Atzilut* (emanation) is superior to the present Law.[50] These and other refinements of the basic *sefirotic* scheme later assisted modern kabbalists in moving steadily toward ever more complex structures. However, as late as the twentieth century, a work based entirely on modern premises (by R. Yehuda Leib Ashlag), was entitled *Talmud 'Eser Sefirot* (The Study of the Ten *Sefirot*), attesting to the endurance of this scheme, at least in nomenclature.

For most medieval kabbalists, theosophy usually closely accompanied theurgy (defined in Kabbalah scholarship as action affecting the divine realm), due to the above-stressed focus on ritual performance.[51] The guiding assumption, probably developing some Talmudic-Midrashic views, was that the human body and the physical world, and especially sacralized objects (such as *tefilin*, phylacteries or *mezuzot*, placed on doorposts), were structurally isomorphic with the world of the *sefirot*.[52] As a result, actions taken in the material world, especially by means of the human body, can enhance, empower, modulate, balance, unify, safeguard and maintain the supernal realm. One variant of these schemes, alluded to just now, is the possibility of causing the restorative ascent of various levels (such as *Keter*) to their proper location. One possible outcome is an overflow of vitality, power and sustenance back to the material realm, and especially to the practitioner and his (on gender roles see below) environment.[53] The need for human action is implicit in structural tensions within the divine realm, as between right and left, higher and lower and especially male and female.

49 Dan, *History of Jewish Mysticism*, vol. VIII, 13–14, 28–32; vol. IX, 449–451.
50 Giller, *The Enlightened Will Shine*, 59–79.
51 Idel, *Kabbalah: New Perspectives*, 173–199; Mopsik, *Les grands textes*, esp. 642–647.
52 Lorberbaum, *In God's Image*, esp. 57, 96–99.
53 Garb, *Manifestations of Power*, esp. 72–136.

In formulations found in twelfth-century Provencal Kabbalah (especially the cryptic writings of R. Itzhak the Blind), these tensions are described as creating events of displacement, falling, rupture and even shattering.[54] These were perceived as being exacerbated by human sin (as in violation of the 'negative commandments' of the Law, especially those pertaining to sexuality and non-Kosher food).[55] As result of such traumas and fissures (as well as the constant potential of seepage from the divine flow to the lowest reaches of material world), the potencies of evil (at times personified as Satan, or as a gendered couple of *Samael* and *Lilith*) were a constant looming threat for many medieval kabbalists, possibly reflecting Gnostic or Iranian influences.[56] The clash with the offspring of the male and female powers of evil is often described in terms of cosmic warfare.[57] At times the demonic world was imagined as the *Sitra Ahra* (Other Side) paralleling the *sefirotic* structure (including its gendered aspects), 'as a monkey imitates a human'.[58] An alternative, rather alchemical image is that of the dross created by the fiery processes of *Gevura*, similar to the image of the dregs of wine.[59] Yet a third set of images, drawing (as often) on the botanical realm, referred to evil as the *qelipa* (husk or shell) surrounding the fruit.[60] Especially in those sections of the *Zohar* with most influence in modernity, the *Idrot* (assemblies, framed as dramatic accounts of special theurgically oriented gatherings), we find the idea of a primal world, whose 'death' or destruction is the source of evil and whose rectification (or enhancement), while being the charge of the kabbalists, was commenced by the emanator himself:

> It has been taught – mysteries of mysteries: when Rabbi Shim'on opened, the earth quaked and the companions trembled: He revealed in mystery and opened, saying, 'These are the kings who reigned in the land of Edom before a king reigned over the children of Israel (Genesis 36:31) . . . who will examine this? who will be worthy of this? . . . May the prayer be accepted, that it may not be considered a sin to reveal this . . .
>
> It has been taught: Before the Ancient of Ancients, Concealed of the Concealed had prepared adornments of the King and crowns of crowns,

[54] Pedaya, *Name and Sanctuary*, esp. 198–200, 242–245.

[55] Negative theurgy is addressed in the current project of Leore Sacks-Shmueli. See for now her 'Castilian Debate'.

[56] Scholem, *On the Mystical Shape*, 56–82; Dan, *History of Jewish Mysticism*, vol. VII, esp. 200–218; vol. IX, 87–124, 163–191; Idel, *Il male primordiale*, esp. 61–115.

[57] See e.g. Dan (ed.), *The Early Kabbalah*, 171–180.

[58] This striking term originated in Talmudic literature. See e.g. Baba Batra 58A. The notion of a parallel, 'left-handed', world of evil was especially developed by R. Itzhak Kohen and his student R. Moshe of Burgos, in thirteenth-century Castile.

[59] Tishby, *The Wisdom of the Zohar*, vol. II, 496.

[60] Farber-Ginat, 'Husk Precedes Fruit'.

> there was neither beginning nor end. He engraved and gauged within Himself, and spread before Himself one curtain, in which He engraved and gauged kings, but his adornments did not endure... All those who had been engraved were called by name, but they did not endure, so that eventually he put them aside and concealed them. Afterward, he ascended in that curtain and was arrayed perfectly... for until He himself was arrayed in His enhancements, all those that he intended to arrange did not endure and all those worlds were destroyed.[61]

The theurgical-ritual focus on the body was closely linked to views of gender and sexuality. Elliot Wolfson has demonstrated that in numerous and foundational texts, the body in question is the male, Jewish, circumcised one. This fact is not surprising, as the entirety of medieval kabbalistic texts were composed by and for men, who were exclusively charged with the great majority of the ritual and liturgy (all of these sociocultural divisions of labor continuing well into the modern period). In these formulations, the goal of theurgical practice is the eventual inclusion of the female aspect within the supernal entities paralleling the phallus or the male body. Interpretations of the commandments and sacral time, as well as one of the most central hermeneutical projects – the mystical exegesis of the Song of Songs – were informed by this phallocentric worldview.[62] Indeed, the hermeneutical process itself, accompanied by experiences of visionary revelation, was at times imagined as a reenactment of circumcision.[63] At the same time, one can also find an intensive theosophical concern with the female genitalia, accompanied by a vivid discourse on the theurgical impact of awakening female sexual desire, as well as theurgical operations designed to elevate the feminine to a higher, even superior position.[64] The somatic concern of medieval Kabbalah, like the above-mentioned psychological concern with the soul and the spirit, also expressed (as in the above-discussed case of cosmology) a certain dialogue with medical theory and other forms of premodern scientific thinking.[65] The marked interest in the act of eating joined this somatic concern, while also expressing a strong tendency in Jewish culture in general.[66] As in the

[61] *Zohar: Pritzker Edition* (trans. and commentary D. Matt), vol. VIII, 325–326, 380.
[62] Wolfson, *Language, Eros, Being*, esp. 142–189, 333–371; Wolfson, *Luminal Darkness*, 144–227; Wolfson, 'Woman'.
[63] Wolfson, *Circle in the Square*, 29–48.
[64] Abrams, *The Female Body of God*, 45–68; Idel, *The Privileged Divine Feminine*, esp. 63–64.
[65] Tirosh-Samuelson, 'Kabbalah and Science', esp. 495–500; Freudenthal, 'The Kabbalist R. Jacob ben Sheshet of Gerona'.
[66] Hecker, *Mystical Bodies, Mystical Meals* and compare to Bynum, *Holy Feast and Holy Fast*, esp. 150–186.

contemporaneous Christian case, this interest did not preclude the constant surfacing of ascetic strains, often reflecting the influence of German Pietism and especially evident in discussions of *teshuva*, or repentance.[67]

In close proximity to theurgy, some schools of Kabbalah absorbed magical notions and practices from both antique sources and contemporary surroundings. Amongst these one should stress manipulations of language (similar to those mentioned above, in the context of hermeneutics), adjurations of angels and at times even demons, and astrological ideas. The latter (their influence peaking in the Renaissance) were focused on the notion of drawing down influx into suitable earthly receptacles.[68] However, one should recall the caveats of Gideon Bohak, and stress that Jewish magic not only predated Kabbalah, but often remained entirely independent of mystical interpretations. Actually, one could posit that some magical traditions entered the kabbalistic world only in the modern period.[69] One should also bear in mind that numerous medieval kabbalists, including Zoharic writers, were ambivalent toward magic, ignored it, opposed it or entirely subsumed it to the *sefirotic* system. Generally speaking, one should beware of inflating the term magic (which often has a rather technical setting) into any discussion of ritual efficacy (which could well refer to theurgy, also in its mode of drawing down influx to the material world).[70] Yet generally speaking, in discussions of miracles, providence and related issues, kabbalists tended to assume far greater contiguity and transference of influence between the supernal and earthly realms than their philosophical counterparts, beyond the at times nebulous question of whether these were couched in theurgical or magical terms.

CHAINS OF TEXTUAL CONTINUITY

The tumult of the transition to modernity, especially the persecutions and subsequent expulsions in Spain and Portugal in the late fifteenth century, coupled with intrinsic factors such as the prevalent esoteric ethos, preclude

67 On Christian influences on the Ashkenazi practices that persisted in both premodern and modern Kabbalah see Fishman, 'The Penitential System', (compare to Bar-Asher, 'Penance and Fasting'). On asceticism in late medieval Kabbalah, see Fishbane, *As Light before Dawn*, 248–271. The relative rarity of monographs such as Fishbane's, covering one medieval kabbalist (the thirteenth-fourteenth-century R. Itzhak of Acre), is less a fault of the field and more an indication of the nonindividual nature of premodern Kabbalah.

68 On medieval astral magic's complex relationship with Kabbalah, see Schwartz, *Astral Magic*, 125–144. On the Renaissance period (further discussed in Chapter 2), see Idel, *Kabbalah in Italy*, 182–190; Ruderman, *Jewish Thought and Scientific Discovery*, 55–92.

69 Bohak, *Ancient Jewish Magic*, esp. 322–326.

70 Kiener, 'The Status of Astrology'; Liebes, *The Cult of the Dawn*, esp. 64–65, 89–91, 98–103.

any assumption as to smooth transmission from medieval centers (especially Spain), to the modern centers.[71] Nonetheless, the self-awareness of the modern kabbalists was bound up with strong commitments to intensive exegesis of a select corpus of medieval texts, resting on a sense of their hallowed authority. The earliest of these is the book *Bahir* (Radiance), pseudo-epigraphically attributed to the Talmudic sage Nehunia ben ha-Qana. This enigmatic and multilayered work, finalized in Provence, is one of the most influential formulations of the doctrine of the *sefirot*, the theurgy of power, the role of sacral time and other core themes (already addressed in this chapter).[72] A later and almost universally authoritative source was the esoteric layer within the highly influential commentary on the Bible penned by the noted Talmudist and communal leader R. Moshe ben Nahman (Nahmanides, 1194–1270) of Catalonia.[73] One example of the percolation of the views of his school (persisting for approximately two generations, often in the form of super-commentaries on his work), is their presence in illustrated manuscripts of liturgical texts (such as the *Haggada* traditionally read at the Passover Seder).[74] A rival Catalonian center (in turn continuing Provencal views), was that of R. Ezra and R. Azriel of Gerona (joined by R. Jacob ben Sheshet Gerondi), whose more philosophically oriented approach may conceivably betray Sufi influences.[75] Though largely suppressed by Nahmanides' opposition, these views were to occasionally surface throughout the history of modern Kabbalah. One striking contribution of this circle was an attempt to provide an internal history of the Kabbalah.[76]

Foremost (though not first), late medieval kabbalists were indebted to the manuscripts of the book *Zohar* (illumination), composed in late thirteenth-century Castile (mostly by R. Moshe De Leon) and the above-discussed *Tikkunei Zohar*. This relatively large corpus, mostly structured as exegesis on the Pentateuch, was first printed and otherwise rendered accessible in the early modern period.[77] Later writers also displayed awareness of the separate

71 Here one must recall that due to such upheavals many preprint texts were lost (and we do not always even have a record of such lacunae).

72 The classic treatment of this work is Scholem, *Origins of the Kabbalah*, 49–198. For its textual history, see Abrams (ed.), *The Book Bahir*, esp. 1–34 and the various studies by Ronit Meroz, esp. 'A Journey of Initiation'. For Christian parallels and influences, see Wolfson, *Along the Path*, 63–88.

73 See Halbertal, *By Way of Truth*, esp. 297–332; Pedaya, *Nahmanides*. A comprehensive intellectual biography by Oded Israeli is currently being written.

74 Halperin, 'The Sarajevo Haggadah'.

75 See Pedaya, *Vision and Speech*, 171–200.

76 See the commentary on the Song of Songs printed in Chavel (ed.), *Kitvei ha-Ramban*, vol. II, 476–479.

77 I cannot enter here the complex question of the authorship of the *Zohar*. The classic discussions remain Scholem, *Major Trends*, 156–243; Tishby, *The Wisdom of the Zohar* (including translations of many key texts).

authorship and approach of *Tikkunei Zohar*, also considered by scholars to be similar to the *Raya Mehemna* (Faithful Shepherd) portions printed with the *Zohar*.[78] Undoubtedly, the vivid literary framework of the *Zohar* and its veneer of antiquity (pseudo-epigraphically invoking the sages of the *Mishna*, especially the second-century R. Shimeon bar Yohai, and again, using the device of pseudo-Aramaic) captured the imagination of numerous authors and motivated the composition of a host of super-commentaries.[79] As we shall yet see further, the *Zohar* itself became a kind of ritual object, its printing study was assigned messianic import and entire portions of it made their way into the liturgy, alongside with influence on Halakha and custom.[80] Indeed, by the onset of modernity, the figure of bar Yohai had well acquired a life of its own, with embellishments on the character portrayed in the *Zohar*, also in songs.[81]

As a result, more than any single book, this work has dominated both scholarly and popular discourse on Kabbalah since the mid-nineteenth century, as reflected most recently in its English canonization through the Pritzker Edition project (led by Daniel Matt).[82] However, several critical comments are called for at this juncture. Firstly, it is wrong to detach the *Zohar* from the floruit of kabbalistic creativity in Castile in the later part of the thirteenth century (replacing the far more reticent approach of Nahmanides). Amongst several prolific schools (such as the above-noted *'Iyun* circle), one should especially stress that of the above-mentioned R. Abulafia. This highly colorful kabbalist traveled to Italy, Greece, Palestine and possibly France, attempting to meet the Pope and absorbing a host of influences, including Ashkenazi mysticism, Sufism and possibly Franciscan thought.[83] Although quite a few central works in premodern Kabbalah (including those extant in Judeo-Sufi circles in Egypt) already include theoretical discussions of prophecy, Abulafia was unique in his claim to have composed works based on prophetic revelation, regarded by him as a new canon (joining the Bible, also for liturgical purposes). Thus, he described his own system as 'prophetic Kabbalah'.[84]

78 Giller, *The Enlightened Will Shine*; Goldreich, 'Investigations'.

79 Another major example of pseudo-epigraphic invocation of early sages is found in the Castilian *'Iyyun* or contemplation circle. See Porat, *The Works of Iyyun*. For the *Zohar*'s literary framework in context, see Benarroch, *Sava and Yanuka*.

80 See Huss, *The Zohar*, 112–115.

81 See Meroz, *The Spiritual Biography*, 174–265.

82 There is a highly erudite French translation by Charles Mopsik.

83 Scholem, *Major Trends*, 119–155; Idel, *The Mystical Experience*; Wolfson, *Abraham Abulafia*. On the question of influences, see below.

84 Idel, *Language, Torah and Hermeneutics*, esp. xi.

True, due to an interdict issued by Nahmanides' main student R. Shlomo ben Aderet (Rashba), Abulafia's numerous works and those of his later followers remained in manuscript until the advent of modern scholarship (in their greater part until the late twentieth century). Yet one can discern important junctures of influence in late medieval, Renaissance and modern (especially late modern) Kabbalah. Their rich array of mystical techniques and experiences of union with the divine, radical views of language and hermeneutics and messianic autobiography, are of far greater significance for the general study of mysticism and religion (while the *Zohar*'s strong exegetical, national-historical and ritual concerns render it of greater significance for Jewish studies).[85] Secondly, the adulation of the *Zohar* was not shared by all kabbalistic centers, as critical or indifferent views are easily locatable in Italy, North Africa and Jerusalem.[86] While kabbalists in other centers, most notably the Byzantine Empire, acknowledged the *Zohar*'s importance, they also developed their own independent thought, which also had some impact on modern Kabbalah.[87]

Most importantly for our purposes, the texts composed within the golden age of Kabbalah in the sixteenth century both reinforced the centrality of the *Zohar* (especially in wake of its printing), and paradoxically supplanted it, presenting themselves as possessing exclusive interpretative keys to this 'sealed' or opaque corpus.[88] For modern kabbalists, the main classics are neither the *Bahir* nor the *Zohar*, although these certainly assisted in crystallizing their 'professional' identity, but rather the sixteenth-century works of R. Moshe Cordovero, R. Itzhak Luria and others. It was especially Luria who restricted the focus of kabbalistic writings to the more anthropomorphic and mythical sections of the *Zohar* (mainly the portions known as the *Idrot*), so that the exegetical concerns of modern kabbalists differ somewhat from those of some modern scholars.[89]

85 Israeli, *Temple Portals*, esp. 20–32, 157–167; Benarroch, 'The Mystery of Unity'. Cf. Verman, 'The Development of Yihudim'; Matt, 'Matnita Dilan'. On mystical union in medieval Kabbalah (and a brief discussion of its modern impact), see Afterman, *And They Shall Be as One Flesh*, esp. 130–224.

86 See e.g. Idel, *Kabbalah in Italy*, 221, 224–226.

87 For premodern critiques of the *Zohar*, see Huss, *The Zohar*, 240–243.

88 Abrams, *Kabbalistic Manuscripts*, 232–233, 257–259, 361, 423–426; Huss, *The Zohar*, 156–177; Garb, *Modern Kabbalah*, esp. 18–25.

89 On the *Idrot* and their influence, see Giller, *Reading the Zohar*, esp. 89–173, as well as the now-classic Liebes, *Studies in the Zohar*, 74–84, 95–98. For a vivid literary and phenomenological reading of the major *Idra*, see Hellner-Eshed, *Seekers of the Face*. For a historically contextualized philological comparison of the two *Idrot*, see Sobol, *Transgression of the Torah*. On the significance of Luria's focus, see Dan, *History of Jewish Mysticism*, vol. XI, 444–445.

To this day, the actual practice of most modern kabbalists, focused on the *kavvanot* (intentions) of prayer, is based on the works of Luria and his later commentators. The ideology of the centrality of the *Zohar*, propagated amongst largely secular audiences, whether by researchers or by nonacademic advocates of Kabbalah, thus reflects their distance from the life-world of the circles continuing the *via regia* of modern Kabbalah.[90] This ideological predilection should be contrasted with the guiding premise of this entire volume, namely that the study of modern Kabbalah should follow and reflect its own autonomy, in both self-awareness and historical context. This context should also restrict comparison of Kabbalah to other mystical systems to those worlds that modern Kabbalah impacted and was influenced by, namely Christianity and to a lesser extent Islam (although global mysticism was to become a factor after the mid-twentieth century).

COMPARATIVE REFLECTIONS

When comparing Kabbalah to the mystical traditions that flourished in the Middle Ages in adjacent cultures, it is important to recall that the main centers, in Provence and in post-*reconquista* Spain, were situated in Christian regions.[91] As Hartley Lachter has stressed, this is the immediate context for understanding what he (somewhat anachronistically) terms 'Kabbalistic revolution'.[92] There is currently some scholarly opposition to speculations around the premodern influence of Marian devotion on the doctrine of the *Shekhina*, or Franciscan influences on Abulafia.[93] However, these hypotheses do rest on the inherent plausibility of contacts, by virtue of location. One broader question is that of the Christian sources of the doctrine of divine sonship, as part of the post-*Bahiric* conceptualization of the *sefirot* as a familial system (the son usually identified with *Tiferet*).[94]

90 Abrams, *Kabbalistic Manuscripts*, 331, 372, 386, 440, 550–552, 586; Meir, 'Hillel Zeitlin's Zohar'.

91 I am not entering here the more speculative question of comparison of Kabbalah to those cultures that only reached its orbit in late modernity, such as Tantra. See e.g. Mopsik, 'Union and Unity'; Wolfson, *Language, Eros, Being*, esp. 321–324.

92 Lachter, *Kabbalistic Revolution*, esp. 24–26, 29–32, 158. The close connection between revolution and modernity (largely in the context of the state) is the subject of numerous studies (such as Fehér [ed.], *The French Revolution and the Birth of Modernity*; Skopcol, *States and Social Revolutions*). Most historians use the more modest terms 'revolt' or even 'protest' when describing medieval uprisings.

93 Green, 'Shekhina'; Schäfer, *Mirror of His Beauty*; Hames, *Like Angels on Jacob's Ladder* and cf. Idel, *Kabbalah and Eros*, 45–49.

94 Idel, *Ben*, esp. 3–4, 387–399, 520, 523, 595–616, mostly opts for the option of shared sources in ancient Judaism (yet see 310, 437–440, 460–467, 545, 551).

A related theme, raised earlier on in the history of the field, is that of Trinitarian influences on the doctrine of the 'three lines', of the *sefirotic* outlay, and similar triune formulations.[95] Another outstanding question is the impact of incarnational theology on notions of divine descent into the material world, or on anthropomorphic views of the *sefirot* as isomorphic with the human form.[96] A neighboring issue is the iconicity of the sacred text (as discussed in the preface) – comparable, according to Wolfson, with the Christological image.[97] Here one should also consider the above-noted possible Christian influence on hermeneutical theory (to which one should add the possible influence of Christian typological interpretation of the Old Testament on Nahmanides) and especially the notion that the Torah accommodates itself to human perception, thus accounting for the multiplicity of possible interpretations.[98] On the level of practice, one should consider the above-mentioned impact of Christian penitential practices on kabbalistic ascetic regimens, as well as Abulafia's portrayal of the mystical path as a highly hazardous struggle (not always crowned with success) against the temptation of Christian influence.[99]

The inverse investigation of kabbalistic influence on Christian mysticism includes queries as to parallels between kabbalistic ideas and images and those found in the works of luminaries such as Meister Eckhart, Ramon Llull and Joachim of Fiore.[100] Moving to less familiar terrain, Valentina Izmirlieva has convincingly argued that one can trace the influence of Kabbalah on Christian mystical-magical practice through the thirteenth-century Slavonic amulet *The Seventy Two Names of the Lord* (this number appearing in Jewish language-mysticism already in late antiquity).[101] In any case, by the Renaissance period the kabbalistic influence on Christian thought is obvious. Beyond the question of contacts and borrowings, kabbalists and Christian mystics shared in medieval culture, including the emotive turn (especially apparent in commentaries on the Song of Songs in both religions). As Judith Weiss has recently suggested (following on from an earlier observation by Bernard McGinn) this ambience may well account for the shared stress on

95 Liebes, *Studies in the Zohar*, 140–145; Benarroch, 'God and His Son'.

96 Wolfson, *Language, Eros, Being*, 190–260, as well as Magid, *From Metaphysics to Midrash*, 201–221 (mostly relevant for the latter periods that are the subject of the present volume).

97 Wolfson, 'Iconicity of the Text'.

98 Benin, 'The Footprints of God', 167–175; Funkenstein, 'Nahmanides' Symbological Reading'; cf. Halbertal, *By Way of Truth*, 219–228.

99 Sagerman, *The Serpent Kills*, esp. 107–177.

100 Wolfson, 'Patriarchy and the Motherhood of God'; Hames, *The Art of Conversion*, 118–189; Scholem, *Origins of the Kabbalah*, 464–465.

101 Izmirlieva, *All the Names of the Lord*.

the love of God, leading to an affective reinterpretation of the *sefirot* (see above).[102] One repercussion (of many) of this internalizing shift within the domain practice can be found, for instance, in the case of the priestly blessing (whose liturgical formulation includes love), that according to the *Zohar* should only be recited by priests who love the congregants or who are beloved by them.[103] In line with this chapter's stress on exegesis, one should recall that both traditions venerated the Old Testament in its received form, and that this is not the case for Islam (in which the veracity of biblical textual transmission is challenged).

Seemingly, Jewish mysticism can be expected to share the Islamic commitment to purist monotheism. However, while this was indeed the case for philosophers (writing in Islamic territory) such as Maimonides, this cannot be said for kabbalists, especially those operating in Christian Spain (such as the authors of the Zoharic works). Besides the questions of anthropomorphic myth and the accompanying fragmentation of the divine into at least ten potencies, the distance of Kabbalah from Islamic theology is well evident in the case of theurgy.[104] While Islamic sources, starting with the *Quran*, generally stress the independence of God from human action, we have seen that kabbalistic writing (again, probably rooted in earlier traditions) made bold claims as to the impact of the *mitzvot* on the divine realm. Thus, paradoxically the shared focus on practical law transmuted into a major point of difference.[105] Here, one can sharpen the distinction between kabbalistic thinking and that of medieval Jewish philosophy, the latter often written in Arabic.[106] This difference is very prominent in the latter's nonliteral interpretation of the idea of creation in the divine image (*tzelem*), as opposed to the rich somatic discourse on this theme in Kabbalah.[107] The move, fueled by the above-discussed affective turn, away from philosophical intellectualism, led to the beginnings of a kabbalistic alliance with *Musar* (self-formation) literature. This coalition is evident already in the case of the thirteenth-century *Sefer ha-Yashar* (The Straight Book, probably influenced by Geronese Kabbalah), and *Sha'arei Teshuva* (Gates of Repentance), written

102 McGinn, 'The Language of Love'. Weiss' project in preparation was presented at Hebrew University in 2016.

103 *Zohar*, vol. III, 147B. On the priestly blessing in this corpus, see Faierstein, *Jewish Customs*, 21–24.

104 For kabbalistic anthropomorphism, see Scholem, *On the Mystical Shape*, 37–55.

105 For a broader comparison of the two mystical systems, see Sara Sviri, 'Jewish-Muslim Mystical Encounters', https://huji.acaemia.edu/SaraSviri/Forthcoming.

106 Tirosh-Samuelson, 'Philosophy and Kabbalah', and cf. Dauber, *Knowledge of God*.

107 Scholem, *On the Kabbalah*, 251–273, and compare to Lorberbaum, *In God's Image*, esp. 57.

by Nahmanides' relative, R. Yona Gerondi (d. 1263?).[108] The early forms of kabbalistic *Musar* were accompanied by a discourse, at times influenced by Sufism, on cultivation of emotional traits such as equanimity and especially affective adherence (*devequt*) to God.[109]

This being said, we have already noted the strong possibility of Sufi influence on the less canonical Kabbalah of Gerona, to which one should add references to Islamic practices in the *Zohar* (joined by some Arabisms found in the artificial Aramaic in which this literature was mostly composed).[110] In the case of Abulafia (who engaged in speculation on the meaning of Arabic words) and his followers, this direct exposure is without doubt. Here is the testimony of Abulafia's student, R. Nathan ben Sa'adia Harar, in his (rare for a medieval kabbalist) mystical diary, *Sha'arei Tzedeq* (Gates of Righteousness):

> The vulgar way is that which, so I have learned, is practiced by Moslem ascetics. They employ all manner of devices to shut out from their souls all 'natural forms', every image of the familiar, natural world . . . Upon inquiry I learned that they summon the name ALLAH, as it is in the language of Ishmael. I investigated further and I found that, when they pronounce these letters, they direct their thought completely away from every possible 'natural form', and the very letters ALLAH and their diverse powers work upon them. They are carried off into a trance without realizing how, since no Kabbalah has been transmitted to them.[111]

Although R. Nathan clearly considers the Sufi path to be inferior, lacking the authentic transmission that he associated with Kabbalah, nonetheless its practices informed both his meditation technique and his views on the powers of holy names and letters. Now it is time to address the Judeo-Sufi school in Egypt and Palestine (paradoxically led by the descendants of Maimonides), where Sufi influences are even more striking and more positively received.[112] However, it is unclear to what extent these groups influenced the kabbalistic tradition. To all this one should add the reciprocal borrowing of magical (such as astrological) practices, some of which entered both mystical traditions, and also the manner in which *Shi'ite*

108 Shokek, 'The Relationship'. 109 Idel, *Studies in Ecstatic Kabbalah*, 106–107, 112–125.
110 Kiener, 'The Image of Islam'.
111 Translated in Scholem, *Major Trends*, 147. On this figure, see Idel and Mottolese (eds.), *Le porte della giustizia*, esp. 47–69. Compare to Hames, *A Seal within a Seal*.
112 See the studies of Paul Fenton, esp. 'Abraham Maimonides'; Fishbane, *Judaism, Sufism, and the Pietists of Medieval Egypt*.

parallels may illuminate the prehistory of kabbalistic views of evil and related topics.[113] The recent dating of some of the studies mentioned just now gives hope that future investigations by a new generation of scholars fluent in Arabic (such as Avishai Bar-Asher's careful discussion of parallels between the famous thirteenth-century Sufi writer Muhyiddin Ibn al-'Arabi's descriptions of paradisial reward and medieval kabbalistic portrayals) will uncover further instances of the influence of a vibrant intellectual culture, whose extension into the heartland of Europe partly survived the *Reconquista* in Spain (which was all but accomplished by the mid-thirteenth century).[114]

In any case, the uniqueness of Kabbalah vis-à-vis its neighbors rests on firm pillars of separatist Jewish identity, fiercely upheld as part of the struggle of an oft-persecuted minority for its continued existence. Nahmanides participated in fraught debates with Christian adversaries, while the *Zohar* claimed that you have no diaspora more difficult to Israel than the diaspora of Ishmael, i.e. Islamic rule.[115] Separatism was often formulated in terms of the division between the Jewish body as well as soul, and that of the Gentiles.[116] Within this framework, one should consider the relative singularity of the stress on family life, as a location of ritual practice (especially around the Sabbath), a source for transmission of tradition, a model for views of relationships and sexuality in the supernal realm, and as a source for reflection on numerous biblical episodes (especially in the book of Genesis).[117] One aspect of Jewish family life (shared with Islam) that influenced the basic social structure of Kabbalah was that of menstrual impurity (associated at times with magical beliefs as to the harm caused by contact with menstrual blood).[118] This factor may well account from a major difference between Kabbalah and other mystical traditions (especially Christian ones), the total absence of medieval female kabbalists (modern aspects of this striking absence shall be discussed in Chapter 7).[119]

113 Ebstein and Weiss, 'A Drama in Heaven'; Heller Wilensky, 'Messianism, Eschatology and Utopia'.
114 Bar-Asher, *Journeys of the Soul*, 439–451 (and earlier studies addressed there).
115 *Zohar*, vol. II, 17A, translated and discussed in Kiener, 'The Image of Islam', 52–53.
116 Wolfson, *Venturing Beyond*, esp. 5, 48–57, 73–107.
117 Idel, *Kabbalah and Eros*, 57–58, 217, 224 (and his above-noted study of sonship); Israeli, 'Honoring Father and Mother'.
118 See Koren, *Forsaken*, esp. 141–143.
119 I believe that this connection shall be discussed in a study in preparation by Ada Rapoport-Albert.

CONCLUSION: KABBALAH IN TRANSITION TO MODERNITY

The great variety of traditions, corpora, locations (as in the unique development of the Kabbalah in Italy or the Byzantine Empire) and interactions with earlier or parallel worlds, make it difficult to assume that there was a singular, consistent and coherent body of thought and practice known as Kabbalah by the end of the medieval period.[120] Kabbalah should be seen as autonomous, rather than independent, in relation to the wider context of medieval life, both Jewish and general, with specific corpora or schools tied to complex strands to cultural forces ranging from German Pietism to Maimonidean philosophy (as in the case of Abulafia). Nonetheless, the kabbalists themselves assumed that there was such a 'reception' (the literal meaning of the term Kabbalah), as well as a social group composed of kabbalistic exegetes and/or practitioners. Furthermore, we have followed the tendency to cluster around canonical groups of texts, even prior to the solidification of canons by the modern advent of print. As a result, the approach taken in this chapter was that of isolating common denominators that, as we shall see, carried forward into the Renaissance and modern periods. Yet all the while, one should recall that modern kabbalists inherited not a doctrine, but a series of tensions, complexities and debates. The manner in which these played out, fueled by the dynamic processes of modernity itself, account for the sheer richness and vastness that is modern Kabbalah. It is this very richness that enabled the crystallization of the professional, discrete identity of the kabbalistic practices and circles.

[120] For an example of a rich, poetic work that had some influence on modern Kabbalah yet is not easily placed within any linear narrative of the evolution of medieval Kabbalah, see Porat, *Sefer Brit Menuha*.

2

The Safedian Revolution of the Sixteenth Century

EARLIER CENTERS

Although several kabbalistic centers rose and declined in different parts of the sixteenth century, especially in the Mediterranean basin, Scholem has correctly located the true beginning of 'new' (in other words modern) Kabbalah in the Galilean town of Safed in the second part of the century.[1] It was here that a veritable spiritual and psychological revolution transformed the worlds of kabbalistic writing and practice.[2] Accordingly, the centers that preceded Safed in the late fifteenth and early sixteenth centuries, influencing Safedian discourse in varying degrees, shall be treated briefly.

The Greco-Turkish center, perhaps the most important representative of the first wave of sixteenth-century Kabbalah, achieved lasting influence through the influential works of R. Meir ibn Gabbai (c.1480–c.1543), most notably his *'Avodat ha-Qodesh* (printed 1567). Here we find a synthesis of earlier views of theurgy, isomorphism and power, yet joined by two modern themes: a move away from Maimonidean philosophical views toward a strong assertion of Man's central place in the universe, and a concomitant stress on the personal power of the righteous.[3] The emergent subcenter in Saloniki was transformed by the arrival of an ex-*converso* from Portugal, Diego Pires, who became Solomon Molkho (1501–1532) after his return to Judaism. As part of his messianic vision (also inspired by the geopolitical

[1] Scholem, *Major Trends*, 288.
[2] For these terms see Heelas and Woodhead, *Spiritual Revolution*; Garb, *Yearnings of the Soul*, 24–25.
[3] Goetschel, *Meir Ibn Gabbay*; Mopsik, *Les grands textes*, 364–383; Garb, *Manifestations of Power*, 238–242.

messianic activism of David Ha-Reuveni, who was in turn influenced by kabbalistic speculations), Molkho left the safety of the Ottoman Empire in a magical attempt to undermine the Christian regime, met Pope Clement VII and was burnt at the stake as an apostate by the Inquisition in 1532.[4] We shall soon examine the influence of Molkho's life and thought on both Jewish and Christian thinkers.

This confrontation with Christianity continued the activity, while still in Spain, of semilegendary figures such as R. Yosef della Reina and other members of the circle of *Sefer ha-Meshiv* (The Book of the Responding Entity), such as the author of the anonymous *Kaf ha-Qtoret* (Pan of Incense).[5] Like Molkho, these writers contended with the growing predicament of Iberian Jewry in the face of escalating Judeo-phobic tendencies culminating with the expulsion in the late fifteenth century (see below) and followed by the activities of the Inquisition against those who chose to convert. These writers, mostly *conversos*, attempted to bring about the downfall of Christian rule through magical techniques (derived partly from angelic revelations, as in the case of the 'responding entity'), and their failure was to dampen the enthusiasm of later kabbalists as to resort to such means. Concomitantly, this corpus reflects disillusionment with the philosophical heritage of Spanish Jewry, for which the medieval Golden Age of dialogue was now but a distant memory. At the same time, their writings clearly reflect the absorption of messianic and incarnational themes from the Christian world. More generally (as demonstrated at length by Shaul Magid) the re-absorption of the *conversos* in the Jewish world in the wake of the expulsion continued to be a troubling issue for Safedian kabbalists.[6] As we shall yet see, *converso* thought continued to shape modern Kabbalah well into the seventeenth century.

Greco-Turkish Kabbalah, by drawing on its roots in the earlier Byzantine Kabbalah, especially influenced a major Egyptian writer, R. David ibn Zimra (known by the acronym Radbaz, c.1480–1573), the teacher of R. Itzhaq Luria, who was to become the most prominent Safedian figure upon immigrating to the Galilee. Like several Safedian figures, Radbaz, whose own Kabbalah focused on the symbolism of the graphic form of the letters, was also a prominent halakhist and a poet. Earlier circles in North Africa, naturally most immediately affected by the emigration from Spain, included the magical-ecstatic kabbalists of Dra'a in Morocco (possibly influenced by the

[4] Benmelech, 'History, Politics and Messianism'.
[5] Vajda, 'Passages anti-chrétiens'; Idel, *Messianic Mystics*, 144–152.
[6] Magid, *From Metaphysics to Midrash*.

practices of their Berber neighbors) and the circle in Fez, especially R. Shimeon ibn Lavi (first part of the sixteenth century), author of a voluminous Zoharic commentary and fierce critic of earlier exegesis (and also of philosophy).[7] Despite vigorous promotion on the part of Spanish émigrés and extensive copying by local scribes, the *Zohar* was less dominant in Italy, where its printing (1558–1560) was accompanied by sharp dispute.[8] Several Italian kabbalists, such as R. Yohanan Alemanno (c.1435–c.1522) and R. David Messer Leon (c.1450–c.1535), adhered rather to Renaissance thought, especially developing the notion of *prisca theologia*, or an antique theology (of Jewish origins) refracted in various faiths.[9] Furthermore, notably in the works of R. Matthias Delacrout (who later moved to Poland) one can discern a reinterpretation of medieval Kabbalah in terms derived from astral and other forms of elite magical thought.[10]

This universalistic Italian cultural tendency had manifold effects. One was a remarkable critique of the historical authenticity of the kabbalistic tradition by R. Eliyahu del Medigo, already at the end of the previous century. Del Medigo was possibly influenced by Renaissance skepticism as to the authenticity of attributions of sacral texts to the antique period.[11] This enterprise should be positioned in the broader context of a growing, modern, awareness of the historical context and role of Kabbalah. A more pervasive effect was extensive contacts with Hebraist and kabbalistic Christians (including copying of manuscripts at their behest).[12] Most prominent amongst Christian writers influenced by Kabbalah, already at the turn of the century, were leading figures such Marsilio Ficino (1433–1499) and Pico della Mirandola (1463–1494). Particularly in the writings of the latter, Kabbalah as an ancient truth obscured by its Jewish reception was enlisted in order to substantiate Christian beliefs. Influenced by his tutor Alemanno, Pico was strikingly indebted to the ecstatic Kabbalah of Abulafia, while the Zoharic option was more extensively represented by the colorful figure of William (Guillaume) Postel. This polymath devoted an extensive translation

[7] Huss, *Sockets of Fine Gold*, 32–38. [8] Huss, *The Zohar*, 191–201.

[9] Tirosh-Rothschild, *Between Worlds*; Lelli, 'Prisca Philosophia'.

[10] Mopsik, *Les grands textes*, 319–335. [11] Huss, *The Zohar*, 243–244.

[12] Following Weiss, *A Kabbalistic Christian Messiah*, 18–23, I generally prefer this term to the more common 'Christian kabbalists'. For we are dealing with Christians (however unconventional) who, amongst other influences resorted to Kabbalah (often in order to advance Christian beliefs, as in the case of Pico) rather than full-fledged kabbalists who happened to be Christians. At the same time, the general thrust of this volume mitigates against reserving the term Kabbalah exclusively for Jewish thought (hence the occurrence of the term Jewish Kabbalah). It may be helpful to note that in Christian texts and their scholarship, the spelling is often Cabala or Qabbalah.

of the *Zohar* and other classics of theosophical Kabbalah, accompanied by rich commentaries (joined by two original works in Hebrew) and actually visited Jerusalem in 1549–1550.[13] As in Jewish Kabbalah in this century, theosophical writing, with strong adherence to the *Zohar*, constituted the mainstream, as also evidenced in the biblical exegesis of Francesco Zorzi.[14]

In Central and Eastern Europe, prior to the Safedian colonization (to be described at the end of the chapter), we find fewer of innovative directions and rather extensive collections of earlier materials, most notably *Shushan Sodot* by R. Moshe ben Yaakov of Kiev. The prayer book by R. Naftali Hertz Treves (d. c.1538), *Mala ha-Aretz de'a* (printed 1560), is especially valuable for scholars, as it preserves Ashkenazi magical techniques. Treves' work, despite his connections with Italy, gives some support to claims that there was a reawakening of interest in German Pietism after the middle of the sixteenth century, especially in Central Europe.[15] In an entirely unrelated development, it was in this cultural domain that kabbalistic forms of Christianity truly came into their own. Influenced by Pico, Johann Reuchlin (1455–1522) employed Kabbalah, and especially its symbolic and linguistic elements, within his project of a 'Pythagorean rebirth' (continuing the Renaissance project of return to the Greco-Roman culture, often under the auspices of *prisca theologia*). Idel has argued that the symbolic interpretation of Kabbalah amongst such thinkers attenuated its Jewish ritual-nomian aspects, yet Wolfson has claimed that in a complex fashion Reuchlin continued the kabbalistic stress on theurgical power of the Hebrew language.[16] Generally speaking (and this is also true of later centuries), kabbalistic Christians stressed *sefirotic* theosophy, rather than the ritual practices of medieval kabbalists. For example, when Giulio Camillo (c.1480–1544) translated kabbalistic ideas into practice in his 'memory theatre' (as part of the Renaissance revival of the classical art of memory), he built it around the seven lower *sefirot*, albeit with astrological and psychological parallels.[17]

While Reuchlin's *De Arte Cabalistica* (On the Art of Kabbalah) was dedicated to Pope Leo X, *De Occulta Philosophia* by the German theologian Heinrich Cornelius Agrippa von Nettesheim (1486–1535) articulated kabbalistic Christianity, alongside with reworking of pagan sources, as an occult

[13] Weiss, *On the Conciliation of Nature and Grace*; Weiss, *Ta'am ha-Te'Amim*.

[14] Busi, 'Francesco Zorzi'. For an extensive overview of what the author terms Christian Kabbalah, see Schmidt-Biggemann, *Geschichte der Christlichen Kabbalah*.

[15] Elbaum, 'Aspects of Hebrew Ethical Literature', 151–152. For the latest stages of the debate on this issue see Fram, 'German Pietism' and cf. Soloveitchik, 'Pietists'.

[16] Wolfson, 'Language, Secrecy'.

[17] Bolzoni, 'Giulio Camillo's Memory Theatre'.

teaching independent of Church doctrine.[18] This bold move had far-reaching cultural implications (see Chapter 7). Here one should add that William Postel was imprisoned by the Inquisition after he envisioned the replacement of the Pope by a female messianic figure who would inaugurate the reign of kabbalistic Christianity. Postel drew on the medieval doctrines of Joachim of Fiore, reflecting continuity with premodern influences of Kabbalah on Christian messianism. Postel's focus on a specific woman (the Venetian nun Joanna), should be contrasted with the *Shekhina*-focused messianism of the prominent cardinal Egidio da Viterbo (1470–1532).[19] Inspired by Shlomo Molkho's geopolitical messianic project, Egidio attempted to persuade his friend Pope Clemens VII and the Holy Roman Emperor Carl V to reform the Church based on kabbalistic doctrine (especially its theory of language). Yet in his case the *Shekhina* is represented, at least overtly, by male leaders.[20] One of the themes of this geopolitical discourse amongst kabbalistic Christians was the contemporary ascendancy of the Ottoman Empire (see below for its effect on Jewish Kabbalah).[21] A more famous example of a contra-ecclesiastical figure influenced by Kabbalah is that of Giordano Bruno (1548–1600), burnt at the stake on the behest of the Inquisition for his heretical opinions that included 'dealing in magic' and upholding reincarnation, in both cases clearly under the influence of Kabbalah. More generally, scholars such as Frances Yates have drawn on such cases in claiming that esoteric-magical beliefs, including numerous kabbalistic strands, contributed materially to the rise of modern science.[22]

The northwards dissemination of kabbalistic Christianity also reached France, as in the work of Postel's student, the poet (also in Hebrew!) and Orientalist Guy le Fevre de la Boderie (1541–1598) and England, as in the famous case of Elizabeth's court magician John Dee (1527–1608). 'The cabala of nature' as a key for restoring the original language and the 'book of nature', or key to complete knowledge of the world, was a major theme in his experience of conversations with angels. It must be stressed that Dee differentiated his mathematical 'real Kabbalah' from that of his predecessors amongst kabbalistic Christians (again reflecting the diversity of approaches

[18] Lehrich, *The Language of Demons and Angels*, esp. 158–159, 186–189, 206–209.

[19] On Postel and Joanna, see most recently Weiss, *A Kabbalistic Christian Messiah*, esp. 116–136.

[20] On this figure, see e.g. Copenhaver and Kokin, 'Egidio da Viterbo's Book'. Edigio's treatise *Scechina* is due to be translated (from Latin into Hebrew) and annotated by Yehuda Liebes and Judith Weiss.

[21] Schmidt-Biggemann, 'Political Theology', esp. 302–303.

[22] Yates, *Giordano Bruno*, esp. 144–156.

in an intellectual current that at times is viewed somewhat monolithically). It is also important to note that kabbalistic knowledge of the secrets of numbers is sharply differentiated from that of 'merchants', thus signifying an alternative to the emergent modernizing forces of early capitalism (especially in England).[23] As Idel has surmised, it is possible that the readiness of kabbalistic Christians to print works of Kabbalah had a reciprocal effect on the move of modern kabbalists toward exotericism.[24] As we shall soon see in greater detail, one striking similarity between kabbalistic Christians and modern kabbalists was a keen interest in current, rather than mythical, history. A prominent example of this trend can be found in the quasi-kabbalistic biblical exegesis of Egidio, who at one point aimed at establishing Renaissance Rome as the new promised land.[25] In and of itself, this move reveals that kabbalistic Christians, whether allied with the Church or antithetical to it, were first and foremost Christians, sharing in the supercessionary approach toward Judaism, soon to be supplanted.

Most proximate to Safed, in space and time, was the center in Jerusalem, especially characterized by the cultivation of trance techniques and nightly messianic prayer vigils. One central figure here was R. Abraham ben Eli'ezer ha-Levi (c.1460–1530), who positively responded to current events, including 'the great man' Luther and his Protestant Reformation, which he took to be a sign of forthcoming redemption. Ha-Levi's interest in this dramatic schism is paralleled by a roughly contemporary testimony from Italy describing the keen interest in Kabbalah amongst the Protestants.[26] Reflecting the inception of globalization (see below), ha-Levi also displayed interest in the process of European colonization. Although after 1530 the Jerusalem center declined, it clearly influenced Safedian writers, and this is its main historical impact, given that almost all of these writings (most notably the very large mystical-magical corpus of R. Yosef ibn Sayyah [c.1500–c.1573], which had some influence on Safedian writers) were only recently printed or still remain in manuscript.

This picture of rising popularity of Kabbalah cannot be comprehended without considering the role of printing (over and above the above-mentioned

[23] De León-Jones, 'John Dee and the Kabbalah' and cf. Harkness, *Conversations with Angels* (the quote on merchants is on p. 176). For a comparison of Dee's enterprise with that of a major sixteenth-century kabbalist (R. Yosef Karo), see Kahana, 'Cosmos and Nomos', 144–147.

[24] Idel, *Kabbalah in Italy*, 190–201, 221, 225–226, 230–235, 306.

[25] Kokin, 'Entering the Labyrinth', 31–40.

[26] Garb, *Shamanic Trance*, 60–65; Robinson, 'Messianic Prayer Vigils'; David, 'The Lutheran Reformation', 125–126; Idel, 'Revelation and the "Crisis of Tradition"', 285–286. For negative views of the Kabbalah in early Lutheranism (including a suggestive statement by Luther himself) see Thon, 'The Power of (Hebrew) Language', esp. 108–109.

case of the *Zohar*), by both Jews and Christians in both fueling and expressing the new popular interest in Kabbalah. Although Italy continued to be the major printing center, toward the end of the century a few works were printed in Safed, home to the first Hebrew press (founded in 1577) in Asia, except for China. Works of modern Kabbalah were already published in Poland and Bohemia around the turn of the century. The printing of a second wave of Zoharic texts (later known as *Zohar Hadash* or new *Zohar*) in Saloniki in 1597 completed the process of canonization of this medieval corpus, just as the decision (based on the negative opinion of Spanish émigrés) not to print other works, such as the Abulafian corpus, set the course for their subsequent reception.[27]

Another common factor is that all of these centers were fed by waves of refugees following the expulsion of the Jews from the Iberian Peninsula at the end of the previous century. Here Idel was correct in modifying Scholem's famous notion of a delayed impact of the expulsion on the national psyche, which for the latter especially spurred the development of a new doctrine on evil and its rectification.[28] Instead, Idel proposed that the expulsion occasioned the transposition of kabbalists into various new centers and often converging onwards on Safed. This set the geographical-sociological stage for the new phase of Kabbalah, as an ongoing interaction, at times tense, between several regional circles.[29] Extending this process of blending of smaller groups of immigrants into a new, stable center, it was at Safed that the Kabbalah truly adopted its new social form, that of the fellowship or fraternity (following a common Ottoman Sufi model). The present chapter shall be structured around an exploration of three somewhat overlapping circles (those of Karo, Cordovero and Luria) and the themes that concerned them, then following the reciprocal impact of the Safedian center on two European centers (Italy and Central Europe) toward the end of the century. Especially in the conclusion, I shall pose the question of general commonalities of Safedian cultural creativity and its tributaries.

KARO AND HIS CIRCLE

Safed's transformation into a hub for émigrés from Spain and other Jewish centers was a direct result of the expansion of the Ottoman Empire, as in the

27 Idel, 'Printing Kabbalah'; Gondos, 'Kabbalah in Print'.

28 Compare to Pedaya, *Walking through Trauma*, who somewhat restores Scholem's argument (developed in his *Major Trends*, 246–251, 286).

29 Idel, 'On Mobility'.

conquest of Syria and Palestine in 1516 and Egypt in 1517 and the subsequent political stability and relatively (especially compared to the above-described expulsions and persecutions in the Christian world) tolerant attitude toward religious minorities. Safed's new administrative (as a regional capital) geographical location, near the trade route joining the commercial centers of Damascus with Mediterranean ports, joined with ancient traditions on the sanctity of cities and graveyards in the Galilee to attract migrants from various Jewish centers. This gradual process tripled its Jewish population between 1525 and 1555, peaking in 1567–1568 with around 1,800 families (prior to the economic and demographic decline of the last quarter of the century). Demographic expansion and economic prosperity facilitated the formation of a network of communal scholastic institutions. Besides Kabbalah, Safed became a center of halakhic and poetic creativity, and this was most apparent in its first major circle. This group was based on immigrants from the Greco-Turkish center, some of whom decided to relocate to Palestine after the following communication from the *Shekinah* experienced by R. Yosef Karo (1488–1575) during a ritual 'order' of all-night study on the eve of *Shavu'ot* (the Pentecost) of 1534.

> Hearken, my pious friends, my dearly beloved . . . blessed are ye . . . for that you have taken upon yourselves to crown me in this night. It is many years since the crown fell from my head and there is none that comforteth me: I am thrown in the dust, embracing dunghills. But now you have restored the crown to its former glory. Therefore be strong my friends, be of good courage my beloved, rejoice and be glad, and know that you are of the exalted few . . . and I have been exalted this night through you.[30]

Karo's mystical experiences and ideas, found in his diary *Magid Mesharim* (see Isaiah 45, 19), had some subsequent impact, especially on the eighteenth-century Hasidic movement and its pietistic predecessors.[31] One of the recurring themes in this work was his intense aspiration toward martyrdom, both expressing his admiration for Molkho and the general preoccupation of Palestinian and especially Safedian kabbalists with mystical death in various forms.[32] The new kabbalistic genres of autobiography and later hagiography expressed the new modern and individualistic social psychology. A proximate facet of this at times morbid psychology was the ascetic sense of sin, shame and guilt. Such emotions were often related to

[30] Translation in Werblowsky, *Joseph Karo*, 109.
[31] Elior, 'Joseph Karo'.
[32] Werblowsky, *Joseph Karo*, 98–99, 152–154; Fine, *Physician of the Soul*, 239–248; Fishbane, *The Kiss of God*, 44–46, 53, 110–117; Garb, *Shamanic Trance*, 33–35, 62.

somatic concerns, such as eating and sexuality, as reflected in Karo's confessions. These take the form of rebukes on the part of angelic-divine, mostly feminine entities (such as the *Shekhina* encountered above) whose revelation he continued to experience throughout:

> Henceforth be careful to perform worldly actions only as far as strictly necessary for life. If there is any pleasure connected with such actions, do not regard the pleasurable side of it but be perturbed, and strongly desire to perform the action without any pleasure. When you eat consider yourself as if a sword were held over your head and hell were gaping under your feet. For if you eat and drink more than is necessary or even if you eat the right amount but intend to derive pleasure from it, then you will be punished. Consider in your heart that you are standing before the King of Kings... whose *Shekinah* is constantly above your head... wherefore all pleasures should be repulsive to you.[33]

Roni Weinstein has speculated that Karo's psychology reflects a Catholic ethos, mediated by returning *conversos* such as Molkho and other immigrants from Spain and Italy.[34] However, there may have been a more proximate influence on Safedian psychology in general (as well as the social-psychological format of fellowships): although the Jews of Safed dwelled in a separate quarter, Sufi orders are known to have been operating in the vicinity, and one should also consider beliefs in reincarnation prevalent amongst the Druze of Galilee.[35] Thus, Karo strikingly records a visit to a Sufi center, although, predictably, he was rebuked by his supernal mentor and experienced guilt (according to Avraham Elqayam's speculation, this feeling was of a sexual nature provoked by possible self-exposure by Sufis in ecstatic dances conducted there).[36] Paul Fenton has pointed at relatively positive evaluations of the spirituality of Ishmael (standing for the Islamic world) within the Cordoverian corpus, as well as at the plausibility of Sufi influence on this kabbalist's discussions of ritual visualization of the spiritual mentor.[37] The latter example clearly joins psychology with the social life of the mystical fellowship.

Furthermore, Haviva Pedaya has argued that the influence of Arabic devotional poetry, evident in the now-canonical works of R. Israel Najjarah (1555–1625), points at a wider contribution of the immediate surroundings to

33 Translated in Werblowsky, *Joseph Karo*, 156. For a more updated biography of Karo, see Altshuler, *The Life of Rabbi Yosef Karo*.

34 Weinstein, *Kabbalah and Jewish Modernity*, 130.

35 Fenton, 'Influences soufies'.

36 Werblowsky, *Joseph Karo*, 138–139; Elqayam, 'Nudity in Safed'.

37 Fenton, 'The Banished Brother', 251; Fenton, 'The Ritual Visualization', 213–221.

the poetic-musical awakening amongst Safedian mystics. However, in evaluating the immediate influence of Najjarah, one must factor in the strong sexual accusations leveled against him, inter alia on the part of Luria's main student Vital (in his own diary).[38] Furthermore, the decline of literary Arabic amongst the Jews of Safed in general, suggests caution as to further conjectures in this direction. At the same time, as noted in the medieval case (see Chapter 1), the more scholars with mastery of Arabic language and mystical culture bring their sights to bear on this topic, the greater the possibility that the state of our knowledge will profoundly alter.

Karo's main renown, as promised by the supernal entities whose communication he experienced, was due to his massive work in the most central domain of Jewish normative life – the Halakha. Karo's works, especially his *Beit Yosef* and its popular summary *Sulkhan 'Arukh*, became the canonical and determinative texts of the entire modern period, to this day. As Weinstein has recently argued, this project reflects the increased Ottoman concern with legal canonization, and in both cases, this endeavor was ascribed messianic portent.[39] Although several Safedian kabbalists were accomplished Talmudists, it was Karo who expressed the kabbalistic-halakhic synthesis that was to dominate much of modern Jewish life. As Moshe Hallamish and others have shown, Karo systematically introduced Zoharic innovations in his reshaping of daily Jewish life, starting with awakening in the morning. One controversial example was the prohibition on women following funeral processions to the graveyard.[40] Furthermore, though it is not beyond doubt (as Scholem had it), it is highly likely that Karo's mystical-messianic beliefs contributed to the 1538 attempt, which he shared with R. Yaakov Berav (1474–1541), to restore the chain of rabbinic ordination and eventually the central legal authority, the *Sanhedrin* (Grand Court), as in the time of the Temple.[41] In any case, Karo, who was ordained by Berav, then ordained the preacher R. Moshe Alsheikh (c.1520–1593?), who subsequently ordained Vital.

The recorder of our opening testimony was Karo's younger associate, R. Shlomo ha-Levi Alqabetz (1500–1576). Alqabetz was to become famous for his mystical poem *Lekha Dodi* (Go Out My Beloved), recited on Friday

38 Pedaya, 'Text and Its Performance'. On the accusations against Najjara, see Chajes, *Between Worlds*, 110–112. On Najjara's influence and his diverse mystical sources, see Seroussi, 'Judeo-Islamic Sacred Soundscapes'.

39 Weinstein, 'Jewish Modern Law'.

40 Hallamish, *Kabbalah in Liturgy, Halakhah and Customs*, 166–173; Karo, *Sulkhan 'Arukh*, *Yoreh De'a*, 359; Katz, 'Post-Zoharic Relations', 302–303.

41 Scholem, *Kabbalah*, 72.

evening in celebration of the onset of the Sabbath. The poem, soon to enter the liturgy of most communities, epitomizes the Safedian spirit expressing redemptive and revelatory hopes, on both national and psychological levels:

> rise up and shake off the dust,
> don your robes of glory my people,
> through the son of Jesse, the Bethelemite [i.e. the Messiah],
> redemption has drawn near to my soul.
> Awaken, Awaken, for your light has come, rise up and shine,
> wake up, wake up, sing a song,
> the Glory of God is revealed upon thee.[42]

This was part of an entire set of practices surrounding this transitory moment, found in earlier sources, yet especially relished in Safed (just like the practice of mystical study on the eve of the festival of *Shavu'ot*). More generally, Safed witnessed a renaissance of devotional poetry, institutionalized in the consolidation of the practice of *baqqashot* (supplications), or communal singing, mostly at night (perhaps continuing the Jerusalemite custom of nightly vigils). This is still an important socioreligious event in some communities (especially those of Syrian origin) to this day. The *maqamat* or musical structures for these chants were clearly influenced by Arabic forms. Thus, a canonical compilation of *baqqashot* by R. Menahem de Lonzano (1550– c.1608), who was in close (though critical) dialogue with Safedian kabbalists, is largely based on Turkish tunes.[43]

In a similar vein, Alqabetz can be seen as the founder of the modern practice of composing personal prayers in a mystical vein. One of these narrates the travails of the expulsion, thus somewhat reinforcing Scholem's above-mentioned thesis regarding its effect on Safedian Kabbalah.[44] Alqabetz also composed several important kabbalistic treatises, including commentaries on the biblical books of Ruth, Esther and the Song of Songs. Here, one can discern a messianic contribution to innovative biblical exegesis, based on the premise that God, the Torah and the soul (also of the exegete) are one essence. The theosophical theory underlying this exegetical enterprise was a complex dialectic in which concealment causes disclosure and disclosure in turn evokes concealment.[45] This dialectical tendency was probably influenced by Scholasticism and its Jewish reception, absorbed through the philosophical

[42] Kimelman, *The Mystical Meaning of Lekha Dodi.*
[43] Yayama, 'The Singing of Baqqashot', vol. I, 22–30.
[44] Werblowsky, 'A Collection of Prayers'.
[45] Sack, *Solomon Had a Vineyard*, esp. 17, 21, 95–123, 137–138, 206–209; Wolfson, 'Divine Suffering', 110–111.

circle in Saloniki. In this regard, Alqabetz is unique amongst Safedian writers, some of whom (such as Alsheikh, of whom he did not approve) were more than reserved toward philosophical inquiry. As an immigrant, Alqabetz valorized the Holy Land, whose very essence (rather than merely the *mitzvot* related to it) is seen as the 'first point of creation' and the source of 'all perfections'.[46] His brother-in-law, a close student, indeed almost an equal, R. Moshe Cordovero (1522–1570), was a descendant of a family of refugees from Portugal or Spain, who established a far more influential and prolific circle around the mid-century.[47] While retaining the theoretical-dialectical interests of his mentor, Cordovero deepened Kabbalah's self-interpretation, producing one of the central canons of modern Kabbalah.

CORDOVERO AND HIS CIRCLE

Cordovero was one of the most prolific, learned and analytic writers in the entire history of Kabbalah. His youthful (at twenty-six) magnum opus *Pardes Rimdesonim* (Orchard of Pomegranates) is composed of a series of syntheses of systems found in medieval and Renaissance Kabbalah, of which he had a panoramic view. This harmonistic impulse is probably related to his general tendency toward unity, expressed in his predilection for 'great chain of being' imagery of cosmic connectivity, as well as his later move toward pantheistic formulations such as this:

> We all come forth from Him and are included in Him and live in His life . . . and all of the existence of beings is Him. And being sustained by creatures that are lesser than Him, such as plants and animals, does not mean that we are sustained by anything outside of Him . . . and He is He, and all is one and there is nothing separate from Him . . . all is included in Him and adheres to Him.[48]

This monistic inclination leads in to an organic view of the unity of the Jewish nation (as well as that of the kabbalistic fellowship itself) that was to have a marked impact over the next centuries.[49]

46 Alqabetz, *Brit Halevi*, 41A.

47 See the biographical details in Raviv, *Decoding the Dogma*, 51–53.

48 *Shi'ur Qoma* (part of *Or Yaqar* yet printed separately and thematically independent), 16B (and cf. Ben-Shlomo, *The Mystical Theology*, 294–313); Idel, *Enchanted Chains*, 57–59, 181–188.

49 Sack, *The Kabbalah of R. Moshe Cordovero*, 205–213. Cordovero's cosmological interests also led him to be the last comprehensive formulator of kabbalistic angelology. See Kadari, *Cordovero's Angels*. This study is invaluable for grasping the diachronical progression of Cordovero's voluminous writing.

Cordovero's 'national Kabbalah' led directly into a critique of contemporary forms of kabbalistic Christianity,

> just as foxes had damaged the vineyard of God . . . nowadays in the land of Italy the priests studies the science of Kabbalah and they diverted it to heresy . . . but blessed is he who gave it [the Kabbalah] to us, because neither they nor the Gentiles distinguish between right and left, but are similar to animals, because, ultimately, they did not fathom the inner [essence of the lore].

As we shall yet see, there were equally negative and more specific attacks on the kabbalistic Christians amongst Luria's later followers. On the other hand, R. Hayyim Vital, a student of Cordovero before he adhered to Luria, dreamt that he taught the Pope 'a bit of the wisdom'.[50] This current engagement should be contrasted with his general assessment of Islam, remaining within the medieval trope of describing Muhammad's prophecy as madness.[51] Such data should give pause before assuming that Safedian kabbalists of European origin immediately shifted to concern with their new cultural surroundings (though in some cases, such as Karo, this hypothesis is indeed borne out).

One of *Pardes Rimonim*'s influential innovations is the foregrounding of the premodern model of the divinity of the soul (propagated inter alia by Nahmanides), the subject of an entire 'gate' of the book. As he succinctly put it (again, under the influence of Alqabetz): 'Man is a part of divinity above.'[52] This formulation is closely related to an oft-recurring binary distinction (also going back mostly to Alqabetz) between the soul-essence and the 'vessel' of the *sefirot*, thus resolving yet another premodern debate on their nature. Demonstrating the constant evolution of his thought, Cordovero's final opus, the recently (fully) published *Elima Rabbati* (Greater *Elima*; see Exodus 15, 27), shows a greater concern with the body, bringing the anthropomorphic imagery found in the *Idrot* and related Zoharic portions to new heights of graphic depiction. Especially, we find a strong stress on the female body, in particular in the sexual sense. Here Cordovero most prominently represents positive valuations of the feminine, moving away from the dominant approach in medieval Kabbalah.[53]

The exemplary work of Cordovero's median period was his commentary on the prayer-book, *Tefila le-Moshe* [The Prayer of Moses; see Psalms 90, 1].

50 Cordovero, *Or Yaqar*, and Vital, *Sefer ha-Hezyonot*, both translated and discussed in Idel, 'Italy in Safed', 248–249.

51 Vital, *Liqqutei Torah*, 124B.

52 Cordovero, *Pardes Rimonim*, Gate 31, chap. 3 (pt. 2, 73A).

53 Wolfson, 'Woman', 177; Abrams, 'A Light of Her Own', 20–23; *Ma'yan 'Ein Ya'acov*, in Sack (ed.), *The Fourth Fountain of the Book 'Elimah'*.

In explicating here the theurgical superiority of the Spanish or Sephardic version of the liturgy, he exemplified the wider process of the displacement of local practices by the mores of the Iberian émigrés. Looking beyond the rite of prayer, this work develops a general theory of action, reflecting Cordovero's keen interest in the theme of power. This extends into everyday life, saturating the day rather than punctuating it, a modern focus that was to peak in Hasidic teachings. As he put it, 'every material action should be accompanied by a hidden spiritual matter', 'spirituality' serving here as another term for the soul-essence.[54]

In general, Cordovero displayed a predilection for anomian techniques, expressed in his fondness for Abulafian linguistic methods. However, the controversial medieval kabbalist is not quoted here by name, thus bypassing the above-mentioned resistance to printing his texts.[55] Likewise, as part of his transhistorical synthesis, Cordovero cultivated the medieval technique of visualization of colors, a theme that also plays a part in his theosophy (the 'vessel' serving as a colored refraction of the colorless soul-essence of the *sefirot*):

> There is no doubt that the colors can introduce you to the operations of the *sefirot* and the drawing down of their overflow. Thus, when a person needs to draw down the overflow of Mercy from the attribute of Grace, let him imagine the name of the *sefirah* with the color that he needs, in front of him. If he [applics to] Supreme *Hesed*, [let him imagine] the outermost white.[56]

Many of these moves were anchored in a new genre of *hanhagot*, or conduct literature, in Cordovero's circle. These practices, such as conducting daily and weekly discussions of one's spiritual state with one's fellows, or monthly conventions devoted to ascetic rites, were directed at 'the society', 'men of [good] deeds' and other designations indicating a shift from smaller circles to more extensive social groupings.[57] At the same time, one must recall that these sectarian tendencies did not go unopposed by halakhists, who as a rule tend to be greatly concerned with uniformity and thus look askance at sectarian innovations.[58]

By far, Cordovero's most demanding project was his exhaustive and intensely analytic commentary on the *Zohar*, *Or Yaqar* (Precious Light),

[54] Cordovero, *Tefila le-Moshe*, translated and discussed in Garb, *Manifestations of Power*, 223.
[55] Idel, *Studies in Ecstatic Kabbalah*, 126–140.
[56] Cordovero, *Pardes Rimonim*, translated and discussed in Idel, *Hasidism*, 67–68.
[57] Hallamish, *Kabbalah in Liturgy, Halakhah and Customs*, 332–346.
[58] Horowitz, 'Notes on the Attitude of Moshe De Trani'.

also composed in his middle years. Like shorter commentaries by figures such as Alqabetz, *Yerah Yakar* by Cordovero's student R. Abraham Galante (d. 1589?), the index to the *Zohar* compiled by the latter's brother R. Moshe Galante (printed 1566), as well as exegetical works composed in the later Lurianic circle, this ambitious interpretative enterprise both expressed the importance of the *Zohar* in the life of Safed and cemented the perception of this canon as a clearly demarcated literary corpus written in the imaginary circle of R. Shimeon bar Yohai.[59] The ongoing (to this day) modern project of rendering the *Zohar* accessible continued into the first years of the next century, as in R. David ben Avraham Shemaria's *Torat Emmet* digest (printed 1605) and R. Yissakhar Baer of Kremnitz's *Pithei Yah* introduction (printed 1609). Here we can find an expression of a wider post-expulsion messianic belief (already voiced in the debate around its printing) that the dissemination of the *Zohar* can accelerate the redemptive process.[60]

One of the prominent expressions of the new wave of admiration for the *Zohar* was the reworking of a folk custom into a rite of pilgrimage to the alleged grave of bar Yohai at Meiron on the outskirts of Safed. This practice was focused in the later Lurianic circle on *Lag* (thirty-third day) *ba 'Omer* (the barley measure), associated with the dramatic mythical occurrences around his death (as described in the *Idra Zuta* section of the *Zohar*). Generally speaking, both Passover and the days of 'counting the *'Omer*', between Passover and the above-mentioned festival of *Shavu'ot*, were foci of Safedian theurgical discourse. According to one legendary account, it was at Meiron that Luria and his circle reconstructed the rite of the *Idra Rabba* as a device for invoking the souls of the alleged Zoharic circle.[61] This being said, as noted above, the pinnacle of mystical attainment for Cordovero was not Zoharic but language-based technique. This surprising move, joined by his indebtedness to the works of the *Sefer ha-Meshiv* circle, reiterates Cordovero's encyclopedic effort to collect, encompass, reconcile and legitimize virtually all existing forms of Kabbalah.[62] Furthermore, the sense that the *Zohar*, in and of itself, is a closed or mysterious text (thus requiring massive hermeneutical effort by the Safedian exegetes), paradoxically enabled them to displace the Zoharic corpus itself from the center of the kabbalistic 'attention space' as they reread and reassembled it within their own system.[63]

[59] Abrams, *Kabbalistic Manuscripts*, 248–252.
[60] Huss, *The Zohar*, 188–189, 201–203.
[61] Benayahu, 'Devotion Practices'.
[62] On encyclopedic Kabbalah in the early modern context, see Weinstein, *Kabbalah and Jewish Modernity*, 31–35, 40–41.
[63] On attention space in sociology of knowledge, see Collins, *The Sociology of Philosophies*, 38–39, 75–76.

Besides this theoretical writing (which is itself not devoid of personal introjections), spontaneous revelations experienced while touring the area of Safed (at times accompanied by his teacher Alqabetz) are recorded in Cordovero's diary-like *Sefer Gerushin* (book of banishments) and described as follows: 'Thanks be to God that we were vouchsafed all this, for these things are all supernal, infused without reflection whatsoever: they are sweeter than honey, the gift of the Queen to them that wander with her in exile.'[64] As evident in this text (and elsewhere in the diary), the *Gerushin* practice was an act of participation in the exile of the *Shekhina*, rewarded by direct messages from Her. Even without subscribing to the above-discussed expulsion thesis, it cannot be denied that Safed as a community was permeated with the pain of the exile and the hope of redemption. R. Abraham ha-Levi Berukhim (c.1515–c.1593), a student of Luria, experienced the following vision of the plight of the *Shekhina* (reminiscent of the above-quoted experience in Karo's circle) at the Wailing Wall in Jerusalem:

> He isolated himself for three days and nights in a fast and {clothed himself} in a sack, and nightly wept. Afterward he went before the Wailing Wall and prayed there and wept a mighty weeping. Suddenly, he raised his eyes and saw on the Wailing Wall the image of a woman, from behind, in clothes that it is better not to describe . . . he immediately fell on his face and cried and wept and said: 'Zion, Zion, woe to me that I have seen you in such a plight.' And he was bitterly complaining and weeping and beating his face and plucking his beard and the hair of his head, until he fainted and lay down and fell asleep on his face. Then he saw in a dream the image of a woman who came and put her hands on his face and wiped the tears of his eyes.[65]

Here weeping, joined by other ascetic behaviors, both leads to and responds to identification with the *Shekhina*, also representing the supernal root of the Holy City, which also guided the widespread visualization and goal of becoming a chariot or chair for its presence. Working from parallel quotes from Berukhim, Wolfson has pointed at the role of intense weeping as a method for enhancing Torah study, especially that of the *Zohar* and at midnight (see below on the latter technique). However, he also parsed a Vitalian approach linking weeping to the nocturnal ascent of the soul to its source, as well as Cordoverian descriptions of the shedding of tears as emending the sin of 'the spilling of seed' or masturbation.[66]

64 Translated and discussed in Werblowsky, *Joseph Karo*, 53.
65 Translated and discussed in Idel, *Kabbalah: New Perspectives*, 80–81.
66 Fishbane, 'A Chariot for the Shekhina'; Wolfson, 'Weeping', 215–222.

The sense of personal identification with *Shekhina-Malkhut* and other *sefirot* (found already in the Kabbalah of Jerusalem) is nowhere clearer than in Cordovero's widely studied (also in a semiliturgical fashion) *Musar* work. This short treatise, *Tomer Devora* (The Palm Tree of Deborah) details refined forms of conduct and emotional self-comportment that emulate the behavior, as it were, of the divine potencies, especially the *sefirot* and the thirteen *middot rahamim.* Reflecting his generally positive view of creation, Cordovero writes in quasi-medical fashion of 'curing the disease of pride':

> I have further found a good medicine . . . That man should train himself to do two things: First, to honour all creatures, in whom he recognizes the exalted nature of the Creator . . . because thy wisdom is attached to them important and great are thy works . . . The second is to bring the love of his fellow-men into his heart, even loving the wicked as if they were his brothers . . . How can he love them? By . . . refusing to look at their faults.[67]

Another popular work of his was *Or Ne'erav* (A Pleasant Light), dedicated to the new ideology of the absolute superiority and necessity of Kabbalah study, at the same time introducing beginners to this form of learning. Ideology, conduct literature and *Musar* were all vigorously disseminated by Cordovero's students, most prominently R. Eli'ezer Azikri (1537–1600) and R. Eliyahu da Vidas (d. 1593?). Like his teacher, Azikri composed a mystical diary, *Mile di-Shmaya* (Words of Heaven), describing his experiences of being constantly accompanied by divine light (also in colors) and on the other hand moments of 'total despair'.[68] This short work is also a treasury of unique practices such as frequent bows (possibly betraying Sufi influence) and officially indenturing himself as God's slave.[69] As in the case of Alqabetz, Azikri is especially renowned for a mystical poem, *Yedid Nefesh* (Soul Friend) also often recited to this day in welcoming the Sabbath. His *Sefer Haredim* (The Book of the God-Fearing), complements *Tomer Devora*'s psychological emphasis in detailing the correspondences between the commandments and the human limbs. In doing so, Azikri also expressed the Safedian desire to perform the entirety of the commandments, including biblically based observances that need to be artificially sought out, such as *Shiluah ha-Qen* (sending away the mother bird before taking her eggs).[70]

[67] Cordovero, *The Palm Tree of Deborah*, 77–79.

[68] Pachter (ed.), *Mili de-Shemaya*, 31, 39, 44, 48, 99, 146, 157, 173; 56.

[69] Ibid., 29, n. 54, 35, 46, 151; 45–48.

[70] Fine, *Physician of the Soul*, 191–192.

This hyper-nomian concern was also evident in the development, starting with Karo, of the requirement of preceding performance of ritual actions with a verbal declaration of one's intention to fulfill the divine commandment and by doing so unify the male Godhead with the *Shekhina*.[71] However, Azikri's writings also continue the anomian, personalized options found in the corpus of his teacher and in the collective activities of the circle. Quoting several authorities, including Luria, Azikri asserts that the practice of weekly self-isolation for personal prayer, while visualizing being contained within the light of the *Shekhina*, is not only superior to any ascetic regimen, but seven times greater than the highest value of normative Jewish life (especially in the modern period) – Torah study. Such experiences of luminosity, joined by various statements on performing the commandments themselves with great joy, balance the darker concerns of Safedian Kabbalah, alluded to above.[72] This balance is most fulsomely formulated in Da Vidas' oft-printed (also in digest form), *Reshit Hokhma* (The Beginning of Wisdom; see Psalms 111, 10), in a passage adroitly counterposing recurrent Safedian themes (including body and soul, isolation and support of popular piety):

> [A]ll the stringent practices which an individual is obligated to perform so as to restore shekhinah have to be carried out with joy . . . a person ought to derive greater pleasure from the joy of serving God and fulfilling His commandments than from all the money in the world . . .
>
> A person who desires to gladden his soul ought to seclude himself for a portion of the day for the purpose of meditating upon the splendor of the letters Y-H-V-H . . . For our soul issues forth from the name Y-H-V-H . . . Therefore, when an individual meditates upon this name his soul lights up and shines wondrously. The soul becomes filled with happiness, and by virtue of the power of this illumination, it is invested with the strength with which to emit sparks. This joy extends even to the body . . . as a consequence of one's love for the King, a person should praise Him and sing before Him in the synagogue, just as it is the custom to sing before a king of flesh and blood. [It is true that] Our Sages, of blessed memory, taught that singing is forbidden. This applies, however, to songs having to do with love between friends and those which praise physical beauty. But a Jew should not desist from singing songs of praise for God, or those that speak of God's compassion. Indeed, it is a custom among all Israel to sing at weddings or at festive banquets in a melodic and joyous way. We have never seen anyone oppose this.[73]

[71] Hallamish, *Kabbalah in Liturgy, Halakhah and Customs*, 48–54.
[72] Azikri, *Sefer ha-Haredim* (chap. 65), 226–227.
[73] Da Vidas, *Reshit Hokhma*, translated in Fine (ed.), *Safed Spirituality*, 151, 154–155.

As Mordechai Pachter has shown, the center of Da Vidas' teaching is love as the perfection of man's soul and interwoven with the classical ideal of *devequt* (see Chapter 1).[74] It is striking that human, especially sexual love, serves as his model for this psychology of adherence to the divine. While Idel has claimed that for Da Vidas, love, directed especially toward the Torah, 'renders the ascetic path unnecessary', Patrick Koch has pointed at the former's employment of ascetic strategies (e.g. fasting), aimed at removing the emotional effects (such as pride) of the demonic invasion caused by sin. Here Koch quotes the following flat declaration 'there won't be any rectification until the husks are crushed by means of fasting, weeping and lamenting'.[75] Koch's analysis, reinforcing Wolfson's above-mentioned treatment of the practice of weeping, underlines two central themes of Safedian mystical culture: an increased concern with the oscillation of emotions and the heightened dramatic sense of a cosmic battle with the forces of evil.[76] The latter characteristic is most evident in the greatly formative teachings of R. Itzhak Luria, to which we shall now turn.

LURIA AND HIS CIRCLE

As noted above, one of Cordovero's students was a Safedian-born scholar of Italian origin, R. Hayyim Vital Calabrese (1543–1620). Vital entered an intense process of seeking a spiritual director after his first mentor passed away. Initially he was fascinated by the mystical achievements of R. Lapidot Ashkenazi, including the detailed diagnosis of the individual's spiritual state provided by this somewhat enigmatic figure. Yet he soon (1571) transferred his alliance to another figure of Ashkenazi provenance. This was R. Itzhak Luria (1534–1572), newly arrived from Egypt. A student of Radbaz and of the halakhic luminary, R. Bezalel Ashkenazi (c.1520–1591), Luria had spent years in an intensive retreat near the Nile River. Luria's writings from this period differ in several significant respects from the teachings of the Safedian period, all of which were mediated through the reception and transmission of his students (chiefly Vital). The former body of texts (the large part of which remained in manuscript until recently) mostly takes the form of commentaries on the *Zohar* (especially the *Idrot*), and thus is looser in nature, both in outbursts of flashes of poetic expression as well as

[74] Pachter, *Roots of Faith*, 289–309.

[75] Idel, *Kabbalah and Eros*, 163, 173–174 (and 192–195); Koch, *Human Self Perfection*, 146–150, 160–163.

[76] On history of emotions in modern Kabbalah, see Garb, 'Shame'.

argumentation in the form of questions and answers. These markedly contrast with the terse, axiomatic style of the later works. This difference is also expressed in far greater indebtedness to Cordovero's dialectics. In keeping with their more derivative nature, the early texts do not contain some of Luria's trademark ideas, such as the doctrine of *tzimtzum*, or contraction of the divine light in preparation for emanation. However, on some issues (such as *mohin*, or intelligences), the level of detail is actually more satisfying.[77]

According to Vital's account, found in his mystical diary, printed as *Sefer Ha-Hezyonot* (The Book of Visions), Luria came not only to Safed, but to the world, in order to teach him and no other, and that 'it was impossible to reveal this wisdom, except through me'.[78] Indeed, Yehuda Liebes has boldly claimed that the main theme of Vital's transmission of Luria's teaching is that of the intricate relationship between the two. In other words, Lurianic Kabbalah is primarily a psychological projection of what one may term a biographical myth onto the cosmic domain.[79] At the very least, it can be granted that this ongoing reflection on the destiny of Luria and Vital has a clear messianic portent. Vital, like others, identified Luria's untimely death (a mere two years after his arrival in Safed) with the mythic, martyr-like death of Messiah son of Joseph, and he envisioned himself as inheriting this role. However, Vital's narrative, couched in highly grandiose terms, was not unopposed. Ronit Meroz has exposed the rivalry amongst the members of the circle, and various legendary accounts attribute Luria's early death (and hence the failure of his messianic project) to these tensions.[80] Vital's main competitors were the ex-Moroccan R. Yosef ibn Tavul (d. 1616) and R. Yisrael Sarug (d. c.1614).[81] Very soon after Luria's death, Vital's circle institutionalized loyalty to his leadership in a *shtar hitqashrut* (contract), a literary form adopted by several later groups throughout the modern period. The focus in this particular document is on preserving the secrecy of Vital's teaching, not pestering him to reveal more and not even revealing what the co-signers themselves had heard directly from Luria without Vital's permission, as they declare their inability to understand it without the latter's mediation. In other words, Vital was thereby accorded total control over the propagation of the Lurianic doctrine.[82]

77 Avivi, *Kabbala Luriana*, vol. III, 1078–1095.
78 Faierstein, *Jewish Mystical Autobiographies*, 48, 156.
79 Liebes, 'Myth vs. Symbol', 226–233; Liebes, 'New Directions'.
80 Tamar, *Eshkolot Tamar*, esp. 187–202.
81 Meroz, 'Faithful Transmission'; Meroz, 'R. Yisrael Sarug'; Fine, *Physician of the Soul*, 341–350.
82 Scholem, *Lurianic Kabbalah*, 262, 264–266.

Luria's system is arguably one of the most intricate and difficult structures in mystical writing as such. Indeed (as stated by Charles Mopsik), the one major change that Safedian Kabbalah brought about was a leap in the sheer complexity of the kabbalistic system.[83] Our understanding of this extensive and (unlike that of Cordovero) highly dense corpus is complicated further by the above-mentioned fact that Luria himself composed only a few short treatises (that have not reached us in their entirety), so that his teaching is mediated by the recordings and reworking found in the writings of his students (again in several competing versions). Furthermore, the resultant sprawling corpus was mostly printed in the late eighteenth century! Prior to that, we have numerous variants in manuscripts, themselves repeatedly noting gaps and 'doubts' in the transmission, and only systematically edited in the mid-seventeenth century. Nonetheless, I shall venture brief sketches of the main variants of the system, stressing those images and terms that are most associated with Luria (rather than his sources) and by necessity overlooking the interpretative quandaries (that arise at almost every point). Following this complex structure will be highly beneficial for the reader, as it is foundational for much of modern Kabbalah.

The one concept most frequently associated with Vital's transmission is the above-mentioned *tzimtzum*. Although this concept has earlier and perhaps even premodern sources, Vital crystallized it for subsequent generations. In this geometric and abstract symbolism, similar to that of the Christian mystic Nicholas of Cusa (1401–1464), the infinite light of the *Ein Sof* vacated a circular central space in order to make way for the very existence of the emanated (and later created) worlds.[84] These were formed by an infusion of a thin line of light into the 'empty space', which then took on the anthropomorphic form known by the semi-Zoharic term *Adam Qadmon* (Primordial Man):

> In the midst of all of this circular emanation light extends through a straight line . . . and this aspect is known in the Torah as the image of God . . . And know that in this emanation there are infinite worlds . . . but now we shall elaborate on one detail that includes the entire reality of this space and from it extend all the worlds, and it is the reality of *Adam Qadmon*.[85]

82 Scholem, *Lurianic Kabbalah*, 262, 264–266.

83 Mopsik, *Les grands textes*, 337, 418–419.

84 On the 'surprising' similarity of *tzimtzum* to Nicholas' *contractio*, see Funkenstein, 'Imitatio Dei', 84.

85 Vital, *Derekh 'Etz Hayyim*, pt. 1, 12B.

Although the general notion of an anthropomorphic entity above the *sefirot* probably owes much to traditions preserved by R. David ben Yehuda ha-Hasid, Vital's explication of the details of this configuration, focusing on its face (with detailed roles assigned to the orifices, hair, especially facial, and skull) was greatly indebted to the *Idrot* sections of the *Zohar*. Indeed, as we have already begun to observe, these were especially favored by modern kabbalists (both Jewish and Christian).[86] In his mystical diary, Vital records that Luria showed him the exact location in which the one of the *Idrot* took place and disclosed that he was of the 'soul root' of R. Shimeon bar Yohai, Vital predictably belonging to that of bar Yohai's main student, R. Abba.[87]

This more mythic component of the cosmogonic account continues with another theme found in the *Idrot* (with plausible earlier roots):[88] that of the 'death of the kings', or as Luria termed it, *shevirat ha-kelim* ('the breaking of the vessels'). In this primordial drama, some of the light emitted by *Adam Qadmon*'s face was too powerful for the receiving vessels of the *sefirot*, or alternatively the vessels themselves were not durable enough. As a result, the light withdrew, while most of the vessels fell outside the realm of divinity into the three created worlds (the fourth being the world of emanation, where the rupture took place). The shattering thus released sparks of divinity throughout the cosmos, an idea echoed in some accounts of the *tzimtzum*, that hold that there was a *reshimu* (trace) of divinity even in the empty space.[89] In any case, it seems that the breaking of the vessels deepened the process of limitation of divine presence commenced by the *tzimtzum*. It transpires here that while for Cordovero connectivity is the organizing trope, for Luria it is that of rupture.

In amending this catastrophic fall, the supernal emanator reorganized the vessels, sparks and returning (as well as 'new') sources of light into the new facial configurations of the five *partzufim* (countenances), again employing the terminology of the *Idrot*: three (*Arikh Anpin*, the long face, or *'Atiq Yomin*, ancient of days, *Abba*, father and *Imma*, mother) paralleling the highest of the *sefirot*; one *partzuf* (*Nuqba*) matching the lowest feminine aspect; and *Ze'ir Anpin*, the short face for the six median aspects. These were characterized by hologramic or fractal interinclusion, a theme found in a more rudimentary form in the writings of Cordovero. This cooperative

[86] Giller, *Reading the Zohar*, 141–157. [87] Faierstein, *Jewish Mystical Autobiographies*, 172.
[88] On parallels to the myth of the breaking of the vessels in antiquity, see Liebes, *Studies in Jewish Myth*, 84–86.
[89] See the Gnostic parallel in Scholem, *Major Trends*, 264. This discussion by Scholem remains one of the clearest expositions of Vital's system in English.

system was what granted the new array its durability. However, part of this process of *tiqqun* (rectification) was left for Adam, as the paradisiacal image or extension of *Adam Qadmon*. Following his primal sin (as described in Genesis 3), which further deepened the cosmic rupture, it then becomes incumbent upon his descendants, and the Jews in particular, to reassemble the scattered sparks and especially to promote the lost harmony of the supernal world by facilitating the *zivug* (intercourse) of its male and female aspects. The various forms of *zivug* (geared toward regular world-maintenance or less frequent infusions of *shef'a*, or influx) are facilitated by the *mayim nuqvin*, female waters awakened by the lower *partzufim*, assisted by the souls of the righteous and accompanied by 'raising' of sparks upward. This process is due to conclude in the messianic *eschaton*, of which, as we have seen, both Luria and Vital were perceived as forerunners. At the same time, Luria strongly rejected the macro-chronic doctrine of *shemitot*, instead seeing cosmic history as a linear process proceeding from Adam's sin to redemption.

One can isolate amongst all these and almost endless other details, some key images: Firstly, containment, as in the entry of light into vessels, as opposed to the surrounding, or more circular lights that remain outside the vessel. This containment was the primary goal of the reorganization of the *sefirot* into the more clearly anthropomorphic form of *partzufim*. It also necessitates the constant diminution of the emanated light as it flows down (in a sense reenacting the primary process of *tzimtzum*). Thus, the light is constantly filtered through a complex lattice of hairsbreadth channels, windows and *neqavim*, or pinholes. A second guiding image is that of movement, characterized by moments of smooth transmission of power, states of rupture and *dilug*, or noncontinuous 'leaps' between states. Further distinctions are drawn between the light merely 'passing through' along its course or moving through dimensions in a more full-bodied form of presence. The direction of movement can be reversed, and as it restarts 'from below to above', accustomed hierarchies (especially in terms of gender) are reversed. As we have already seen, a third, psychological image is that of the soul. When the lower subaspects of the higher *partzufim* 'enclothe' themselves in the higher subaspects of the lower ones, they become their soul. And one of the pinnacles of Vitalian theurgy is the creation of new souls through the *zivug* process. Finally, perhaps reflecting Vital's own early alchemical studies (that his teacher actually frowned upon), we have the notion of constant, cathartic refinement, as a central component of the process of *tiqqun*, through which the grosser aspects are constantly 'deferred' downwards.

The transmission of R. Yisrael Sarug, a senior disciple of Luria, is unique in dealing with processes that took place prior to the *tzimtzum*, especially movements of pleasure within the *Ein-Sof.* As Wolfson has shown, the Cordoverian theme of divine self-pleasure as a motive force for emanation of the supernal world becomes explicit here.[90] One can also posit that Sarug conceived of the earliest phases of the creation in terms of a series of uterine contractions.[91] These created atom-like points, which then turned into letters (the letter *yod* itself having the form of a point), whose interweaving produced a garment, equivalent to the primal Torah and later folded inwards, in a *tzimtzum*-like process. In other words, language and textuality are the most primordial of processes, just as the breaking of the vessels is likened to the scattering of letters. It is possible that one can discern here the influence of earlier Ashkenazi language-mysticism, perhaps mediated through the earlier Jerusalem center.[92]

Furthermore, even in Vital's transmission there is a certain emphasis on language, balancing the anthropomorphic and geometric emphases discussed just now. For example, the highest aspects of *Adam Qadmon* are comprised of *milui'm*, or expansions of the letters of the Tetragammaton, with a special emphasis on the letter *yod*. These correspond in a complex manner to the various components of the Torah scroll (letters, vowels, musical cantillation notations and decorative 'crowns'). Overall, the Sarugian transmission was more diffuse than the more tightly controlled teaching of Vital: thus, Meroz has discerned an early phase, and later a split into Eastern and Italian branches, with marked contrasts between these three variants. For example, while the Eastern tradition sees the shards of the vessels as requiring astro-magical or angelological utilization rather than repair, early texts set forth a new myth of 'kings' related to Cain (again going back to Genesis) who are beyond repair.[93]

In contradistinction, Tavul's more coherent transmission records explicit disagreements with Vital.[94] One of his particular innovations was a cathartic and national view of *tzimtzum* and *shevira*, which for Tavul are ultimately the same process: according to this account, the roots of the attribute of judgment were mixed in the entire divine reality. As a result, the *tzimtzum* process entailed a disclosure and concentration of these (feminine) powers

90 Wolfson, *Circle in the Square*, 69–72.

91 Compare to Jacobson, 'The Aspect of the Feminine', 245 (Hebrew readers may locate this study in the collection Jacobson, *Truth, Faith and Holiness*).

92 Idel, *Golem*, 148–153.

93 Meroz, 'Contrasting Opinions', 200–202 (and Meroz, 'The Saruq School').

94 Avivi, *Kabbala Luriana*, vol. I, 154–157, 180–185.

as a result of the withdrawal of the (male) attribute of mercy, like dust in the sea becoming evident once the water recedes.[95] Therefore, the 'one spark' emanating from *Adam Qadmon* contained even more explicitly negative potencies as it 'was divided into two: the kernel (*moah*) and husk, the root of Israel in the kernel and the root of the nations in the husk, and in this spark the root of the nations was prior to the root of Israel'. Hence, the breaking of the vessels was aimed at purifying the primordial realm from the demonic presence of the national other.[96] Scholem (basing his argument on Isaiah Tishby's analysis), described this doctrine as dualistic and Gnostic, true to his general interpretation of the thrust of kabbalistic history.[97] This negative view of mundane reality, in contradistinction from Cordovero's more harmonistic approach, can also be readily located in Vital's transmission: 'This earth is the utmost denseness of the *qelipot*, and hence all the occurrences of this world are difficult and bad and the wicked prevail in it.'[98] Of Luria's minor students, the most influential was R. Moshe Yona, whose one book survives in oft-copied manuscripts. The relative success of his *Kanfei Yona* lies in its offering a synopsis of the entire Lurianic doctrine. Yona's transmission uses somatic imagery in order to explain the earliest stages of emanation, rather than the spatial-geometric or linguistic language that we have encountered up to now. Thus, the primal condensed 'one point' is likened to human flesh that is comprised of the classical four elements, yet these are not visibly apparent in it. Similarly, Yona uses body–soul interaction in order to illustrate the condensation of the 'inner' light into the vessel (as opposed to the 'surrounding light' that remains above it).[99]

While Scholem, Tishby and others have focused on the narrative of *tzimtzum–shevira–tiqqun* found in the initial 'gates' of the theosophical treatises, Pachter has pointed at the salience of what I would term the psychosomatic structure, as found in later gates.[100] Especially, he underlined the development of the *partzufim* from pregnancy through birth, lactation and childhood to maturity, sexual and psychological. The later process is mostly a matter of the lower *partzufim* (based on those vessels that bore the

95 Tishby, *The Doctrine of Evil*, 56–59; Wolfson, 'Divine Suffering', 118–122.

96 Tavul, 'Drush Heftzi Ba', translated and discussed in Tishby, *The Doctrine of Evil*, 42.

97 Scholem, *Major Trends*, 267 (see at greater length in Fine, *Physician of the Soul*, 144–149). Cf. the complex harmonistic move in Avivi, *Kabbala Luriana*, vol. III, 1035–1036, n. 4, 1184–1190 (somewhat supported by Wolfson, 'Divine Suffering', 122, 136).

98 Vital, *Derekh 'Etz Hayyim*, pt. 2, Gate 42, chap. 4, fol. 91A. See also Dan, 'No Evil Descends from Heaven', 103; Tishby, 'Gnostic Doctrines'.

99 See the manuscripts quoted in Avivi, *Kabbala Luriana*, vol. I, 195, 198–199.

100 Pachter, *Roots of Faith*, 186–233.

brunt of the *shevira*) being completed by the *mohin* flowing from the *zivug* of the higher ones. Consequentially, the divine image or *tzelem* is constructed and refined.[101] Yet, as we have seen, some versions of Luria's teachings locate similar themes in earlier phases of the emanation. Indeed, it is not entirely clear to what extent the original version of Luria's teachings upheld a linear (as opposed to fractal or circular) view of cosmogony. At the very least, one can discern competing images of lines and circles.[102]

As opposed to Cordovero's positive view of femininity, the various Lurianic traditions, true to their dourer outlook, mostly uphold the model of the absorption of the female aspects within the male and phallic body (as argued by Wolfson). Yoram Jacobson has proposed a somewhat different reading, according to which the initial feminine force (described as the 'world of points' that disintegrated in the breaking of the vessels) is 'distorted and impaired', and only after the appearance of the masculine principle can a balanced world be established. Through this process of rebuilding of the vessels, the feminine is reconstituted as a productive and creative power. This transformed femininity is expressed in the three mundane worlds below the divine world of *Atzilut*:

> [A]ll parts of these three worlds of Beriah, Yetsirah and Assiyah are the aspect of the female . . . and they do not include a male (aspect) whatsoever . . . Because all of them are the hosts of Malkhut and her army, and were built and configurated by the mentioned purification process of the seven Kings [i.e. the seven lower sefirot whose vessels broke].

The ongoing purification of the feminine (perhaps reflecting the halakhic rite of the monthly purification of women after menstruation) is closely related to the ongoing theurgical process: 'All the created beings and the souls of the righteous people as well, are the result of the purification of these Kings. Day by day, they are cleansed and raised as female waters (from the chaotic mixture) to upper levels of restored existence, in the course and as a result of our prayers.' The term *mayim nuqbin*, 'female waters', refers to the Zoharic notion of the sexual awakening of the feminine aspect initiating theurgical processes.[103]

What I have elsewhere termed the psychological revolution of Safed is most markedly present in the intense concern with metempsychosis in Luria's circle, especially as recorded in Vital's *Sha'ar ha-Gilgulim* (Gate of

[101] Magid, *From Metaphysics to Midrash*, 200–213. [102] Pachter, *Roots of Faith*, 130–184.
[103] Wolfson, *Language, Eros, Being*, 80–81, 179–186, 386–388; Jacobson, 'The Aspect of the Feminine' (the text is translated and discussed on 254–255).

Reincarnations).[104] Here, the more rudimentary ideas found in medieval and Renaissance Kabbalah were greatly elaborated in a complex system of 'soul roots', or psychic families, whose ultimate origin lies in the primal soul of Adam (and thus their reincarnations are repeated attempts to emend his sin).[105] It is instructive that unlike Luria, Cordovero felt that it was unadvisable to seek out esoteric knowledge of one's personal reincarnation history. The general Safedian interest in reincarnation had diverse sources, the most immediate of which were the Greco-Turkish kabbalists (as in the anonymous *Gallei Raza*, Revelation of the Mysteries, 1552–1553), whose ideas were also mediated through the above-mentioned Radbaz. The theoretical concern with *gilgul* was accompanied by the theme of *'ibbur*, or 'impregnation' by another soul during one's lifetime.[106] Vital's diary is replete with accounts of such occurrences, echoing the theoretical concern with the process of pregnancy (as described above). Concomitantly the practice manuals based on Luria's teachings, especially *Sha'ar Ruah ha-Qodesh* (The Gate of the Holy Spirit), contain techniques designed toward enabling adherence to the souls of the departed righteous.

The parallel to *'ibbur* is that of spirit possession (later acquiring the term *dibbuq*), mostly befalling women (and frequently involving improper sexual behavior), who were then exorcised by (male) kabbalists, beginning with Karo. Here too, the Lurianic practice manuals are highly instructive as to technique, combining linguistic, angelological and meditative strategies. As J. H. Chajes has argued, one can discern here the influence of the Iberian origin (both Jewish and general) of much of Safedian mystical culture.[107] From his psychological-anthropological perspective, Yoram Bilu has contrasted *dibbuq*, as possession trance, with what can also be regarded as a somewhat separate domain of experience – nonpossessive trance experience involving a *magid* or angelic mentor.[108] Although this was part (though by no means the greater part) of Karo's experience, we shall soon see that this was not the case for other Safedian circles.

As a whole, Lurianic theory is indelibly wedded to a remarkably detailed set of mystical and at times shamanic practices: the refraction of the cosmic flaw at the individual level is diagnosed by a set of quasi-medical methods, especially pulse-taking and metoposcopy. As Lawrence Fine has noted, this

[104] Garb, *The Yearnings of the Soul*, 24–40. [105] Scholem, *On the Mystical Shape*, 229–241.

[106] On the lines of influence and difference between Safedian views of reincarnation and earlier Kabbalah, see Ogren, *Renaissance and Rebirth*, 290–292.

[107] Chajes, *Between Worlds*, 35–56, 68–85, 104–106. On the Iberian context, see 26–31, 139.

[108] Bilu, 'Dybbuk and Maggid'.

was supplemented by direct communication with the soul, aimed at reaching more subtle layers of the supplicant's psychic being.[109] However, for Luria, as for other early modern kabbalists, *tiqqun* is mostly brought about by a vastly complex system of *kavvanot*.[110] Though these are firmly embedded in the traditional ritual-liturgical structure, Luria's focus on technique led to a certain anomian tendency (similar to that which we encountered in the case of Cordovero's circle). For instance, in *Sha'ar ha-Yihudim* (The Gate of Unifications), a treatise devoted to the central method of unifications of divine names (through mentally combining their constituent letters) it is stated that:

> Involvement with the unifications is greater than engagement with the Torah for the unification is engagement with the Torah . . . Thus it is good to unify these unifications constantly every day, for this will help him more than engagement with Torah. Moreover, by means of this he will draw down upon himself the souls of the righteous who want to be impregnated in him for they very much desire these unifications.[111]

In other words, the practice of unifications, not as a mere daily practice of technique but saturating the entire day, is not only equivalent to but actually superior to Torah study (recalling Azikri's formulation mentioned above). For just as the aim of Torah study is cleaving to the root of one's own soul, the practice of unifications leads to the revelation of the souls of the departed righteous, experiences described in detail in Vital's diary (and often taking place at the former's gravesites).[112] In true shamanic fashion (and elaborating on a Zoharic motif), at times the righteous vouchsafe mystical knowledge by taking on the form of birds.[113] Through *yihudim* and similar techniques, including diagnosis of one's spiritual well-being through the state of the letters of the divine name shining on the forehead, the linguistic pole of the Lurianic teaching (most evident in Sarug's transmission) comes to fore.

Despite this intense mystical-occult concern, Luria explicitly opposed recourse to 'practical Kabbalah', or magic, giving various reasons for his firm stance. Here one can discern some similarity to Cordovero, who converted the terminology of astral magic to the theurgical trope of the

109 Fine, *Physician of the Soul*, 150–167.
110 On *kavvanot* in the sixteenth century, see Safrai, 'Give Strength to God'.
111 Translated and analyzed (in a somewhat different manner) in Wolfson, 'Weeping', 211–212. For an analysis of sample *yihudim*, see Fine, *Physician of the Soul*, 277–281.
112 On Torah study and the soul in Lurianic and modern Kabbalah, see Garb, *Yearnings of the Soul*, 150–153.
113 See e.g. Vital, *Sha'ar Ruah ha-Qodesh*, vol. I, third treatise, 47.

righteous drawing down influx from the internal aspect of the *sefirot*. Cordovero and Luria also shared significant reservations concerning the role of angels as sources of mystical knowledge, here distancing themselves from Karo (as well as Renaissance Italian kabbalists, Jewish and Christian).[114] As we have just seen, for Luria the superior goal is obtaining revelations from the departed souls of the righteous.[115] There is a certain move here away from the more positive attitude toward magic found amongst diverse figures in the first part of the century, including Jerusalemite kabbalists, Molkho (and other *converso* figures), as well as Luria's own teacher Radbaz.[116] However, this slightly ambivalent renitence did not persist amongst the next generation. Vital compiled magical and alchemical techniques (including spells in Turkish and European languages) and consulted (as did his son Shmuel) with Arab practitioners, as well as writing numerous amulets, as did Yona.[117]

We would err if we saw Luria merely as interpreting and expanding existing ritual structures. He produced messianic hymns for the Sabbath meals as well as hundreds of new customs and stringencies. One of the most widespread amongst the former was that of seven *hakafot*, or festive circles with the Torah scrolls on the festival of *Simhat Torah* (Rejoicing in the Torah) at the end of the *Sukkot* festival.[118] Luria also made the first steps toward what was to become canonical in many quarters as 'The Ari's prayer-book'. At the same time, he provided a kabbalistic rationale for the plurality of versions of the liturgy found amongst the immigrant populations of Safed, ascribing them to twelve windows in heaven for each of the tribes of Israel. However, as an Ashkenazi and in contrast to Cordovero, Luria himself set great store by the Ashkenazi hymns.[119] However, once the notion of a Lurianic version of prayer crystallized amongst the following generation of editors of his writings, at a time when genealogies traceable to areas of origin became increasingly blurred, it was described as the thirteenth window.[120] Luria's Ashkenazi loyalties were also expressed in his development of the rites of penitence designed by the German Pietists, under the new rubric of

114 Kadari, *Cordovero's Angels*; Werblowsky, *Joseph Karo*, 15, 72, 77–79. On angelology in Renaissance Kabbalah, see Lelli, 'Poetry, Myth and Kabbala', esp. 61. Compare also above on John Dee.

115 Garb, 'The Cult of the Saints'.

116 On Radbaz, see Garb, 'The Kabbalah of R. Joseph ibn Sayyah', 262. For wider discussion informed by a somewhat different approach, see Idel, 'R. Nehemia ben Shlomo the Prophet on the Star of David' (esp. 48 on R. Moshe Yona).

117 Boss, 'Hayyim Vital's Practical Kabbalah', esp. 60; Chajes, *Between Worlds*, 93, 177.

118 On Luria's innovation and its later development, see Faierstein, *Jewish Customs*, 69–72.

119 Idel, 'On Nehemia ben Shlomo'.

120 Hallamish, *Kabbalah in Liturgy, Halakhah and Customs*, 106–110.

tiqqun. These practices included fasts atoning for negative emotions, especially anger.[121] The interpretation of repentance as *tiqqun* dovetailed with a wider Safedian attempt to impact society, often by means of homilies, in bringing about mass repentance. These efforts range from R. Yehuda Hallewa's early endeavors, through Azikri's short-lived fellowship dedicated to repentance (1588–1589) to Vital's failed attempts in his later period in Damascus.[122]

Perhaps the most important and influential Lurianic rite was that of *tiqqun hatzot* (Rectification at Midnight) greatly developing the Jerusalemite practice of nocturnal activity. This practice included obvious ascetic elements, such as placing ashes on one's forehead and rubbing one's eyes in dust, in identification with the lowly state of the *Shekhina*. Yet the second, more upbeat phase of the ritual involves consoling the *Shekhina* through participation in her erotic preparation for *zivvug* with the male potencies.[123] More broadly, *tiqqun hazot* epitomized a larger Safedian shift toward nocturnal activity, including intensive recording of dreams. Here is a description of the manner in which the above-mentioned Berukhim (d. 1593) spent his nights: 'Every night [he] would rise at midnight and walk through all the streets, raising his voice and shouting bitterly: Arise . . . for the Shekhina is in exile . . . and he would call each scholar by his name, not departing until he saw that he had left his bed. Within an hour the city was full of the sounds of study.'[124] Elliot Horowitz has suggested that this flurry of late-night activity is related to the appearance of coffee, mentioned rather approvingly already by Radbaz and by 1580 available in a Safedian coffee house.

Like the members of Cordovero's circle, Luria and Vital would walk in the valleys and hills of the Galilee, especially frequenting graves of the righteous, many of which were identified by Luria.[125] Curiously, he also located the grave of Jesus.[126] Another similarity to Cordovero's group can be found in the propagation of the new kabbalistic ideology: an oft-quoted text by Vital, printed as an introduction to his magnum opus *Derekh 'Etz Hayyim* (The Tree of Life), composed soon after his master's death (probably as an eulogy) is (in Rachel Elior's words) 'a bold religious document, expressing a transformation of religious awareness'.[127] As in Cordovero's *Or Ne'erav*, Vital

[121] Fine, *Physician of the Soul*, 167–186. [122] Idel, 'R. Yehudah Ḥallewa', 122–124.
[123] Magid, 'Conjugal Union'. [124] Translated and discussed in Horowitz, 'Coffee', 27.
[125] Giller, 'Recovering the Sanctity', 158–167.
[126] Vital, *Sha'ar ha-Gilgulim*, introduction, 37, 182. As Faierstein, 'The Possession of Rabbi Hayyim Vital' has noted, this passage was censored in some printings.
[127] Elior, 'Messianic Expectations', 38 (the book is popularly known as *'Etz Hayyim*). The relatively widespread genre of eulogies by and for kabbalists requires further study.

insists on both the necessity and primacy of the study of Kabbalah. Vital's Cordoverian leanings are also apparent in the former's oft-printed *Musar* work, *Sha'arei Qedusha* (Gates of Holiness), directed toward the attainment of prophecy, with the rectification of one's *middot* as a prerequisite. Another example of a *Musar* text merging Cordoverian and Lurianic influences is *Midrash Shmuel*, a popular commentary on the Mishnaic tractate *Avot* (a common genre in Jewish writing in general and in kabbalistic literature in particular), by R. Shmuel Uceda (d. c.1603). Like *Sha'arei Qedusha*, this work upholds the need to focus both on the commandments and on the virtues of one's inner and emotional life. As noted in the concluding discussion, Vital's claim in *Sha'arei Qedusha* that prophecy is readily accessible (like Cordovero's *gerushin* method), reflects a wider aspiration toward revelatory experience. However, other aspects of Vital's ideological tract underline his distance from Cordovero's pluralistic approach. Not only is Luria's mystical power given place of pride in the first of a series of hagiographical flights, but the bulk of earlier Kabbalah are actually rejected as rather trite, lacking as they do the support of revelation, especially that of Elijah: thus, in the above-mentioned introduction/eulogy Luria's revelatory teaching is positioned at the heart of a newly narrow and esoteric canon (with Vital's own status as 'single student' projected on earlier periods):

> And each of the known sages of this wisdom . . . would study it in great secrecy . . . and would only disclose it to the single student of his generation, and this too only in chapter headings,[128] mouth to mouth, revealing one handbreadth and concealing a thousand. And this wisdom was steadily collapsing from generation to generation until Nahmanides, the last of the true Kabbalists. Now all the books of the later Kabbalists who came after Nahmanides, do not come close to them – for from Nahmanides onwards the way of this wisdom was hidden from the eyes of all of the wise, and they only possessed a few branches of introductions without their roots, and upon these the later Kabbalists, of blessed memory, constructed their teachings with the human intellect. And you yourself can tell that the sharp student can encompass and know most of their introductions and principles in four or five days. And most of their sayings are duplications in different words and all of the fruit of their introductions is that there are ten *sefirot* and they piled up books on this matter that can be summarized in two or three treatises.[129]

[128] See *Hagiga* 13A.

[129] *Derekh 'Etz Hayyim*, introduction, 8 (and compare to 10 and the discussion in Garb, *Modern Kabbalah*, 14–21).

SAFED IN EUROPE

Despite the resistance, especially on the part of R. Hayyim Vital, to the proliferation of Lurianic Kabbalah, it soon made its way to kabbalistic centers throughout the Diaspora. Although it also had some influence in North Africa and Yemen, it mainly took root in two European centers toward the end of the century, at the same time as the Safedian center itself declined to a tithe of its former strength. As we shall see further, the travels of R. Israel Sarug (d. 1610) in northern Italy and Central Europe ensured that this form of Lurianic doctrine, viewed with great suspicion in the Near East, became a dominant form of European Kabbalah, also outside the Jewish world. More than a decade earlier, Tavul's version of this teaching had already reached the shores of Italy through his student R. Shimson Baqqi.

Unencumbered by the Vitalian politics of internal esotericist bans, the Kabbalah of Cordovero also found numerous Italian devotees. One of the most striking of these was his student R. Mordekhai Dato (1525–1597?), a poet and preacher who spent the year 1560 in Safed and Jerusalem. His magnum opus *Migdal David* expresses apocalyptic and acute messianic expectation, focused on the year 1575. At the same time, in typically modern autobiographic mode, he admits that this prediction could be colored by his 'powerful desire to bring the redemption closer'. As an exegete, Dato focused on the figure of David as an emblem of messianic destiny, both here and in his commentary on Psalms. As Jacobson has surmised, this urgency was fueled not only by the Iberian expulsion, but closer to home, by the deterioration of the status of Italian Jewry, peaking with the burning of the Talmud at the bequest of Pope Julian III in 1553 (itself exemplifying the shadow side of the move to print culture) and the expulsion of the Jews from the Papal states in 1569. Conversely, Dato was encouraged by the renewal of immigration to the Holy Land that he himself witnessed.[130] Such juxtapositions further reflect the shift on the part of modern kabbalists toward heightened attention to the course of external history. Dato's contribution to the dissemination of the system of Cordovero (whom he continued to visualize conversing with him even after the latter's death, in Safedian fashion) is found in his detailed annotation of *'Asis Rimonim* (Juice of Pomegranates), an abridgment of *Pardes Rimonim* by his colleague R. Shmuel Gallico (c.1530–1582?).[131] One of the refractions of Cordoverian doctrine in Dato's

[130] Jacobson, *Along the Paths of Exile and Redemption*, 17–19, 37, 183–184, 187.

[131] On the mystical connection with Cordovero, see ibid., 323, n. 467.

elaborate historiosophy is his repeated stress on the organic nature of the Jewish nation and the superiority of the Jewish soul.[132]

Yet this Safedian colonization, like the earlier Zoharic proliferation, was not unopposed. For example, the physician and scientific writer R. Avraham ben Hanania Yagel (1553–c.1623) acknowledged Vital's greatness, yet relegated him to the locality of Galilee, possibly implying that his lore is irrelevant for the Italian context.[133] The disparity between Yagel's approach and the Safedian outlook is glaringly apparent in the former's willingness to 'search in the pouches of the ancients, either from our blessed sages, or from the rest of the sages of the nations', here referring primarily to the above-mentioned Heinrich Cornelius Agrippa.[134] In other words, Yagel's writing, heavily influenced by Alemanno, was a bulwark of Renaissance *prisca theologia* universalism in face of the far more insular approach imported from the Galilee. Accordingly, he presaged later Italian developments in identifying the power of the *sefirot* with the Platonic ideas.[135]

Yosef Avivi has now uncovered the Central European channel of circulation of Lurianic writing and its editing. Already around 1613, a manuscript containing extensive Sarugian teachings was copied in Frankfurt, containing detailed notes by R. Alexander Katz (d. c.1606). These texts, and others mixed with Cordoverian doctrines, were to form the basis for the dissemination of Safedian Kabbalah in both Central and Southern Europe in the course of the next century. In some of these, we find references to the transmission from Sarug (in turn based on his time at Luria's table), to Katz's own mysterious teacher. A further indication to the early reception of Lurianic practice in this area is the reference to 'our custom in Ashkenaz' with regard to *kavvanot*. Yet another manifestation of Ashkenazi self-consciousness is the presence of theological discussions continuing pantheistic views found in the medieval corpus of German Pietism.[136] For all of the differences that Avivi duly notes, these views are reminiscent of the Hasidic theology developed two centuries later in Eastern Europe.[137] Caution dictates, however, that Avivi's findings should be contrasted with the testimony of R. David of Fuld, himself a conduit of textual transmission from the Land

132 Ibid., 153, 84–85.

133 Idel, 'Italy in Safed', 253–254.

134 *Beit Ya'ar ha-Levanon*, translated and discussed in Ruderman, *Kabbalah, Magic and Science*, 110–111, 117, 144–149.

135 Ruderman, *Kabbalah, Magic and Science*, 156.

136 Pantheism in German Pietism and its influence shall be addressed in a study in preparation by Itzhak Melamed and myself.

137 Avivi, *Kabbala Luriana*, vol. I, 435–467.

of Israel, as to the scarcity of kabbalistic knowledge (and the derogatory attitude toward it in philosophically oriented circles) in Germany in 1595.[138]

In Poland, local agents, such as R. Issakhar Baer Ha-Kohen of Shebreshin, who may have visited the Land of Israel, compiled Zoharic customs in his *Mar'eh Kohen* (printed 1589).[139] A consultation from Lvov with R. Hayyim Vital on supernatural phenomena in 1620 reflects the authoritative status of Safed amongst the Galician elite.[140] At the same time, alongside with the Ashkenazi critique of Karo's halakhic project, local authorities, such as R. Shlomo Luria (1510?–1573) boldly rejected the influence of Kabbalah on halakhic decision-making. Karo's main protagonist in the halakhic realm, R. Issakhar Baer's own teacher R. Moshe Isserles, or Rema (1525–1572) of Cracow, sharply criticized the popular propagation of Kabbalah in Central Europe, especially amongst those lacking knowledge in basic Jewish texts. Some Italian rabbis absorbed this Ashkenazi critique, so that R. Moshe Provinicialo went so far as to describe a Zoharic ruling as the words of a mistaken student.[141] Despite existing reservations as to the thesis of a resurgence of philosophy in sixteenth-century Ashkenazi culture, one can certainly discern a certain openness toward philosophy in Isserles' *Torat ha-'Ola*.

In some senses, Isserles' center of Cracow, attracting immigrants from several areas in Europe, can be seen as a counterpart to Safed and its insular approach. As Lawrence Kaplan has argued, Isserles' defense of philosophy was part of a wider defense of Ashkenazi-Polish tradition, paralleled by his halakhic positions.[142] From this perspective, it is far from coincidental that after the fierce campaign waged by R. Joseph Ashkenazi (c.1530–c.1582) against the printing of philosophical works failed in Poznan (1559), he made his way to Safed and joined Luria's circle. This immigration was a portent of cultural mediation, as Ashkenazi transmitted the late medieval Ashkenazi tradition to his namesake Itzhak Luria Ashkenazi.[143]

However, such confrontations amongst the elite were overshadowed by the steady process of popular dissemination of Kabbalah through conduits such as *Musar* and especially *Drush*, or homilies (these two genres often merged). What is sociologically significant in this literature is that the masses created by the demographic explosion in Jewish Poland–Lithuania are regarded as theurgical auxiliary forces, as it were, for the emergent class of

138 Zimmer, *The Fiery Embers of the Scholars*, 30–33.
139 Gries, *Conduct Literature*, 41–42.
140 Ruderman, *Kabbalah, Magic and Science*, 81–82.
141 Katz, *Halakhah and Kabbalah*, 108.
142 Kaplan, 'Rabbi Mordekhai Jaffe', 267–269.
143 Reiner, 'The Attitude of Ashkenazi Society'; Scholem, *Lurianic Kabbalah*, 127–128, 134.

kabbalists. Thus, in R. Judah ha-Kohen's compilation of Safedian nocturnal rituals, he writes that the prayer of those ignorant of the proper *kavvana* joins with that of the kabbalists, so that they are 'bound as one'.[144] Here the Cordoverian notion of the organic unity of the nation comes into full play. From this perspective, it is telling that already this Safedian master made strategic use of the term *hamon ha-'am*, or the masses, and related the dialectic of concealment and disclosure in the divine realm to the 'political distinction', as Wolfson put it, between the elite and the masses.[145]

CONCLUSION: SAFED AS A MYSTICAL CULTURE

Our survey has noted marked differences between the three major Safedian circles and mention of more minor figures would have easily multiplied these. The hagiographical tradition reflects these disputes in accounts of Karo repeatedly falling asleep in Luria's classes (demonstrating his unsuitability) and Luria arriving in Safed straight after Cordovero's funeral (signaling that a new era had begun). Yet, the plurality of Safedian Kabbalah should be ascribed not only to the diversity of circles (including the internal disputes within Luria's fellowship) and channels of reception, but also to immigration from various earlier centers, joined by extra-Jewish influences. This plethora is reflectively marked in the Safedian theory (admittedly developing Jerusalemite formulations) of all but endless interpretative exegetical possibilities based on one's 'soul root'. Here too, there is the possibility of external influence, that of Renaissance thinkers such as Bruno.[146] On the theosophical level, Vital records a statement that: 'In this *Atzilut* there are infinite kinds of worlds', so that *Adam Qadmon* is only 'one detail', encompassing as it may be.[147]

Despite these divergences, we have already begun to discern threads of commonality running through the Safedian enterprise as a whole. Looking back at Renaissance and medieval Kabbalah, one can point at a far greater readiness to accommodate new revelations, as opposed to transmission and interpretation of existing traditions on the one hand and philosophical speculation on the other. The privileging of visions and pneumatic attainment over discursive processes was part of a wider aspiration in sixteenth-century Kabbalah, as in the *converso Meshiv* circle and its offshoots and *Galia Raza*.

[144] Ha-Kohen, *Order and Tikunim of the Recitation of the Shma before Bedtime*, translated and discussed in Elbaum, 'Aspects of Hebrew Ethical Literature', 158.

[145] Wolfson, 'Divine Suffering', 113; Twersky, 'Talmudists, Philosophers, Kabbalists', 436, 447.

[146] Idel, *Absorbing Perfections*, 93–96.

[147] Vital, *Derekh 'Etz Hayyim*, pt. 1, Gate 1, Branch 2, 12B.

This shift can be comprehended against the background of the decline of philosophy in most circles, as in the following declaration by Alqabetz (debating the views of R. Israel di Curiel, an exception who proves the Safedian rule): 'The Torah, which is man's perfection . . . being more perfect than any wisdom or science. And this [statement] is such as does not require explanation.'[148] In broader terms, the authority of revelation replaced that of the 'human intellect' that was set aside alongside with much of medieval Kabbalah. The yearning for revelation was declared poignantly in the concluding stanza of Azikri's *Yedid Nefesh* poem, beginning with the call 'please reveal yourself . . . my dear one'. An interesting nexus of vision and gender, reflected in Vital's contacts with female visionaries, can be found in the writings of R. Asher Lemlein Reutlingen, a messianic Ashkenazi who operated in Northern Italy at the beginning of the century (and possibly reached Safed), who reports messages from a feminine figure, including critiques of the present state of Kabbalah (especially in its Sephardic form).[149]

This quest for otherworldly communications was most frequently captured by the trope of communicating with the legendary figure of the prophet Elijah qua psychopomp.[150] Most strikingly, it led to the dissolving of the partitions between the waking state and dreams (again recorded copiously by Vital), and especially between the 'lands of the living' (Psalms 116, 9) and the world of the dead. The intensive search for mystical exchanges with the spirits of the departed, often at graveyards, led R. Moshe Alsheikh to describe Safed as 'city of interred dead'.[151] For example, de Vidas' graphic descriptions of Hell are based on an encounter with a departed soul in a dream.[152] Yet here too this concern (deepening in the next century and expressing wider cultural trends) extends beyond Safed:[153] *Gey Hizayon* (Valley of Vision), composed in 1578, by Yagel, again a thinker critical of Safedian colonization, takes the form of a dream tour of the afterworld guided by the soul of the author's father.[154] One may speculate that the ancient, cross-cultural association of the dream world and the world of the dead manifests here, in both cases reflecting the aspiration to go beyond the everyday world and its intellectual products.

148 Translated and discussed in Pachter, *Roots of Faith*, 241.

149 Chajes, *Between Worlds*, 101–104, 113–118: Idel, *Messianic Mystics*, 140–142. On the scope of his reception, also in the Christian world, see Campanini, 'A Neglected Source'.

150 Wolfson, 'Weeping', 212–215; Idel, 'Enoch and Elijah', 362–370.

151 Chajes, *Between Worlds*, 33–34.

152 Da Vidas, *Reshit Hokhma*, 59.

153 See e.g. Davies, *The Haunted*, 111–116.

154 Ruderman, *A Valley of Vision*; Ruderman, *Kabbalah, Magic and Science.*

Azikri's above-mentioned stanza climaxes with the demand: 'hurry beloved, for the time has come'. Even if one does not follow Scholem *in toto*, the accelerated revelatory turn is clearly tied up with the messianic drive, as in the case of Lemlen. As noted above, the specific Safedian context may well be the messianic atmosphere created around Suleiman II ('the magnificent'), the Ottoman emperor and conqueror.[155] We have already noted the impact of Ottoman ascendancy on kabbalistic Christians and their geopolitical messianism. However, one should beware lest the blanket term of messianism occlude the autonomy of related concerns such as repentance, rectification and victory over demonic evil (as in exorcism). All of these developments converged in a heightened sense of individual self-awareness (also present in the personalized relationship with the divine evoked by Azikri). As a result, numerous Safedian texts repeatedly stress the distinction between 'external' and 'internal' aspects.[156] The internal is also associated with the internal dimension of the Torah (and prayer), or Kabbalah, whose superiority lies at the core of the Safedian ideology. As an example of an extreme case, in a treatise on redemption probably penned in Safed around 1570 (by R. Shlomo Turiel) we find that the kabbalists will be above the rule of the Messiah himself in the rapidly approaching eschaton.[157] In other words, one should avoid reducing the new kabbalistic ideology to Messianism.

Whether through revelation or the time-tested method of exegetical effort, Safed witnessed an explosion of new lore, joining a massive reorganization of existing knowledge, perhaps reflecting broader cultural transformations. While Weinstein's arguments as to scientific language in Safedian Kabbalah (as part of its encyclopedic tendency) are somewhat strong, it is true that Luria (according to Vital's transmission) employed semimedical imagery for the *tiqqun* of the soul, while both he and Cordovero explicitly referred to 'the wisdom of anatomy'.[158] More generally, Assaf Tamari has pointed at the salience of medical knowledge and imagery in the writings of Vital (extending beyond his transmission of Lurianic teachings).[159] It was this unique combination of complex, detailed and often well-organized knowledge with passionate ecstatic, poetic and musical expression that paved the way for the penetration of Safedian thought and practice into numerous domains of Jewish thought and life by 1700, as described in the next chapter.

155 See further in Garb, *Yearnings of the Soul*, 26.

156 Scholem, *Lurianic Kabbalah*, 229; Margolin, *The Phenomenology of Inner Religious Life*, 45–48.

157 Scholem, *Lurianic Kabbalah*, 108, 121–123.

158 Garb, *Yearnings of the Soul*, 39–40; Weinstein, *Kabbalah and Jewish Modernity*, 28–31, 38–39; Cordovero, *Pardes Rimonim*, Gate 31, chap. 8, 75B.

159 See Tamari, 'The Body Discourse'.

3

The Kabbalistic Crisis of the Seventeenth Century

In December 1665, Henry Oldenburg (c.1619–1677), secretary of the scientific Royal Society (founded only five years earlier) wrote as follows to Baruch Spinoza (1631–1677; sadly, we do not have the philosopher's reply):

> As for politics, there is a rumor everywhere here concerning the return of the Jews, who have been dispersed for more than two thousand years, to their native country . . . may it please you to communicate to a friend what you have heard regarding this matter, and what you think of it . . . if the tidings prove to be true, it is sure to bring about an upheaval of everything in the world.[1]

The Sabbatean movement was not only (per Scholem) the 'largest and most momentous Jewish messianic movement in Jewish history subsequent to . . . the Bar Kokhva Revolt' (in second-century CE Palestine against the Roman Empire), but also the first social movement engendered by kabbalistic doctrines and visions.[2] This represents a marked enhancement of the sixteenth-century pattern of fraternities, and set the stage for further modern kabbalistic movements in later centuries. In its scope and in the fierce responses it provoked, Sabbateanism was truly international, bridging the Ashkenazi and Sephardic worlds, and also Western and Eastern Europe.[3] The movement ranged as far afield as Yemen, whose iconic devotional poet, R. Shalom Shabazi (1619–c.1680) wrote a passionate declaration of affection for its leaders.[4] As an interpretation of Lurianic Kabbalah, Sabbateanism

[1] Spinoza, *Letters*, translated and corrected in Scholem, *Sabbatai Sevi*, 544.
[2] Scholem, *Kabbalah*, 244. [3] Ruderman, *Early Modern Jewry*, 145.
[4] Tobi, 'Two Poems' (and see Yaakov, *God Came from Yemen*, 219–224).

continued the Safedian revolution (as well as intellectual patterns harking back to premodern Kabbalah). However, as Stephen Sharot first suggested, Sabbateanism also epitomizes what some historians term 'the general crisis of the seventeenth century'.[5]

While Sharot referred to the effects of economic decline on *conversos* and other Sephardic communities, one can speak more broadly of a crisis of authority, undermining the successful canonization of Safedian writing.[6] In this sense, the link with Spinoza, through *converso* communities such as that of Amsterdam, is more than incidental. Rather, the figures of the would-be Messiah Shabbetai Tzevi (1626–1676) and the excommunicated philosopher converge as figurations of the early modern crisis of rabbinical Judaism.[7] Scholem, who devoted much of his scholarly eros to uncovering the hidden history of the movement, was essentially correct in depicting Sabbateanism as the forerunner of revolutionary, reform and nationalistic trends in modern Judaism.[8]

However, the power of this narrative, vividly portrayed in Scholem's masterpiece *Sabbatai Sevi: The Mystical Messiah* (that reads like a historical novel), has occluded the extensive scope of intellectual and social processes in seventeenth-century Kabbalah, starting obviously with the half century before Tzevi's messianic declaration. This period especially witnessed the consolidation of the Safedian revolution, through the emergent process of the ever-morphing proliferation of Lurianic Kabbalah, yet also by means of the residual influence of the Kabbalah of Cordovero. The Italian philosophical interpretation of these doctrines did much to inaugurate the transformation of Kabbalah into a widespread, continuous presence in European intellectual life. Through the further mediation of a new generation (now mostly Protestant) of kabbalistic Christians, leading political, scientific and philosophical figures were exposed to this lore in its updated form.[9] It was precisely this success that engendered the first sustained critique of Kabbalah, as in the works of R. Yehuda Arye de Modena (1571–1648). Yet avoiding a Eurocentric approach requires attention to the spread of Lurianic theosophy and ritual throughout the Middle East,

[5] Sharot, *Messianism, Mysticism and Magic*, 110–114.
[6] Ruderman, *Early Modern Jewry*, 136–158.
[7] On affinities between 'cosmoerotic' theories found in the writings of Nathan of Gaza and those of Spinoza, see Idel, *Kabbalah and Eros*, 199–200.
[8] Scholem, *Major Trends*, 304, 320; Scholem, *The Messianic Idea*, 155, 159.
[9] See the overview (reaching into the early eighteenth century) in Kaennel, 'Protestantisme et cabale'.

especially in the strong center of Jewish learning (as well as international trade contacts) in Aleppo (Haleb).

It was not long before Tzevi's dramatic announcement of his messianic identity that Eastern Europe witnessed the first massive annihilation of Jewish communities: the Chmielnicki uprising (1648–1649). Polish Kabbalah, as a rapidly emergent doctrine amongst a fast-growing and relatively new Jewish center, was deeply haunted by this tragedy. Viewed more widely, this early form of ethnic cleansing foreshadowed the profound insecurity of Jewish life in modern Europe. Symbolizing this connection, R. Shimson Ostropoler (d. 1648) saw himself as a redemptive magician, so that for him his sacrificial death in the pogroms stemmed the tide of the demonic assault by the Christian world. This troubled Jewish European existence was a major factor in the nationalization of modern Kabbalah, most pronounced in the doctrines of the superior Jewish soul and language, and especially well established amongst the kabbalists of Prague during the course of the century. In the early twentieth century, this process resulted in yet another social movement (the Rav Kook circle).

These then shall be the foci of this chapter: Sabbateanism and its rejection, the competing versions of Safedian Kabbalah in Europe and the triumph of Lurianism in the Middle East, the philosophical impact of Kabbalah within and without the Jewish world (and the resultant critical reaction) and nationalizing responses to insecurity in Jewish Europe. Further notable developments, such as the further spread of *Musar* literature and other forms of the consolidation of kabbalistic quotidian practice, shall be woven into this narrative.

SABBATEANISM: THEOLOGY, IDEOLOGY AND SOCIOLOGY

As a messianic ideology resting on kabbalistic theology and engendering a mass movement, the Sabbatean phenomenon thus has three central facets, each of which has attracted a scholarly approach. The clearest exposition of the ideology of the movement was offered by Liebes. Overturning interpretations such as that of Oldenburg seen above (later joined by Zionist historians and thinkers), who perceived Sabbateanism as a political effort to restore the Jewish people to their ancestral homeland, Liebes has correctly captured its key message as one of religious transformation.[10] In doing so,

[10] Liebes, *Studies in Jewish Myth*, 93–113.

he provided ideational sketches of the three dramatis personae, to be presented now:

Shabbetai Tzevi, born in Izmir (Symrna), a community with a strong *converso* presence, was troubled in his youth by strong mood swings, accompanied by sexual anxieties as well as 'bizarre acts', some of an antinomian nature. These trials and exultations have been read by Elqayam (following Foucault) in terms of the figure of the divine fool (that disappeared under the assault of rationalism around this time). In doing so, he has posited a plausible connection between messianism (in terms of radical disruption of the normal order of things) and madness (see also on R. Nahman of Bratzlav in Chapter 5). However, to the almost entirely Eurocentric framework in which Foucault operated (his writing on Iran being a classic example of an exception that proves the rule) Elqayam adds the Islamicate context within which Tzevi increasingly operated. Besides offering a reverberation of the medieval Jewish polemic against the prophet Muhamad as a madman, Elqayam points at the prevalence, in the Ottoman context, of two Sufi orders (the *Khalwattiya* and particularly the *Bektāshiyya*) known for their socially disruptive antinomian conduct.

These persuasive claims give a specific geographical-cultural focus to the clear (and previously recognized) connections between Tzevi's self-perception as the 'absolute fool' and the long-standing Sufi tradition of divine madness. Almost certainly, these highly personal, often ineffable experiences were the crucible for Tzevi's unique theology, known as 'the secret of faith'.[11]. This rich setting is further expanded by Fenton's earlier observations of the parallels between the current geopolitical dimensions of Tzevi's apocalyptic-messianic vision, namely expectation of the downfall of Poland (in divine retribution for the Chmielnicki massacres) and the eschatological significance ascribed to the 1672 Ottoman victory over the Polish army by his Turkish contemporary Muhammad an-Niyāzi (1618–1694, who was also influenced by the *Bekhtāshis*).[12]

Tzevi's clearly modern discovery of the 'true' or personal God, the special 'God of Shabbetai Tzevi', usually identified with the median aspect of the divine world, engendered a radical critique of Jewish religiosity, culminating in his conversion to Islam following his anticlimactic encounter with Sultan Mehmed IV (1642–1693) on September 16, 1666.[13] On the mundane political level, this took place on pain of death by arrows, yet for Tzevi this was at the

[11] Elqayam, 'The Horizon of Reason'; Foucault, *Madness and Civilization*, esp. 21–24, 35–37, 64.
[12] Fenton, 'Shabbatay Sebi'. Compare to Scholem, *Sabbatai Sevi*, 287, 623–624.
[13] Beck, *A God of One's Own*, 104–117.

command of the true God. In his initial explanation of the conversion, it was a punishment for the Jews' forgetting of the true God. Yet even prior to this break, which predictably ended the mass following of the movement, he had rejected the doctrine of Luria, stating that the latter, in his intricate yet impersonal structure, had 'made a wonderfully beautiful chariot, but did not say who was riding in it'.[14]

Even if we do not follow Scholem's claim that it was the Jerusalem-trained Lurianic kabbalist R. Nathan Ashkenazi of Gaza (1643/4–1680) who reframed Tzevi's psychological suffering as messianic destiny, it is evident that he was the central formulator of Sabbatean ideology:[15] reinterpreting Lurianic Kabbalah in his *Sefer ha-Bri'a* (Book of Creation), one of the most important of unpublished modern kabbalistic works, Nathan developed a highly innovative theology revolving around two opposing poles: the 'thoughtless light', representing Shabbetai Tzevi, maintaining chaos even after creation, and the 'thoughtsome light', or Nathan, controlling it so as to enable the emergence and persistence of the cosmos.

However, Matt Goldish has reminded us that this was not merely a theological reading of personal destinies but also a mystical or shamanic experience. In March 1665, shortly before he met Tzevi, the youthful Nathan had the following visionary encounter (described in an epistle from around 1673 first uncovered by Scholem): 'The spirit came over me . . . I saw visions of God all day long and all night, and I was vouchsafed true prophecy . . . And with the utmost clarity my heart perceived toward whom my prophecy was directed [that is, toward Sabbatai Sevi] . . . but it remained hidden in my heart till the redeemer revealed himself in Gaza and proclaimed himself the Messiah.'[16] This anticipated declaration by Tzevi took place on May 31.

And later in that year (on the *Shavu'ot* festival, as in the sixteenth-century case of Karo):

> In the middle of the night a great sleep fell on Nathan . . . he leaped and danced in the room, shedding one piece of clothing after another until his underclothes alone remained. He then took a great leap and remained flat on the ground . . . He was like a dead man. Presently, a very low voice was heard . . . 'Take care concerning my beloved son, my Messiah Sabbatai Zvi'.[17]

[14] 'Raza de-Razin' (of unclear authorship), translated in Scholem, *Sabbatai Sevi*, 904.
[15] Scholem, *Sabbatai Sevi*, 207–228. Cf. Tishby, *Paths of Faith*, 246–258.
[16] Translated and discussed in Scholem, *Sabbatai Sevi*, 203–205 (the original text of the manuscript is transcribed in Scholem, *Major Trends*, 417–418, n. 18).
[17] Barukh of Arrezo, '*Likharon li-bnei Yisrae'l*', translated and analyzed in Goldish, *The Sabbatean Prophets*, 63–66.

Scholem has correctly deciphered this experience in terms of trance, and I would add here the phenomenon of automatic speech.[18] Although Nathan was a highly advanced student and practitioner of Lurianic Kabbalah (indeed Tzevi first approached him in pursuit of the Lurianic rite of the rectification of his troubled soul), his visionary independence led him to boldly annul its system of *kavvanot*, stating that continuing them in the messianic era would be like performing weekday tasks on the Sabbath. This abrogation undermined the very heart of the Safedian canon. As Scholem has noted, it is striking that this occasioned no protest on the part of R. Shmuel Vital, R. Hayyim Vital's son and editor, who was enlisted as a supporter of the movement.[19]

Third, we have the ex-*converso* Abraham Miguel Cardozo (1627–1703), arguably the leading theologian of the movement. Cardozo's philosophical-theological University training in Spain impelled him toward a certain demythologization of Sabbatean theology, so that for him the Messiah is not seen as part of the divine world, as he was for Tzevi himself (as well as for Nathan and others). This internal critique of the movement's central theology, accompanied by extensive polemics, rested on Cardozo's reiterated assumption that as Messiah son of Ephraim or Joseph, his understanding of the 'secret of faith' was superior to that of Tzevi himself (the Messiah son of David). He strongly suggests that this vantage point is related to his *converso* origins.[20] At the same time, throughout his voluminous writing, Cardozo preserved the movement's core ideology: the exile of the Jews is problematic mostly because it leads to the forgetting of the true God. As he put it in his treatise *'This is my God and I will Praise him'* (see Exodus 15, 2), while 'all of us moderns', Jewish, Christian and Muslim, worship a remote First Cause, it is the God of Israel (similar to Tzevi's personal God) and the feminine *Shekhina* who together created the world and are thus the source of its salvation.[21]

As evident in this text, questions of gender and sexuality were at the core of Cardozo's doctrine, also in comparative discussions of Mariology and of the absence of the divine feminine in Islam. In a detailed analysis, Wolfson has shown that for this thinker, the restoration of the primal androgyny through the integration of the female divinity within the male epitomized the messianic state. Thus, it is not surprising that besides the two Messiahs and Moses (a traditional messianic figure, especially in *Tikkunei Zohar*),

[18] Scholem, *Sabbatai Sevi*, 218. [19] Ibid., 268–290.
[20] See e.g. Scholem, *The Messianic Idea*, 95.
[21] Halpern (ed.), *Abraham Miguel Cardozo*, 240–241.

Cardozo adds a fourth, heraldic, figure, who may be a woman.[22] Certainly, Tzevi himself proposed to emancipate women from their secondary status in Jewish religious life, as recorded by the Dutch clergyman Thomas Coenen (who worked in Smyrna) in his eyewitness account of the movement:

> As for you wretched women, great is your misery, for on Eve's account you suffer agonies in childbirth. You are in bondage to your husbands and can do nothing small or great without their consent... give thanks to God then, that I have come to the world to redeem you from all your sufferings, to liberate you and make you as happy as your husbands, for I have come to annul the sin of Adam.[23]

In an extensive exploration of this remarkable statement, Ada Rapoport-Albert has merged sociohistorical factors, such as the destabilization of traditional structures in the Ottoman Jewish world in general (and Smyrna in particular) due to successive waves of immigration (including *conversos*), literary-theological influences, such as premodern critiques of the subservience of women found in the anonymous *Sefer ha-Qana* (penned in the Byzantine area taken over by the Ottomans), known to have influenced Tzevi, and ideological-revolutionary drives, such as a utopian conceptualization of the messianic era. In terms of the movement's social practice, Rapoport-Albert has pointed at accounts (especially, by Coenen) of Tzevi's intimate contact with numerous women, which had more of a ritual than a sexual nature, as well as the inclusion of women in public religious activity (condemned as 'outlandish' by the derogators of the movement) by later figures, such as Yehuda Hasid (who, as we shall see, led a Sabbatean immigration to the Land of Israel in 1700).[24]

It was this profound discontent with normative Judaism that generated profound interest in other religions: Christian influences on Nathan are suggested both by his doctrine of the spiritual union of the Sabbatean collective through love and by his deification of Sabbetai Tzevi, a possibility reinforced by Nathan's qualification of the precise error of Jesus and his efforts to rectify his soul, joined by a magical rite that he performed at the Vatican.[25] However, Abraham Elqayam has also emphasized the influence of Sufi orders (especially the *Qalandariyya*) on Nathan's ecstatic practices and

[22] Ibid., 249. Wolfson, 'Constructions of the Feminine', esp. 29–35, 57–89. Cf. Idel, *The Privileged Divine Feminine*, 130–132.

[23] Scholem, *Sabbatai Sevi*, 404.

[24] Rapoport-Albert, *Women and the Messianic Heresy*, 107–144.

[25] On the spiritual union, see Wirshubsky, *Between the Lines*, 226–236; On Nathan and Jesus, see Idel, *Messianic Mystics*, 202–206. See also Scholem, *Sabbetai Sevi*, 285.

experiences in Ottoman Gaza (also reflecting his upbringing in Jerusalem, an important Sufi center at the time). The state of almost complete nudity described in the eyewitness account cited just now is an expression of transgressive ecstasy with a long Sufi pedigree. Despite the differences in the mix of influences, these observations reinforce the commonalities between the cultural horizons of Tzevi and his prophet.[26] And indeed, at times it is difficult to parse the extra-Jewish sources of the Sabbatean heresy: thus, the discourse around the posthumous 'uplifting' (also in the sense of divinization) and 'disappearance' of Shabbetai Tzevi, to be followed by a 'second revelation', could reflect either *Shi'ite* (the occultation of the Hidden *imam*, or quasi-divine leader) or Christological (the ascension of Christ and second coming) influences, as the respective terms indicate.[27] Questions of historical influence aside, Scholem was certainly right on target in foregrounding the diverse phenomenological parallels between the two messianic movements, Christianity and Sabbateanism, including the paradox of the suffering messiah, antinomianism (accompanied by a strong stress on the redemptive power of faith) and Trinitarian formulations (Cardozo displaying explicit awareness of Christian parallels).[28]

It is thus not surprising that Sabbateanism begot various syncretistic sects, the first of which was that of the *Dönme* (Turk. converts). Originating from the 'believers' who remained loyal to Tzevi even after the conversion (and his death in 1674), this group was notorious for orgiastic rites (such as 'extinguishing the lights'), perhaps disclosing residues of paganism in Asia Minor mediated through the above-mentioned *Bekhtāshi* order. While still shunned by the Jewish collective, the sect had a marked influence on the Young Turk movement that secularized Turkey in the early twentieth century.[29] Strengthening the cross-religious connections, the eighteenth-century Frankist movement in Eastern and Central Europe, culminating in mass conversion to Christianity, maintained close ties with this group. In more general terms, the blurring of boundaries between religions joined the processes affected by the *converso* communities.

Liebes' seminal insight, with which we opened this section, coupled with the notion of the general crisis of the seventeenth century, well account together for the emergence of the movement and for its persistence amongst

[26] Elqayam, 'Liberating Nudity'. [27] Schatz Uffenheimer, *The Messianic Idea*, 103, 111–113.

[28] Scholem, *Major Trends*, 307–308; Scholem, *Sabbatai Sevi*, 211–212, 217. On Cardozo, see Wolfson, 'Constructions of the Feminine', 34, 39, 55–56.

[29] Scholem, *The Messianic Idea*, 142–166. For a history of the *Dönme*, based on Ottoman archives, see Sisman, *The Burden of Silence*.

what he terms 'the hard core', yet not for its striking mass appeal, for which sociological analysis is required. Yet first, one should pause to contemplate the extensive geographical reach of such a heretical movement and its temporal duration, in one form or another, well into the eighteenth century. The role of the *converso* network in the initial sociogenesis of the movement has already been alluded to.[30] Here one should also return to the phenomena of trance states and prophetic visions that were the determinative factor in the mass appeal of the movement.[31] These phenomena were but part of a wider wave of prophetic 'enthusiasm' throughout Europe, just as Sabbateanism fueled milleniaristic expectations in the Christian world.[32] In terms of the Sabbatean transvaluation of gender, it is striking that many of the participants in these events of mass ecstasy were women, and that Tzevi's wife Sarah was herself a leading prophetic figure.[33]

THE FINALIZATION AND TRIUMPH OF THE SAFEDIAN CANON

At the beginning of the seventeenth century, it was still possible for a writer with a strong interest in Kabbalah (such as R. Judah Loewe of Prague, of whom we shall have more to say anon) to be oblivious of the Safedian corpora. Yet two events taking place in the middle of the century guaranteed that this would be rendered impossible in its later part. In 1640–1643, R. Yaakov Tzemach, then in Jerusalem, began to convert the chaotic manuscripts of Vital into coherent books such as *Otzrot Hayyim* and *'Olat Tamid*, concisely yet systematically summarizing Lurianic theosophy and practice. His student R. Meir Poppers took this process one step further. Working with what he described as 'disordered' and 'scattered' texts, he merged *Otzrot Hayyim* and other works, creating what was to later become the canonical Lurianic work – *Derekh 'Etz Hayyim* (*The Tree of Life*, see Proverbs 3, 18), as well as a companion volume on *kavvanot* – *Pri (Fruit of) 'Etz Hayyim*.[34] While Tzemach's corpus spread in Italy and North Africa, Poppers' works were disseminated in numerous manuscripts, and eventually (1780s) printed, in Central and Eastern Europe. Around this time, the

30 Barnai, 'Christian Messianism'.
31 Wolfson, 'The Engenderment', 207; Goldish, *The Sabbatean Prophets*, esp. 122.
32 Goldish, *The Sabbatean Prophets*, 16–40; Rapoport-Albert, *Women and the Messianic Heresy*, 75–76 (and 77–78 on Islamic parallels for the role of women).
33 Van der Haven, *From Lowly Metaphor to Divine Flesh*.
34 The quotes are from Poppers' introduction to *Derekh 'Etz Hayyim* (not paginated in the edition used here).

Shemona She'arim (*Eight Gates*), edited in 1649–1654 by R. Shmuel Vital, became the authoritative version of Lurianic Kabbalah in the Near East.[35] Some of the figures we shall discuss soon, especially Ramaz and R. Nathan Shapira, continued this great wave of editing that effectively ended together with the century. Thus the eighteenth century was already the golden age of interpretation, and later printing, of a sealed canon formed in the mid-seventeenth century.

While located in the Near East, as an ex-*converso* Tzemach was well aware of European developments, such as kabbalistic Christianity. In his *Tiferet Adam* (Glory of Man), he wrote the following rationale for his vast editing project:

> There are books by Gentile astronomers and philosophers, old and new, in Latin and Spanish, and in some of these there are a few matters in the holy tongue [i.e. Hebrew], with tables and circles . . . and drawings. Therefore I ordered . . . in this book a compilation of all the books of the *Zohar* . . . and Rabbi [Luria] in whose mouth was the true Torah and the truth will show its way . . . so that none shall lapse [*yikashel*] in reading those books.[36]

Elsewhere, Tzemach was more pointed: 'The Gentile who wrote *De occulta philosophia*, named Heinrich Cornelius Agrippa . . . mixed the mundane with the impure . . . for he found a few circles and tables . . . and drawings, and did not possess knowledge for God did not grant him apprehension of the truth, only to his own people.'[37] The repeated mention of charts is not incidental. As Yossi Chajes has shown, the utilization of detailed diagrams by mid-century Lurianic writers, including Tzemach's own student Poppers, reflected parallel trends in natural philosophy, as manifested in the predilection of thinkers such as Gottfried Wilhelm Leibniz (1646–1716) and Spinoza for geometric, diagrammatic argumentation.[38]

Such connections to wider European culture were far more significant for both the setting and effect of our second foundational event. In the last decade of the sixteenth century, Luria's student R. Yisrael Sarug arrived in north Italy and according to an eyewitness account made a strong impression on local elites. According to one key witness, R. Yehuda Arye de Modena (of whom we shall say more below), he 'used to say that there was no difference between philosophy and Kabbalah. Everything he learned

35 Avivi, *Kabbala Luriana*, vol. II, 600–755.

36 Tzemach, *Tiferet Adam*, introduction, 1.

37 Ibid., 110.

38 Chajes, 'Kabbalah and the Diagrammatic Phase'. This study is due to be expanded into a book-length treatment.

from Kabbalah, he would explain in a philosophical manner.'[39] Sarug's Italian following was diverse, yet one should focus on two formative figures: R. Menahem 'Azzariya (Ram'a) da Fano (1548–1620), a notable halakhist, community leader (and also banker), who operated in Venice and elsewhere in Northern Italy, and R. Avraham Kohen de Herrera (1562?–1635?), to be discussed below.

Ram'a's encounter with Sarug accelerated his transition from Cordoverian to Lurianic Kabbalah (in its Sarugian form with some influence by R. Moshe Yona as well), leading him to posit that just as Cordovero greatly transcends non-kabbalistic writing, so does Luria eclipse Cordovero.[40] Together with the assignation of Cordovero's texts to the level of *pshat* (or the simple meaning), this can be seen as a strategy for maintaining these works within the Safedian canon, while according Luria's corpus the pride of place. Similarly, as Pinchas Giller has remarked, R. Avraham Azulai, a prolific writer operating in the Judean town of Hebron, excised any Cordoverian statements that contradicted Lurianic tenets, even while popularizing the former's commentaries on the *Zohar* and other contributions.[41]

Typically of Italian writers, Ram'a maintained an independent stance, not hesitating to critique both Sarug and Vital. Furthermore, despite his known connection with R. Avraham Yagel, Ram'a's writing discloses little of Sarug's reported philosophical inclination, and is based on dense interpretation of biblical and rabbinic texts, interwoven with complex Safedian structuring. Reaching beyond the Italian context, his works betray influences of the far less conceptual Ashkenazi form of Kabbalah later developed in Poland, as in his use of numerology. The difficulty of approaching his writings, accounting for the late and partial interest in him in academic scholarship, is compounded by his endless labor of rewriting and reediting, to which he ascribed theurgical import.[42] Nonetheless, it is possible to extract some theoretical themes from his substantial corpus.

Ram'a introduced a crucial distinction between the *ba'al ha-ratzon* ('master of the will') and the divine will, where the *tzimtzum* took place. This formulation was later important for Cardozo, who adopted a metaphorical interpretation of the *tzimtzum*, and as we shall observe in the following chapters, it also had a seminal effect on the intensification of

[39] *Ari Nohem*, adduced from manuscript, translated and discussed in Dweck, *The Scandal of Kabbalah*, 139.
[40] Introduction to Menahem 'Azzariya da Fano, *Pelah ha-Rimmon*, 5–7.
[41] Giller, *Reading the Zohar*, 26–27 (and 20–21).
[42] Abrams, *Kabbalistic Manuscripts*, 703–712.

mid-modern kabbalistic discourse on volition, paralleling central moves in general philosophy. For Ram'a, the will was also the *anima mundi*, or world soul, and he also employs a nomian simile: the light that remains in the vessel after the *tzimtzum* parallels the regular obligation of the law, and the light that remains above the vessel parallels the *humrot* (extra stringencies) designed at 'increasing holiness'. Here one can discern the beginnings of the kabbalistic rationale of *humrot* that was elaborated throughout the modern period, in justification of the general move of Halakha in this stricter direction.[43]

Despite Sarug's marked influence, the first part of the century was characterized by residual loyalty to Cordovero, in northern Italy and further north. The proliferation of this pre-Lurianic corpus was reinforced by extensive printing of major texts as well as shorter summaries. For example, already at the end of the sixteenth century, two major works (*Pardes Rimonim* and *Tomer Devora*) were printed in Poland. This development has been contrasted with various restrictions (also in the aftermath of Sabbateanism) on the dissemination of Lurianic texts and its much belated printing (as noted above).[44] The most influential formulator of Cordoverian Kabbalah in this period was R. Sabbetai Sheftel Horowitz (1565–1619) of Prague, who wrote the following on the doctrine of evil in *Pardes Rimonim*: 'these are all the words of the living God and who can come after the king, especially a king like him . . . they [Cordovero's words] are as a crown on my head, and as a candle lighting my path and system'.[45] The central theoretical innovation of this largely summarizing writer was that of coming down firmly in favor of the divinity of the Jewish soul in his much-cited *Shef'a Tal* (printed 1612).[46] One of the main devices for the sharpening of the ontological divide between Jews and non-Jews (posited already in premodern Kabbalah) was the ascendancy of this very doctrine.[47] It was spread to Eastern Europe (and hence to Hasidism) in R. Aharon Shmu'el of Kremintz's *Nishmat Adam* (printed 1617 though written somewhat earlier).

One of the most effective vehicles for propagation of Cordoverian doctrine was the constant reprinting of the *Musar* texts of his school. These were joined by the further development of the largely kabbalistic genre of 'conduct literature', often translated into Yiddish. As Zeev Gries has shown at length, this form of writing was the main conduit for the penetration of Lurianic

[43] Idel, 'Conceptualizations of Tzimtzum'. The quote is from *Kanfei Yona*, 3–5.

[44] Idel, *Hasidism*, 41–42. [45] *Shef'a Tal*, Gate 6, 61B.

[46] Sack, *Shomer ha-Pardes*; Sack, 'The Influence of Cordovero'.

[47] Wolfson, *Venturing Beyond*, 114–120.

Kabbalah into the vast world of *minhag*, or semihalakhic custom. Gries has also called our attention to the customized, so to speak, variants of this literature directed at specific sectors, including women at time of birth, midwives, cantors and ritual slaughterers (*shohatim*).[48] In sociological terms, one can say that the Kabbalah in this century not only became an elite profession, but also reshaped nonelite professions. One striking example offered by Gries is that of de Modena's *Sod Yesharim*, partly devoted to tricks for conjurors seeking to 'astound the onlookers'.[49]

A major landmark in the development of Lurianic rites was *Sha'arei Tziyon* (Gates of Zion) by R. Nathan Net'a Shapira Hannover (d. 1683), who immigrated to Italy after surviving (and chronicling) the Chmielnicki pogroms. This compilation, first printed in 1666 and subsequently in dozens of editions, both Lurianized conduct literature and standardized the Lurianic practice of *tiqqunim*, especially the midnight vigil of *tiqqun hatzot*. One of the striking features of Shapira's rendering of this rite is that the male worshipper sounds the mournful voice of the exiled *Shekhina*, in the wake of the pogroms. Shapira's shaping of nocturnal practice was also reflected in the development of the Lurianic liturgy and meditation around the bedtime recitation of the *Shem'a* prayer (based on Deut. 6, 4–9), seen as protection against nocturnal emissions and other forms of sexual-demonic invasion that we shall explore very soon.[50]

Another striking subgenre of this ritual corpus was that of guidebooks accompanying dying and mourning, as well as the closely related corpus of ethical wills, in which the need to preserve family memory was explicitly linked to the Chmielnicki massacres. Avriel Bar-Levav has shown how such writings can be read as ego-documents, thus joining hagiography and autobiography as three expressions of the early modern fashioning of individual self-awareness.[51] From a phenomenological point of view, texts such as *Ma'avar Yaboq* (the Passage of Jabbok, printed 1626) by Ram'a of Fano's student R. Aharon Berakhia of Modena (d. 1639) or *Sefer ha-Hayyim* (the Book of Life) by R. Shimeon Frankfurt (printed 1703) can be compared to works such as the late medieval Tibetan *Bardo Thodol* (Book of the Dead). Bar-Levav has sharpened our understanding of the phenomenology of death reflected in such texts by focusing on the need for magical protection of the body and soul of the departed from demonic forces. These include temptations to blaspheme precisely at the moment of death, and here Bar-Levav has

48 Gries, *Conduct Literature*, 41–102. 49 Quoted in ibid., 95.
50 See Nabbaro, 'Tikkun', esp. 65–71, 95–105.
51 Bar-Levav, 'Jewish Ethical Wills', esp. 56–57.

well noted Catholic parallels, especially in the Italian setting.[52] Indeed, R. Aharon Berakhia's uncle, R. Yehuda Arye de Modena, whom we shall encounter more fully below, exclaimed already in 1619: 'why should we be different from other nations [with regard to such guidebooks]'?[53]

Demonology, with a sexual slant, played an important part in the development of the ascetic rites of *tiqqun* performed during the six or eight (in the case of a *shana me'uberet*, leap or 'pregnant' year) winter weeks of the *shovavim* (literally mischievous) season. Concomitantly, *shovavim* was a term for the products of illegitimate seminal emissions. This rite, whose possible origins are Safedian, was especially popularized through a manual penned by Ramaz but fully kabbalized only toward the end of the century by his student's student R. Shmuel Ottolenghi (d. 1718).[54] Ottolenghi reported that a '*shovavim* society' was established in Padua, ending the period in festive song. Asceticism was also prominent in the continued popularity of ritualized fasting and other aspects of the *tiqqunei teshuva* (see Chapter 2), that according to a contemporary account circulated in 'streets and markets'.[55]

Bar-Levav has well captured the sociogenesis of the literature on death in linking it to the phenomenon of *havurot* (fellowships) dedicated to care for the dying and ill as well as to social welfare in a more general sense. As in the parallel setting of the Catholic revival, this extension of the Safedian model of the mystical fellowship can be viewed as part of a general evolution of a 'spiritual civil society' in early modernity.[56] Economics too played an important modernizing role, as evidenced in the rite of the *pidayon nefesh* (Soul Ransom), or donation of charity in sums equaling the *gematria* of divine names. One of the earliest sources for this practice is found in the fascinating ethical will of R. Naftali Katz (1645?–1719), a highly colorful figure who was expelled from Frankfurt am Main after being accused of burning down the Jewish quarter as part of a magical experiment.[57]

Indeed, the contested, yet pervasive, spread of magic reached far beyond the context of death-related fears and rites. One major indication of this process was the printing of *Sefer Raziel ha-Malakh* (The Book of the Angel

52 Bar-Levav, 'Death and the (Blurred) Boundaries'.

53 Translated and discussed in Bar-Levav, 'Ritualisation of Jewish Life and Death', 75.

54 Nabbaro, 'Tikkun', 80–84; Hallamish, *Kabbalah in Liturgy, Halakhah and Customs*, 567–594.

55 R. Yehuda Kohen, 'Seder ve-Tiqqun Qriat Shem'a 'Al-Ha-Mita', quoted in Elbaum, *Openness and Insularity*, 204, n. 82.

56 Compare to Ruderman, *Early Modern Jewry*, 57–98.

57 Bar-Levav, 'Ritualizing Death and Dying'.

of Divine Secrets), a compendium of magical traditions from various periods, in Amsterdam (1701).[58] The rabbinic opposition to its printing was verbal enough to be noted by the famous bibliographer Johann Christoph Wolf, yet such anonymous or pseudo-epigraphical printing continued nonetheless.[59] Another expression of the spread of magical concerns was the continued prevalence (in this age of witch-hunting), of narratives of *dybuks.* These can be found in what Chajes has termed 'polemical demonology' (responding to the increase of skepticism in this period), as in the case of Menasshe ben Israel (who shall be discussed below). A less obviously polemical case (though it aroused the ire of later writers belonging to the Jewish Enlightenment) was that of a well-publicized event in 1696, in which a detailed manual for exorcism made available by a leading rabbinical figure in Nickelsburg, Moravia, was put into practice by R. Moshe Graf of Prague (whose theoretical work will be described below).[60]

Halakha, as a method of study and as a ritual system, was another powerful mechanism for the transformation of Kabbalah, especially in its Safedian form, into the dominant form of Jewish spirituality in early modernity. Highly influential Polish commentaries on the Sephardic and kabbalistically oriented *Sulkhan 'Arukh*, such as *Magen Avraham* (Shield of Abraham) R. Avraham Abele Gombiner (c.1635–1682), a survivor of the Chmielnicki massacres, or *Turei Zahav* (Rows of Gold) by R. David ha-Levi Segal (c.1586–1667, who sent his family to pay homage to Shabbetai Tzevi), overcame earlier Ashkenazi reservations and freely (also not always accurately) incorporated Lurianic and other kabbalistic sources in their elaborate discussions. A more clear-cut case is that of R. Mordekhai Yaffe (1530–1612), who wrote commentaries on both the halakhic canon (in which he described kabbalistic customs as 'The Law given to Moses at Sinai'[61]) and Safedian texts. At the beginning of the century, R. Yissakhar Baer ben Ptahia of Prague listed over 250 laws arising from the Zohar in his *Yesh Sakhar* (see Jeremiah 31, 15).[62]

An interesting test case for the infiltration of Kabbalah into the halakhic realm was that of donning *tefilin* in *hol ha-mo'ed*, the intermediate festival days (during *Sukkot* and Passover). Under the influence of Safedian rulings, central Ashkenazi authorities such as Segal were willing to dilute the fiercely

[58] Rebiger, 'Sefer Razi'el ha-Mal'akh'. [59] Chajes, 'Too Holy to Print'.

[60] Chajes, *Between Worlds*, 120–121, 126–140; Tzfatman, *Jewish Exorcism.*

[61] Yaffe, *Levush ha-Tkhelet*, quoted in Elbaum, *Openness and Insularity*, 369. On ha-Levi's indebtedness to Ram'a of Fano's synthesis between Halakha and Kabbalah, see Bonfil, 'Halakhah, Kabbalah and Society', 61.

[62] Gondos, 'Kabbalah in Print'.

defended Ashkenazi custom and omit the accompanying blessing (thus drawing closer to the *Zohar*-based Sephardic convention of entirely avoiding the practice on those days). Around the end of the century, Italy, a contested territory between Sephardim and Ashkenazim, witnessed a crescendo of disputes around this litmus test of loyalty to the Zoharic ruling (reinforced by the Safedian authority of Karo). This culminated in 1716 when the kabbalist R. Emmanuel Hai Ricci demonstratively tore up a verdict by R. Samson Morpurgo defending the Ashkenazi custom, as R. Morpurgo's view contradicted 'the soul of the Torah', or the Kabbalah. Although Italian rabbis rejected such extreme actions, they accepted the authority of the community as a whole to override customs not aligned with the kabbalistic direction.[63] This flurry of disputation and interpretation was not restricted to Europe: as Avital Sharon has shown, Vital's student R. Hayyim ha-Kohen of Aleppo (c.1585–1655) reinterpreted the laws of the Sabbath in terms of the relationship between body and soul, paralleling the national divide between Jews and Gentiles, yet according legitimacy to both. Sharon has shown that ha-Kohen's halakhic-kabbalistic synthesis displays a profound concern with the body, adding mythical depth to Halakha as an ultimately somatic practice.[64]

All in all, the dissemination of popular works (also in digest form) on ritual, Halakha, liturgy and *Musar*, facilitated by the further development of print technology, contributed to the popular spread of Safedian Kabbalah far more than abstruse works discussing the dynamics of the supernal worlds. Phenomenologically speaking, the myths of Safedian Kabbalah invoked the mythical past and messianic future, while *Musar* focused on the present, also in the sense of everyday life, especially that of the body, through its cycle of birth, sexuality and dying. As Weinstein has put it, the concern with the body bifurcated into two practices, ascetic and what I would term sacramental, in other words mobilization of the body as a vehicle for manifestation of the divine within the mundane.[65] Both approaches were enhanced throughout the next two centuries. In his case study of the Italian manuscript on sexual and other guidance, *Tiferet Bakhurim* (The Glory of Youth), by R. Pinhas Barukh ben Pelatiyah Monselice, Weinstein has pinpointed clear parallels in advice literature penned in Italy as part of the Catholic Revival.[66] To some extent, *Musar*'s horizon of the present included the

[63] Katz, *Halakhah and Kabbalah*, 111–120.
[64] Sharon, 'The Hida's Kabbalah'; Hallamish, *Kabbalistic Customs*, 34, 241.
[65] Weinstein, 'The Rise of the Body'.
[66] Weinstein, *Juvenile Sexuality*, 129–199, 288–289, 298–300.

socioeconomic-political realms. In his much-printed (including translations into both Yiddish and Ladino) work, *Qav ha-Yashar* (The Just Measure), R. Tzevi Hirsch Koidanover of Frankfurt wrote the following:

> The final redemption shall also come about due to the merit of women, and thus women need to be more modest than men, and should not follow the impulses of their hearts in following the dress codes of the uncircumcised, as I have seen now new developments within a short period of time. There is an increase in transgressors who walk around dressed like the daughters of the uncircumcised and there is no distinction between Jews and the uncircumcised and this causes much evil in the world . . . secondly that they create envy and hatred amongst the nations that cast their eyes on us because the daughters of Israel comport themselves with greater importance than the ministers of the nations, and we are in the bitter exile, and are required to wear black and mourn.[67]

This striking text can certainly be interpreted in the terms of nationalization that we shall develop anon (as demonstrated in the attack on learning French, which follows in the text). However, it is worth pausing here to notice the concern that the new Jewish bourgeoisie will arouse the envy and antagonism of the non-Jews. In the terms developed in a controversial work by Yuri Sletzkin, we can see here the anxiety caused precisely by success and resultant acculturation. For the author, this confident comportment subverts the proper exilic consciousness that, coupled with correct gender values, is the path to redemption. As David Sorotzkin has correctly claimed, Koidanover's polemic reflects the segregationist response to the modern Jewish predicament, a stance that gained widespread acceptance throughout the modern period.[68] The kabbalization and nationalization of *Musar*, moving away from more philosophical and thus universalistic concerns found in its premodern forms, should be placed within this broader cultural history.

As they spread throughout Central Europe, the various strands and offshoots of Safedian Kabbalah tended to merge:[69] the most significant example of this process is found in *'Emeq ha-Melekh* (The Valley of the King), an extensive, multilayered and rich work by R. Naftali Bakrakh, printed in 1648. Bakrakh, most of whose writings have not reached us, freely

[67] *Qav ha-Yashar* (chap. 82), 189. Koidanover relies heavily on earlier sources, in particular *Yesod Yosef* by his teacher R. Yosef of Dovna.

[68] Slezkine, *The Jewish Century*; Sorotzkin, *Orthodoxy*.

[69] This account differs from that of Idel, who deemphasizes the spread of the Lurianic doctrine. See esp. his *Messianic Mystics*, 175–182, 185–187.

merged Vital and Sarug, though ultimately foregrounding the latter, who actually sojourned in Poland and Germany. *'Emeq ha-Melekh* was a highly influential conduit for Lurianic practice (as in the *tiqqunei teshuva*) as well as hagiographical accounts, stressing Luria's superiority over Cordovero and the missed messianic opportunity that terminated with the former's premature death. Bakrakh joins here a previous wave of Ashkenazi hagiographical valorization of Luria. A Moravian Jew, R. Solomon Shlomiel Dresnitz (c.1547–1632?), wrote a series of letters on the mystical powers of the Safedian kabbalists, especially in communicating with the souls of the departed. These were disseminated in print by Bakrakh's erstwhile student R. Yosef del Medigo (to be discussed soon), and the former may well have been his source.

In exploring the realms that preexisted the *tzimtzum* process, Bakrakh developed the Sarugian theme of the pleasures or *shasu'im*, in the higher realms of the divine. As Bakrakh puts it, the mere thought of the future appearance of righteous Jews and their good deeds generated pleasure and movement, setting in motion the process of creation, itself a manifestation of dominance (one of the adages subsequently much quoted from *'Emeq ha-Melekh* is that 'there is no king without a people' to rule over). The striking economic-somatic simile that he uses is that of a person who contemplates future profit, creating excess blood in the spleen and generating movement.[70] Besides the obvious Safedian influences, Bakrakh's work displays affinities to Polish Kabbalah in continuing earlier Ashkenazi mysticism and its predilection for *gematria*, linguistic magic in general and angelology.[71] Another Ashkenazi characteristic of his writing, setting him apart from the Italian writers with whom he was in contact, was his disdain for philosophy, as in describing Aristotelians as 'stupid donkeys'.[72] Though Bakrakh visited the land of Israel, his main link to Lurianic Kabbalah was R. Alexander Katz (d. 1606?), a somewhat mysterious figure who facilitated the flow of manuscripts into Central Europe, reediting Ram'a's Italian texts in the process.[73] Another recipient of Katz's textual transmission was R. Nathan Net'a Shapira of Cracow (1585–1633, not to be confused with the writer of the same name discussed earlier), whose *Megale 'Amuqot* (Revealer of the Depths), became a classic of the new Polish Kabbalah, which shall be discussed further below.[74]

70 Bakrakh, *'Emeq ha-Melekh*, 'Gate of Shasu'im of the King', chap. 1, 1A-B, 2B.
71 Baumgarten, 'Comments'.
72 Bakrakh, *'Emeq ha-Melekh*, 'Gate of Shasu'im of the King', chap. 1, 1B.
73 Avivi, *Kabbala Luriana*, vol. I, 433–451, 463–467.
74 Paluch, *Megalle 'Amuqot*.

As Liebes has argued, Bakrakh is probably the only substantial source for Scholem's interpretation of the *tzimtzum* as a metaphor for exile.[75] Bakrakh's messianic vision, though it had a certain personal flavor, was largely expressed in the idea of the ultimate expansion of the Land of Israel throughout the Diaspora. In the terms developed by Michael de Certeau, one can describe this as a move from a discourse on vertical movements of ascent and descent (though these too are found in this work), toward horizontal extension and expansion.[76] This relatively moderate form of messianism, formulated as it was before the 1648–1649 massacres and the activity of Shabbetai Tzevi, serves as a useful backdrop for the much stronger messianic ferment that was soon to appear. Both the printing of Vital's esoteric lore and its incorporation within a Sarugian framework aroused the ire of Near Eastern kabbalists, such as the above-mentioned R. Hayyim Kohen, as well as Italians of similar views, such as R. Isaiah Bassan, of the Ramaz school (see below).

An example of the influence of *'Emeq ha-Melekh* can be found in an influential work printed in Dessau (Saxony) in 1698. *Va-Yakhel Moshe* (Moses Assembled), by the above-mentioned R. Moshe Graf, represents a move away from the kabbalistic texts penned in his city in the earlier part of the century (as discussed above), toward the Lurianic ideology and Sarugian metaphysics of *'Emeq ha-Melekh*, quoted toward the end of this deliberately short treatise (Graf's longer work *Haqal Tupuhuin*, Field of Apples, remains one of the major lost books of modern Kabbalah). Attacking both excessive use of *gematria* (probably referring to works such as *Megale 'Amuqot*) and the current admixture of Cordoverian and Lurianic Kabbalah, Graf presents the latter as the culmination of a long historical process of *tiqqun*, as well as hastening the redemption. Exemplifying an advanced stage of the process of blending of *Musar* and Lurianic Kabbalah, *Va-Yakhel Moshe* also contains detailed discussions of the theurgical effect of positive and negative *middot*.

A work with some similarities with *'Emeq ha-Melekh* was written (though printed much later) at the beginning of the eighteenth century (and rather influencing Hasidism). *Sha'arei Gan Eden* (The Gates of Paradise) by R. Yaakov Kopel Lipshitz (d. 1740), of Mezeritch in the Ukraine, went even further in resuscitating the doctrine of *shemitot*, claiming that the present-day law reflects a fall from the Torah of the world of *Atzilut* to that of *Beri'a*, and thus will be superseded to some extent by a 'new Torah' as the messianic era approaches.[77] Intriguingly, Lipshitz's insistence that the present *shemita*

[75] Liebes, 'The Author of "Emek ha-Melekh"', 116. [76] De Certeau, *The Mystic Fable*, 289.
[77] See the text cited and discussed in Scholem, *On the Kabbalah*, 84–85.

is governed entirely by the laws of nature opens a space for a moderate form of naturalism, not divorced from contemporary developments in general culture. This antinomian thrust probably reflected Lipshitz's sympathy with Sabbateanism (as evident in his extensive borrowing from the works of Nathan of Gaza).[78] Shaul Magid has pointed at Lipshitz's innovative theology of the divine kingdom (echoing Bakrakh's concerns with kingship). For him, the *sefira* of *Malkhut* can embody the *tzaddiq*, thus merging two of the dominant mythical structures of premodern Kabbalah. One outcome of this synthesis is that *Malkhut* plays a similar role to that of the *tzaddiq* in its descent to the lower worlds. In a striking reversal, it is precisely *Malkhut*'s emptiness, possessing nothing of its own (as the *Zohar* famously put it), that links it to the infinity, rather than rendering it susceptible to demonic invasion.[79] One can discern here a key moment in the development of the theme of *Malkhut de-Ein Sof*, or the kingdom of the infinite, throughout the next two centuries.

Moving outside Europe, Morocco represents a 'control case', in which one can still discern the influence of local forms of sixteenth-century Kabbalah, but somewhat less Safedian influence. Here the presence of the *Zohar* withstood its incorporation by Safedian exegetes and preserved its independent dominance. This is evident in the works penned in the circle of the students of R. Moshe Elbaz in southern Morocco, a highly scholastic textual community that also spread into Algeria.[80] The most prominent work penned in this school, R. Yaakov Ifergan's *Minha Haddasha* (written 1619), displays marked continuity with premodern themes such as the *shemitot* doctrine, extensive angelology and demonology, and *heikhalot* cosmology. One modern concern that one can discern here is the freer discussion of reincarnation of souls. Another is Ifergan's testimony as to the spread of skepticism regarding the entire esoteric-mystical project.[81]

PHILOSOPHICAL AND CULTURAL RECEPTION

A form of Kabbalah rather different from all of those just discussed was to develop in northern Italy. Again, the pivotal event here was Sarug's arrival in the Venneto. His above-mentioned student Herrera was of *converso* origin, like several other figures that we have already encountered. Herrera, who operated mainly in Venice and later in Amsterdam, explicitly responded to 'what is being discussed in the schools and universities', and at times went so

[78] Tishby, *Paths of Faith*, 204–226. [79] Magid, 'Metaphysics of Malkhut'.
[80] Idel, 'The Kabbalah in Morocco', 118. [81] Hallamish, *Kabbalah in North Africa*, 94–95.

far as to travel disguised as a Christian.[82] Indeed, his self-described theology often betrays intimate acquaintance with medieval and early modern Christian Scholastic writing, as well as classical, medieval and Renaissance philosophy. Herrera's classics, *Puerto del Cielo* (The Gate of Heaven) and *Casa de la Divinidad* (House of God), were both composed in Spanish (though rendered into Hebrew in a truncated form in 1655). Not surprisingly, they were soon translated into Latin (1677–1684) as part of the large project of *Kabbala Denudata* (Kabbalah Unveiled) by the major Hebraist Christian Knorr von Rosenroth (1636–1689).[83] One can view this shift in language as a landmark in the Europeanization (also in the vernacular sense) of modern Kabbalah.

While in many ways, such as his understanding of Kabbalah as part of *prisca theologia*, Herrera continued Renaissance discourse (especially that of thinkers with a strong kabbalistic interest such as Ficino and Pico della Mirandola), one should not ignore the strikingly modern aspects of his thought, explicitly stated in his references to thinkers whom he himself described as modern, specifically '*los modernos cabalistas*'.[84] Indeed, Herrera's rather loose employment of Sarugian and other forms of Safedian Kabbalah position him as an ultimately independent thinker, as we have seen in the case of Ram'a. In his writing, the allegorical and philosophical, especially Neo-Platonic interpretation of Luria's doctrine is explicit: one can describe his rendering of these teachings as political, as in the interpretation of *tzimzum* as a restriction of divine potency, and psychological, as in identifying the Lurianic trope of *shevira* with the fall of the soul from intellect to imagination, or describing the goodness of God in terms of a monopoly on power.[85] More broadly, such directions can be seen as part of what Idel has described in terms of a shift responding to developments in European culture, from metaphysical to epistemological and psychological descriptions of the kabbalistic universe.[86] As we shall see in the following chapters, this transition was to accelerate in later periods.

82 Altmann, 'Lurianic Kabbalah', 22. For a comprehensive study of this figure, see Necker, *Humanistische Kabbala im Barock*.

83 The Christian Knorr von Rosenroth Society devoted an entire issue of its journal *Morgen-Glantz* to this work (no. 16, 2006).

84 De Herrera, *Gate of Heaven*, 312.

85 Yosha, *Myth and Metaphor*, 201–202, 285–288; Krabbenhoft, 'Syncretism and Millennium', 69.

86 Idel, 'Divine Attributes and Sefirot', 87–88. There is currently strong scholarly interest in the reception of *tzimtzum* in European culture, see e.g. Schulte, *Zimzum: Gott und Weltursprung*.

At the same time, as Ronit Meroz has shown at length, Herrera's notion of *tzimtzum she lo ki-peshuto*, or a nonliteral interpretation of the divine contraction, was foundational for the eighteenth-century debate around this theme. In exploring the pantheistic implications of this approach, Meroz cites Sarugian formulations identifying the material world with the *Ein Sof*, or describing the world as an illusion.[87] In other words, while largely indebted to the Italian philosophical context, Herrera's reading of *tzimtzum* also continues a variant locatable within the Lurianic corpus itself. Actually, even a text from Vital's transmission states that the processes surrounding *tzimtzum* are not literal but rather should be regarded as 'a metaphor and simile in order to understand the reality of the creation of the worlds'.[88] Therefore, one should be wary of either overstressing Herrera's originality or the scope of Sarugian influence. Idel was correct in describing such Italian interpretations of Safedian Kabbalah as de-mythologizing, and thus also de-messianizing moves.[89] Amongst writers such as Herrera there was also little concern with the theurgical effect of the performance of the commandments. It was precisely these cultural adaptations that rendered works such as Herrera's convenient for reception in general European culture. For example, Herrera's strong focus on the perfect figure of *Adam Qadmon*, both expressed a general anthropocentric tendency in this circle (again continuing Renaissance trends) as well as aroused interest amongst Christian writers, as this theme naturally lends itself to Christological reworking.

Glancing at the broader context, it is significant that Italian Kabbalah maintained a strong affinity with philosophy (just as the latter orientation declined in the Middle East and Eastern Europe), as well as displaying an interest in Christian theology that presaged that of Sabbatean thinkers such as Cardozo. These observations also hold true for Herrera's associate, R. Yosef Shlomo del Medigo (Yashar) of Candia (Crete, 1591–1656), who later lived in Vilna (after traveling in the Near East). Like later Italian kabbalists, del Medigo studied medicine in Padua University, open to Jewish students, and a major hub for the emergence of modern scientific thought (as in the case of his own famous teacher Galileo Galilei). Del Medigo was accused by Bakrakh of plagiarizing his manuscripts during the former's sojourn in Frankfurt am Main, as part of his extensive travel itinerary. As del Medigo's *Ta'alumot Hokhma* was part of Spinoza's library (no. 30 in the catalog), he was evidently a strong link between Sarugian pantheism and the

87 Meroz, 'An Anonymous Commentary', esp. 320–322.
88 Avivi (ed.), *Qitzur Seffer (!) ha-'Asilut*, 120.
89 Idel, 'Conceptualizations of Tzimtzum', 48–49.

Dutch philosopher. In terms of del Medigo's own self-awareness, he saw himself as a follower of Ram'a of Fano, whom he described as 'The teacher of all the Kabbalists of western countries.'[90] Inter alia, this statement exposes a sense of Western Kabbalah (presumably in opposition to that of the Middle East), based on his exposure to various centers in Europe.

There is actually a rather heated scholarly debate around whether del Medigo should be seen as a kabbalist or rather a modern critic of Kabbalah.[91] This very dilemma underscores the complex nature of kabbalistic identity in this period. While Herrera's interpretation of Kabbalah is more philosophical-theological, del Medigo's bears the imprint of the scientific theories of his time. For example, he rendered the Lurianic image of divine sparks and points in atomistic terms. As Idel has argued, such theories may reveal the influence of Giordano Bruno, who was a marker of the transition from magic to science in early modernity.[92] Del Medigo's interest in the science of the time is expressed in his entirely modern understanding of alchemy as an experimental science (including an exchange of letters with the Karaite alchemist Zerah ben Nathan (b. 1578):

> The [true] natural science is to know how to create a creation or a formation, not to waste time in logical and philosophical discussions... But I do praise the inventors of definite works for the benefit of many, and the occupations of those who transmute metals, the sages among the philosophers of alchemy, who show manifestly the truth of their philosophizing, and likewise those [who work] in seafaring and in agriculture and in the devices of bringing water, and the like... for truly they are the accomplished sages who have invented marvels, and not the philosophers who write empty words.[93]

Following Cordovero and Sarug (and probably more immediately indebted to Bakrakh, as we have just noted), del Medigo emphasized divine self-pleasure as a motive force for creation, as an act of bestowing God's goodness. While this is partly a Platonic theme, del Medigo places a special stress on motion as the immediate cause of *tzimtzum*.[94] This can be seen as a form of dynamism, helping to explain the reception of the kabbalistic thought of this circle amongst thinkers such as Leibniz, as we shall now see.

90 Del Medigo, *Mezaref la-Hokhma*, 32A.
91 Barzilay, *Yosef Shlomo Delmedigo*, esp. 107–108, 218, 265–267, 292–296 and cf. Ruderman, *Jewish Thought and Scientific Discovery*, 131–152, which is more convincing.
92 Idel, 'Conceptualizations of Tzimtzum', 45–46.
93 Patai, *The Jewish Alchemists*, 402–406 (the quote is on 405, from *Ta'alumot Hokhma*).
94 Del Medigo, *Shever Yosef*, 60A–61A.

We have already mentioned Herrera's influence on Knorr, who was for many years the advisor to the Prince Christian August of Anhalt-Zerbst (1690–1747). A striking indication of the popularity of kabbalistic Christianity amongst German royalty and beyond can be seen to this day in the highly Christianized representation of the *sefirot* in the *Lehrtafel* (educational board) of Princess Antonia of Württemberg (1613–1679) found in the Protestant church of Bad Teinach in the Black Forest. It is more than likely that the Princess herself appears as one of several feminine figures in the triptych, which was also aimed at a wider viewing audience.[95] The German reception of diagrammatic representations of the kabbalistic universe (as mentioned above in the text by Tzemach), is also apparent in the greatly influential illustration of the Tree of Life in *Oedipus Aegyptiacus* by the Jesuit scholar Athanasius Kircher (1601–1680). Another possible example of the seepage of Kabbalah throughout Europe and beyond elite circles can be found in *Paradise Lost* by John Milton (1608–1674), who corresponded with the above-mentioned Henry Oldenberg. Though most studies promoting this conjecture are far from thorough, John Steadman, in a careful examination, has pointed at a parallel in Reuchlin's *De Arte Cabalistica*.[96]

Knorr, who studied Kabbalah from manuscripts and a Jewish teacher (Meir Stern) in Amsterdam, was connected to Francis Mercurius van Helmont (1614–1698) whose importance shall be discussed below, as well as Henry More (1614–1687) and Anne Conway (1631–1679), both of the circle of Cambridge Platonists (a possible conduit for the influence of Kabbalah on the esoteric manuscripts of no less than Isaac Newton).[97] Their writings appear alongside with Knorr's own, together with translations from Hebrew works of Kabbalah (emphasizing the *Idrot* and including extensive quotes from Bakrakh) in his *Kabbala Denudata*. Amongst these, he included an alchemical treatise, *Esh Metzaref* (The Refiner's Fire), which expresses the approach of 'spiritual alchemists' (including both himself and Prince Christian August), who employed kabbalistic correspondences in 'healing' impure metals.[98]

Knorr spent a month with Leibniz at Sulzbach in 1688, while Von Helmot, who subsequently influenced another major philosopher (John Locke) was in close contact with Knorr since 1671. Kabbalistic themes such as the

[95] Betz, *Licht vom unerschaffnen Lichte*; Morlok, 'The Kabbalistic "Teaching Panel"' (image available at http://pamela2051.tripod.com/kabbalism.htm).
[96] Steadman, 'Adam'. Cf. Werblowsky, 'Milton'.
[97] Cf. Goldish, *Judaism in the Theology of Sir Isaac Newton*, 157–161.
[98] Coudert, 'Kabbalistic Messianism', 114–117.

Lurianic points (reworked into Leibnizian monads) and the transformation of the soul (based on the doctrine of *gilgul*) are apparent in the leading German philosopher's vast corpus, as Allison Coudert has demonstrated at length. This may account for Leibniz's possible reciprocal influence on Italian Kabbalah in the early eighteenth century.[99] In this context, one should mention the strong presence of kabbalistic themes (such as the power of the Tetragrammaton and *Adam Qadmon*) in the voluminous alchemical-mystical writing of Jacob Böhme (1575–1624), which had a strong effect on German idealism and Romanticism in general.[100] Finally, one should note the contribution of converts from Judaism, such as Johann Kemper of Uppsala (1670–1716), to the Zoharic faction amongst kabbalistic Christians.[101]

One of the cultural agents who contributed most to the philosophical reception of Kabbalah was Menashe ben Israel, or Manoel Dias Soeiro, born (1604) into a *converso* family and possibly Spinoza's tutor. Menashe was instrumental in the gradual return of the Jews to Oliver Cromwell's Commonwealth of England after three centuries (and himself arrived in London in 1655). This endeavor was part of a messianic vision of resettlement of natives of South America, whom he sought to identify as the lost Ten Tribes of Israel. Here, as in the later writings of Padua-trained R. David Nieto (1654–1728, leader of the Jews of Iberian descent recently arrived in London), one can discern the effect of global discovery on mystical-messianic thought (as in Menashe's discussion of the Jewish-kabbalistic origins of Hinduism).[102] As Richard Popkin has uncovered, Menashe's vision was developed in close collaboration with Millenarian Christian thinkers and thus stresses universalistic themes (as also evident in his continuing the Renaissance tradition of *prisca theologia*). This universalistic tendency was espoused by R. Nathan Shapira of Cracow (to be discussed soon), who went so far as to partly legitimize the messianic status of Jesus.[103]

The first Hebrew press, founded in Amsterdam by Menashe, published the works of del Medigo (following some dispute, in which Herrera upheld their legitimacy) and one of Menashe's own works received the latter's approval. Therefore, it is justifiable to see him as part of a semikabbalistic

99 Coudert, *Leibniz and the Kabbalah*; Coudert, *The Impact of the Kabbalah* (see esp. 271–307, on Locke and esp. 179–200, 208–219, on another important influence – on the Quakers, through Anne Conway).

100 Wolfson, 'The Holy Kabbalah of Changes'.

101 Wolfson, 'Messianism in the Christian Kabbalah'.

102 Ben Israel, *Nishmat Hayyim*, 73B (and Goldish, 'The Spirit of the Eighteenth Century').

103 Popkin, 'Jewish-Christian Theological Interchanges'; Popkin, 'Jewish-Christian Relations'.

circle in the Dutch Golden Age. Certainly, Menashe shared with those Italian kabbalists their Platonic and psychological interests. His main Hebrew work, *Nishmat Hayyim*, reflects the conjoining of these two themes.[104] Spinoza, Menashe's possible student, should be placed in this context of the cultural ferment in Amsterdam around the mid-century. As Miquel Beltrán has plausibly argued, Spinoza's discussions of the relationship of infinity and finite beings may well be a reworking of themes found in Herrera's *Puerto del Cielo*.[105]

It is not surprising then, that toward the end of the century Amsterdam was the site of a wave of controversies including questions of pantheism. In 1703, the above-mentioned Nieto was attacked by communal leaders in London and Amsterdam as a pantheist (in the Spinozist vein) after a he delivered a sermon declaring the identity of God and nature. As Ruderman has shown, Nieto's stance reflects the influence of Newtonian scientific thinkers such as Samuel Clarke (1675–1729).[106] One of the former's main adversaries was R. Shlomo Ayalon (c.1660–1728), forced out of London in 1703 due to his Sabbatean beliefs. Nieto was soon defended by the leading halakhist Tzevi Ashkenazi (1658–1718). In his *Hakham Tzevi* responsum, Ashkenazi wrote as follows:

> If it [the complaint] is because he says that there is no nature that encompasses all of reality, and they consider it beneath the dignity of the king of kings to operate without mediators then know that those who seek the mediation of nature for the general conduct [*hanhaga*] are close to fall in a web, while those who believe in God's providence over everything will walk safely wherever they turn. And if they thought that the sage's words referred to the particular nature, and sought to decipher his claim as insinuating that the heating or humid element is divine – this is something one cannot suspect of even the most stupid heretic in the world.[107]

In other words, it is actually those who insist on placing a nondivine category of nature between God and particular objects who are the true heretics. All of these figures were to resurface in another controversy only ten years later. Nehemia Hayon (c.1655–c.1730), of Balkan origin, was accused of Sabbateanism by the community in London. The Ayalon and Hayon scandals in London were but two of a series of 'Sabbatean controversies', some of which drew in the entire European Jewish world, enacted

[104] Chajes, *Between Worlds*, 118–138; Ogren, *Renaissance and Rebirth*, 294–297.
[105] Beltrán, *The Influence of Abraham Cohen de Herrera's Kabbalah*.
[106] Ruderman, *Jewish Thought and Scientific Discovery*, 315–324, 329–330.
[107] Ashkenazi, *Hakham Tzevi*, #318, 14 A–B.

throughout the following century.[108] Hayon (unlike Cardozo, who was influenced by other *converso* theologians such as Herrera) interpreted the Lurianic doctrine of *tzimtzum* literally, while later (1715) Nieto, as a pantheist, devoted a rich tract (*Esh Dat*) to assailing this very idea. While Ayalon and other opponents of Nieto supported Hayon, Nieto's defender R. Tzevi Ashkenazi was one of Hayon's main persecutors, joined by R. Moshe Hagiz (1671–1751?), who played a lead role in subsequent 'witch hunts' against the Sabbateans.[109] This time, however, it was the foes of Sabbateanism who had to leave town. Ashkenazi especially found fault with Hayon's assertion that Kabbalah can be studied without transmission from a teacher (reflecting in turn the erosion of traditionalist concepts of religious authority throughout the century).[110]

Sarug's Italian following, whose ideas and influences we have traced at length, was countered by a major school in Italy in the second part of the century: R. Moshe Zacuto (Ramaz, c.1610–1697) of Amsterdam and later Venice and Mantua, also of *converso* origin, was a major halakhist, yet he also composed in an impressive variety of genres, including liturgy, poetry, theater (influenced by Dante), magic, ritual (e.g. the above-mentioned *shovavim* rite), etc. However, for present concerns one should focus on his extensive Zoharic exegesis and his encyclopedic writing. Here one should especially note his *Shorshei ha-Shemot* (The Root of Names), which as indicated by its title, delves into the biblical origins of the divine names employed in *kavvanot* (to which Ramaz devoted separate tracts). One can regard this as an example of a prevalent attempt to anchor the ever-proliferating details of modern Kabbalah in the earliest sources of Jewish tradition. Despite his earlier studies in Poland, Ramaz followed the Near Eastern tradition in a purist loyalty to the transmission of Vital, as edited by R. Ya'akov Tzemach, who addressed at least one epistle to him (Ramaz also received this tradition in Venice from Vital's student R. Benjamin ha-Levi, c.1590–1671). Ramaz's propagation of the Lurianic corpus was greatly facilitated by his collaboration with the above-mentioned R. Nathan Shapira (d. 1667?), erstwhile of Cracow, who came to Venice to collect funds for the Jewish community in Jerusalem.[111]

[108] See Carlebach, *The Pursuit of Heresy*, 75–121 (esp. 114–116).

[109] The reference to the early modern 'witch craze' is not merely ornamental. On Cardozo's metaphorical approach to such Lurianic themes, see Yosha, *Captivated by Messianic Agonies*, 163–164, 197–215, who accentuates the difference between this writer and Hayon.

[110] See the documents assembled in Maciejko (ed.), *Sabbatian Heresy*, 91–103.

[111] Volume 96 of the journal *Pe'amim* (2003) was devoted entirely to Ramaz. In English, see esp. Bregman, 'Moses Zacuto'; Chajes, *Between Worlds*, 87–95. The obvious need for further

Unlike the earlier Italian circle around Sarug, the larger one of Ramaz displayed a strong mystical-messianic interest that rendered it susceptible to Sabbateanism once the movement appeared on the stage. While Ramaz was only attracted to Sabbateanism in its heyday, his close students R. Avraham Rovigo (1650–1713) and R. Benjamin Kohen (1651–1730) were part of the post-conversion Sabbatean underground, with ties reaching into Central and North-Eastern Europe. They also met Ayalon during his sojourn in northern Italy. Another Sabbatean writer who corresponded with them was R. Heshel Tzoref of Vilna (1633–1700). Tzoref, who had marked influence on both the Hasidim and their opponents in the next century, wrote thousands of pages of prophetic revelations in his *Sefer ha-Tzoref*. Rovigo and Kohen were especially fascinated by *magidic* revelations experienced by kabbalists from the strong Sabbatean center in Prague, such as R. Baer Perlhefter and R. Mordekhai Ashkenazi. As we shall yet see, this preoccupation with supernal communications continued in northern Italy well into the eighteenth century. These mystical and messianic concerns contrast markedly with the Sarugian school's more abstract preoccupations, and indeed Ramaz explicitly and strongly critiqued del Medigo in a letter.

CRITICAL RESPONSES

It was precisely the success of Safedian Kabbalah and especially its unintentional reinforcement of kabbalistic Christianity that provoked a variety of critical responses (some echoing the reservations that we have already encountered). The most notable figure here was R. Yehuda Arye de Modena, a highly colorful intellectual who studied literature, music (later leading an *academia de musica*) and dance. As in the case of Herrera, de Modena chose to communicate in the vernacular, as in his Italian sermons. De Modena met repeatedly with Sarug and is an important source of information on this towering student of Luria, though he was not in the least impressed by him. In regional terms, one may say that this Italian rabbi resisted the ongoing process of cultural colonization by Safedians. In his polemical *Ari Nohem* (Roaring Lion), de Modena bluntly describes the Kabbalah as a later innovation, rather than a hallowed transmission from antiquity. He goes on to expose the non-Jewish influence on central kabbalistic formulations: 'Anyone of reason . . . will see that these [the kabbalistic ideas] are but the children of the Gentiles, the vain notions of the Greek philosophers, that

research will be partly addressed in a current project led by Yuval Harari and Gerold Necker (which also promises to reinvestigate the question of the Ramaz–Sarug relationship).

entered the ears of some of our later scholars, who mixed them and enclosed them with order and names according to their own opinions.'[112]

In this sense, de Modena, his colleague Simone Luzzatto (1583–1663) and later figures such as R. Yaakov Emden presaged modern critical approaches! Indeed, in his illuminating study of Modena's critique, Yaacob Dweck has underlined his skepticist concern with freedom of thought, and its parallels in the European thought of the time. Likewise, Evelien Chajes has pointed at the contacts between figures such as Luzzatto and French libertines displaying a keen interest in Kabbalah.[113] It is also instructive that de Modena was especially troubled by the co-option of the Kabbalah by Christian writers, as well as the reciprocal influence of writers such as Pico on none less than his own student R. Yosef Hamiz (d. c.1676). In sum, the new critique of Kabbalah, in contrast to its widespread acceptance in the medieval period, should be seen as a response to its success, greatly enhanced by the printing press, in becoming a cultural agent in modern Europe. It is in this context that one should view proto-academic philological critiques of the editions of the Zohar, as in R. Aharon Zelig's *'Amudei Sheva* (printed 1645).[114]

As in the case of the Sarugian circle that he opposed, de Modena's own circle extended beyond Italy. His student, R. Shaul ha-Levi Mortera (1596?–1660), erstwhile of Venice and one of Spinoza's early teachers (and incidentally also an early teacher of Ramaz), blamed the Kabbalah for the prevalence of the belief (popular amongst *conversos* for obvious reasons), that punishment for sin is not eternal. Mortera correctly noted that the Lurianic doctrine of *tiqqun* through *gilgul* effectively undermines the traditional, prekabbalistic image of the afterlife. One can posit that the Lurianic approach represents a modern shift away from the 'world-to-come' to 'this world', just as the belief that the Jewish soul is not subject to eternal damnation reflects the process of nationalization, to be discussed below. It is interesting that the Christian writers discussed above (Knorr and von Helmont) also saw the kabbalistic stance as a resource for challenging mainstream views of eternal punishment within their own faith.[115] Mortera's position was challenged by Herrera's student R. Itzhak Aboab de Fonesca, whose rebuttal was taken up by another probable tutor of Spinoza, R. Menashe ben Israel, whose ties to the Sarug circle we have already noted.

112 De Modena, *Ari Nohem*, 52.

113 Dweck, *The Scandal of Kabbalah*, 16–17, 135–136; Chayes, 'Visitatori libertini', esp. 133–136.

114 Abrams, *Sefer Hibbur 'Amudei Sheva'*.

115 Coudert, *The Impact of the Kabbalah*, 100–136.

The now well-entrenched dominance of the Kabbalah can be gauged from the fact that it was Mortera who was forced by the community to retract.[116]

De Modena was also involved in the defense of a prominent Dutch figure, R. David Farar (d. 1624), who was attacked, amongst others, by R. Yoel Sirkis (1561/2–1640), a leading halakhic writer in Poland (and a follower of Cordoverian Kabbalah), when he wrote mockingly of both the Kabbalah and the nonlegal portions of the Talmud (*Aggada*).[117] Farar's critique was amplified by an excommunicated *converso* in Amsterdam, Uriel Da Costa (1583/4–1640), who also targeted the doctrine of reincarnation. Generally speaking, this century saw a renaissance of writing on *Aggada*, often interwoven with kabbalistic sources (as in the highly popular *Yalkut Reuveni* by R. Avraham Reuben Sofer of Prague (printed 1681), or comments, as in the case of Maharal of Prague (see below) and the vastly influential Polish commentator R. Shmuel Edeles (1555–1631, known as Maharsha). Nonetheless, the latter noted that the absence of any mention of the Kabbalah in rabbinic texts shows that it is highly esoteric – and should remain so![118]

While the Italian-Dutch critique of Kabbalah in the first part of the century is rather well known, this is not the case for the later Ashkenazi criticism that was to continue in the next century. For instance, the independent-minded German halakhist R. Yair Bakrakh (1639–1702), in his *Havat Yair* responsum, sought to restore mysticism to the enclosure of the esoteric few, and went further than Edeles in claiming that belief in its sanctity is not essential. For Bakrakh, the Kabbalah was like the Land of Israel – though its holiness was indisputable, few have actually entered it, so that one could in fact have a full religious life without it.[119] Furthermore, Bakrakh is the conduit we have for a lost book, *Shemen ha-Ma'or*, by R. Moshe Shimshon Bakrakh. In attacking Ashkenazi disseminators of Safedian Kabbalah, as by his namesake R. Naftali Bakrakh, R. Moshe Shimson emphasizes the economic motivation of the accelerated copying of kabbalistic manuscripts: 'hasten and speed only to gain monies, and the buyers rush'.[120]

The constant employment of Kabbalah, especially in its Safedian form, by Sabbatean propagandists, motivated by an ideological impetus toward exotericism, further reinforced critiques of its proliferation. These peaked in the repeated renewal of the ban, found already in the writings of the above-

[116] Altmann, 'Eternality of Punishment'. [117] Fishman, *Shaking the Pillars of Exile*, 49, 64.

[118] Maharsha on *Hagiga* 13A, and see also on *Qiddushin* 71A, critiquing 'invention of tradition'.

[119] Twersky, 'Law and Spirituality'.

[120] Quoted in Avivi, *Kabbala Luriana*, vol. II, 837 (my translation).

mentioned R. Aharon Berakhia of Modena, on studying Kabbalah before the age of forty, together with strong reservations penned by central Polish commentaries on the laws of Torah study in the *Sulkhan 'Arukh*. The most prominent example is the following statement in *Siftei Kohen* (printed 1646) by R. Shabbetai Rapoport (1621–1662):

> The Kabbalists and other later sages [*ahronim*] stressed that one should not study Kabbalah until 'filling one's belly' with the Talmud and some wrote not to study before the age of forty as it says [*Avot* 5, 21] 'forty for *Bina*,' also as one requires holiness and purity and alacrity and cleanliness for this, and most of those who trespassed on this wisdom before the proper time were 'crumpled' before their time, as all is this is set forth in the words of the sages of truth [i.e. kabbalists].[121]

It is interesting that Rapoport enlists the kabbalistic tradition itself (including the association of Kabbalah with *Bina*, and thus with the age of forty) in support of his stringent restrictions and warnings, aimed at restoring the unchallenged supremacy of the Talmud in Ashkenazi culture. Finally, the Central European critique of Kabbalah was not confined to the Jewish world: Yossi Schwartz has shown that writers such as Johann Georg Wachter (1673–1757) and Juan Caramuel Lobkowitz (1606–1682) tied the Kabbalah to the new scepter of atheism. It is particularly interesting that elements of negative theology found in kabbalistic views of the *Ein-Sof* were also enlisted in this charge.[122] This was a fitting finale for the century in which Kabbalah developed its closest ties to heretical thinking.

THE NATIONALIZATION OF KABBALAH

It was the Ashkenazi world that repeatedly printed and quoted the *Shela* (*Shnei Luhot ha-Brit*, The Two Tablets of the Covenant) by R. Yesh'ayahu Horowitz (c.1570–1626) of Prague (and later Jerusalem), the nephew of R. Shabbetai Sheftel (whose national psychology we have discussed above). An eclectic mixture of Cordoverian Kabbalah (mostly), biblical exegesis, *Musar* and *minhag*, this large and untidy work dramatically impacted the Hasidic movement in the next century. Horowitz was instrumental in the development of rites of death, the *shovavim* practice and other components of the post-Safedian kabbalistic ritual complex. In particular, the *Shela* was amongst the shapers of a new, largely kabbalistic ideology in Central and Eastern Europe surrounding the study of the Torah, as a manifestation of

[121] 'Siftei Kohen' on *Yore De'a* 246, 6. [122] Schwartz, 'On Rabbinic Atheism'.

holiness rather than as a merely intellectual project. An important component of this reinterpretation was the effacement of the widespread distinction between *nigle* (exoteric), and *nistar* (esoteric), as separate realms of knowledge.[123] As we shall see further, it is reasonable to attribute the remarkable wave of intensive learning, in Yeshivas and places of enclosure (*kloiz*) to various tributaries of this belief system.

For Horowitz, the mere pronunciation of the Hebrew letters, even without conceptual understanding, has a powerful theurgical effect due to their supernal root. As he wrote in the *Shela*'s long preface, just after addressing the merit of even rudimentary Torah study:

> the name for a certain thing is really the name for what is above... Therefore our language is called a Holy Language because all of the names and words exist above in their root, in the supernal place of holiness... when something descends and is extended from this holy place, this manifestation is called by that [supernal] name as a metaphor.[124]

Reversing views of conventional language found in Jewish philosophy, the true meaning of the Hebrew word is its supernal denotation, whilst its material use is merely metaphorical. In these terms, the exoteric is an emanation of the esoteric, the continuum between them being firmly asserted. Though it has some medieval sources, this understanding of the sacrality and superiority of the Hebrew language was actually part of a wider national Kabbalah, encompassing the divine origin of both the Jewish soul and body (as the true *tzelem*) and a reinvigorated stress on the holiness of the Land of Israel. It is not surprising then, that Horowitz blamed the current wave of printing of kabbalistic works for the undesirable phenomenon of its spread outside the Jewish world: 'Would they had not publicized the matters of the wisdom of the Kabbalah . . . Since then, they have begun to call out the name of God among the gentiles. And the sages... said "the teachings of the Torah are not to be transmitted to a gentile" [BT *Hagiga* 13A], all the more so the Secrets of the Torah.'[125]

However, a third and eventually most influential national thinker in Prague, R. Yehuda Loew (Maharal, c.1520–1609), did not seem to have been exposed to Safedian texts (as mentioned above). Therefore, following Sorotzkin's insights, one should regard his nationalization of Kabbalah and of Jewish thought in general less in panoramic terms of literary influence, and more as

[123] Katz, *Halakhah and Kabbalah*, 98–99.
[124] Translated in Krassen, *Isaiah Horowitz*, 151–152.
[125] Translated and discussed in Dweck, *The Scandal of Kabbalah*, 168.

Figure 1 Old Jewish Cemetery in Prague (burial site of Maharal) Source: © Jorge Royan 2008 / http://www.royan.com.ar / CC BY-SA 3.0. Available at: https://commons.wikimedia.org/wiki/File:Old_Jewish_Cemetery_in_Josefov,_Prague_-_8220.jpg Accessed 25.4.2020

an expression of the increasing problematization of Jewish identity in the context of the rise of the nation state in early modernity.[126] It is true that Maharal was the teacher of R. David Gans (1541–1613), whose writing displays a keen interest in science (especially in the new astronomy), he himself reputedly met with Emperor Rudolf II (who was known for his strong interest in the occult) and Ruderman has attempted to locate Protestant influences on his thought.[127] Nonetheless, Maharal repeatedly insisted on the radically separate ontic status of the Jews. This is especially apparent in a book dedicated to their election, *Netzah Israel* (The Eternity of Israel), as in the following credo of national ontology, penned as a rebuttal of the Christian argument from the lowly status of the Jews to their supersession:

> Because Israel are the beginning of reality they are the main [aspect] of reality, and the nations that are not the beginning do not have this, and thus are only an addition, and that which is an addition is not the essence and main [aspect] of reality … for God who is one in the world, how can he

[126] Sorotzkin, *Orthodoxy*, esp. 167–173, 191–194.

[127] Ruderman, *Jewish Thought and Scientific Discovery*, 95–99.

> not have one nation that belongs to him . . . so that one needs no proof that Israel are the main reality in this world, as they are the ones that are specifically described as 'man' [*adam*, see BT Yebamot 61A] . . . and from this the eternity of Israel is explained.[128]

Although such texts were not influential at the time (Maharal had a contentious personality. . .), they substantially affected numerous kabbalists in the twentieth century. Far from being mere theology, Maharal's national mysticism carried over to his view (common in Prague) of the secondary status of converts, as well as his insistence (in the face of prevalent rabbinic leniency) on upholding the prohibition on consuming wine touched by gentiles.[129] In this respect, it is interesting that the modern development of the ancient legend of the Golem, or artificial hominoid, attributed to Maharal the creation of the 'Golem of Prague', created to protect the community against anti-Semitic assaults. This figure has since had numerous folkloristic, literary, artistic and cinematic elaborations in both high and popular (reaching to Tarantino and Sleepy Hollow) culture.[130]

A related theme reflecting nationalization was that of the opposition between the power of the Jews and that of the nations. This is especially developed in *Aspaklaria ha-Me'ira*, a commentary on the Zohar written by R. Tzevi Hirsch Horowitz (d. 1689) of Lithuania (at the time united with Poland in one commonwealth). National concerns were indeed most obviously apparent amongst Polish kabbalists, especially in the works composed around the 1648–1649 Chimelinicki pogroms. Most striking amongst these are the writings of R. Shimshon Ostropoler, who was murdered by the insurgents. Building on R. Nathan Net'a Shapira's *Megale 'Amuqot*, R. Shimshon waged magical warfare against the demonic forces of Christianity. Remarkably, he presaged and actively prepared for his own death in describing his destiny as that of martyrdom, following biblical and rabbinic precedents, including those of his namesake Samson and Messiah the son of Joseph. In his self-perception (as described by Liebes), this sacrifice would advance the holy war against Christianity, precisely because of his profound knowledge of that religion. I would even take this innovative reading one step further and speculate that he saw it as a Jewish counterpart of the crucifixion.[131]

128 Loew, *Netzah Israel*, 60–62.

129 Katz, *Exclusiveness and Tolerance*, esp. 143–145. On wine as an important theme in Kabbalah, see Putzu, 'Bottled Poetry'; Morlok, 'Zwischen Ekstase und Gottesfurcht'.

130 Idel, *Golem*, 251–258.

131 Liebes, 'Mysticism and Reality'.

Finally, one of the main foci of discourse in national Kabbalah was that of the Land of Israel. Again turning to Maharal: 'other countries are lacking, but the Land of Israel alone lacks nothing and is perfect . . . and this resembles [the people of] Israel'.[132] More generally speaking, this focus was reinforced by emissaries from the Land of Israel, such as R. Nathan Net'a Shapira, who devoted his *Tuv ha-Aretz* to the merits of the land, thus inaugurating a subgenre of kabbalistic writing reaching well into the twentieth century. One should again recall the Sabbatean immigration in 1700, the first of a series of such immigrations over the next two centuries. However, some Sabbateans, most notably R. Nathan of Gaza, opposed such relocations, and as we shall see, its Frankist offshoot (as well as some Hasidic leaders) adopted a 'territorialist' approach of loyalty to their own countries.

CONCLUSION

From a perspective wider than the customary focus on Sabbetianism, one can view seventeenth-century Kabbalah as more than a transitional stage between Safed and the famous Hasidic movement. Rather, the interplay of canonization and counter-canonization that characterizes much of the kabbalistic life of this period can be seen as pivotal for the transformation of Kabbalah into a significant player in European intellectual and cultural history. More significantly, at least on the quantitative level, it was through these very transformations that Kabbalah consolidated its status, not only as the theology, but also as the lifestyle of much of the Jewish world (in complex dialogue with Halakha, *minhag* and magic). And it was this double success that occasioned an external critique of the sanctity of Kabbalah, as well as internal criticism of its proliferation, especially insofar as it breached the boundaries of the Jewish world.

The ongoing crisis of the century (the 'general crisis' of historians actually ended just before the Sabbatean outbreak) was also reflected in tensions between individual self-fashioning and fellowship culture, nationalization and interaction with Christianity, mystical experience and philosophical speculation. Besides general European challenges such as skepticism, the specific Jewish trauma of the Chmielnicki pogroms had effects on the kabbalistic way of life that that reached beyond the regional context of Poland (though undoubtedly formative for the historical memory of that community, including its mystics).

[132] Loew, *Derekh Hayyim*, 246.

Writing of the period between 1670 and 1730, Scholem stated: 'originality in the work of kabbalists who remained outside the Shabbatean camp was limited. Continuators rather than original thinkers . . . Hence the predominantly conservative character of the "orthodox" Kabbalah from 1700 onward.'[133] In a similar vein, Idel wrote: 'the last decades of the 17th century and the early decades of the 18th century are much less creative and even less innovative. With one major exception, the thought of R. Moshe Hayyim Luzzatto, Ramhal, the mystical writings originating from this period are rather poor.'[134] As we conclude here and gradually move into the eighteenth century in the next chapter, beginning with Ramhal's circle and its wider context, it can be quite safely said that such negative judgments are exaggerated.

[133] Scholem, *Kabbalah*, 80. [134] Idel, 'Qav ha-Yashar', 123.

4

Canonization

The Eighteenth Century

Just as in the age of revolutions in Europe and America and the formative 'twenty-five years of philosophy' (especially in Germany), the eighteenth century was the definitive period of modern Kabbalah.[1] To this day, the great majority of kabbalistic schools adhere to canonical corpora and detailed ideologies dating to this period. Unlike previous forms of Kabbalah, characterized by relatively small circles and one short-lived mass movement, the second part of the eighteenth century witnessed the emergence of a mass social movement strongly influenced by Kabbalah. Despite its rapid proliferation into very many submovements and other striking changes unfolding over the following centuries, the Hasidic social structure and ideology is still highly successful. Alongside with the reshaping of Kabbalah in this time of high modernity, we shall follow clear lines of continuity with the previous early modern centuries.

The activity of the founder of Hasidism, R. Israel Ba'al Shem Tov (c.1699–1760), around the mid-century, marked the watershed between the its first half, in which Sabbateanism was still a looming presence and other forms of seventeenth-century Kabbalah still held sway, and its second half, in which the true innovations of this period, reaching into the early decades of the nineteenth century, took hold. It was in these later decades that the Lurianic teachings of the sixteenth century were most fully developed in the circle of R. Shalom Shar'abi (Rashash, 1720–1777) in Jerusalem, though with merely noticeable connections to the dramatic changes in European Kabbalah.

[1] Forster, *The Twenty-Five Years of Philosophy.*

Far closer to the end of the century, and thus reaching even further into the successive one, a puzzling synthesis of post-Sabbatean messianism and dour reticence toward the ecstatic forms of mysticism (that Hasidism brought to the fore), was promoted by R. Eliyahu Kremer (Zalmanovitch) the Gaon (genius) of Vilna (1720–1797). This approach, going far beyond mere opposition to Hasidism (*hitnagdut*), developed into yet another social and ideological force that is still markedly with us. Viewed in tandem, sharing as they do numerous values and sources, Hasidism and *hitnagdut* reflect the shift of the center of kabbalistic gravity toward northern and eastern Europe over the course of the century.[2]

These then were the four main moments of eighteenth-century Kabbalah: the residual forms of Sabbateanism, especially in Italy, the Hasidic movements, the school of Rashash and the movement inaugurated by R. Eliyahu of Vilna. While the Near Eastern kabbalists operated in relative isolation, all of the three European developments were interlinked in numerous ways, this itself being an expression of one of the cultural characteristics of high modernity. As mentioned, R. Eliyahu's school exhibited a complex response to seventeenth-century Kabbalah, especially evident in its indebtedness to a semi-Sabbatean Italian messianic writer, R. Moshe Hayyim Luzzatto (Ramhal, 1707–1746?). Even if one is to follow Tishby in rejecting (or at least modulating) Scholem's description of Hasidism as a neutralization, or deflection of Sabbatean messianism, one cannot deny that the new movement drew heavily on kabbalistic *Musar* literature, earlier and contemporaneous, including works swayed by Sabbateanism.[3] More generally, one of the main theological innovations of Hasidism, the nonliteral interpretation of the doctrine of *tzimtzum*, was an extension of seventeenth-century Italian kabbalistic writing.

Despite the utility of our quadripartite scheme, it should not lead us to ignore a host of independent figures, only some of whom can be described here. Fueled by the near-final shift from manuscript culture to almost unfettered printing (which tripled in the Jewish world), the common denominator of the century was sheer quantity of figures, works, ideas and practices. While many of these were formed within the four central canons or were at the very least co-opted by them, many others remained outside their respective orbits. The future of further research lies precisely in these less charted side streams and gullies.

[2] For an interesting argument as to the closeness of Hasidic theory and that of R. Eliyahu of Vilna, see Fraenkel, *Nefesh HaTzimtzum*, vol. II.

[3] Scholem, *The Messianic Idea*, 178–202; Idel, *Hasidism*, 4–17; Piekraz, *Beginning of Hasidism*.

MESSIANISM AND THE RESIDUAL PRESENCE OF SABBATEANISM

As we have seen, following Shabbetai Tzevi's apostasy in the late seventeenth century, the Sabbatean movement went into underground mode, calling forth a network of 'witch hunters' who sparked a series of public controversies. The distinction of the later, eighteenth-century polemics was their scope, trans-European and in some cases including parts of the Near East. In two of these, surrounding the above-mentioned Luzzatto and R. Yonatan Eybeschütz (1690–1764), the dramatis personae were either identical or else in close contact. The age of the Sabbetean controversies both peaked and ended in a mass Eastern European movement surrounding the colorful, even shocking figure of Ya'akov Frank (1726–1791). These more obvious story lines should not obscure a host of less central figures, some of whom composed in the ever-popular genre of kabbalistic *Musar*.

Operating in the first decades of the century, Luzzatto's extensive corpus merged the thought of the previous one and presaged the new ideas and social forms of his time. On the one hand, he was a close student of R. Benyamin Kohen, of the circle of Ramaz. As such, he imbued Sabbatean theology, especially that of R. Nathan of Gaza.[4] However, his outreach program led him into close contact with a group of students at Padua University, sharing some of the scientific and philosophical interests of writers such as Del Medigo. The most prominent of these was R. Moshe David Valle (1696–1777), a polymath who offered a kabbalistic interpretation of numerous cultural, political and scientific developments in Europe and even America. It was one of these students, R. Yekutiel Gordon of Vilna, who leaked details of Luzzatto's mystical-messianic activity and thus, in 1729, sparked the controversy that led to Luzzatto's containment, and subsequently excommunication and eventual exile and early death. However, upon his return to Eastern Europe, Gordon also ensured the survival and subsequent influence of this banned corpus. While Luzzatto himself was dedicated to the vocation of divine worship and did not enroll in University, the scientific atmosphere of his fellowship was expressed, inter alia, in his highly systematic restructuring of the Vitalian transmission of Luria's doctrine.

Luzzatto's rich experiences were described not only by Gordon but also in his own correspondence, which has largely survived as part of the

[4] Tishby, *Messianic Mysticism*, 223–288; Mopsik, *Les grands textes*, 533–543.

excommunication file.[5] Beginning with angelic revelations, in a mode that we have encountered in Safed, Luzzatto progressed to internal dialogue involving mythical figures, especially Abraham, Moses, Rabbi Shimeon bar Yohai, the Messiah and his precursor the prophet Elijah (again in a Safedian vein). His identification with bar Yohai and Moses (to whom the *raya mehemna*, or faithful shepherd, layer of the *Tikkunei Zohar* literature is attributed) was also expressed in voluminous writing in Zoharic Aramaic. More significantly, the dialogue with messianic figures formed part of a detailed theory of his messianic destiny, as well as the theurgical-messianic tasks of his students, including the composition of personal prayers focused on the theme of hope.[6] It is likely that there was some division of labor with Valle, who adopted the role of Messiah son of David, with his younger colleague being assigned the more turbulent task of Messiah, son of Joseph.[7] As such, Luzzatto saw himself as rectifying the errors of previous aspirants, especially Shabbetai Tzevi.

Although Luzzatto's self-perception was thus that of a critic of Sabbateanism, his revelatory-messianic writing aroused the ire of rabbinical authorities, first the Rabbis of Venice, and gradually drawing major Sabbatean-hunters outside Italy, one of whom, R. Moshe Hagiz, we already know from the earlier Hayon controversy.[8] Their first and limited achievement, compromising with Luzzatto's defenders, was to ban writing in Zoharic Aramaic and receiving dictation from angelic mentors or souls of the exalted departed. The 1730 truce was experienced by Luzzatto as the suspension of the circles' messianic project. This setback instigated a profound shift in Luzzatto's writing, now disguising his mystical doctrine in the form of commentaries on canonical texts and even as non-kabbalistic treatises on history.

The latest of these, printed as *Da'at Tevunot* (translated as *The Knowing Heart*), contains Luzzatto's most central theoretical innovation: God's good nature leads Him to desire to bestow of himself by self-revelation. The only attribute that can be grasped, *via negativa*, is God's oneness, in the sense of absolute power and sovereignty. This quality can only manifest through negation of the illusion of any competing force in the arena of history. In other words, it is the overcoming of evil through redemption that offers the fullest apprehension and thus enjoyment of divine radiance:

[5] Garb, *Kabbalist in the Heart of the Storm*.

[6] The trope of personal prayer, like other elements in the discourse of the circle, goes back to *Tikkunei Zohar*.

[7] Garb, 'A Renewed Study' and cf. Tishby, *Messianic Mysticism*, 289–372.

[8] Carlebach, *The Pursuit of Heresy*, 195–246.

> The more forcefully evil brings itself to bear against men, the more manifest will be the strength of God's oneness and the omnipotent sway of his reign . . . And this, in effect, is the orientation of the exile, wherein He has concealed His countenance more and more, so that evil has asserted itself to the fullest extent . . . the purpose of this concealment is only ultimate revelation.[9]

It is not difficult to discern the traces of Sabbateanism even when couched in this historiosophical and dialectical genre (also possibly reflecting Leibnizian influence).

Allegations as to breaching of the truce, fueled by Luzzatto's travel toward Amsterdam, a major printing center, led to a renewed and far more severe outburst of the controversy in 1735. Luzzatto's new writings were seized at Frankfurt am Main, some later destroyed and thus lost to us. The writs of excommunication, signed by most rabbinical authorities in Europe, forbade him to engage in any writing or teaching of Kabbalah and contained dire threats against anyone assisting him with such activities. As a result, his fellowship was disbanded, with Gordon returning to Eastern Europe, and setting up his own circle, not only preserving some writings but also composing new works, some of which have been erroneously attributed to Luzzatto.

As for the latter, he found refuge, like other marginalized Jewish figures, in Amsterdam, where he moved entirely to nonkabbalistic writing. Of several works composed in this period, the most important was his *Musar* treatise, *Mesilat Yesharim* (the Path of the Upright), which was to acquire canonical status in subsequent generations, especially in Eastern Europe. Structured in a classical mode of a ladder of ascent, this dense and exquisitely crafted treatise subtly demarcates a trajectory leading toward inner worship, pervaded by eros (see further below) and exemplified by the true Hasidim, or exalted individuals:

> One who truly loves the creator . . . will not endeavor and intend to fulfill his obligations by means of the duty . . . but will react in very much the same manner as a son who loves his father, who, even if his father gives only a slight indication of desiring something, undertakes to fulfill his desire as completely as he can . . . we notice [this] at all periods and at all times between all lovers and friends . . .
>
> The same holds true for one who strongly loves his creator; for he too is one of the class of lovers. The mitzvoth, whose behests are clear and widely

[9] Luzzatto, *The Knowing Heart*, 49–50, 55, 57.

known, will serve [*levad*, merely[10]] as an indication to him of the will and desire of the Blessed one.[11]

The Hasidim adopting this hyper-nomian approach (the *mitzvot* being a 'slight' or 'mere' indication of God's deeper intention) are contrasted elsewhere in the work to the external Hasidim (probably including early forms of the Eastern European movement), who engage in ascetic practice rather than inward cultivation. Thus Luzzatto skillfully concealed the work's spiritual-mystical background and aspirations in highly conventional terms. However, Luzzatto was not content with this restricted activity, and in 1743 he emigrated to the Galilee, only to die from the plague with his family around 1746. After the dispersion of the fellowship, R. Moshe David Valle, while long outliving his erstwhile protégé, significantly moderated his messianic-mystical discourse. The diary-like experiential accounts gave way to what is evidently the most thorough kabbalistic commentary on the Bible. His vast, largely unresearched corpus (including volumes in Italian) focuses, in a very modern manner, on the inner life of biblical heroes, especially his own personal model, David. At the same time, it continues Valle's ongoing engagement with Christianity, ranging from vociferous critique though detailed acquaintance with doctrines and practices to a bold (yet highly ambivalent) recognition of Jesus as yet another failed messianic figure.

One of Luzzatto's early detractors was R. Yosef Irgas of Livorno (1685–1732). His popular presentation of kabbalistic ideology, *Shomer Emunim* (Guardian of Faith), was highly influenced by the other major form of seventeenth-century Italian Kabbalah, especially the writing of Hererra, while sharply assaulting Hayon. Its main thrust is that Lurianic Kabbalah in general, and the doctrine of *tzimtzum* in particular, was merely a metaphor. For him, a literal understanding of the constriction of the divine presence would be anthropomorphic. Thus, *tzimtzum* is merely a limitation of God's operative power.[12] A kabbalist based in Italy who traveled throughout the Jewish world (including Safed), Immanuel Hai Ricci (1689–1743) devoted a sharp monograph, *Yosher Levav* (Straightness of Heart) to negating Irgas' assertions. According to his argument, *tzimtzum* is a *mysterium*, inaccessible to ordinary reason, and rather granted to perceptions 'Shining in the spark

[10] Here I reinserted a telling word omitted by the translator.
[11] Luzzatto, *The Path of the Upright*, chap. 18, 217–219.
[12] Irgas, *Shomer Emunim*, second debate, section 43, 74.

of one's soul'. However, it is still necessary to claim that God is not found in unclean places and generally in the material world.[13]

Like Luzzatto, Hai Ricci was justly suspected of Sabbatean leanings, joined for him with dream revelations on his messianic destiny.[14] However, Hai Ricci's main achievement, outlasting his death at the hands of bandits in 1743, was his extensive summary of Lurianic Kabbalah, *Mishnat Hasidim*. Despite its scope, reaching to the Shar'abian centers in the Near East, Hai Ricci's reception was shadowed by charges of Sabbateanism, which are far from ungrounded.[15] The main doctrinal impact of Sabbatean thought can be seen in *Yosher Levav*, where he stresses that worship must be focused exclusively on the *Ze'ir Anpin*, or median aspect of the divine world. This view extends to a rejection of veneration of the feminine aspect, to which the infinite light does not extend. Here he is continuing his approach to the *tzimtzum*, which he identified with the 'judgment', or restriction of divine presence traditionally associated with the feminine. Hai Ricci's approach should be contrasted to the approach of Luzzatto's fellowship, devoted to the veneration of the *Shekhina*, which was radically described as superior to the ordinary love of God.[16] This divergence can be assigned to an internal dispute within the Sabbatean framework, for as we have seen, thinkers like Cardozo promoted a highly positive view of the feminine, probably reflecting the contemporary phenomenon of fellowships devoted to Marian worship.

One of Luzzatto's most outspoken and effective foes was R. Ya'akov Emden (1698–1776), the son of R. Tzevi Hirsch Ashkenazi. As part of his harsh critique of Jewish society, Emden fearlessly exposed covert Sabbateans, regardless of their standing (frequently joined by Hagiz).[17] The most prominent of these was the above-mentioned R. Yonatan Eybeschütz, a master Talmudist and communal leader in Prague and later Hamburg-Altona, who weathered two waves of accusations, in 1725–1726 (when Eybeschütz himself joined an anti-Sabbatean ban) and 1751–1756. Although the rabbinical establishment, including the Council of Four Lands (a major body of Jewish self-government), supported Eybeschütz, Emden succeeded in dividing communities in Europe, from Holland to Hungary, so much that at one point the

[13] Hai Ricci, *Yosher Levav*, first house, room 1, chap. 13, 28–29.

[14] Morgenstern, *Mysticism and Messianism*, 19–36.

[15] Giller, *Shalom Shar'abi*, 100–102.

[16] Hai Ricci, *Yosher Levav*, second house, room 3, chap. 10, 130–131; Wolfson, 'Divine Suffering', 134; Chriqui (ed.), *The Letters of Ramhal*, 268–269.

[17] Sorotzkin, *Orthodoxy*, 290–295, 309–321, 346–348.

government of Hamburg forbade further discussion of the topic and the police intervened to prevent clashes.[18]

Eybeschütz's own doctrine is found in a work most likely penned by him, *Va-Avo Hayom el ha-'Ayin* (And I Came This Day to the Fountain), which merged graphic sexual symbolism (unprecedented even for a kabbalist...) with a radicalization of Nathan of Gaza's doctrine of the hostility to the world of the 'thoughtless light', going so far as to describe creation as defecation and at the very least as God's exile.[19] These moves were continued by his son, Wolf Jonas, who attempted to synthesize Christianity (which had earlier interested his father) and Kabbalah.[20] A far more philosophical work of doubtful authorship that was attributed to Eybeschütz during the controversy was *Shem 'Olam*. However, it appears to follow the approach of Hayon (who was freshly excommunicated in 1726, after accepting restrictions reminiscent of those imposed on Luzzatto) with some resonance with contemporary deistic approaches. If this understanding is true, one can discern here an early effect of secularization, or at least the formation of liminal identities, on kabbalistic discourse.[21]

Paradoxically, at least according to Liebes, Emden's campaign, which extended to in-depth study of the doctrine of his opponents, was fueled by his own self-perception as one of a series of temporary Messiahs, charged with combating the messianic pretenders of each generation. In a striking reversal of habitual messianic doctrine, Emden used the Talmudic term 'the days of the Messiah' to refer to this generational, present-day activity, rather than the utopian period after the final redemption.[22] Furthermore, his attitude to Christianity (as well as Islam) was generally positive enough as to attract the attention of Moses Mendelssohn (1729–1786), the major thinker of German Jewish Enlightenment.[23] Thus, we are not dealing with a mere ideologue, but rather with a writer who expressed (also in his remarkably frank autobiography *Megilat Sefer*) the contradictions of accelerated modernization.

For all of the extremity of his formulations, Eybeschütz drew the line at the next manifestation of Sabbateanism, led by Ya'akov Frank.[24] Starting in 1755, Frank gathered a large following in Ukraine, Galicia and other areas,

18 Schacter, 'Rabbi Jacob Emden', 370–498; Maciejko, 'The Jews' Entry into the Public Sphere'.

19 Maciejko (ed.), *And I Came This Day unto the Fountain*. A comprehensive treatment of the works of R. Eybeschütz will appear in Joshua Maierson's dissertation.

20 Liebes, *On Sabbateaism*, esp. 77–102.

21 Feiner, *The Origins of Jewish Secularization*.

22 Liebes, *On Sabbateaism*, 198–211.

23 Schacter, 'Rabbi Jacob Emden, Sabbatianism and Frankism'.

24 Leiman, 'Rabbi Jonathan Eibeschuetz's Attitude toward the Frankists'.

engaging in a series of disputations with Jewish communal representatives, leading to their vindication by representatives of the Catholic Church and the burning of thousands of copies of the Talmud. In these debates, the Frankists also upheld the Passover blood libel against the Jews, a charge prevalent in Eastern Europe (and elsewhere) well into the next century. This far-reaching transgression of the bounds of identity, accompanied at times by anti-Semitic language and an episode of conversion to Islam, culminated in the mass conversion of the sect to Catholicism in 1759, although Frank was soon imprisoned as a heretic. Indeed, Frank radicalized nihilistic and erotic themes, in total rejection of existing religions and regimes. As the compilation *Slowa Pańskie* (The Sayings of the Lord) has it: 'wherever I set foot all will be destroyed, for I came into this world only to destroy and annihilate'.

In proto-Nietzschian terms, the 'warriors' engaging in this combat against law, reason and order need to 'enter the abyss' in order to 'reach freedom under their own power'.[25] This transvaluation received particular expression in the sexual realm, including validation of incest and ritualized wife swapping. The adoption and immediate heretical adaptation of Catholic values was expressed in the Mariological myth that Frank developed around the divinization of his daughter Eva, probably affected by the icon of the Black Madonna of Częstochowa (where he was detained in 1760).[26] However, Hillel Levine has offered an alternative account, according to which rather than absconding from the world, Frank developed a complex political strategy, aimed at addressing the plight of Polish Jewry in face of the weakening of their mainstay, the monarchy. Certainly, Frank was one of the early figures attempting to organize a Jewish army, as part of his adoption of Poland as the promised land (thus presaging nineteenth-century territorialist moves amongst Eastern European Jewry). Furthermore, he attracted the support of the Habsburg empress Maria Theresa.[27] Generally speaking, Frankism can be seen as part of the growing embroilment of kabbalists in the shifting balance of power in Europe, which was to accelerate around the Napoleonic Wars.

[25] *Slowa Pańskie*, translated and discussed in Scholem, *The Messianic Idea*, 130–131. Harris Lenowitz's annotated translation is found at https://archive.org/details/TheCollectionOfTheWordsOfTheLordJacobFrank. See the anti-Semitic locutions cited (from Fanya Scholem's Hebrew translation) in Elior, 'Jacob Frank's Book', 17–20.

[26] Maciejko, *The Mixed Multitude*, 150, 170, 174–179 (cf. Kriegel, 'Theologian of Revolution or Adventurer').

[27] Levine, 'Frankism as Worldly Messianism'; Maciejko, *The Mixed Multitude*, 159–161, 233.

The offspring and mutations of Sabbateanism in Italy and Central Europe were joined by figures in Poland-Lithuania following upon the circle of Herschel Tzoref, and with perhaps wider impact, the continued impact of Cardozo's thought in the Ottoman Empire.[28] Prominent amongst his students there was R. Eliyahu Itamari (1659–1729) of Izmir. The most influential of his works (translated into both Yiddish and Ladino) was *Shevet Musar* (Rod of Chastisement, printed 1712). The approach contained in this book is individualistic, relative to the *Musar* genre. Expanding a Lurianic idea, Itamari warns against ignoring one's desire to study a particular aspect of the tradition (including Kabbalah), as this is precisely one's guide as to the *tiqqun* required for one's present incarnation. Furthermore, the very challenges confronting the performance of a specific commandment indicate that this is the destiny of the root of one's soul. The study of Torah instigates a process of fiery transformation of body into soul, the simile being the exposure of a shining jewel covered by rust and dirt. Elsewhere, we see that this is not mere metaphor, as through study it is possible to acquire the magical powers of various jewels. Thus, throughout the book, transformation leads to personal empowerment.[29] It is permissible to speculate that this is a trace of the Sabbatean notion of the personal God, and further reflect on the prominence of this tendency in modern religion in general, as highlighted by Ulrich Beck.[30]

A similar work was the highly popular (to this day) *Hemdat Yamim* (printed in Izmir in 1731), attributed erroneously to Nathan of Gaza, but probably composed by one or more Sabbatean sympathizers (again first exposed as such by Emden) in Turkey.[31] The book's main goal can be described as the saturation of time by intensive religious consciousness and practice, including numerous new prayers. For example, when describing preparations for the Sabbath, the authors advise verbally describing one's intention to unify the sixth *sefira* (paralleling Friday, the sixth day of the week) and the seventh *sefira* (paralleling the Sabbath), as well as articulating one's intention to dedicate every single object purchased that day to the

28 On the scope of Sabbatean activity in Poland, see Scholem, *Studies and Texts*, 83–116.

29 Itamari, *Shevet Musar*, 3 A–B, 4 A–B, 13 A–B. On fiery transformation and empowerment in modern Kabbalah, see Garb, *Shamanic Trance*, esp. 36–45, 82–96 (and 122–125, 128–131, on *Musar* and Torah study). For Itamari's social thought (also informed by the belief in reincarnation), see Lehmann, *Ladino Rabbinic Literature*, 111–117, 128–130.

30 Beck, *A God of One's Own*. Beck's historical starting point (104–115) is the sixteenth century, contemporaneous with the advent of kabbalistic modernity.

31 See Tishby, *Paths of Faith*, 163–167 for Itamari's influence in this work (and 44–45 for the influence of Nathan of Gaza).

Sabbath. The main author attests that he repeatedly rebuked women who made the beds on Thursday, thus betraying that it was not deliberately in honor of the Sabbath (and its union with the sixth day). Later on, there is a lament (one of many), decrying those who feast on profane days while skimping on the expenses in honor of the Sabbath.[32] And all this is far from exhausting the topic... The hyper-nomian ritual innovation pervading this lengthy work is expressed, for instance, in a Passover-like *seder* or ritual meal (based on fruits) on the minor agricultural festival of the fifteenth day (*tu*) of the Hebrew month of Shevat. These and similar writings (also in Yiddish) demonstrate that rather than being an anarchistic or nihilistic movement, Sabbateanism developed into an intricate network, linked by what Ludwig Wittgenstein described as family resemblance. While the adherence of some of the figures discussed here to Sabbateanism has been questioned (often with apologetic motivations), one cannot deny their belonging to the wider category of Messianism.

HASIDISM: THEOLOGY, IDEOLOGY AND SOCIOLOGY

From its inception, Hasidism was a success story. Emerging from one of numerous kabbalistic circles, by the end of the century it transformed into a rapidly spreading movement, conquering entire communities throughout Eastern and Central Europe. The beginning of Hasidism is largely the story of a rather mysterious, in some ways legendary figure – R. Israel Ba'al Shem Tov, or the Besht. He developed his spiritual path in dialogue with somewhat nebulous circles of mystics. These included R. Nahman of Hordenka (c.1680–1765) and R. Nahman of Kossov (d. 1746), the latter accused by Emden of Sabbateanism. Claiming transmission from a biblical prophet, Ahija the Shilonite (Elijah's teacher according some traditions), the Besht was one of a series of *Ba'alei Shem* (masters of the name, see further below).[33] These shaman-like wonderworkers employed the power of divine names and language in general for healing and other social needs, reflecting the proliferation of kabbalistic *segulot* (charms) in the first part of the century.[34] These can be seen as what Raymond Williams termed 'residual practices' against the background of the ascendancy of modern medicine.[35]

[32] *Hemdat Yamim*, vol. I, 30–37. On the influence of this work on the Sabbath liturgy, see Hallamish, *Kabbalistic Customs*, 97, 235.

[33] Weiss, *Studies in Eastern European Jewish Mysticism*, 5–8, 27–42 (cf. Piekraz, *Beginning of Hasidism*, 136–137); Etkes, *The Besht*, 47–78. On the history and practices of the *Ba'alei Shem*, see Hundert, *Jews in Poland-Lithuania*, 143–152.

[34] Gries, *Conduct Literature*, 96–99.

[35] Williams, *Marxism and Literature*, 122–133.

Here in a nutshell, we already have four salient features of Hasidism: the focus on the personal power of individuals, the centrality of language, openness to magical applications and responsiveness to the needs of the community. The Besht emerged into public view in Podolya, today Ukraine, but in that period a borderland that had passed from the Ottoman Empire to Poland.[36] His origins in Wallachia may have also exposed him to the mystical-magical activity (especially in the domain of healing) of the *starets* (elders) and more generally the neo-Hesychast movement in the Orthodox church. This highly complex cultural crossroads, bringing into contact forms of Catholic, Orthodox, Sufi (again especially *Bekhtāshi*) and Tatar religiosity (as well as residual Shamanic elements amongst recent Maygar converts to Catholicism), may offer a partial explanation of the uniqueness of the Besht's message. For example, his foundational decision to 'uplift' both tales and melodies with extra-Jewish origin is plausibly placable against the background of this diverse setting.[37]

This doctrine is clouded by a thick layer of later hagiography (in Hebrew and Yiddish), the literary prototype being *In Praise of the Ba'al Shem Tov*, printed only in 1815. Indeed, 'the praises of the righteous' (partly imitating the seventeenth-century accounts of Luria and his powers), drawing on oral transmission, were a major literary medium for bolstering the Hasidic ideology surrounding the roles and powers of the *tzaddik*.[38] While such later accounts are not very useful in deciphering the ideational aspects of the movement, they are highly informative as to its sociology. In his studies of this vast literature, Yoav Elstein has stressed the adaptation of Eastern European folklore, the subversive tension between internal-ecstatic values and external norms, and the fluidity of external reality, in line with the belief in divine immanence.[39] This analysis was reinforced by Eli Yassif, who also pointed at the tensions between ideology and sociology in Hasidic folktales, both championing the common people and expressing the desire for status and wealth.[40]

One document that places us on relatively firm ground in understanding the Besht's innovation is the epistle on his ascent of the soul (again reflecting regional Shamanic influences) penned to his brother-in-law R. Gershom of Kitov (d. 1761) around 1752. As R. Gershon was possibly a member of the

[36] For a historical study see Rosman, *The Founder of Hasidism*.

[37] See Idel, 'Israel Ba'al Shem Tov'; Idel, 'Early Hasidism and Altaic Tribes' (esp. 16–17); Tourov, 'Hasidism and Christianity'.

[38] Gries, *The Book in Early Hasidism*, esp. 36–37.

[39] Elstein, *The Ecstatic Story*, esp. 62, 110–112, 160–169.

[40] Yassif, *The Hebrew Folktale*, 393–397.

fraternity of Rashash, we have here a loose connection to another central school. The epistle has several versions and has engendered conflicting interpretations. This is from the Koretz version:

> On *Rosh ha-shanah* of the year 5507 (1746), I performed an incantation for the ascent of the soul . . . and in that vision I saw wondrous things, which I had never seen until then . . . And it is impossible to relate and to tell what I saw and learned in that ascent hither . . . But when I returned to the lower Paradise, I saw the souls of living and of dead persons . . . numberless, in a to-and-fro movement, ascending from one world to the other through the pillar known to adepts . . . and I asked my teacher and master[41] that he come with me as it is a great danger to go and to ascend to the supernal worlds . . . and these were mighty ascents . . . So I ascended degree after degree, until I entered the palace of the Messiah.
>
> I asked the Messiah: When do you come? [Sanhedrin 98A] And he answered: You will know [the time] which is when your doctrine will be revealed in public and it will be disclosed to the world and 'your fountains will well outside',[42] what I have taught you . . . and also they will be able to perform the unifications and the ascents [of the soul] as you do, and then the shells will be abolished, and then there will be a time of good-will and redemption. And this [answer] surprised me, and I was deeply sorrowful because of the length of time when this will be possible; however, from what I have learned there, the three things, which are remedies and three divine names, it is easy to learn and to explain. [Then] my mind was calmed and I thought that it is possible for my contemporaries to attain this degree and aspect by these [practices].[43]

Although there are some ineffable, mysterious elements here, one can glean the following from this powerful mystical-shamanic testimony: the Besht practiced the techniques of ascent of the soul to the heavenly realm and of communication with the spirits of the dead, as popularized in Safed. His imaginal conversation with the Messiah points at the messianic thrust of the new movement, reflecting some continuity with the post-Sabbatean atmosphere.[44] It is highly likely that the Besht's disappointment with the Messiah's deferment of immediate fulfillment of such hopes was temporary. After all, he suggested that there are mystical-magical recipes that can hasten the process. In the meantime, it will be promoted through the proliferation and exotericization of the Besht's teachings (and abilities), a core component of Hasidic ideology. Furthermore, the visionary element evident in this

[41] Probably Ahija. [42] Prov. 5, 16.
[43] Translated and discussed in Idel, *Ascensions on High*, 143–146.
[44] Tishby, *Studies in Kabbalah*, vol. 2, 475–519.

formative text demonstrates certain continuity with the prophetic impetus of Sabbateanism and its offshoots.[45]

The Besht's conversion of a series of scholars, often through demonstration of his mystical or shamanic powers (and shifting them away from ascetic regimens), marked the establishment of his circle, which evolved from his group of origin, in a similarly loose fashion.[46] Yet from this point on, his teaching is refracted through its complex reception and transmission. Therefore, we shall not dwell further on attempts to isolate the teaching of the Besht per se, but rather follow the early variants of his doctrine, that were soon to crystallize into submovements.[47] The first printed Hasidic books, composed by R. Ya'akov Yosef Katz of Polonnoy (1705–1783), were published in the early 1780s. Like most Hasidic writing, these works, most centrally *Toldot Ya'akov Yosef* (The Generation of Jacob–Joseph; see Genesis 37, 2), were transcribed from their oral source in the nonelite Jewish language of Yiddish (which plays a central role in Hasidic identity to this day).[48] They clearly reflect the self-perception of the secondary elite of itinerant preachers, and more generally are highly valuable resources for appreciating the social structure of the new movement (somewhat similar to that of Sabbateanism). At their core is the interrelationship between the *tzaddik* and the masses, the latter term reflecting a new modern awareness instigated by demographic explosion.[49] Although socialist interpretation of Hasidism as an uprising against the primary elite of scholars (and its alliance with wealthy lay leaders) is unfashionable, it cannot be entirely dismissed.[50] Yet in a history of Kabbalah the more concrete sociological dimensions of the new movement cannot occupy center stage.

The disruptive aspects of Hasidic teaching are clearly visible in doctrines such as the descent of the *tzaddik* into the *qelipot*, the uplifting of 'strange thoughts' (distractive but including sexual fantasies), that assail one during prayer, to their supernal source. This radicalization of existing themes in turn forms part of a cluster of ideas including the notion that evil is but 'a chair for good'. These antinomian tendencies enhanced trends found in

45 Scholem, *Major Trends*, 333–334. Cf. Idel, 'On Prophecy'.

46 Hundert, *Jews in Poland-Lithuania*, 173–175. As in other cases, the term 'circle' is at times overly reified in academic writing.

47 Pedaya, 'The Besht'; Pedaya, 'Two Types of Ecstatic Experience'.

48 Gries, *The Book in Early Hasidism*, esp. 49–50, 64–65.

49 Weiss, *Studies in Eastern European Jewish Mysticism*, 12–17; Dresner, *The Zaddik*, 75–86, 94–122, 165–172.

50 Compare Dynner, *Men of Silk*, esp. 13–15, 36–38 (though dealing with a later period), 120–128.

Musar and *Drush* (sermon) literature of the century and its predecessor, popular especially amongst preachers.[51] These more radical inclinations are joined by a more moderate, anomian teaching, according to which:

> even a man's food, his clothing, his home and his business – all these belong to the sparks of his own soul which he is called upon to lift up. Even the fact that he sometimes loses in a [business] transaction or brings it to a good conclusion depends on the state of his sparks . . . this, then is the hidden meaning of the verse 'By *all* your ways know him [Prov. 3:6] – because everything serves man to concentrate his mind and to lift up the sparks of his own soul, which are, at the same time, the sparks of the Shekinah.'[52]

In other words, reaching beyond the elite, R. Ya'akov Yosef reframes everyday life (a realm receiving increasing attention in this historical period), as part of the Lurianic practice of *birur* (sifting prior to uplifiting) of the soul-sparks. One should note that the *Shekhina* here is not a gendered theosophical concept (as in earlier forms of Kabbalah), but rather expresses the idea of pan-psychism, or divine immanence mediated by the soul. Elsewhere, he describes the uplifting of one's individual soul sparks as the raison d'être of the historical reality of the Exile.[53] Above all, expanding on ideas propagated by the highly popular *Musar* literature of the Cordovero circle, R. Ya'akov Yosef established *devequt* as the central Hasidic ideal.[54]

Amongst the other students of the Besht, we shall briefly address three: Pinchas Shapiro of Koretz (1726–1791) may be more of a colleague than a student. In any case, from his nonsystematic teachings, one can discern a particular emphasis on kabbalistic practice, including angelology, dealing with the non-Jewish authorities through modulating emotional responses and dream work (as in sleeping in the same room with one's small children in order to share dreams).[55] The equally dispersed teachings that we have in the name of Yehiel Michel, the Magid (preacher) of Zlotshov (c.1726–1781), point at the continuation of Beshtian emphases on magic, messianism and ascent, alongside with an early form of positive psychology, based on the ideas that one can approach God from any situation in which one finds oneself, and that one can acquire greatness precisely from self-nullification,

[51] Piekraz, *Beginning of Hasidism*, esp. 213–221, 277–279, 283–291.

[52] *Toldot Ya'akov Yosef*, adduced and translated in Scholem, *The Messianic Idea*, 189. See further sources and discussion in Wolfson, *Along the Path*, 89–101; Kauffman, *'In All Your Ways Know Him'*.

[53] See the text translated and discussed in Scholem, *On the Mystical Shape*, 248–249.

[54] Sack, 'The Influence of Cordovero'.

[55] Frankel (ed.), *Imrei Pinhas*, vol. I, 42, 423.

like a drop becoming part of an ocean. This sense of exaltedness was expressed by 'royal' clothing and comportment. The latter statement echoes the general role of clothing in the construction of Hasidic identity.[56] R. Yehiel Michel's student, Meshulam Feibush Heller of Zbarzah (1743?–1794) contributed greatly to the crystallization of Hasidic ideology in his *Yosher Divrei Emmet* (The Justness of Words of Truth).[57]. A later figure, yet the son of the Besht's daughter Adel, and thus rather close to the source, was Moshe Hayyim Ephraim of Sudilkov (c.1748–1800). His *Degel Mahane Ephraim* (see Numbers 2, 18), continued along his grandfather's path of shamanic ascent and magical healing, while balancing his love-focused approach with a more ascetic stress on 'inner awe', paradoxically assuaging the fears evoked by the known dangers of ascent.[58]

A rather different approach is contained in the morass of teachings attributed to R. Dov Baer Freidman (1704–1772), the Magid of Mezeritch, who emerged as the Besht's most influential student. As far as it can be reconstructed, the Magid's approach rests on three pillars: psychologization (or, as Margolin has termed it, internalization), an even more central role for language and the doctrine of *'ayin* (nothingness).[59] The first element represents a shift not only away from Messianism but also away from Lurianic *kavvanot*: according to one teaching, one must 'dwell within the letters' in both prayer and study. While 'the earlier ones' used the key of *kavvana* to open the door inwards, 'today we have no *kavvanah* save for the brokenness of heart', the simile being a thief who smashes open the door.[60] This text, besides containing the second element, is highly instructive on two more levels: it represents the modern historical sense of a break between 'the earlier ones' and 'today', and it demonstrates an increasing openness to melancholy and other downcast emotional states. The second element shall be addressed more fully later, and for now it suffices to say that for him psychology is as much cognitive as emotive. And as for him (in a move reminiscent of the psychoanalytic system of Jacques Lacan), thought itself,

[56] Horowitz (ed.), *Torat ha-Maggid mi-Zlotchov*, 43; Ha-Kohen (ed.), *Mayim Rabim*, 15A, 40A (and Altshuler, *The Messianic Secret*). On clothing in early Hasidism, see Gries, *The Hebrew Book*, 234–236.

[57] Krassen, *Uniter of Heaven and Earth.*

[58] Brill, 'The Spiritual World', esp. 45–49.

[59] Margolin, *The Human Temple*, esp. 184–186, 190–191; Matt, ''Ayin'. On the formidable philological challenge of parsing the Magid's teaching from that of his associates, see Moseson, 'From Spoken Word', esp. 295–296.

[60] See the texts translated and analyzed in Schatz-Uffenheimer, *Hasidism as Mysticism*, 216–218 (utilizing a reasonable phenomenological comparison to quietisitic doctrines of nondoing in seventeenth-century Catholicism that can well be expanded to Far Eastern materials).

including its 'early' or unconscious forms, is a linguistic process, much of the Lurianic system can be described in terms of language (an approach broadly similar to that of Sarug and his reception).[61]

The third element, phenomenologically similar to Buddhist teachings, and in any case containing some antinomian potential, consists of separation from corporeality, culminating in union with God, in which one ceases to exist. This trajectory is closely related to psychologization, as one reaches *'ayin* 'only if man does nothing but which pertains to the soul'. In this state, even while the plain sense of prayer entails requesting material improvement, one cannot 'turn to any thing of the world at all', seeing that one does not exist![62] Joined, with the negation of Lurianic *kavvanot*, this a-cosmic tendency forced a reinterpretation of the entire theurgical project, now reframed as giving pleasure to God through exposing his concealed presence (like a child in a game of hide and seek).[63] The close link between the doctrines of nothingness and language can be found in what Idel has termed 'immanentist linguistic'.[64] One can decode this paradoxical doctrine in the following manner: the fragility and relativity of material being derives from its radical dependence on the power of divine language, as expressed in the 'speech act' of creation, while it also serves to conceal this divine source.[65]

One can appreciate the complexity of the Hasidic worlds, even at this relatively earlier stage, if one recalls R. Ya'akov Yosef's embrace of the mundane. The complexity of the Magid's own teachings is reflected both in the difficulty of isolating a clear textual record of transmission (despite the printing of his main work, *Maggid Devarav le-Ya'akov*, as early as 1781) and in the sheer number of disciples, each with his own unique interpretation of his teacher's path, adapted also to the geographical-cultural areas in which they planted the movement.[66] As also supported by an external eye-witness report (see below), the Magid himself deliberately adapted his discourses to each of his listeners. One should also recall that it is possible that this

61 Scholem, *The Messianic Idea*, 214, 216–217, 226–227; Scholem, *On the Mystical Shape*, 133–134, 139; Mayse, *Speaking Infinities*. For Lacanian readings of Hasidism, see Pedaya, *Expanses*, esp. 207–208, 215–216, 240–246, 289–290, 314–316.

62 See the texts translated and discussed in Schatz-Uffenheimer, *Hasidism as Mysticism*, 73–74, 77. The psychology of nothingness in the Magid's writings shall be addressed in a study in preparation by Menachem Lorberbaum.

63 Compare to Idel, 'Ta'anug'; Idel, *Kabbalah: New Perspectives*, 151–153. On a-cosmism in Hasidism, see Elior, *Israel Ba'al Shem Tov*, vol. I, 421–422, 426.

64 Idel, *Hasidism*, 215–221.

65 Mayse, *Speaking Infinities*.

66 Both the complexity of the Hasidic worlds and the salience of regional-geographic elements have been emphasized by Baumgarten, *La Naissance du Hasidisme*, esp. 19–22. For a wide selection from the Magid's students see Green et al. (eds.), *Speaking Torah*.

divergence reflects the complexity of the Besht's own teaching, though this is very difficult to determine.

The Magid's son, fittingly known as Avraham ha Malakh (the Angel, c.1741–1776), deepened the internalized and contemplative elements of his father's teaching, but by doing so removed himself, even before his early death, from the role of successor and leader of what was now becoming a full-fledged movement. Thus, one should but note that the stress on the intellect, in his work *Hesed la-Avraham* (see Micah 7, 20), may possibly reflect the eighteenth-century revival of Maimonidean philosophy. R. Menahem Nahum Twersky of Chernobyl (Ukraine, 1730–1797) was the only one of the students known to have studied with the Besht. His *Ma'or Enayim* (see Prov. 15, 30) reveals the continued influence of *Musar* literature on Hasidic writing, and as such can be seen as an antipode to R. Avraham's formulations.[67] To the extent that there is a major ideational innovation in this work, it lies in the development of the notion of redemption of the individual soul, rather than that of the collective (see above in our discussion of R. Ya'akov Yosef). According to R. Menahem Nahum, 'every time there is a unification of thought and speech, this is the restoration of the aspect of the Messiah, but it is not permanent'.[68] Another prominent student who had some contacts with the Beshtian circle and transmitted (in the name of the Magid) a reversal of customary views of exile was R. Uziel Meizels (1744–1785), who operated in central Poland. In his main work *Tiferet 'Uziel*, he cites a parable of a king who is most accessible when away from his home.[69] In these variants or developments of the Magid's teachings, the collective and historical elements of the mystical-messianic approach of the Besht are further individualized and spiritualized.

Another veteran student was R. Barukh of Kossov (c.1725–1780), who followed R. Avraham Hererra in a systematic nonliteral, most psychological interpretation of the Lurianic system.[70] In 1777 another prominent student, R. Menahem Mendel of Vitebsk (1730–1788), following an earlier immigration (1764, by members of the Besht's circle) led a group of immigrants to the Galilee, founding a center in Tiberias that continues in diverse forms to this day. R. Menahem Mendel radicalized the teachings of the Maggid on *'ayin*, through stating that the Lurianic system should be not only psychologized

[67] Sagiv, *Dynasty*, esp. 255–258, 332–334.

[68] Translated and discussed in Idel, *Messianic Mystics*, 231–233 (see also 221–226, 286–287). For an English translation of part of the work (soon to be expanded), see Green, *The Light of the Eyes*.

[69] Meizels, *Tiferet 'Uziel*, 137A.

[70] Liebes, 'The Novelty'.

but bypassed through access to the infinite via faith. This rather Paulinian approach (phenomenologically similar to some Sabbatean formulations) is accompanied by a downplaying of detailed work with the emotions, à la *Musar*, in favor of spontaneous inspiration and including a sense of mystical unity amongst the fellowship.[71] The Lithuanian sect of Karlin, led by R. Aharon 'the great', Perlow (1736–1772), continued to be loyal to the teachings of the departed master.[72] Perlow is famous for his probable authorship of the devotional hymn *Yah Ekshof No'am Sabbath* (Yah, I yearn for the pleasantness of Sabbath), which has become a pan-Hasidic anthem today.

A slightly later student, R. Levi Yitzhak of Berditchev (c.1740–1810), displayed an interest in political affairs reflecting the beginnings of aspiration toward leadership of the Jewish community as a whole.[73] While his fame, as defending the case of the Jews and bringing their plight before God, is largely due to later hagiographical accounts, his *Qedushat Levi* (Holiness of Levi), partly published in his lifetime, offers a relatively direct glance at the early development of the Maggid's thought. Here *'ayin* enters a dialectic with *yesh*, or 'somethingness', that set the tone for much of later Hasidic writing.[74] R. Ze'ev Wolf of Zhitomir (d. 1798), is especially notable for bringing the largely premodern (Abulafian) method of combination of letters to the forefront of Hasidic teaching.[75] R. Ze'ev Wolf is further outstanding in preserving Beshtian traditions that capture the world-negating dimension of the practice of uplifting sparks, which (at least momentarily), uncovers the nothingness concealed in material objects. Scholem famously marshaled such texts against the popularizing interpretation of Hasidism by Martin Buber (see Chapter 6), and indeed R. Ze'ev Wolf critiqued more popular forms of Hasidism, rather promoting an elitist practice, culminating in the transformation of the adept's very perception of the world.[76] Yet it is safer to say that they reflect the gap between the reception of the Besht's nonsystematic lore on the part of R. Ya'akov Yosef and that of the Magid (again, as refracted by his various disciples).

[71] On parallels between Hasidic and Christian thought, see Magid, *Hasidism Incarnate*.
[72] For a history of Karlin see Brown, *'Like a Ship on a Stormy Sea'*.
[73] Loewenthal, 'Early Hasidic Teachings'. [74] Elior, 'The Paradigms'.
[75] Idel, *Hasidism*, 56–60, attempts to generalize from this move to the thrust of Hasidism as a whole.
[76] For a range of interpretations around these issues, see Scholem, *The Messianic Idea*, 241–244; Scholem, *On the Mystical Shape*, 130; Brody, 'Open to Me the Gates of Righteousness'; Green et al., *Speaking Torah*, vol. I, 43.

Arthur Green has correctly noted that the innovative focus of Hasidism lies in the ways of *'Avodat Hashem* (servitude or worship of God) rather than in abstract theology.[77] Indeed, Hasidic writing is remarkably replete with advice on the ups and downs of spiritual life. However, one should be careful not to reduce this shift to the inner life of emotional or contemplative worship.[78] Rather, we are speaking of a shift in practice, encompassing sociocultural and not merely spiritual dimensions (and codified in the Hasidic adaptations of the *hanhagot* genre). In other words, the confluence of new ideas, practices and social structures constituted a new habitus. In this revitalization of Jewish life, prayer moved to a more central place, somewhat demoting the classical idea of Torah study as the pinnacle of religious life. Study itself was reframed in devotional terms, following on from moves that we have already encountered in seventeenth-century Prague.

As indicated above, this shift in values was accompanied by a new form of leadership, that of the charismatic *tzaddik*, not always accompanied by the pedigree of Talmudic learning. Hasidic practices included regular immersion in the *miqve*, or ritual bath, at times accompanied by an innovative set of *kavvanot*, set forth in the name of the Besht, in R. Shabbetai of Rashkov's prayer book (written 1755, published 1797) and elsewhere.[79] Other trademarks of Hasidic life were a different approach to the laws of ritual slaughtering (the use of special knives) and the replacement of the traditional Ashkenazi liturgy with versions based on Luria. Earlier in the century, a Polish halakhist, R. Shlomo Rapoport of Chelm (c.1717–1781), critiqued not only the pretentious study of Kabbalah in his time but also an entire bodily and emotional comportment, including vocal prayer accompanied by melodies, groans, waving of arms and donning of white clothing. Many of these mannerisms, some originating in Sabbateanism, can be noted amongst the Hasidim.[80] To this somatic-sonorous array, one should add the innovation of numerous *nigunim* (tunes), some attributed to the Besht and other founding figures, and the importance attributed to group dancing.[81] These had a special part in the construction of Hasidic sociality, especially around the Sabbath and festivals.

77 Green, 'Early Hasidism', 445 (and Hisdai, 'Eved haShem').

78 Cf. Margolin, *The Phenomenology of Inner Religious Life*, esp. 274–275, 353–364.

79 Kallus, 'The Relation of the Ba'al Shem Tov', esp. 156–159.

80 Rapoport, *Markevet ha-Mishne*, unpaginated introduction (and Faierstein, *Jewish Customs*, 30). On Hasidic practices and Sabbateanism, see Liebes, *On Sabbateaism*, 98–100.

81 Gries, *The Hebrew Book*, 239–240.

For all of David Assaf's correct emphasis on fluidity and movement (ideologically sanctioned in notions of pilgrimage to the court of the *tzaddik*) across national and regional boundaries (as well as shifts in the boundaries themselves), Hasidism as a way of life was molded by the cultures of those areas of Eastern and Central Europe to which it constantly spread. As Assaf duly notes, this geographical tendency includes the preservation (to this day) of the memory of specific locales, after which the various branches are named. Yet it also extends to loyalty to national entities.[82] However, it must be stressed that it was only toward the end of the century, largely through penetration into the densely populated Jewish communities of Poland, when Hasidism transformed from a set of circles, in a recognizable pattern, to a social movement. The figure most associated with this change of social form was the leader of Hasidism in southwest Poland, R. Elimelekh Weisblum of Lyzansk (c.1717–c.1786). His somewhat cryptic *No'am Elimelekh* (Pleasantness of Elimelekh) provides the accompanying ideology, focused on the role of the *tzaddik* in drawing down influx, materializing as concrete benefits for the masses.[83] As Ada Rapoport-Albert has shown, Weisblum gave doctrinal support for the decentralized and continuous proliferation of autonomous 'courts' of *tzaddikim*, while assuming a soul-connection between them and their respective adherents.[84]

THE NEAR EASTERN HEGEMONY OF R. SHALOM SHAR'ABI

A striking, though largely unrelated parallel to the mid-century change in the dominance of European Kabbalah can be found in the Near East. While the Hasidic movement enveloped large parts of the spiritual life of Eastern and Central Europe, within two generations Near Eastern Kabbalah accepted the hegemony (as Giller fortuitously put it) of the system of R. Shalom Shar'abi (Rashash). The main difference between the two roughly contemporaneous developments is that the latter largely remained within the Lurianic (and especially Vitalian) mode of an elite fellowship (though this pattern was to change somewhat toward the twentieth century). However, one should not miss the magnitude of the shift in internal power relationships. Rashash was soon to be imagined as Luria returning to earth to

82 Assaf, 'Polish Hasidism or Hasidism in Poland' (compare to Teller, 'Hasidism and the Challenge of Geography'; Stampfer, 'How and Why Did Hasidism Spread'); Schor, *Studies*, 588–609.

83 See the texts translated and discussed in Idel, *Hasidism*, 116–117.

84 Rapoport-Albert, 'Hasidism after 1772'.

complete his project, and his writings were accorded a status equal to that of the Safedian master. Just as Rashash himself, in his letters to the sages of the 'West', or Tunisia, warned against any attempt to challenge Luria's teachings through Zoharic passages, it was soon assumed that his innovations were impregnable to questioning based on the Lurianic corpus.[85] One ingredient of the enduring power of the Rashashian hegemony was its base in the young Jerusalemite Yeshiva, *Beit El* (The House of God) that he joined and soon headed. Unchallenged until the late nineteenth century, this total institution of kabbalistic learning and practice operates till this very day.

On the one hand Rashash, unlike most European kabbalists (yet like Ramaz) adhered strictly to the Vitalian transmission, merging the familial editing of R. Shmu'el Vital (highly popular in the Near East) and the later phase of Zemach's Jerusalemite rendition. He was particularly fierce in his attacks on any vestige of Sabbateanism.[86] However, from the very beginning of his magnum opus *Nahar Shalom*, he thinly veiled his discontent with Vital's interpretation of Luria, politely saying that it reflects the former's early, immature understanding. The specific point at issue there can illustrate the scope of Rashash's innovation. While Vital differentiated between the relatively lower *partzufim* affected by the breaking of the vessels, and the higher ones that were not, Rashash boldly asserted that a three-dimensional view of the depth dimension reveals that there is no part of the supernal world unaffected by this cataclysmic event.[87] As he put it elsewhere in a gloss on the Vitalian *Derekh 'Etz Hayyim*, 'these matters [Luria's teachings] are not literal and thus several questions fall, and if it was possible to understand the truth of all the matters there would be no room for difficulties'.[88] Based on a version found in some manuscripts, there is reason to believe that the term 'truth of all the matters' refers to a three-dimensional perspective. Thus, while a two-dimensional, vertical, hierarchical and linear perspective can differentiate between higher and immune aspects and lower and vulnerable ones, seeing through to the depth dimension reveals a seam of fracture running through the entire cosmos.

Returning to our main text, while explaining that all aspects were subject to fracture, Rashash specifies that when stating that a certain *partzuf* remained intact, this is only relative to the ones below it, and here sets forth

85 Giller, *Shalom Shar'abi*, 10–12; Garb, *Modern Kabbalah*, 22, 72–75.

86 Shar'abi, 'Nahar Shalom' (printed at the end of Vital, *Derekh 'Etz Hayyim*), 32A, 34A. On the possible presence of Sabbateans in the early days of Beit El Yeshiva, see Barnai, 'On the History of the Sabbatian Movement', 67–68.

87 Shar'abi, 'Nahar Shalom', 2A–B. On 'height' versus depth see e.g. 13B.

88 Gloss on Vital, *Derekh 'Etz Hayyim*, Gate 14, chap. 3, pt. 1, 71A.

a meta-principle: 'For all is based on the relative terms [*'erkei ha-kinnuyim*] alone, but there is no change between them [the various aspects] at all, except that according to the refinement of the lights and the changes in the elevation of the locations thus is the change in the diminution of their sensation [*hargashatam*] in the lower aspects.' We shall soon see how this cryptic statement was decoded later in the text (and also in the next generation of the *Beit El* school); however, for now one can glean two observations: one is that there is some form of nominalism here, as indicated by the phrase 'relative terms'. That is to say, difference lies in description rather than in reality. Second, the reference to sensation probably reflects the influence of Hai Ricci's perspectivism, or subordination of the plethora of aspects in the Lurianic system to the relative point of view from which they are observed.[89]

Based on these guidelines, Rashash was able to develop a complex system of 'details of details till the last detail that one can detail'.[90] This method builds on the earlier notion that each aspect includes all of the others in a hologramic manner. Rashash not only took this subfraction to the fourth level (e.g. the three higher *sefirot*, of the six lower *sefirot*, of the three higher *sefirot*, of the six lower *sefirot*), but also developed a complex system of interchange, in which, for example, the *Keter* of *Hokhma* was changed into the *Hokhma* of *Keter* and then back again.[91] This seemingly technical enumeration is what enables three-dimensional movement throughout the entire structure: thus, while, for instance vertically speaking *Malkhut* is well below *Keter*, one can navigate in the dimension of depth from the *Malkhut* of *Malkhut* to the *Malkhut* of *Keter* (especially since it was once the *Keter* of *Malkhut*), thus linking seemingly disparate realms, creating 'one unity' reaching all the way to the *Ein-Sof*.[92] As we shall now see, the resultant flexibility was highly fruitful for the conversion of theory into practice.

Despite the magnitude of these theoretical offerings, Rashash's main contribution, and the key to understanding his sway, was to develop the Lurianic system of *kavvanot* into a fully detailed repertoire.[93] The guiding theory behind this reconstruction is the foregrounding of the soul.[94] On a more practical level, he filled a major lacuna in the weekly implementation of Lurianic practice – the intentions of the Sabbath prayers, as well as cementing the practice of undoing all curses uttered during the week before

[89] On the question of the influence of Hai Ricci on Rashash (despite the latter's assertions of purist restriction to the Vitalian corpus), see Giller, *Shalom Shar'abi*, 100–102.
[90] Shar'abi, 'Nahar Shalom', 4A. [91] See e.g. ibid., 10A. [92] Ibid., 34A.
[93] Giller, *Shalom Shar'abi*, 67–77. [94] Garb, *Yearnings of the Soul*, 43–44.

the Sabbath.[95] Rashash's interest in time led to another major innovation, the existence of an entire *partzuf* focused on the festivals. According to his reading of the opening chapter of Genesis, the first day of creation inaugurates the '*partzuf* of days', while the creation of the luminaries, designed 'for signs, and for seasons, and for days and years' (Genesis 1, 14) on the fourth day began the separate '*partzuf* of times'.[96]

This foregrounding of the temporal dimension is closely accompanied by the startling assertion that the daily practice should actually be understood as a tri-daily process, in which each day retroactively affects the previous day.[97] In a similar move, Rashash drew close to the doctrine of *shemitot* in writing that the completion of the *tiqqunim* for each cycle of six thousand years retroactively renders the previous cycle more 'refined' or closer to the infinite. Fittingly, he concludes this discussion by saying: 'and this is enough for he who understands for we cannot expand more on what needs to be said for these are deep deep matters and the enlightened one will understand'.[98] The new hegemony did not rise entirely unchallenged. R. Shlomo Molkho (1747?–1788, not to be confused with his sixteenth-century namesake), of Saloniki and later Jerusalem, repeatedly wrote in his *Shemen Zayit Zakh* (Pure Olive Oil), that there are no difficulties that necessitate Rashash's 'inventions' as all is 'simple and clear'. Again and again he proposes linear solutions in lieu of three-dimensional moves and especially resists the foregrounding of the soul in *kavvanot*, dryly noting that if this theme is of such importance, Luria should have mentioned it himself.[99]

The above-mentioned similarity between Rashash's approach toward Vital and that of a major Italian kabbalist is not coincidental. To some extent, Italy preserved its earlier status as bridge between East and West. Thus, one of Rashash's disciples, R. Yosef Hayyim David Azulai (known by the acronym *Hida*, 1724–1826, descendant of R. Avraham Azulai) lived in Italy in his later years (as part of his extensive and well-recorded travels throughout the Mediterranean, being hosted on one occasion by none less than opponents of Luzzatto). Azulai's extensive legal writings also mark the incorporation of Rashashian practice within the world of Halakha.[100] Prominent amongst his ritual innovations was a practice popular throughout the Near East – *tiqqun karet*, ritual learning and prayer, usually throughout Thursday night, aimed at avoiding the punishment of untimely death (known as *karet*). Azulai greatly contributed to the adoption of a custom

[95] Hillel, *Ahavat Shalom*, 10–11; Hallamish, *Kabbalistic Customs*, 97.
[96] Shar'abi, 'Nahar Shalom', 13A, 37B, 39B. [97] Ibid., 24A. [98] Ibid., 13A.
[99] See e.g. Molkho, *Shemen Zayit Zakh*, 89, 337. [100] Sharon, 'The Hida's Kaballah'.

that became one of the most important catalysts for widespread exposure to Kabbalah. The custom of daily recital of *Hoq le-Israel* (see Psalms 81,5), or daily reading of a sample of canonical texts, including Zohar, had some Lurianic sources, but was actually established in Egypt around 1740, rapidly spreading to the new Hasidic world, acquiring messianic portent and becoming all but universal in communities across the Middle East well into the twentieth century.[101] A second major student, R. David Majar, effectively summarized his teacher's abstruse system in his oft-quoted *Hasdei David* (see Isaiah 55, 3). Yet his independence is evident in moving away from Vitalian purism, and quoting Sarug.[102]

However, Rashash's main student, taking his teaching to new levels of detail, sophistication and creativity, was R. Hayyim de la Rosa (d. 1786), author of *Torat Hakham* (Teaching of the Sage). Just as Rashash claimed to set forth the true meaning of Luria's doctrine (even if seemingly contradicted by Vital), de la Rosa claimed to have received transmission 'from between the eyelashes' of his teacher, even if it clashed with the plain sense of his texts.[103] This self-confidence should be contrasted with the confession on the part of Rashash's son (and one of his successors in the leadership of the Yeshiva), R. Hizkiyahu Yitzhak Mizrhai Shar'abi (d. 1808), as to his lack of true understanding of his father's *kavvanot*.[104] Radicalizing the principle of relativity, de la Rosa employed it in order to interpret central Lurianic themes in a nonliteral manner. In a move reminiscent of the allegorical interpretations of *tzimtzum*, he repeatedly states that there is actually never any withdrawal of *mohin*, and even where this is indicated by the texts in question this is merely nominal (*mekhane otam be-shem*). In this context, he goes so far as to say that one should assume that Luria deliberately wrote inaccurate statements in order to conceal his true view. One implication of these moves pertains to gender: according to de la Rosa, contrary to textual appearances, the feminine aspect cannot receive *mohin* directly from the higher countenances, but is rather dependent on the mediation of the male aspect of *Ze'ir Anpin* at all times.[105] A closely related innovation was to render relativity in terms of quality: in other words, quantitatively, in the dimension of depth, all the worlds are equal, and the entire differentiation in

[101] Hallamish, *Kabbalah in Liturgy, Halakhah and Customs*, 327–328.
[102] Giller, *Shalom Shar'abi*, 103; Ehrenfeld, *Yira'ukha im-Shemesh*, 604–631.
[103] Garb, *Modern Kabbalah*, 76.
[104] See the text adduced and translated in Giller, *Shalom Shar'abi*, 19.
[105] De la Rossa, *Torat Hakham*, 160A (and 171B).

the vertical dimension should not be taken literally, but rather refers to qualitative and thus relative, perception-dependent, differences.[106]

The close relationship between Rashash and his students, balancing his own towering status, is evident in the charters of the fellowship (which came to be known as *Ahavat Shalom*, love of peace). Here we find an egalitarian structure in which the members of the fellowship are adjured to express their 'great love' and sense of unity (each considering the other to be 'as if he was literally his limb'), by abstaining from any honorific gestures, as 'we should behave as if we are one man, with no advantage of one over the other'.[107] Indeed, as in the case of the early masters of Hasidism, it is often difficult to distinguish between Rashash's own teaching and the editing and reworking of his disciples; his prayer book (containing the incredibly intricate system of *kavvanot*), being a clear example.

Toward the end of the century, *Beit El* was headed by R. Yom Tov Algazi (1780–1802), a major halakhist and communal leader. While representing the Yeshiva in Europe, he attracted the attention of Ashkenazi luminaries such as R. Moshe Sofer (to be discussed below). The above-mentioned correspondence between Rashash and the sages of Tunis, and the seepage of *kavvanot* 'according to the opinion of the Holy R. Shar'abi', facilitated the gradual spread of Rashashian Kabbalah in North Africa.[108] Typically for this area, summaries of theosophical systems were accompanied by poems, as well as experiences of messages from Luria in dreams. The first printed commentary on the entire *Zohar*, *Miqdash Melekh* (Sanctuary of the King, printed 1750), by the sage R. Shalom Buzaglo (d. 1780, of the prolific circle in Marrakesh, Morocco), largely subordinated the exegesis of the medieval canonical text to the Lurianic schemes and was frequently quoted in Eastern Europe, especially by the Hasidim. Ironically, in his less-known *Hadrat Pnei Melekh* (Majesty of the Face of the King) commentary devoted to the *Idrot*, he espoused the literal view of *tzimtzum* that was anathema to the Hasidim. Another indication of what can be described in terms of globalization was the appearance, around 1800, of a North African commentary on Polish Kabbalah.[109]A specifically Moroccan phenomenon, apparent already in 1708, was the custom of bringing numerous amulets to the home of a new-born child, a practice that was banned by rabbinic interdict.[110]

106 Ibid., 23B, 152A.

107 My translation of the text cited in Benayahu, 'The Fellowship Charters', 64–65.

108 Hallamish, *Kabbalah in North Africa*, 74, 107.

109 Ibid., 117, 138–141 (see also 120–123 on poetry and 158–159 on dreams).

110 Ibid., 121.

The most striking representative of this period in Morocco was a pre-Shar'abian figure, R. Hayyim ben 'Attar (1696–1743), widely known as 'the Holy One'. His poetic commentary on the Bible, *Or ha-Hayyim* (Light of Life) soon acquired canonical status (also as part of *Miqre'ot Gedolot*, the most widespread format of the Hebrew Bible) and aroused especial admiration amongst the Hasidim.[111] The mystical contents of the work are not readily evident on first reading, yet careful scrutiny uncovers not only quotations from the *Zohar* but also erotic-experiential formulations: 'You should know that there is no yearning in the world as pleasant and dear and desirable and loved and passionate and hoped for the created – and particularly for the spiritual part that apprehends and knows the light of God – as the adherence [*hitdabqut*] to His blessed light', or 'if people would sense the sweetness and pleasantness of the good of the Torah, they would go mad and burning after her'. These joined dreams of combating the male and female forces of darkness.[112] In terms of historical context, one should note ben 'Attar's discussions of the state of Moroccan Jews under Islamic rule. Thus Genesis 1, 2: 'darkness was upon the face of the deep' is interpreted as follows: 'This hints at the bitter exile in which we are sunk, in an endless deep, for 1671 years, and as if the length of the exile was not enough, we have darkness, that hints at . . . the servitude to the nations and the weighty burden of taxes . . . Happy is he who has not seen this, especially in our West [the Maghreb].'[113] This strong sense of exile was accompanied by a keen messianic self-consciousness, expressed, inter alia, in ben 'Attar's emigration to the Galilee in 1742.[114]

R. ELIYAHU OF VILNA AND HIS SCHOOL

For all of their roots in kabbalistic *Musar* literature, the Hasidic innovations were bold enough to call forth (starting with 1772) a series of rabbinical bans and interdicts, on both published works (such as *Toldot Ya'akov Yosef*, which was actually burnt) and practices.[115] The latter included the demotion of Torah study from pride of place, praying with the Lurianic liturgy, divergent laws of ritual slaughter (with a polished knife) and other instances of what was described as a 'new religion'. The genre of anti-Hasidic writing,

[111] Manor, 'R. Hayyim ben Attar'.
[112] *Or ha-Hayyim* on Genesis 2, 1; Deuteronomy 26, 11; Genesis 49, 11.
[113] Compare to *Or ha-Hayyim* on Leviticus 6, 2, which reflects a sense of missing a possible messianic 'exit date' a year later.
[114] Ibid., on Deuteronomy 15, 7.
[115] Elior, *Israel Ba'al Shem Tov*, vol. II, 17–21.

accompanied by bans, flourished until the turn of the century. Works such as the first-printed (1772) anti-Hasidic tract, *Zemir 'Arizim ve-Harbot Tzurim* (Pruning of Tyrants and Knives of Flint), ridiculed resort to magic, and suggested that the Hasidic leaders were in fact charlatans seeking material gain in return for wonder-working. Predictably, the shadow of Sabbateanism loomed in the background.[116]

Toward the end of the century, the *mitnagdim* (opponents) succeeded in enlisting the support of a reclusive and immensely learned figure, the above-mentioned R. Eliyahu of Vilna. In his response the more theoretical (see also above on psychologization) side of the debate is prominent: in a letter whose authenticity is not certain, R. Eliyahu wrote: 'How they have deceived this generation, uttering these words on high: "These are your Gods o Israel; every stick and stone" [see Exod. 32:8]. They interpret the Torah incorrectly regarding the verse: "Blessed be the name of the glory of God from His dwelling place" [Ezek. 3; 12] and also regarding the verse: "You enliven everything" [Nehemia 9, 6]'.[117] Despite his opposition to Hasidism, it is possible that R. Eliyahu had a more positive view of Sabbateanism, and in any case he stayed on the sidelines in the Eybeschütz-Emden controversy.[118] Furthermore, his circle, if not his own doctrine, was significantly indebted to the messianic thought of Luzzatto and Hai Ricci.[119] As already mentioned, R. Eliyahu's circle was influenced by R. Heshel Tzoref, who also had a marked impact on the Besht and other early Hasidic masters.[120] As we shall yet see, the influence of Sabbateanism and other forms of Messianism grew stronger amongst those members of the circle who actually did emigrate to Ottoman Palestine.

While acknowledging these influences, we can discern R. Eliyahu's remarkable independence in his divergence from the Lurianic doctrine (at times denied amongst the later generations of his school). Amongst several examples noted by Avivi, the following is most important for appreciating his complex and dialectical approach to Kabbalah: both Luria and R. Eliyahu agree that there are two forms of *zivug* (erotic unification between *partzufim*) – the permanent one taking place between *Abba* and *Imma*, and the impermanent one, between *Ze'ir Anpin* and *Nuqba*, dependent on human action. The point of difference lies in the relative value assigned to each:

[116] For an overview of this 'hostile phase', see Wilensky, 'Hasidic-Mitnaggedic Polemics'.
[117] Translated and discussed in Hundert, *Jews in Poland-Lithuania*, 204–205.
[118] Leiman, 'When a Rabbi Is Accused of Heresy'.
[119] Shuchat, *A World Hidden*, esp. 121–130, 144–151.
[120] Liebes, *The Zevi and the Gaon*, 283–360.

while for Luria the significant *zivug* is the impermanent one, the keystone of theurgical practice, for R. Eliyahu it is the permanent one, for it is the hidden source of vitality in wisdom, as opposed to the more external *zivug*, which he identifies with speech.[121] The overall significance of this dispute will soon become apparent.

Yet more generally, R. Eliyahu's writings take the form of terse commentaries on rabbinical or Zoharic texts, and include numerous works based on student notes and thus of mixed authenticity. The most influential and consistent of his authentic writings is his commentary on *Sifra de-Tzniuta* (Book of Modesty), a Zoharic treatise probably belonging to the *Idrot* literature. The constantly unwinding argument (like the snakes that are the central mythical images in the text) needs to be extracted from constant citation and interpretation of texts from this Zoharic layer (as well as *Tikkunei Zohar*, to which R. Eliyahu devoted a late printed commentary that was subject to heavy editing), as well as frequent resort to Lurianic writings, though not cited as such. The opening move differentiates between two levels: that of 'modesty', assigned to the hidden highest layers of *Keter* and touching on the Infinite, and the beginnings of revelation in wisdom. As this is the case, 'all study of Kabbalah is entitled wisdom', however this study must constantly be accompanied by modesty, 'the general principle (*'iqar*) of this wisdom is to conceal (*le-hatzni'a*)'.[122]

This self-reflection on the kabbalistic project opens into a wider analysis of discourse: The three highest *sefirot* (*Keter* being modest and hidden), *Hokhma*, *Binah* and *Da'at* correspond to thought, writing and reading (out loud as is the traditional custom in Jewish learning), speech and narrative. These *mohin*, especially Hokhma, are the source of vitality and 'the life of man'.[123] These statements reinforce the superiority of the higher *zivug*, as discussed just now. They also inform a wider intellectualist approach, in which the Torah and its innovative study is the absolute value: the higher *zivug* corresponds to the giving of Torah on Sinai, whilst the end of the period of Torah (in which there is no true innovation but rather mere commentary), ushered a return to chaos. It follows that the eschaton is characterized by a 'new', innovative Torah.[124] The Torah is the supreme

121 Avivi, *The Kabbalah of R. Eliyahu*, 36–42.

122 Kremer, *Commentary*, 1A–B, and see also 17B.

123 Ibid., 3A (and see Wolfson, 'From Sealed Book to Open Text', 151–156).

124 Ibid., 2B, 8A; Avivi, *The Kabbalah of R. Eliyahu*, 59–61. On the Gaon's messianic thought, see Shuchat, *A World Hidden*, esp. 166–200, 247–259. On the theme of 'new Torah', see Idel, '*Torah Haddasha*'.

manifestation of the covenant, as the symbol of connectivity between the human and divine (together with circumcision, to be discussed below).[125]

The second move, located at the heart of the commentary, shifts the focus to *Ze'ir Anpin* (also identified with the people of Israel), just as in the thought of Hai Ricci and his Sabbeatean sources):

> the tetragammaton is all the level of *Ze'ir Anpin* and it guides the world, and this is the name of the infinite, which is revealed by it . . . for the main intention of the infinite was that His name will be revealed in the world . . . And thus he descended rank after rank till *Ze'ir Anpin* and was revealed there . . . and thus the name of *Ze'ir Anpin* is the main special name and all other, prior names . . . are subsidiary though higher.[126]

It is highly likely that the focus on the Tetragammaton reflects a similar stress in the premodern *Sh'arei Orah* by Gikatilia, a work recommended by the Gaon as an introduction to Kabbalah. There is no contradiction between the focus on *Ze'ir Anpin* and R. Eliyahu's devaluation of the *zivug* between this aspect and its feminine consort, *Nuqba*. For R. Eliyahu shared in Hai Ricci's marginalization of the lower feminine aspect. For him, the *Nuqba* cannot be a source of innovation, for 'all she has no rectification except through adherence to the male' (this adherence, epitomized by the rite of circumcision, being the unification of the two messiahs, son of Joseph and son of David).[127] This is no mere point of doctrine, but actually crucial for appreciating R. Eliyahu's polemic against Hasidism: his position toward the *Nuqba*, which is usually associated with the divine in-dwelling in the material world, is part of a wider reticence toward immanence, as in his insistence that the divine soul is hidden and removed from human perception, but rather assists (again, in intellectual form!) surreptitiously from above, just as for him, divine providence (identified with *Ze'ir Anpin*), rather than divine presence can be found in the world.[128]

One may possibly link this approach to R. Eliyahu's austere mystical path, as described in the introduction to the commentary penned by his main student, R. Hayyim of Volozhin: according to this much-quoted text,

> He only allowed [himself] to show his soul satisfaction [Eccl. 2:24] with his own effort . . . One of the heavenly messengers very much pressed him, but

[125] Kremer, *Commentary*, 15A; Avivi, *The Kabbalah of R. Eliyahu*, 51–58.

[126] Kremer, *Commentary*, 20B (compare to 15B). Cf. Idel, *The Privileged Divine Feminine*, 150–152.

[127] Kremer, *Commentary*, 9A, 10B, 11B. On the centrality of circumcision in the Gaon's writing, see Wolfson, 'From Sealed Book to Open Text', 149–150, 157.

[128] Avivi, *The Kabbalah of R. Eliyahu*, 42–48; Kremer, *Commentary*, 6B.

> nevertheless he... answered him that... I do not want my depth of understanding which I have not toiled for and applied my own wisdom to... this was especially the case with revelations which were without Torah, 'his soul abhorred them' [Zecharia 11:8].[129]

In other words, R. Eliyahu saw the effortful study of Torah as the sole means of connectivity to the divine, rejecting other avenues of divine presence, as with the Hasidism (probably alluded to here), and their prophetic revival. This championing on the exclusivity of Torah study, joined with an ascetic distancing from the material realm, is also reflected in polemical works penned in his circle, around the turn of the century.

LESSER-KNOWN TRIBUTARIES

One circle explicitly exempted from some of the above-mentioned strictures on Hasidic practices was that of the *Kloiz* or enclosure in Brody. This was one of a set of institutions devoted to full-time learning and supported by private funding.[130] This circle produced a set of dense, unresearched writings, such as the works of R. Hayyim ben Menahem Zanzer (d. 1735) and R. Moshe ben Hillel Ostrer (d. 1785). The most influential of these was *Eretz Tov*, by R. Yesh'aya Ya'akov ha-Levi, written at the end of the century. Ha-Levi's book is focused on the Lurianic term 'central point', identified here with power, the Messiah and the Land of Israel. These concerns can be seen as a reflection of the continued messianic preoccupation and the awakened interest in the Land of Israel that characterized the turn of the century. Characteristically for the century, ha-Levi and other *Kloiz* members also expressed keen scientific interests. Thus, for example, R. Eliezer Fischel of Strizov, in his *'Olam Hafukh* (Inverted World), compares medieval and modern optics.[131] The above-mentioned R. Gershon of Kitov is a rare example of the link between this elitist circle and the Hasidic movement (which possibly borrowed from it the ritual recitation of Psalm 107 before the Sabbath).[132]

One illustrious figure who received his early training in the *Kloiz* was the major halakhist R. Yehuda Landau (1713–1793), the chief rabbi and head of the Yeshiva of Prague. Driven partly by anxiety (fueled by the Eybeschütz

[129] Translated in Fraenkel, *Nefesh HaTzimtzum*, vol. II, 500–502.
[130] Reiner, 'Wealth, Social Position and the Study of Torah'.
[131] Fischel, *'Olam Hafukh*, 171–172 (and Kahana, *From the Noda be Yehuda to the Chatam Sofer*, 148–149).
[132] Hallamish, *Kabbalah in Liturgy, Halakhah and Customs*, 135–137.

controversy and the Frankist movement) as to the infiltration of Sabbateanism into rabbinic literature, Landau spearheaded a complex critique of popularization of Kabbalah. Landau particularly resisted the insertion of theurgical themes into liturgy. For instance, Landau staunchly opposed the spread of the custom to preface performance of the commandments with the formula (similar to those that we encountered in *Hemdat Yamim*), 'For the sake of the unification of the Holy-one-Blessed be-He (here representing the *sefira* of *Tiferet*) and his *Shekhina*.'[133] Landau's efforts were joined by the 1757 ban on study of Kabbalah before 'filling one's belly' with the Talmud and legal codes (continuing halakhic opinions we have already seen), with a specific interdiction on studying the *Zohar* before the age of thirty, probably reacting to the popularity of trends similar to Hasidism amongst youth.[134]

Kahana has traced the profound influence of Landau, also in an agonistic manner, on another highly independent and complex figure, R. Moshe Sofer (1762–1839), known by the titles of his voluminous Talmudic commentaries, response and homilies entitled *Hatam Sofer* (Scribe's Seal). Though his reign, as the major halakhist of the Habsburg Empire, reached well into the next century, Sofer's background was indelibly marked by his early tutelage under the controversial visionary and magical kabbalist R. Nathan Adler (1742–1800). This charismatic figure was twice excommunicated by the Frankfurt am Main community as result of a set of innovative and schismatic practices, some overlapping with those of the Eastern European Hasidim, and some rather unique (such as tying ritual fringes, traditionally reserved for men, in women's clothing, changing the times of the beginning of the festivals and abstaining from eating with 'outsiders').[135]

Despite the efforts of figures such as Landau, the eighteenth century marked one of the high points in the proliferation of Kabbalah. Along with the printing of the Lurianic canon (accompanied with printing of Lurianic hagiographies) toward the end of the century, line-by-line close readings of these works appeared and soon became classics, such as *Yaffah Sha'a* and other works by R. Shlomo ha-Kohen (also a prominent halakhist).[136] However, the genre of kabbalistic *Musar* continued to be the main vehicle of popularization, especially shaping the experience of the Sabbath and festivals

133 Kahana, *From the Noda BeYehuda to the Chatam Sofer*, esp. 40–53, 62–76, 85–91, 105–118. Cf. Flatto, *The Kabbalistic Culture*.

134 Hundert, *Jews in Poland-Lithuania*, 179–181.

135 Elior, 'R. Nathan Adler'.

136 At a later point in his somewhat mysterious itinerary, ha-Kohen encountered the works of Rashash and expressed profound admiration for them.

(as we have also seen in the case of Hasidism). Two influential works contributing to this deepening of the kabbalistic hold on the Jewish calendar were Aharon ben Mordekhai of Vilkatz's *Sha'ar ha-Melekh*, especially stressing the month preceding and preparing for the High Holidays at the beginning of the year, and *Yesod ve-Soresh Ha-'Avoda* (The Foundation and Root of Worship), by R. Alexander Ziskind of Grodno, Lithuania (d. 1793), who was revered equally by the Hasidim and their opponents.

Magic continued to be another major vehicle for the spread of kabbalistic ideas, alchemy being a particularly widespread interest in this century (also amongst Christian writers influenced by Kabbalah). Emden read alchemical works in German and upheld alchemy and herbology as alternatives to the rise of modern medicine, perceived by him as a deist move. As part of this rearguard action, Emden critiqued the scientific interests of *Kloiz* scholars (see also above).[137] Following on from the return of the Jews to England in the seventeenth century, London joined the ever growing list of kabbalistic centers. One pioneer was Samuel Falk (1700–?), the controversial Ba'al Shem of London, who dealt in charms and amulets and was part of a network of magicians and mystics including Freemasons.[138] Amongst these one should especially note the Swedish visionary Immanuel Swedenborg (1688–1772) whose extensive writings may well reflect kabbalistic influences (especially surrounding the doctrine of the *Ein-Sof*), reflecting the earlier interest in phenomena such as Sabbateanism in Sweden.[139] Predictably, Falk aroused the ire of Emden, who obviously differentiated between alchemy and magic.

The former was but the first of a series of luminal figures operating in London at the turn of the century, such as George Levison, aka Mordekhai Gumpel Schnaber (?–1797), who employed Newtonian physics, proto-Darwinian notions of evolution and new technologies such as telegraphy to convey kabbalistic cosmology, or Jacob Hart, aka Elyaqim ben Avraham (1745–1814), who critically engaged with Newton as well as other English thinkers, such as John Locke and David Hume.[140] To these one should add Christianized kabbalists, such as Immanuel Frommann (d. 1735), who composed a kabbalistic commentary on Luke.[141] The Sabbatean ideas reflected in

137 Kahana, 'An Esoteric Path'.

138 For the spread of Masonic adaptations of Kabbalah already in this period, see Aptekman, *"Jacob's Ladder"*, 44–82.

139 Oron, *Samuel Falk*; Akerman-Hjren, 'Emanuel Swedenborg' (and Schuchard, *Emanuel Swedenborg*).

140 Ruderman, *Jewish Thought and Scientific Discovery*, 332–370.

141 On the effect of Sabbateanism on conversion to Christianity in the eighteenth century, see Carlebach, *Divided Souls*, 81–87.

this text can be said to echo, in turn, the ongoing Christian influence on the Jewish messianic movement.[142] Such figures demonstrate that the blending of Kabbalah into European occult as well as philosophical and scientific culture accelerated in the eighteenth century, alongside other processes of modernization. In terms of religious history, one should note the influence of kabbalistic ideas, indirectly, through Jacob Böhme and directly, through Cappel Hecht (a Jewish admirer of Böhme), on Pietistic (or as some have it, early evangelical) figures such as Friedrich Christoph Oetinger (1702–1782).[143]

The beginning of the *Haskala*, or Jewish enlightenment, a new player in the field of European Jewry, was accompanied by increasing ambivalence toward the Kabbalah. Moshe Mendelssohn (1729–1786), the giant of German Jewish enlightenment, corresponded with Emden (and was approvingly noted by his antagonist Eybeschütz), and adopted the former's critique of the *Zohar* (as described below).[144] An indication of Mendelssohn's connection to the kabbalistic culture at large can be found in the fact that his early mentor R. Israel of Zamosch was approved by R. Joel Ba'al Shem, one of the Besht's predecessors in his magical capacity (although R. Israel himself was a critic of Hasidism).[145] Figures of the Italian Jewish enlightenment, such as Shmuel David Luzzatto (Shadal, 1800–1865), went even further than Mendelssohn, denying that there are any ancient portions of the *Zohar* and in fact blaming the Kabbalah for hundreds of years of darkness amongst the Jews.[146] At the same time, Mendelssohn, like Naftali Hertz Wessely (1725–1805), whose works spread the Berlin *Haskala* in French and Italian, attempted to isolate elements of speculative philosophy in this and other kabbalistic texts. The full development of this distinction is found in *Imrei Binah* (see Prov. 1, 2) by Itzhak Satanov (1733–1804), who worked in Germany yet continued to be involved in the intellectual life of Galicia (including the printing of core Lurianic texts). Satanov sought correspondences between Kabbalah and philosophy, the first such attempt since early seventeenth-century Italy, and an expression of the general philosophical revival alluded to above (which was spearheaded by Mendelssohn).[147]

The keen interest in geometry that R. Eliyahu of Vilna displayed and some positive statements on learning science attributed to him, enabled his

142 Wolfson, 'Immanuel Frommann's Commentary'.
143 Herzog, *European Pietism*, 133–134.
144 Freudenthal, *No Religion without Idolatry*, esp. 165–174.
145 Kahana, *From the Noda be Yehuda to the Chatam Sofer*, 166–171.
146 Huss, *The Zohar*, 283–284.
147 On this still under-studied figure see Schulte, *Die Jüdische Aufklärung*, esp. 119–137.

adoption as a mascot of the Eastern European branch of the *Haskala*, as propagated by figures such as Satanov.[148] The Lithuanian kabbalistic response to *Haskala* was most developed in the bestseller *Sefer ha-Brit* (The Book of the Covenant), by R. Eliyahu Pinhas Horowitz of Vilna (1765–1821), who had connections to the circle of his namesake the Gaon. Horowitz surprisingly interpreted Vital's *Sha'arei Qedusha* through an extensive survey of the natural world. This was based not only on Jewish writers such as the above-mentioned Levison, but also modern non-Jewish scholars (although he remarkably predicts that their innovations will in turn be nullified by the discovery of new scientific instruments).[149] Like other Lithuanian kabbalists, R. Pinchas commented on R. Immanuel Hai Ricci's *Mishnat Hasidim*, which is not surprising, as the latter kabbalist upheld a staunchly literalist interpretation of *tzimtzum*, useful for resisting Hasidic a-cosmism.

In terms of general intellectual history, a more important interface between Kabbalah and the spread of *Haskala* into Eastern Europe can be found in the autobiography (written around 1792) of Shlomo Maimon (c.1753–1800). Maimon, who later became a central interlocutor of both Moshe Mendelssohn and Immanuel Kant, provides there a rather critical eye-witness account of the court of Magid of Mezeritch and the charismatic modus operandi of its leader (alluded to above). As Itzhak Melamed has shown, Maimon's early study of Kabbalah had a formative effect on his influential critique of Kantian metaphysics and early modern philosophy in general, especially his engagement with Spinozian pantheism. As Melamed has noted, Maimon is a crucial link between the debate on Pantheism or a-cosmism (a term coined by Maimon himself) amongst Eastern European Jewry and a no less lively polemic in the philosophical circles with which we opened this chapter.[150]

EIGHTEENTH-CENTURY KABBALAH AS SPLIT CANONIZATION

Reflecting as a whole on the trajectory of Kabbalah in early modernity, one can roughly speak of the following dialectic: the eighteenth-century displays

148 For exaggerated claims on the Gaon's tendency toward critical, philosophical and scientific thought see Stern, *The Genius*. On the Gaon's reception in the Haskala movement, see Etkes, *The Gaon of Vilna*, 37–41.

149 Ruderman, *A Best-Selling Hebrew Book*, 20, 40–51.

150 Melamed, 'Spinozism, Acosmism, and Hassidism' (and Melamed, 'Salomon Maimon and the Rise of Spinozism', esp. 79–83).

far greater diversity than any previous century of kabbalistic writing, and indeed the sheer scope of composition (accompanied by extensive printing of canonical works, including premodern texts, and their attendant commentaries, in the second part of the century, especially in Eastern Europe) necessitated the omission of some important figures (especially within the Hasidic world) in this account.[151] While the previous early modern centuries were characterized by processes of intensive canonization (of Safedian corpora), this high modern century can be readily described in terms of split canonization, or the formation of new, looser and more diverse canons (see especially above on Hasidic critiques of the Lurianic system of *kavvanot*).[152] This relative fragmentation is especially evident in the remarkable proliferation that we followed when addressing the Hasidic movement that already by the end of the century unfolded into numerous distinct paths.

This complex process, not yet fully comprehended by academic research (despite the recent intensification of interest in the century within Jewish studies) should be understood as an ongoing response to the challenges and crises of the seventeenth century. In particular, one should note, as in the residual underground presence of Sabbateanism, an ongoing crisis of authority, instigating new forms of leadership (such as that of the *tzaddik*). In the course of the century, the sense of crisis was reinforced by both Jewish and extra-Jewish developments, such as the decline and eventual (1764) dissolution of the self-governing body, the Council of Four Lands, the repeated partitions of Poland (toward the end of the century) and what is best described as proto-secularization, especially in Western Europe. One expression of this tumult was the recovery (toward the end of the century) of messianism, after its repression (as in the Luzzatto affair) in the wake of Sabbateanism. However, the complexity of the connections, influences and polemics of the century confound binary descriptions in terms of 'secularization' and 'orthodoxy' (ironically the extremely bold R. Moshe Sofer, devoted pupil of a twice-excommunicated maverick, and a messianic and semiprophetic aspirant in his own right, was presented in earlier scholarship as a bastion of Orthodoxy).[153] Liminal figures such as Frommann or Maimon best confound such facile distinctions.

[151] On changes in location, quantity and genre of printing in this period, see Gries, *The Book in the Jewish World*, 69–79.

[152] An unresearched case study of anxiety around challenges to canonization is the defense of the Lurianic-Vitalian corpus in R. Naftali ben David's work *Ben David*, printed in Amsterdam in 1729.

[153] Samet, *Chapters in the History of Orthodoxy*, esp. 268. Cf. Kahana, *From the Noda be Yehuda to the Chatam Sofer*, 427–433.

It is no coincidence that the conflicted and polemical R. Ya'akov Emden repeatedly emerged here as a hub for both the tensions and advances of this pivotal century, all the while haunted by the ever present shadow of Sabbateanism (and thus mistakenly viewed at times as a bastion of conservative reaction). One image that captures Emden's role as a harbinger of high modernity, is his scientific-technological description of the process of *tzimtzum* through the images of a 'magnetic stone' and an air pump.[154] This is but one select expression of manifold imprints of modernity in the kabbalistic systems of the century: individualization, greater focus on everyday life and what one can describe as a search for totality, expressed in the constant stress in some Hasidic writings on every person, place, movement, etc. This can be contrasted to the medieval worldview, focused on hierarchies, gradations and insistent differentiation.[155]

The controversy-laden, fraught and hence dialectic nature of the period is reflected in the persistence and at times deepening of skepticism. Critical responses within the traditional Jewish world to the spread of Kabbalah by no means abated, at least in the first part of the century. Here again Italy played a major role: Samson Morpurgo (1681–1740) republished a poem (by Jacob Frances) critiquing the excessive study of Kabbalah in Italy. Morpurgo's move was occasioned, inter alia, by Christian employment of kabbalistic argumentation in inter-faith debate. Solomon Aviad Sar Shalom (c.1680–1749), a student of Ramaz and an associate of Luzzatto (who also devoted a work to the defense of the Kabbalah against its detractors) responded at length in his *Emunat Hakhamim* (Faith in the Sages). Yet he himself attempted to buttress kabbalistic and Aggadic beliefs by means of contemporary scientific discovery.[156] Here too, Emden's role is striking: in his 1768 work *Mitpahat Sefraim* (Book Cloth), reacting to the exclusive valorization of the *Zohar* by the Frankists, he dared to challenge its authenticity, employing philological-historical tools in a pioneering manner. He predated a prevalent view in modern scholarship by ascribing some of the *Zohar* to Moshe De Leon, while claiming that one can also uncover an ancient stratum, in effect proposing a scientific edition. Emden here radicalizes seventeenth-century critical philological studies of the *Zohar*, such as *'Amudei Sheva*. One can say then, that modern research joins most other forms of kabbalistic learning extant today in tracing its antecedents to the

[154] Emden, *Mitpahat Sefarim*, 111–112.
[155] Compare to Elior, *Israel Ba'al Shem Tov*, vol. I, 419.
[156] Ruderman, *Jewish Thought and Scientific Discovery*, 214–228.

eighteenth century.[157] Yet these critical voices, joined by later enlightenment figures, represented only the elite. Amongst the general population, this was the time of the Kabbalah's greatest sway. One indication can be resulted from the above-mentioned Yiddish vernacularization (which actually began as early as the late sixteenth century), which is especially evident in the *Musar* genre and including translations of premodern texts such as the *Zohar*.[158] This linguistic process facilitated access of kabbalistic ideas to much larger numbers of women, who both read and wrote *tehines* or personal supplicatory prayers (based inter alia on works such as *Hemdat Yamim*). One of these, *Imrei Shifre*, attributed to the late eighteenth-century Shifre bas Yosef and analyzed by Chava Weisler, focuses on the theurgical significance of the rite of lighting the Sabbath candles (traditionally entrusted to women).[159] Finally, Yiddish remains an informal language of learning (including Kabbalah study) for the Ashkenazim (who prior to the Holocaust comprised the great majority of Jews) to this day. Here is another example of the manner in which the kabbalistic world as presently observable has deep roots in the eighteenth century.

157 On this period in *Zohar* critique and apologetic responses, see Huss, *The Zohar*, 255–276.

158 Faierstein, 'Kabbalah and Early Modern Yiddish'; Baumgarten, 'Yiddish Ethical Texts'; Baumgarten, 'Quelques échoes de Shabbetaï Tsevi' (esp. 164–167).

159 Weisler, 'Woman as High Priest'.

5

Beginnings of Globalization

The Nineteenth Century

GEOPOLITICS AND THE KABBALAH: AN OVERVIEW OF THE CENTURY

In 1798 and again in 1801, R. Shneur Zalman (Rashaz, c.1745–1812) of Liadi (Belorussia), was arrested and taken to the Russian capital of St. Petersburg for investigation by its Senate.[1] The charges were diverse, but included transferring funds to the Land of Israel (thus supporting the followers of his teacher, R. Menahem Mendel of Vitebsk). From the point of view of the Russian authorities, this activity supported the Ottoman Empire, clashing with Russia's southward drive (peaking in the 1853–1856 Crimean War and the 1877–1878 Russo-Turkish war). The arrests were instigated by informants amongst the *mitnagdim* (opponents), in a last-ditch attempt to block the spread of the teachings of R. Menahem Mendel in Lithuania and Belorussia.[2] Although they also targeted the Karlin branch, they were especially troubled by the increasing success of what came to be known (from 1805) as the Habad (acronym of *Hokhma*, *Bina* and *Da'at*) movement headed by Rashaz.

Ironically, as the youngest student of R. Dov Baer of Mezertich, Rashaz's claims to represent and later to inherit R. Menahem Mendel of Vitebsk were also challenged by the selfsame Karlin branch. R. Menahem Mendel's close student and fellow immigrant R. Avraham of Kalisk (1741–1810) contested

[1] The constant shifting of borders in Northeastern Europe during this period can be confusing. Regional identifications usually refer to present-day geography. In the Jewish context, terms such as Poland or Lithuania could refer to cultural identities rather than to precise geopolitical demarcations.

[2] To this day, informing on Jews to the non-Jewish authorities is a taboo from the point of view of Jewish mores, expressing the beleaguered consciousness of an oft-persecuted minority.

what he perceived as an excessive stress on intellectual comprehension of kabbalistic themes, as well critiquing their extensive, open propagation.[3] Rashaz's power and eventual takeover of Hasidic Lithuania rested on a combination of organizational precision, halakhic erudition (as expressed in the new *Sulkhan 'Arukh* that he composed) and most notably mystical experience and its eloquent expression in writing.[4] This is evident in his masterpiece *Sefer ha-Tanya* (derived from the opening quote from a Talmudic passage), one of the most-printed Jewish books of all times.[5] The first part, *Sifram shel-Benonim* (The Book of the Median), declaredly moved away from the magical figure of the *tzaddik* (as developed especially in Polish Hasidism) toward a focus on 'everyman'. In doing so, it mandated exceedingly high spiritual standards (such as never sinning in practice) for all who wish to escape the Talmudic category of 'the wicked'. This elitism, paradoxically coupled with an expansionary thrust, was to remain a hallmark of the Habad movement well into the twentieth century. The second part of the book, *Sha'ar ha-Yihud va ha-Emuna* (The Gate of Unity and Faith), set forth Rashaz's all but a-cosmic belief in divine immanence (albeit mediated through language), and thus a strongly nonliteral interpretation of *tzimtzum*.

The influence of *Sefer ha-Tanya*, amongst Hasidim and beyond, drew from its combination of measured, precise, scholastic prose with outbursts of mystical passion, as exemplified in the following quote:

> Another Method to find true joy in your soul, particularly when, on those specific occasions when your heart becomes desensitized . . . what you could do then is probe deeply in your mind, picturing mentally and cognitively, the concept of G-d's genuine nonduality . . . and even how this lowly physical world is filled with His glory . . . Now, when you will probe this extensively, your heart will be gladdened . . . Now, imagine the immense joy of an ordinary person . . . if a human king were to come close to him by lodging and living with him in his house. All the more so, to an immeasurably greater extent, G-d the blessed king of kings, making his intimate home (with you)![6]

3 Gries, *The Hebrew Book*, 357–389; Schor, *Studies*, 489–541.

4 For an English-language sampling of the literature, see Foxbrunner, *Habad*, Etkes, *Rabbi Shneur Zalman*, as well as the study by Loewenthal, *Communicating the Infinite*. The most comprehensive Hebrew-language collection is Grunwald (ed.), *Ha-Rav*.

5 Nidda 30B.

6 Tanya, pt. 1, chap. 33, 41B–42A, translated in Miller, *The Practical Tanya*, 369–373. For R. Shneur Zalman's psychology, see Jacobson, *Truth, Faith and Holiness*, 279–421.

Rashaz's release and clearance of charges, in edicts issued on behalf of Emperor Paul I (1754–1801) and his successor Alexander I (1777–1825), marked the beginning of an alliance with the Russian Empire that was to last (in the face of ebbs and flows in the status of Russian Jewry in general), until the 1917 October Revolution.[7] This bond was cemented during the Napoleonic Wars. The above-mentioned Land of Israel was to continue to play a major role in this century (up to and including the first Zionist Congress of 1897). Carrying over from the previous century, Jerusalem saw the solidification and expansion of the circle of Rashash, which itself split at the end of the century. As we shall see, the Hasidim, the most prolific kabbalistic group of the century, were joined in immigrating to the Holy Land by some of the followers of R. Eliyahu of Vilna. This bifurcation of R. Eliyahu's school was also a factor in the moderation of the opposition to Hasidism in these circles (the fierceness of which had been epitomized in complaints to the non-Jewish authorities). The geopolitics around the Napoleonic Wars and other external events mentioned here (some directly affecting events in the Holy Land) expressed one of the central processes of the century – globalization.[8] So it is to the globalization of Kabbalah, inside and outside the Jewish world, that we shall turn at the end of this chapter.

THE CHANGING OF THE GUARD IN HASIDISM

The Napoleonic Wars did more than rearrange the political structure of Europe for a century (the order produced in the 1814–1815 Congress of Vienna lasted for this long).[9] They also instigated a sharp divide within the leadership of the now well-established Hasidic movement. As conveyed vividly in Martin Buber's novel, *Gog and Magog (for the Sake of Heaven)*, some Hasidic leaders, such as R. Menahem Mendel of Riminov (1745–1815, known as the Riminover) saw Napoleon's dramatic rise and aspiration to unite Europe, West and East (under one revolutionary hegemony) as an instigator of the messianic redemption. Others, most notably Rashaz, stressed the spiritual dangers entailed in Napoleon's offer of emancipation to the Jews, embedding a demand to adapt their religious practices to the

[7] Lurie, *The Lubavitch Wars*, esp. 181–254. For a contrary approach (expressed in opposition to the Russian takeover of Poland) within the later Ger dynasty, see Mark, 'The Son of David'.
[8] See e.g. Osterhammel, *A Global History*.
[9] On the effect of the Congress of Vienna on nineteenth-century Hasidism, see Biale et al. (eds.), *Hasidism: A New History*, 264. This volume provides historical surveys of nineteenth-century Hasidism.

requirements of citizenship.[10] This was a clear contention around a central agent of modernization, reflecting the deepening engagement with various aspects of modernization in the Jewish world throughout this period. The rapidly proliferating genre of Hasidic tales, a nascent form of internal historiography, traced the unusual coincidence of demise of all of these leaders around the final years of the wars to a magical clash between the rival aspirations of these *rebbes* (masters). In other words, this first global conflict was seen as an earthly reflection of a mystical-magical clash.[11] The continued vibrancy of Hasidic messianism can also be gauged by the case of R. Shlomo of Karlin, whose eschatological aspirations were curtailed when murdered by a Russian soldier during the war with Poland in 1792 (which had also evoked divided loyalties amongst Hasidic leaders). This event was equated with the Talmudic-legendary prediction of the death of Messiah, son of Joseph (*Sukka* 52A).[12]

The main hero of the later tales surrounding the death of the leading *rebbes* was R. Yaakov Yitzhak ha-Levi Horowitz, the Seer of Lublin (1745?–1815), student of R. Elimelekh Weisblum, who reportedly fell to his death while bringing about the downfall of Napoleon. His title was based on the belief that he was possessed of a panoramic ability to see distant events (though he was also described as later beseeching God to significantly restrict his range. . .), a logical requirement for involvement in geopolitics. . .

The Seer's own teaching is of interest, especially in its antinomian suggestions that would be taken up in subsequent generations of his school.[13] However, his main impact lay in training a large group of intense mystics, who continued his mission of spreading Hasidism in Galicia and beyond, while adopting fiercely independent stances. This 'holy rebellion' was evidenced most distinctly by R. Yaakov Yitzhak Rabinovitz of Psischa (1766–1813), widely known as the Holy Jew, who famously quarreled with his teacher (and this, according to some Hasidic stories, was the reason for his own death a mere two months after that of the Seer).[14] The Holy Jew did not demonstrate the same affinity for visionary trance states that one can find amongst other students of the Seer, such as R. Qalman Qalomymus Epstein (1751?–1823) of Cracow, author of the markedly influential *Maor*

10 Levine, 'Should Napoleon Be Victorious'.

11 On the global nature of the Napoleonic Wars, see e.g. Mikaberidze, *The Napoleonic Wars*; Esdaile, *Napoleon's Wars*.

12 Schor, *Studies*, 1058–1081.

13 Gellman, 'Hasidic Existentialism?'.

14 Cf. the skeptical approach of Gellman, *The Emergence of Hasidism in Poland*, 201–203. Gellman's argument that it is hard to imagine that such a rift could remain unmentioned in contemporary sources underestimates the secrecy often surrounding such sensitive episodes.

va-Shemesh (see Psalms 74, 16). The following testimony there by Epstein reflects the atmosphere surrounding the Seer that the Holy Jew moved away from to an extent: 'It is known and I have seen that the great *Tzaddiqim*, when they cleave to the supernal worlds and divest themselves of the material trappings, then the *Shekhina* resides on them and speaks from their throats and their mouths speak words of prophecy and of the future and these *Tzaddiqim* do not know later what they themselves said.'[15]

Fittingly, the Holy Jew's own student R. Simkha Bunim Bonhart of Psischa (1765–1827) rebelled against him. R. Simkha Bunim's career can be seen as an illustration of relative modernization, as he doubled as a business man.[16] The controversy evoked by Psischa's breakaway can be gauged through the episode of the great wedding held in 1821 in Ustila (Uścilug, Ukraine), a veritable summit of Hasidic leadership. Although it is hard to separate fact from fiction here (as Uriel Gellman has shown in detail), it is clear that the excommunication of Psisicha was on the table (as it were) at this gathering.[17] According to many accounts a central adjudicator here was the cross-regional leader R. Avraham Yehoshua Heschel of Apt, Poland (1748–1825), a long-lived student of R. Weissblum, who was able to assemble teachings from successive generations of Hasidic leaders. The distillation of his accumulated lore in *Ohev Israel* (Lover of Israel), focuses on consensual values such as careful observance of the commandments, the *tzaddik* and *teshuva* and as a result is still one of the most-read Hasidic works.

Despite these ongoing schisms, there appears to be a common denominator between the first two leaders of the Psischa branch: the stress on in-depth Talmud study as a primary path to spiritual attainment.[18] To some extent, this shift reversed the displacement of study in favor of rival values such as prayer and *devequt* amongst some early Hasidic leaders (probably including the Besht himself).[19] In doing so, the masters of Psischa (as well as most leaders of Habad) moved closer to the *mitnagdim*, a rapprochement echoed by a moderation of the ideological and practical stance of the opponents themselves. Methodologically speaking, Gellman is correct in claiming that the avoidance of writing in the formative stages of the Psischa movement renders prevalent scholarly constructions of its approach questionable. Yet he himself acknowledges that this is true for much of the

[15] Translated and discussed in Garb, *Shamanic Trance*, 124.

[16] Rosen, *The Quest for Authenticity*, 330–348. Cf. Gellman, *The Emergence of Hasidism in Poland*, 207–208, 280–281.

[17] Gellman, *The Emergence of Hasidism in Poland*, 248–250.

[18] Cf. Ibid., 250–261 (concurring as to the later branches of Psischa).

[19] Katz, *Tradition and Crisis*, 197–199.

Hasidic movement, characterized as it is by a predilection for more fluid oral discourse.[20] One should also recall that in the course of the nineteenth century, both textual borrowing and study with several teachers confound sharp ideological distinctions.

The stress on Talmudics was continued by R. Simkha Bunem's student, R. Menahem Mendel of Kotzk (1787–1859), who brought the 'holy rebellion' to a crescendo (while intensifying the avoidance of writing and indeed of systematic doctrine as such). The Kotzker, as he is commonly known, was one of the most striking Hasidic figures of all time. Fiercely committed to authenticity and critical of the institutionalization of charisma in the ever-expanding movement, he spent the last twenty years of his life in embittered isolation. This melancholy disposition was similar to that of the Seer, who was rumored to be suicidal.[21] Abraham Joshua Heschel, direct descendant of his above-mentioned namesake, has fruitfully compared the Kotzker's individualistic, critical and existentialist stance to a contemporary Christian spiritual giant, Søren Kierkegaard (1813–1855).[22]

Rarely for this stream, the Kotzker's main student, R. Yisrael Meir Alter (Rotenberg) of Ger (1799–1866) remained loyal to him throughout. The latter's main dynastic successor was R. Yehuda Leib Alter (1847–1905), who further reinforced the focus on Talmudic learning (upheld by this large and powerful group till recently). Both this approach and a renewed stress on the importance of the Land of Israel were shared by the Sochatchov (Poland) dynasty, founded by the Kotzker's son-in-law (husband of Sara Tzina), R. Avraham Borenstein (1839–1910), author of now-classic halakhic works.[23] The return to Talmudics was also espoused by R. Hayyim Halberstam of Zanz, Galicia (1797–1896), who composed seminal halakhic responses to modern phenomena such as industrialization.[24] At the same time, his *Divrei*

[20] Gellman, *The Emergence of Hasidism in Poland*, esp. 213, 261–267.

[21] On these rumors, occasioned by his early death, see Assaf, *Untold Tales*, 97–119. The melancholy of the Seer and of other nineteenth-century masters can be compared to that of their contemporaries the Romantics (see also Mark, *Mysticism and Madness*, esp. 3, 141–146, 210–212).

[22] Heschel, *A Passion for Truth* (partial translation of Heschel's Yiddish-language work. Further portions have been translated into Hebrew).

[23] At the same time one must recall the ideology of the exile as an ideal setting for Torah life (coupled with a Jewish identity centered solely on the Torah), found especially in the writings of Galician figures such as R. Shlomo Halberstam, the *rebbe* of Bobov (see Piekraz, *Ideological Trends*, 214, 227–231, and also 220–224 for the claims as to the spiritual passion fostered paradoxically in exile, found in the Sochatchov dynasty itself!).

[24] The 'Zanzer Rabbi' was mainly the student of R. Tzevi Hirsch Eichenstein. He is especially famous for this extensive campaign (starting in 1869) against R. Avraham Yaakov Freidman of Sadigura, Bukovina (1819–1883), the son of R. Israel of Ruzhin, who was accused of being

Hayyim (Words of Life) commentary on the Bible discloses a mastery of Kabbalah, pioneering the reception of the system of Rashash as well as that of the Luzzatto circle (some of whose works were printed by Hasidic agents). As an independent thinker, Halberstam is described as Ultra-Orthodox, yet, as seen in the following quote, he developed, at least theoretically, the antinomian tendencies that we shall soon encounter in other streams of the Lublin school:

> The statement of the Sages [*Nidda* 61B]: 'The commandments will be cancelled in the future' is known, and the *tzaddikim* have interpreted that the matter of the commandments is only that of advice, that is to say advice as how to come to *dvekut* to God. For the purpose of the creation of all of the worlds was in order to worship God... and God created Adam with utmost perfection... so as to possess the power to cause the blessed and exalted *Shekhina* to reside in this world... but because he did not observe God's commandment, and the Holy One blessed be He removed his *Shekhina* from this world... and [later] He chose his servant Abraham and his seed after him, and they drew the *Shekhina* down on Mount Sinai and the Temple. Yet because all of the worlds were not yet amended, and there was still resistance to His blessed glory... The Holy One blessed be He granted the Torah to his people of Israel six hundred and thirteen forms of advice... until the entire world will be amended... and the Glory of God will be seen and revealed... And all shall rejoice... and as a result there will be no more need for the commandments, for each person will see what he needs for worship and *devekut*.[25]

Alter's loyalty to the Kotzker was not shared by R. Mordekhai Yosef Leiner of Izbiche (1801–1854), who performed the final act of the holy rebellion in breaking with his teacher in late 1839 (or 5600, a year with messianic portent, going back to a Zoharic source). Reawakening and enhancing the antinomian tendencies of the Seer, Leiner went so far as to challenge the very notion of free will. First, through a historiosophical view of a process of *birur*, in which it will be clarified that 'he [Adam] only ate the good [of the fruit of the tree and good and evil] and the sin was only in his perception [*lefi d'ato*] as an onion peel [i.e. a thin surface layer of reality] and no more'. Second, as part of a national view according to which Jews cannot sin by definition, so that 'a Gentile who gives... to charity so that his son lives is

overly modern and castigated for following the 'regal way' (see below). On this episode, see Assaf, *Beguiled by Knowledge*.

25 Halberstam, *Divrei Hayyim*, vol. II, 111. Terms such as Orthodoxy and Ultra-Orthodoxy should be employed only when the materials and setting call for them.

wicked, and in the case of a Jew he is a full *tzaddik* [*Rosh ha-Shana* 4A], and this is because God testifies that the depths of our heart are purified according to His will'. Third, through a psychological doctrine based on the notion that 'whoever's heart is drawn after the will of God, even if according to the shade of color [i.e. surface perception], it seems as if he sometimes strays from the way of the Torah, this is also the will of God'.[26]

Not surprisingly, although Izbiche was far less demographically and politically significant than the rival branch of Ger, it has drawn more attention from academic writers (who tend to neglect more consensual writing, even if it is far more prevalent).[27] Leiner's son and heir, R. Yaakov of Radzin (1814–1878) somewhat moderated his stance.[28] His own son, R. Gershon Hanokh (1839–1891) revitalized the school by moving beyond the textual scope of his ancestors in extensive incorporation of Zoharic and Lurianic texts.[29] A highly learned and creative Talmudist, he also proposed a radical halakhic move, renewing the light blue (*tkhelet*) threads of the *tzitzit* (ritual fringes). Here he drew on travels to the Naples aquarium (assisted by his knowledge of modern languages) in studying the ink-fish from which the correct dye would be derived, as well as ascribing the innovation itself messianic portent.[30] The hopes surrounding the *tkhelet* (also in Bratzlav and later circles), expressed a rabbinic chain of images leading from these threads to the divine throne and beyond.[31] As we shall see, this merger of messianism and modernity is a major thread throughout the century. Yet another embellishment of R. Mordekhai Yosef's doctrine is found in the writings of his student R. Zadok ha-Kohen of Lublin (1823–1900), whose numerous, highly learned works (including a dream diary) later facilitated the penetration of Izbiche teachings into the mitnagdic Lithuanian Yeshiva world.[32]

The study of Kabbalah was far more pronounced amongst the branch established by the Seer's student R. Tzevi Hirsch Eichenstein of Ziditchov,

[26] Leiner, *Mei ha-Siloach*, vol. I, 15, 178; vol. II, 40.

[27] For the main English-language studies, see Weiss, *Studies in Eastern European Jewish Mysticism*, 209–248; Faierstein, *All Is in the Hands of Heaven*.

[28] Yet for the exegetical and psychological profundity of his teaching see Wiskind-Elper, *Wisdom of the Heart*.

[29] On his writing see Magid, *Hasidism on the Margin*.

[30] Magid, 'A Thread of Blue'. On the earlier history of *Tkhelet*, see Sagiv, 'Dazzling Blue'.

[31] Hullin 89A.

[32] Liwer, 'Oral Torah' (and Brill, *Thinking God*). Another student of R. Mordekhai Yosef Leiner, R. Leibele Eiger, was the son of R. Akiva Eiger, author of Talmudic works venerated in the Lithuanian Yeshiva world. Interestingly, the former regarded the Seer as his 'root teacher'.

Galicia (1763–1831), author of dense commentaries on the *Zohar* as well as on a Lurianic manual of *kavvanot*. The scope of Eichenstein's thought ranged far beyond exegesis, extending to radical views of the *tzaddik* as managing and maintaining the world (with God relegated to the role of a constitutional monarch, as it were).[33] This copious literature was greatly expanded by his nephew, R. Yitzhak Eizek Yehuda Yehiel Safrin of Komarno (1806–1874). The Komarner, as he is widely known, brought together several competing strands of the Seer's heritage in his effort to blend in-depth Talmudic-halakhic analysis with Zoharic and Lurianic Kabbalah, as in his *Sulkhan ha Tahor* (Pure Table).[34] At the same time, he was critical of most forms of post-Lurianic Kabbalah (including the Luzzatto school and Habad). Through his diary, *Megilat Setarim* (Scroll of Secrets) we have a glimpse into his visionary life, again harking back to that of the Seer:

> 1846. On the first day of *Rosh Hashana*. I did several spiritual exercises on behalf of the community of Israel in Russia. I overcame their guardian angel . . . On the second day, I did what I had to do and at night I saw the above-mentioned guardian angel with a drawn sword . . . Afterwards, I saw the guardian angel of Edom and he assured me that he would not do anything bad as result of the decree and I blessed him with the blessing for the king, and then awoke.[35]

These extensive testimonies were accompanied by rare expressions of self-negation, expressed in self-description as 'a little worm literally, literally nothing'.[36] Of all of his various massive projects, Safrin's successors especially continued his exegesis of the *Zohar*. A complementary path was taken by another nephew-student of Eichenstein's, R. Yitzhak of Radzil (1790–1848), who expressed constant self-doubt as to his very suitability for the role of *tzaddik*, that should be contrasted with the 'regal way' of Ruzhin, to be described soon.

A rather different path was chosen by the highly influential R. Tzevi Elimelekh Shapira of Dinov (1783–1841), author of the series *Bnei Issaskhar* (see Genesis 46, 13) who had the following to say of the *Haskala*:

> It appears to me that in this generation that the insolent have increased, and the dark is recognized for itself and the light for itself and the insolent wicked are apparent to all as part of the sects of the mixed multitude

33 Haran, 'Olam Hafuch'. One can speculate on the effect of nineteenth-century political life on this doctrine.

34 Kahana and Mayse, 'Hasidic Halakha', 406–407.

35 Translated in Faierstein, *Jewish Mystical Autobiographies*, 286.

36 Translated and discussed in Garb, *Shamanic Trance*, 114 (see also 83).

> [see Exodus 12:38] . . . If the people of Israel shall firmly remove them from their tents . . . Then he [the Messiah] shall arrive speedily in our days . . . and those who follow the stubbornness of their hearts [Deut. 29, 18] after the external [secular] wisdoms and cast off the restraints of the yoke of Torah, know that they are not part of our people . . . and thus this is close to the days of our Messiah, their perfidy is revealed to all.[37]

In other words, Shapira ascribed messianic portent to what he saw, within his generational analysis, as a sharp divide between the Torah-loyal Jews and secularizing aliens. Drawing on a tradition going back to the medieval *Tikkunei Zohar*, the latter are described as 'the mixed multitude'. Especially amongst his descendants, founders of the Munkatsh dynasty in Hungary (and its associated branches) we can locate the roots of fierce opposition to Zionism in large parts of the Hasidic world.[38] In terms of kabbalistic writing, the most prominent of these was his descendant R. Tzevi Hirsch Shapira (1850–1913), a student of the Zanzer Rabbi and author of an extensive commentary on *Tikkunei Zohar* (thus expressing the predilection of many branches of Lublin, starting with the Seer himself, for the Zoharic corpus). This adversarial position vis-à-vis modernity was passionately shared by a prominent student of the Seer's, R. Moshe Teitelbaum (1759–1841), whose successors, the Siget (and later Satmar) dynasty consolidated the Hasidic presence in Hungary.

A more proactive response to the processes of late modernization was offered by the demographically and politically powerful dynasty founded by R. Teitelbaum's fellow student, the magical healer R. Shalom Rokeah (1783–1855) of Belz (Galicia, today's Ukraine). His successor R. Yehoshua (1825–1894), promoted (1871) the society *Mahziqei Dat* (Upholders of Religion), allied with R. Menakhem Mendel Hager (1830–1884), son-in-law of R. Israel of Ruzhin and founder of the large Romanian Viznitz dynasty, in order to combat the *Haskala*. The society, which was seen as theurgically-magically combating the Other Side, published a newspaper and sent representatives to the Austrian parliament.[39] Opposition to secularization was indeed a trademark of Hasidism in the Austro-Hungarian Empire (after the

37 *Ma'ayan Ganim*, discussed in Sorotzkin, *Orthodoxy*, 354–355 (and see 354, n. 571, on the messianic hopes that Shapira cast on the year 5660.

38 On Hasidic opposition to early Zionism, see Biale et al. (eds.), *Hasidism: A New History*, 382.

39 Sagiv, *Dynasty*, 352. This political involvement was shared by some followers of R. Simha Bonim, most notably R. Itzhak Kalish of Worke (1799–1848), whose ideology of intercession ushered in the age of the Hasidic leader acting on behalf of the entirety of Polish Jewry (a model globalized in twentieth-century Habad). See Wodziński, *Hasidism and Politics*, esp. 178–206.

Congress of Vienna including Galicia), in a sense patrolling the border with Western Europe, which remained all but immune to Hasidic influence.[40] In sum, the various branches of the court of the Seer, despite their divergence (as well as geographical dispersion) can be seen as the backbone of nineteenth-century Hasidism, exemplifying the gamut of its ideological possibilities, such as: messianism, zealotry, antinomianism, and return to Talmudism, cultivation of visionary and magical powers.

There was one figure that transcended these options: a Ukrainian descendant of the Besht who was fascinated by Napoleon and demanded daily updates on his progress, R. Nahman of Bratzlav (1772–1810).[41] Napoleon's dramatic rise and fall inspired R. Nahman, in 1816, to compose the tale of the 'two sons who were reversed', one of a series of fairy-tales (or, to use a more contemporary term, a fantasy literature) that increasingly captivated the Jewish literary imagination.[42] Nahman's literary ability was fueled by a remarkable gift for associate thinking (inspired inter alia by *Tikkunei Zohar*), creating lengthy and creative chains of 'aspects'. This move to tales, while reflecting the success of this genre throughout this century of Hasidic life, was a strategic choice (facing what he perceived as a form of spiritual sleep and perhaps reflecting relinquishing messianic hopes or alternatively their reformulation). This shift was formulated in Lurianic terms in the following *Tora* (in the sense of teaching) in his kabbalistic masterpiece *Likutei Moharan* (*Collectana* of Our Teacher R. Nahman):

> For there are people who sleep through their days, and even though it appears to the world that they are worshipping God . . . even so God has no satisfaction [*naches*] from them, for all of their work remains below . . . for the main vitality is the intelligence [*sekhel*] . . .[43] but when it [the worship] falls to the smallness of intelligences [*mohin*], the aspect of sleep, it cannot ascend above.
>
> For the intelligence is the face . . . and the quest for the face, that is to return and seek his face, depends on emending the heart . . . [when the heart is spoiled], through this one loses the face and falls into the aspect sleep and when one wishes to show him [the sleeper] his face and waken him from sleep, one needs to garb the face in stories . . .

[40] Brown, 'The Two Faces', 352–358.

[41] Green, *Tormented Master* (cf. Piekraz, *Studies in Braslav Hasidism*, esp. 219–246).

[42] Collected in Mark (ed.), *The Complete Stories* (see 313–322 for the tale of the two sons, as well as Wiskind-Elper, *Tradition and Fantasy*, 29–31, 70–71, 93–103). For fantasy writing in contemporary Bratzlav, see Doron, *The Warriors of Transcendence*.

[43] See *Likutei Moharan*, Torah 1.

> And there is one who has fallen from all of the seventy faces [of Torah[44]], until he cannot be awakened by any means, except by means of the stories of early days, that all the seventy faces . . . receive vitality from.[45]

This oft printed (and translated) work, as well as writings that did not survive, joins the stories themselves as a second expression of his exceptional religious genius, a third being ritual innovations such as *tiqqunim* for sexual sins and rites of pilgrimage to his gravesite. Continuing the Besht's focus on *Rosh ha-Shana*, later generations focused the occasion of this oft-hazardous voyage on the New Year. Liebes has ascribed some of these practices to Sabbatean influence. Though it is true that the accompanying theurgical formulation, *ha-tiqqun ha-klali* (the general rectification) is found not only in Sabbatean writings but in Luzzatto's circle, the time gap is considerable. In contradistinction, Zvi Mark (alongside with other reservations) has contested this link.[46] Finally, we have R. Nahman's rarely detailed vision of the messianic process, with himself as the lead figure, transmitted secretly over the generations, and now published by Mark.[47] From a phenomenological point of view, it is understandable why R. Nahman has attracted the attention of academics and others seeking impact on the wider culture (see Chapter 6), yet in his century he was barely quoted and indeed he and his successors, well into the twentieth century, suffered waves of bitter persecution (including physical violence) on the part of rival Hasidic groups.[48]

In a characteristically maverick fashion, R. Nahman's deliberately short (and with messianic motivations) trip to the Galilee in 1798–1799 was part of the Hasidic movement's growing relationship with Ottoman Palestine, and contributed to the radicalization of his own teachings. His somewhat bizarre behavior during this journey reflected his engagement with madness, also in the form of melancholy (similar to the figure of the mad Yogi in Indo-Tibetan Buddhism).[49] This was accompanied by an exalted self-consciousness, including the radical rite of confession to the *tzaddik*, which of course may betray Christian influence.[50] In subsequent generations of Bratzlav, commencing with *Liqutei Halakhot* (on the *Sulkhan 'Arukh*) by R. Nahman's scribe and editor R. Nathan Sternhartz of Nemirov

44 The formulation 'The Torah has seventy faces' has late antique and medieval sources, and was much embellished in Kabbalah (Scholem, *On the Kabbalah*, 62–67).

45 *Likutei Moharan*, Torah 60, 6. Compare to Wineman, *The Hasidic Parable*, for a related Hasidic literary form.

46 Liebes, *Studies in Jewish Myth*, 115–150, 184–210; Mark, *Revelation and Rectification*, 115–153.

47 Mark, *The Scroll of Secrets*.

48 Assaf, *Untold Tales*, 120–153.

49 Mark, *Mysticism and Madness*.

50 Weiss, *Studies in Eastern European Jewish Mysticism*, 99.

(1780–1844), this ever escalated toward near-divinization, expressed in a constant imperative of adherence to the soul of R. Nahman, with R. Nathan himself framed as the prime conduit. However, it must be stressed that the very sense of absence that evoked such veneration (accompanied by a rapidly expanding hagiographical corpus) also led to the fragmentation of the movement after R. Nathan's death.[51] Notwithstanding this, Sternhartz was the most influential amongst several creative writers, and greatly expanded the genre of personal prayer in his *Liqutei Tefilot*.[52] Indeed, in terms of technique, *hitbodedut*, or isolation for personal prayer (preferably in Yiddish), is probably Bratzlav's main contribution.

Though this move is not unproblematic, Joseph Weiss, correctly advocating the diversity of Hasidism, has contrasted Bratzlav's faith-centered approach to Habad's 'contemplative mysticism'.[53] The above-mentioned death of the latter's founder Rashaz occasioned a political and ideological split in the ever-growing movement, between his son, R. Dov Shenuri (1773–1827) and his close student, R. Aharon Horowitz of Staroselye (1766–1828).[54] While Horowitz somewhat radicalized Rashaz's a-cosmic tendencies and cultivated emotional-enthusiastic states (in a manner that challenges Weiss' dichotomy), Shneuri cultivated contemplative-meditative states. His successor, R. Menahem Mendel Schneerson (1789–1866), took up the halakhic mantle of his grandfather Rashaz, as in his book of *responsa*, *Tzemakh Tzedek* (Plant of Righteousness; see Jer. 23, 5). His vast corpus reflected the sheer proliferation of Habad literature as well as his own tendency to systemize various corpora. For example, in facing the challenge of the *Haskala* movement, he incorporated medieval Jewish philosophy in his *Sefer ha-Haqira* (Book of Inquiry). He is also notable for reviving the medieval and Renaissance genre of kabbalistic discourse on the reasons for the commandments. However, his containment of Habad's innovations within classical erudition should be seen as part of the institutionalization of charisma, both in weakening a-cosmic, ecstatic and meditative elements and in the attempt to normalize dynastic succession. After his death the movement again split between the main Habad branch, led by his son R. Shmuel Schneerson (1834–1882, whose writing represents further moderation of the mystical ferment of the movement) and the short-lived, though

[51] The vast bibliographical history (reflecting the drive to reestablish R. Nahman's presence through propagating his teachings) can be found in Assaf, *Bratzlav*.

[52] Meir, 'R. Nathan Sternhartz's Liqquṭei Tefilot', 94.

[53] Weiss, *Studies in Eastern European Jewish Mysticism*, 43–55.

[54] Elior, *The Paradoxical Ascent*, esp. 167–172, 191–200; Loewenthal, *Communicating the Infinite*, 100–138; Steinbock, *Phenomenology and Mysticism*, esp. 67–88.

influential Kapost dynasty, headed by R. Shmuel's brother R. Yehuda Leib Schneerson (1808–1866).[55] As formulated by R. Yehuda Leib's successor, R. Shlomo Zalman (1830–1900), the mentalist-contemplative position of R. Shmuel was opposed by a return to a more heart-based approach, reminiscent of that of R. Aharon Horovitz in the second generation. In other words, one can discern an ideational continuity between the challenges to what became the Habad mainstream. This recurrence is explained by the ongoing discrepancy between the intellect-based approach of Habad and the Hasidic mainstream.[56]

A similar process of routinization took place in the large Ukrainian dynasty of Chernobyl, in which R. Menahem Nahum Twersky was succeeded (after some disputation) by his son R. Mordekhai (1770–1837) whose sparse writing is informative, but lacks the innovative thrust of his father's. Furthermore, in several cases (most famously R. Israel Perlow of Stolin of the Karlin dynasty), very young children (*yenuqot*) received the mantle of dynastic leadership.[57] The Chernobyl movement subsequently split into numerous subgroups, most prominently Trisk, led by R. Avraham (1806–1889), author of the still-popular work *Magen Avraham* (Shield of Abraham). Generally speaking, this writing distanced itself from the unique characteristics of Hasidic thought and came to resemble kabbalistic *Musar*, also in its ascetic predilection (especially focusing on sexual purity).[58] While Hasidic discourses, from the outset, reflected the popular nature of the movement by being couched in the form of sermons (*drashot*) on the weekly Torah reading or festivals, this tendency grew more pronounced over time.[59] Another expression of popularization was the frequent use of *gematria*, as in the unresearched *Zemakh Tzadik* (see Jeremiah 23, 5), by the above-mentioned R. Menahem Mendel Hager, or *Zer'a Qodesh* (see Isaiah 6, 13) by R. Naphtali Zvi Horowitz of Ropshitz (1760–1827), the main student of the Riminover.[60]

These phenomena seemingly support a major thesis on post-Napoleonic Hasidism, as 'retreating' from mysticism or 'substituting for it', now

55 It is likely that R. Barukh of Meizibuch (1757?–1811), grandson of the Besht, was the first to develop a theory of dynastic succession. See Green et al. *Speaking Torah*, vol. I, 56. This colorful figure was one of the main foes of R. Nahman of Bratzlav (amongst others).

56 Several prominent twentieth-century Jewish intellectuals, such as Hillel Zeitlin, came from Kapost families.

57 Sagiv, 'Yenuka'.

58 Sagiv, *Dynasty*, esp. 269–273, 320–323.

59 Polen, 'The Hasidic Derashah'.

60 See the literary description in Potok, *The Chosen*, 135–141.

eloquently championed by Benjamin Brown.[61] As he duly notes, there are some later sources that support this interpretation (which paradoxically blends with the current scholarly perception of the nineteenth century as the Golden Age of Hasidism).[62] For example, the above-mentioned R. Shlomo Zalman Schneerson of Kapost dates this process, writing that the departure of the *tzaddiq* brings about a state of exile for his followers, ending the flow of the river from Eden that symbolizes his influence (using a prevalent Zoharic image based on Genesis 2, 10[63]). He goes on to say that the 'river' beginning with the Besht's revelation around 1728 flowed for 150 years, thus ending around the time of writing in 1867. Now, bemoans R. Shlomo Zalman, we must make do with after-growths. The example that he tellingly gives, while confessing that he does not want to elaborate on it, is that of the increase of knowledge together with the decline of *'avoda* (worship) after the first two leaders of Habad.[64]

It must indeed be granted that the decease of some many leading figures, with which we began this chapter, changed the nature of the movement into a form of social identity or lifestyle. This process naturally reflected Hasidism's proliferation (also due to subdynasties in the usual case in which a leader had more than one son) and the resultant adaptation to diverse geographical and cultural contexts.[65] The long-term effects of this shift can be observed to this day in the streets of Jerusalem or Brooklyn, in which Hasidic groups diligently preserve their distinctive outfits, culinary preferences (reflecting, just like the names of the groups, their regions of origin) and particular dialects and accents of Yiddish. Though it is hard to speculate as to their mystical experience, it would be difficult to claim that the average devotee has acquired a significant knowledge of kabbalistic concepts. As a result, though the history of Hasidism undoubtedly overlaps with that of modern Kabbalah, it also begins to diverge from it in this period.

Certainly, Hasidism began to acquire economic clout and consequentially material as well as spiritual considerations came to play an increasing role.[66]

61 Brown, *Substitutes for Mysticism* and cf. Idel, *Hasidism*, 221, as well as the judicious approach of Gellman, *The Emergence of Hasidism in Poland*, 192, 290; Sagiv, *Dynasty*, 409–415.

62 See the overview of this Hasidic century in Biale et al. (eds.), *Hasidism: A New History*, 257–287.

63 Hellner-Eshed, *A River Flows from Eden*, esp. 229–251.

64 Schneerson, *Magen Avot*, vol. I, letter printed as unpaginated introduction.

65 Dynner, *Men of Silk*, esp. 96–109, 201–208.

66 Here one should mention the role of wealthy women (the best known being Temerel Sonnenberg of Warsaw, d. 1830) as patronesses (Dynner, *Men of Silk*, 94–97, 102–109 and compare to Rapoport-Albert, *Women and the Messianic Heresy*, 1–10, who refutes an

The most striking illustration of this tendency is that of R. Israel Freidman of Ruzhin, Ukraine (1796–1850) a direct descendant of R. Dov Baer of Mezeritch. Freidman was famous (or notorious) for his court-like lifestyle (cultivated especially after his move to the Austrian Empire), including an estate, coach, private orchestra and contacts with leading Jewish financiers such as Moses Montifiore. This 'regal way', centering on Freidman's 'kingship', was ascribed messianic portent (especially around the year 5660).[67] Tellingly, some of his successors, most notably R. Menahem Nahum of Itskan (1879–1933) were remarkably open to modern phenomena such as philosophy and Zionism.[68] In other words, the crystallization of socioeconomic forms of Hasidism should not be viewed merely as a defensive reaction to modernity.[69]

Rather, one can follow Moshe Rosman in assessing Hasidism as 'perhaps ... implementing the most successful nineteenth-century Jewish modernizing strategy'. Especially, he has argued that one can view the Hasidic headquarters or court, combining a network of communication with distant 'cells' and seasonal convention-style gatherings, as typical of modern forms of organization.[70] Zooming out, one should recall here Craig Calhoun's now-classical claim that 'The early nineteenth century was fertile ground for social movements as perhaps no other period was until the 1960's.'[71] It is highly significant for our present discussion that Calhoun has pointed at identity as the central axis of these movements, noting (early) feminist, nationalist, socialist and also religious forms, all of these comprising the heterogeneity of intensive modernization.

More generally, in various schools in the post-Napoleonic era one can notice a growing emphasis on sociality, rather than individual ecstasy. In many ways, Hasidic thought itself became an identity-based ideology, perhaps best captured in works like the collection known as *Yosher Divrei Emet* (The Straightness of Words of Truth), by R. Meshulam Feisbush Heller of Zbarazh (1744?–1795, a student of R. Yehiel Mikhel of Zlotchov), or the more

anachronistic feminist interpretation of the role of women in nineteenth-century Hasidism (and see Dynner's comment on the exceptional status of figures such as Temerel, 181).

67 Assaf, *The Regal Way*, esp. 72, 93, 146, 191–198, 212–225, 233–238, 257–261, 275.

68 Assaf, *Untold Tales*, 154–205. For qualified openness toward modernity in at least one branch of Karlin Hasidism, see Brown, *"Like a Ship on a Stormy Sea"*, 117–122.

69 Pedaya, 'The Development of the Social-Religious-Economic Model'.

70 Rosman, 'Hasidism as a Modern Phenomenon', 221.

71 Calhoun, 'New Social Movements', 392 (and 418). See especially 387–388, for his critique of the neglect of spiritual and religious cases in the study of new social movements. As he takes care to note (419, n. 5), the early nineteenth century is for him a starting point, not an end point.

extensive works of R. Hayyim Tirrer of Chernovitz (c.1740–1817), who facilitated the spread of the movement toward the Balkans.[72] Moderation of pietistic and ecstatic elements is a hallmark of such writings, influential to this day.[73] A striking example of intense kabbalistic activity curtailed by the series of deaths of leaders in 1814 is that of R. Israel Hopstein of Koznitz (c.1733–1814), a very late student of R. Dov Baer of Mezeritch (and later mostly of Weissblum), and an opponent of Napoleon, who published and commented on hitherto neglected medieval kabbalistic texts, emphasizing details of mystical technique.[74] Another case is that of the above-mentioned Riminover (rarely and tellingly of German origin) who famously championed a radical approach to revelation. As R. Naftali Tzevi of Ropshitz records: 'I heard from the mouth of our master, teacher and rabbi from Rymanov... discussing the verse "One thing God spoke, Two I heard" [Psalms 62, 12] that it is possible that we heard from the mouth of the Holy One, blessed be He, only the letter *aleph* of *anokhi* [that is, the first letter of the Hebrew word I that begins the First Statement in Exodus 20, 2].'[75] In other words, the proof-text in Psalms is read to say that God spoke one letter and all the rest was heard by the recipients of revelation. Such formulations belie prevalent scholarly descriptions of such figures as Ultra-Orthodox. At the same time, it is true that some of the Riminover's spiritual heirs, especially in Hungary, were prominent in what can be described as a rearguard operation in the face of modernization (see further anon).[76]

In evaluating the development of Hasidism as an identity, one should recall that there was some crossover between regions as well as the sanctified practice of pilgrimage to teachers, often well outside the region in which certain Hasidim dwelled.[77] The ongoing process of urbanization, epitomized

[72] Krassen, *Uniter of Heaven and Earth*. The process of identity formation included the nascence of Hasidic historiography. See Rapoport, 'Hagiography with Footnotes'.

[73] Again, one's ability to observe the descendants of the Hasidic groups *in situ* yields valuable insights, such as the gap between the canon studied in academic intuitions and the quotidian Hasidic curriculum.

[74] Gries, *The Hebrew Book*, 314–356.

[75] Translated and discussed in Sommer, *Revelation and Authority*, 89–91. On the reception of this teaching (reaching to figures such as the postmodern thinker Jean-François Lyotard), see Harvey, 'What Did the Rymanover Really Say'.

[76] Salmon, 'The Precursors of Ultra-Orthodoxy'. Salmon himself (140, n. 90), acknowledges the cardinality of kabbalistic-mystical ideas in the Riminover's *Ilana de-Hayye* (Tree of Life). To cite one example from this work (that was heavily edited by followers of the Psischa school and thus mixed with teachings from numerous other masters): Discussing the binding of Isaac, it describes Abraham's body as operating autonomously, without conscious volition, in what could best be described as a trance state (fol. 10A).

[77] Wodziński and Gellman, 'Toward a New Geography'.

by the growth of Warsaw and Lublin as Hasidic centers, further mitigated regional loyalties and variations.[78] In other words, personal charisma, fortressed by the doctrine of the *tzaddiq*, still predominated over social identities. If one is correct in seeing the branches of the Lublin as the core of nineteenth-century Hasidism, it is hard to deny the ongoing ferment galvanized by its mystical, kabbalistic, antinomian and messianic possibilities. Zealotry should be seen as a continuation of ideological vitality rather than its mitigation.

Furthermore, like economics, the typical components of Hasidic daily life, such as the Yiddish language, daily ritual immersion, dance, music (*nigunim*), ethnic foods (especially the *kugel* pudding) and clothing were all ascribed mystical-spiritual value.[79] Here is an example penned by the above-mentioned Komarner: 'One should strive to wear four white clothes on Shabbat . . . And this vestment is worthy of any son of Israel . . . and one should accept insults and suffering . . . And don white clothing on the Sabbath.'[80] The portent of the case of music goes beyond mere lifestyle, as it relates both to the role of the *tzaddiq* as composer (at times extending from his meditations, as in the case of Habad), performer, etc. Furthermore, the borrowing of tunes (folk melodies, marches, etc.) from various strata of non-Jewish society challenges (as do R. Nahman's folktales) the still-prevalent image of Hasidic insularity.

Another way of approaching the question would be to question the usefulness of the etic term mysticism, accompanied by endless debates and definitions (see Chapter 1). Rather, following Green's thesis, one could opt for the emic term *'avodat hashem*, translated as divine worship. This characterization of the goal of Hasidic discourse and practice is epitomized by Eichenstein, who opted to explicate the *Zohar 'Al derekh ha-'avoda* (according to the path of worship).[81] In these terms, the proliferation of approaches during the nineteenth century should be best seen as an ongoing refinement and selection of options of *'avoda* (divine worship). In yet other terms, the Hasidic schools and subschools, like Kierkegaard and other European theologians, contended with the question of the individual facing

[78] See further Biale et al. (eds.), *Hasidism: A New History*, 585–587.

[79] Fishbane, *The Exegetical Imagination*, 173–184; Seroussi, 'Music'; Mark, *Mysticism and Madness*, esp. 97–130, 161–168; Idel, *Il male primordiale*, 317; Nadler, 'Holy Kugel'.

[80] Safrin, *Sulkhan ha-Tahor*, 178. On the Riminover's preoccupation with dress codes for both men and women, see Salmon, 'The Precursors of Ultra-Orthodoxy', 128–129. Generally speaking, the Riminover vigorously opposed adaption of extra-Jewish mores. In other words, national, group and gender identities converge, as often.

[81] Segal, *The Path of Worship*.

God, increasingly in a modern context. As we have seen, this issue was perhaps most frontally confronted by Leiner.[82]

THE MODERATION OF THE VILNA GAON'S SCHOOL

Following the death of R. Eliyahu, the Gaon of Vilna at the end of the eighteenth century, his following split into two branches (as shown by Aryeh Morgenstern):[83] One, led by R. Menahem Mendel of Sklov (d. 1827), will be addressed in the next section, as it operated in the Galilee. The main, European branch was spearheaded by R. Hayyim Itzkovitz of Volozhin (1749–1821), whose main achievement, institutionally speaking, was to establish a central, donor-supported Yeshiva in that Lithuanian town. This became the prototype for an entire institutional and intellectual world, that of the Lithuanian Yeshiva, that has continued successfully (despite its near-decimation in the Holocaust), to this day. This institutionalization shifted the focus of R. Eliyahu's school from a more reclusive, ascetic pattern to a form of identity-based sociality, mirroring processes within the Hasidic context described above. Thus it is not coincidental that the core principles of Itzkovitz's ideology are set out in his 1802 call for financial support for his new Yeshiva: the dependence of the very existence of the Jewish people, and indeed the entire world, on Torah study and the towering stature of R. Eliyahu himself as the exemplar of the supreme value of toil in this study.[84]

As in the Hasidic case, the shift to identity-based and institutionalized ideology set in motion a steady process of moderation: in his magnum opus, *Nefesh ha-Hayyim* (Soul of Life) Itzkovitz toned down the scope and the virulence of critique of Hasidism, while taking care to curb mystical aspirations in favor of the above-mentioned focus on toil in Torah, joined by minute performance of the details of the law.[85] This dual move is epitomized in his approach to a-cosmism: while he acknowledged that 'there is literally absolutely nothing else apart from Him in all of the worlds . . . to the extent that it can be said that no creation or world exists here at all but all is filled with his Absolute Sublime Essence', he also made sure to restrict this realization within two perimeters – first, 'too much intellectual engagement in this concept [clearly referring here and elsewhere in the book to Hasidic theological discourse] is extremely dangerous', and second

[82] Garb, *Yearnings of the Soul*, 61. [83] Morgenstern, 'Between the Sons and the Disciples'.
[84] Fraenkel, *Nefesh ha-Tzimztum*, vol. II, 525–539.
[85] Magid, 'Deconstructing the Mystical'.

> relative to us, according to the way in which we are commanded by the Holy Torah with respect of observance of Torah and *Mitzvot*... God has hidden [Proverbs 25, 2] from us the level of [His] filling the worlds... without this... perspective, there would be no scope for Torah and *Mitzvot* alone. This is even though in truth from God's perspective... all being a pure Absolute Unity... nevertheless we are unable and also not permitted to intellectually engage in this awesome concept.[86]

Thus, through perspectivist epistemology (reminiscent of that of his contemporary, the German philosopher Immanuel Kant), theological speculation is channeled toward the strict nomian framework.

Another example pertains to the study of *Musar*: Itzkovitz restricted it to 'a short period' in the midst of many hours of Talmudic study.[87] Indeed, the toil in Torah was framed as the exhaustive in-depth Talmudic analytics that were to become the hallmark of the Lithuanian Yeshiva. Building on earlier principles of theurgical world-maintenance, *Nefesh ha-Hayyim* casts the Torah, as a cosmic entity, rooted in the 'highest of the supernal worlds – called the Worlds of the *Ein Sof*'.[88] The theurgical focus on Man as 'the one who opens and closes a myriad of powers and worlds according to the detail of his behavior... as if he [man] were also the source of their power', through constant study and performance of the law, shifted aside the God-intoxicated 'religion of the heart' championed by both Hasidism and its sources in kabbalistic *Musar*.[89]

In contradistinction, other students of R. Eliyahu preserved both his ascetical tendency and his hostility to Hasidism. Most prominent amongst these was R. Pinehas of Polotsk (1767–1822), whose *Keter Torah* (Crown of Torah) includes statements such as 'do not seek after anything in this world of yours beyond that [which is absolutely essential] to remove hunger or cover nakedness'. The more metaphysical-theoretical dimension of this adjuration lies in its radical body-soul dualism, with the latter struggling every moment to escape the body (which is under 'no form of divine providence'). With regard to the absolute primacy of Torah study, R. Pinehas almost explicitly identifies Hasidic counterarguments with the voice of the *yetzer ha-r'a* (evil impulse).[90]

[86] *Nefesh ha-Hayyim*, Gate 3, chaps. 2–4, 6, as translated in Fraenkel, *Nefesh ha-Tzimtzum*, vol. I, 478–480, 484, 492–494, 504–506.

[87] Ibid., Gate 4, chap. 7, vol. I, 656 (compare to vol. II, 611).

[88] Ibid., Gate 4, chap. 10, vol. I, 664.

[89] Ibid., Gate 1, chap. 3, vol. I, 116 (and Campbell, *The Religion of the Heart*).

[90] Nadler, *The Faith of the Mitnagdim*, esp. 84–102, 153–170 (the translated quotes are from 93–94, 96); Etkes, *The Gaon of Vilna*, 165–167.

Itzkovitz's moderating move was further developed by his son and heir (in leadership of the Yeshiva) R. Itzhak (1780–1849). In *Milei de-Avot* (Words of the Forefathers), a commentary on the Mishnaic tractate *Avot*, his radically passive approach to prayer (reminiscent of early Hasidism), extends to imagining, in a-cosmic fashion, that one does not exist, as 'Man should know that he really does not have any self-reality'.[91] However, Itzkovitz senior's main student was R. Zundel of Salant (1786–1866), who distilled the principles of theurgical prayer found in *Nefesh ha-Hayyim* into an accessible and simplified set of *kavvanot*. These are mostly based on the technique developed by R. Yosef Karo: focusing on the image of the letters of the words of prayer and on their general theurgical effect. R. Zundel, who immigrated to Jerusalem in 1837, and his son-in-law Samuel (1816–1909), the student of R. Yitzhak Itzkovitz, were part of the leadership of the pre-Zionist old *yishuv* (settlement) in the second part of the century.

The leading figure of the fourth generation, soon to eclipse all others, was R. Zundel's close student, R. Yisrael Lipkin of Salant (1810–1883). Salanter (as he is generally known) adopted his teacher's instruction to base his inner work on Luzzatto's *Mesilat Yesharim*. This choice epitomized the shift from overtly kabbalistic discourse to rationalistic formulations more resonant with the spirit of the emergent Lithuanian Yeshiva world. While respectful of Kabbalah (as we shall see, he was quoted by a leading kabbalist on the place of Kabbalah study after 5660), he removed overtly kabbalistic works from the curriculum of his new social-ideological faction, to become known as *tenu'at* (the movement of) *ha-Musar*.[92] Although his original intentions were oriented toward the wider public and even Western Europe, the movement soon settled in the Yeshiva world, after a fierce but brief controversy. While several of his students discreetly studied Kabbalah, the initial focus of the movement was on the study of human psychology, especially motivation and self-interest, and on self-mobilization through a form of auto-suggestion. Individual introspection was joined by a form of group work, later crystallized into the format of *va'adim* or group sessions.[93]

This interest in pragmatic psychology (reminiscent of that of a slightly later figure, William James, 1842–1910), not only reinforced the move away from metaphysics but also lent itself to borrowing from the literature of the *Haskala*, such as *Sefer Hesbon ha-Nefesh* (Book of Soul-Searching), by

[91] Itzkovitz (I.), *Milei de-Avot*, 23A. Compare to 23B.

[92] Brown, *The Lithuanian Musar Movement*, downplays the role of Kabbalah (as well as medieval philosophy) in the thought of its leaders.

[93] For a vivid literary portrayal, see Grade, *The Yeshiva*, vol. II, 251–265.

Mendel Lefin (1749–1826), itself based on the self-help writing of Benjamin Franklin.[94] It cannot be coincidental that the *Musar* movement emerged soon after a similar shift from metaphysics to incisive self-critique amongst Hasidic figures such as the Kotzker. Indeed, Salanter was in close contact with several Hasidic leaders.[95] In other words, his highly successful project (again lasting, though in diminished form, to this day), represented the last stage of a move from hostility to Hasidism to its near-imitation. The dual focus on Talmudics and psychology, in tandem with the forging of the alliance with the donor-supported Yeshiva, further explains the most striking move away from the thought of the Gaon: the avoidance of Messianism. This was far from the case for the minor branch of the Gaon's school, to which we shall now turn.

THE EASTERN EUROPEAN IMMIGRATIONS TO OTTOMAN PALESTINE

Following the failed immigration of the Gaon of Vilna (who gave the Land of Israel a significant role in his messianic thought), a group of his students settled first in the Galilee (c.1808) and then in Jerusalem (1815).[96] Together with the ongoing reinforcement of the Hasidic enclave in Tiberias (culminating in the establishment of a Yeshiva of Slonim Hasidim in 1899) and Hebron (settled by Habad in 1819) this wave continued the immigrations of the eighteenth century and presaged the far more massive relocations related to the Zionist movement toward the end of the century.[97] The geopolitical context was the growing involvement of the imperial powers in the Near East. As Morgenstern has briefly noted, the possibility of reestablishment of Jewish presence in Ottoman Palestine was enabled by the decline of this empire (as reflected in the temporary conquest of Palestine by the armies of the warlord Muhammad Ali Pasha).[98]

The most significant kabbalistic figure amongst the students of the Gaon in the Land of Israel was R. Menahem Mendel of Shklov (d. 1827). He

[94] Etkes, *Rabbi Israel Salanter*, 123–134 (cf. Goldberg, *Israel Salanter*, 300–301, n. 110). Lefin is considered to be the instigator of the *Haskala* in Galicia.

[95] Kaplan, *Selected Writings*, 17; Gellman, *The Emergence of Hasidism in Poland*, 247, n. 28.

[96] Morgenstern, *Hastening Redemption*, 51–57, 130–131; Shuchat, *A World Hidden*, 59–72.

[97] Founded by R. Avraham of Slonim (1804–1883), this dynasty combined allegiance to the path of Habad's more emotive rivals amongst Lithuanian Hasidim with a highly intellectual approach (their Yeshiva associated itself with Lithuanian Talmudics). On Karlin Hasidism in the Land of Israel, see Brown, *"Like a Ship on a Stormy Sea"*, 93–107, 203–220.

[98] Morgenstern, *Hastening Redemption*, 168 (and 62–63, 192).

showed greater fidelity to the ascetic path of his teacher than the institutionalized branch discussed above. Tellingly, his circle was known as *prushim*, or ascetics. Although the extent of messianic motivation for this immigration (and its relationship to the Zoharic prediction of redemption in the year 5660) has been hotly debated, one cannot set aside the reports amongst British diplomats of messianic awakening throughout Jewish Eastern Europe around 1840.[99] Furthermore, while these messianic hopes foundered on the reality of restoration of Ottoman rule of Palestine in 1840 (and its negative repercussions for the Jewish communities), as well as the destruction of Safed and Tiberias in the 1837 earthquake, they still echoed the constant weakening of the Ottoman hold.

The case for R. Menahem Mendel's messianic orientation has been strengthened by Liebes, pointing at the surprising influence of Sabbeteanism on his difficult writings.[100] It is also significant that recently published manuscripts of his include a commentary on the antinomian *Sefer ha-Pli'a*, an important source for Shabbetai Tzevi. At the same time, R. Menahem Mendel also harked back to other premodern sources alien to the dour thought of his teacher, such as the ecstatic Kabbalah of R. Avraham Abulafia and *Brit Menuha*, both texts that had some influence on Hasidic thought.

Liebes has also pointed to another striking echo of Hasidic thought (albeit with some earlier sources): the stress on the Jewish 'inner point' or core national-religious identity (as prevalent in the school of Psischa).[101] Indeed, one of the more general characteristics of nineteenth-century Kabbalah was an increasing focus on national identity.[102] To note but one more example, part of the messianic outlook of Sofer, who is usually associated merely with a rearguard action against the *Haskala* and reform, was the belief in the legislative power of the loyal Jewish public, as an expression of the 'light of the Israelite national collective'.[103] R. Aqiva Yosef Schlesinger (1837–1922), the son of one of Sofer's students, further developed these ideas, influenced by Hungarian nationalism and buttressing 'Israelite' national identity

[99] Tuchman, *Bible and Sword*, 175. For the debate, see Morgenstern, *Hastening Redemption*, esp. 36–41, 169–173; and cf. (e.g.) Bartal, 'Messianic Expectations'; Etkes, 'The Vilna Gaon and His Disciples'.

[100] Liebes, *The Zevi and the Gaon*, 123–173 (and the speculative suggestions as to Sabbatean influence on the Gaon himself in 105–119, 177–282).

[101] Liebes, *The Zevi and the Gaon*, 146–162 (compare to Piekraz, *Ideological Trends*, 125–153 and to the doctrine of *yiddishe natur*, or Jewish nature in the writings of R. Shenuri's student R. Itzhak Eizik Epstein of Homil).

[102] Salmon, 'Precursors of Ultra-Orthodoxy', 130–132.

[103] Kahana, *From the Noda BeYehuda to the Chatam Sofer*, 395–405 (the quote is from 403).

(using the term nation explicitly) around names, language and dress.[104] Around his 1870 immigration to Jerusalem (also joining the *Beit El* Yeshiva), Schlesinger took his fiercely independent approach a step further in envisioning a Jewish state, complete with flag and militia. Actually, he was but one of a series of proto-Zionist writers and activists influenced by Kabbalah to various degrees, such as the messianic thinker and magical practitioner R. Eliyahu Guttmacher, rabbi of Grütz, Poland (1796–1874), or R. Yehuda Hai Alkalai (1798–1888), who moved from Bosnia to Jerusalem, and whose messianic optimism (again centered on the year 5660) extended to a positive view of the emancipation of Western European Jewry (despite the accompanying secularization process).[105] In conclusion, one may hazard the claim that such figures support the broad thrust of Morgenstern's claim that Zionism, a largely secular movement, was preceded by religious, often messianic-kabbalistic ventures.

Another (related) general characteristic of the Kabbalah of this century was the growing focus on the sanctity and centrality of the Land of Israel (already noted in the case of some of the branches of Lublin). One striking example is the Hasidic work *Bat 'Ayin* (see Psalms 17, 8), by R. Avraham Dov of Ovruch (1765?–1840), who immigrated to Safed in 1833 after occupying a central rabbinic role in the Ukraine. To cite a representative example:

> It is known that the main perfection of speech is in the holy tongue, and this too particularly in the Holy Land, but abroad the language of lies [see Proverbs 12, 19] dominates . . . when we shall reside on our land . . . speech will be perfected, in the aspect of truth, but not now when we are in exile . . . and this will be the aspect of breasts [as opposed to the exile, see Song of Songs, 8, 8], the aspect of influx.[106]

R. Menahem Mendel's main European student (though only at a very young age), R. Itzhak Haver Wildmann (1789–1853), who commented on some of his teacher's writings, did not seem to share some of his more radical tendencies, yet clearly followed his emphasis on the nation. This independent path included an elaborate historiosophical construction indebted to the works of R. Luzzatto. Another major influence, Maharal of Prague, led him to sharply differentiate between the natural and supernatural realms (echoing the writings of R. Yehuda Leib Alter of Ger), with the Jewish people being ascribed to the latter realm. This move also led into a

[104] Silber, 'A Hebrew Heart'.
[105] Bartal, 'Messianism and Nationalism', 14–15; Lehmann, *Ladino Rabbinic Literature*, 159–160.
[106] *Bat 'Ayin*, vol. II, 374–375. For his biography, see Assaf, 'From Volhynia to Safed'.

frontal assault on the *Haskala*, with the Kabbalah in the vanguard, as in his magnum opus *Pithei She'arim* (Opening of the Gates):

> When the root of all of the . . . souls came out of Egypt . . . the mixed multitude also went out with them [see Exodus 12, 38] who are from the aspect of the knowledge of good and evil which is the seductive force in man . . . and from this was rooted the evil impulse in their souls in following generations and from this came the sinners in all of the generations . . . and from them in these generations in which the deniers of the beauty of the supreme wisdom [Kabbalah] have increased and they cast down its radiance because they have been attracted to human research the counterfeit wisdom. And those who depart from the received ways of Torah in all details of the *mitzvot* . . . they are literally the souls of the mixed multitude . . . and thus it was decreed that the soul of Moses will be reincarnated in every generation and be in exile amidst the mixed multitude . . . and these are the true scholars in Israel . . . who stand in the breach . . . and this is in the period of the footsteps of the Messiah [*Sanhedrin* 97A, *Sotta* 49B] when . . . the light of the Torah and the supreme wisdom shall be revealed to all.[107]

The historiosophical approach carried over into the fourth generation, as in the works of Haver's student Itzhak Kahana Ashkenazi (d. 1900), who immigrated to Jerusalem in 1853 and authored a super-commentary (*Toldot Yitzhak*; see Genesis 25, 19) on the Vilna Gaon's commentary on *Sefer Yetzira*. The main innovation here was to extrapolate a hermeneutic grid based on the teachings of the Gaon: the Torah is seen as a template for the course of each and every generation and individual life course. Kahana also bolstered the perception of the Gaon as representing the Messiah son of Joseph.[108] Around this time, we witness a certain return to messianism in the anonymous work *Qol ha-Tor* (see Song of Songs 2, 12), of various versions and of dubious provenance.[109] Here, the Jewish settlement in the Land of Israel is seen as a naturalistic 'awakening from below' of the redemption, accompanied by the development of scientific thought (espoused already by the Gaon's Galilean student, R. Yisrael of Shklov, 1770–1839), and even a form of socialism. This text, for all of its difficulties, can be regarded as an

[107] *Pithei She'arim*, Part. II, 73B–74A (and see also Liebes, *The Zevi and the Gaon*, 162–167).

[108] Shuchat, 'The Theory of the General and the Specific'. Kahana's work is also notable for its engagement with Rashashian Kabbalah.

[109] The skeptics as to the messianism of the followers of the Gaon have contested the authenticity of this text. For a more balanced approach (supported by oral testimonies I have heard), see Hershkovitz, 'Reevaluating Kol ha-Tor'.

expression of the influence of central nineteenth-century developments on kabbalistic thought.[110]

CONTINUITIES AND DIVERSITIES IN THE NEAR EAST

Rasashian Kabbalah continued to proliferate, develop and solidify throughout the nineteenth century, becoming a voluminous, intricate (and almost entirely unresearched) canonical literature. Dynastic-familial continuity (as in the case of the Hasidic masters of the century) was expressed in the central status of Rashash's grandson (and eventual successor as dean of the *Beit El* Yeshiva, from 1808), Rafael Avraham Mizrahi Shar'abi (1775–1827) author of *Divrei Shalom* (Words of Peace), an authoritative collection of practices. According to one legendary account, he employed magic in protecting Jerusalem from the effects of the political unrest that (as we have seen) also affected the Ashkenazi immigrants in the Galilee.[111] Others of the successive heads of *Beit El* Yeshiva continued the pattern of doubling as religious (and to a large extent political) leaders of the Jewish community in Palestine. Thus, for example, R. Hayyim Avraham Gagin (1787–1846), was the first *Hakham Bashi* (Chief Sage), or officially recognized caretaker of the autonomous Jewish community under the Ottoman *millet* (nationality) system (following the constitutional reforms known as *tanzimat*). Institutionally speaking, one can observe a gradual transition from an intensive fellowship, to that of a Yeshiva, in the life of which lengthy prayer (and thus the *sliah tzibur* or prayer leader) plays a central role. The self-confidence of the Rasashian school in this period is apparent in several leniencies in the laws of prayer, aimed toward facilitating and prioritizing the lengthy and demanding *kavvanot* developed by its founder.[112]

Space permits addressing only two of several unstudied, yet important figures. Schlesinger's teacher, R. Aharon Ferera (1815–1887) can be regarded as a super-commentator on the works of de la Rossa as well as those of Rashash. Recently published manuscripts demonstrate his intensive, diarized, visionary and dream life as well as its messianic aspects (including visions regarding the son of Joseph and the son of David) as well as his dialogue with colleagues on their meaning. Here are two appetizers:

[110] On Socialism and Kabbalah in the nineteenth century see Stern, *Jewish Materialism*, 128–130.

[111] Giller, *Shalom Shar'abi*, 86.

[112] Morgenstern, *Yam ha-Hokhma-2010*, 116–118.

> I dreamt a dream . . . that we were in the Temple, all of Israel and all the great ones of Jerusalem . . . and there were many trees like straight cedars surrounding it [the temple], and I saw a fire go up in one tree from below to above all of the tree one flame and I feared that the other trees around it will catch fire and that the Temple will be burnt and all of the great ones and sages are looking and are not trying to put it [the fire] out, for it was Friday night [the diarized time of the dream] and they would not desecrate the Sabbath, and soon God granted me strength and I grasped the tree with great might and uprooted it and threw it to the ground . . . and later . . . I put it [the fire] out and all of the trees were saved . . . and when I awakened a verse fell in my mouth . . . and the solution [of the dream] seems to be that there was a man who wanted to begin a dispute and burn . . . in our synagogue or in Jerusalem . . . and I cast him down . . . and others solved the dream for me [see *Berakhot* 55B for this ancient Jewish practice] that it was the tree of the husk that I cast down to the ground.
>
> Today . . . the holy Sabbath day I dreamed during the day that I was told: Here is the rainbow in front of you, and I lifted my eyes eastwards and I actually saw the rainbow unclouded in shining colors, and I immediately made the full blessing [*Berakhot* 59A] with its correct formula [*matbe'a*], the *kavvana* of the blessing as is known in full . . .[113] and then I saw a ladder in front of me and wished to climb it and a man came from behind me and held me the way one holds a baby who begins to walk, and lifted my entire body from the ground around one or two cubits [around thirty inches], and lifted me above and I saw a whole Torah scroll . . . open . . . and the letters inscribed on the parchments on both sides like the tablets given to Moses . . . and I greatly wondered, and said that there is not such a Torah scroll in the entire world. And the solution seems to me that I shall merit the revelation of the *Shekhina* face to face like Moses . . . and thus some colleagues solved for me . . . and may we merit to ascend above, not according to the way of nature, through one person who is unified in the utmost unity who assists us.[114]

However, the most prominent Rashashian theoretician of the century was R. Yedidiya Raphael Hai Abulafia (c.1807–1869, known by the acronym Yare), student of Rafael Shar'abi and (from 1848) dean of the *Beit El* Yeshiva and its prayer leader. The Yare not only produced the authoritative version of the Rashashian prayer-book with *kavvanot*, but more generally represented what Thomas Kuhn has described as the 'normal science' of the paradigm (opposing any non-Rashashian *kavvanot*).[115] In particular, the

[113] This being one of the most-discussed themes in Rashashian *kavvanot*.

[114] Turgeman (ed.), *Ginzei ha-Rav Ferira*, vol. I, 46, 48. For the two messiahs see 46, 50.

[115] Kuhn, *The Structure of Scientific Revolutions*, esp. 10–52.

Yare upheld what Giller has termed the 'archeological' approach to Shar'abi's development over time.[116] Moving away from the often idiosyncratic views of de la Rossa, he systematically developed a set of sophisticated philological tools to reconstruct the authoritative later opinion (in face of the various changes in Rashash's positions over time on key topics).[117] In the more public domain, the Yare urged Sephardic activists to join Ashkenazic legal authorities in opposing the importation of secular studies from Europe to Jerusalem.

This enterprise was later contested by various scholars, mostly notably (also on the basis of dream revelations) R. Eliyahu Mani (1824–1899) of Hebron and the Bosnian-born R. Moshe Sasson Bakher (c.1823–1903), the Yare's eventual successor as dean of the *Beit El* Yeshiva, who wrote:

> and I don't know where he got this from . . . But know that this is his [the Yare's] own conclusion from the questions that he found . . . And this I wrote that it should be known and famous that all the words of Rashash are as the words of the living God, and on this we say that one should not change his words and say this is earlier or later edition . . . for all this is merely our lack of understanding and knowledge.[118]

Beyond this debate, his multivolume *Shemen Sasson* (see Psalms 45, 8), containing massive bibliographical detail, have duly become (within the world of Sephardic kabbalistic Yeshivas) indispensable tools not only for the study of Rashashian Kabbalah (especially the *kavvanot*), but also for the Lurianic corpus itself.

The centuries-long hegemony of the *Beit El* Yeshiva was first challenged at the end of the century (1896), presaging the multifocal Rashashian Yeshiva world of the twentieth century. The breakaway institution, *Rehovot ha-Nahar* (see Genesis 36, 31) was founded by the wealthy Nissim Nahum of Tripoli (1864–1927) who also funded a wave of printing of post-Rashashian texts (see further below).[119] However, the spiritual authority here was R. Hayyim Shaul ha-Kohen Dweck (1858–1933), who immigrated (1890) from the strong center of Aleppo, where he served as the leading rabbinic authority and was one of several students of R. Mordekhai 'Abadi (d. 1883). The

[116] Giller, *Shalom Shar'abi*, 96.

[117] This and other examples of indigenous textual scholarship shall be discussed in a study of mine (based on a 2017 lecture kindly hosted by Columbia University's Institute for Israel and Jewish Studies). For now see Ehrenfeld, *Yira'ukha im-Shemesh*, 432–504.

[118] *Petah 'Enayim* (fourth volume of *Shemen Sasson*), cited in ibid., 503. Bakher married a granddaughter of Ferreira's.

[119] Meir, *Kabbalistic Circles*, 37–46.

occasion for the schism, expressing earlier tensions (see Feirera's solution to his dream) was a sharp dispute over the proper *kavvanot* for the sabbatical year. Rashash himself initially regarded the *kavvanot* as a kind of 'labor' that could be performed without compromising the holiness of the Sabbatical rest. However, he grew increasingly troubled by this inconsistency and in the last year of his life, a sabbatical, he refrained from performing the intentions, the very heart of kabbalistic life. His circle attributed his early death to this error, though this was part of a wider story of failed messianic effort.[120] As a result, de la Rossa (joined by another independent-minded figure, R. Avigdor 'Azriel), spearheaded a return to the original practice, in the following sabbatical year (1784). Toward the sabbatical year of 1896, Dweck boldly broke with this precedent in upholding Rashash's final, and thus for him most authoritative, decision (thus joining the approach of the Yare). As noted by Giller, it is probably not a coincidence that shortly after, another kabbalistic immigrant and legal authority, R. Avraham Itzhak Ha-Kohen Kook, aroused controversy in finding a way to permit actual labor during the sabbatical year of 1910.[121] Venturing this neo-historicist interpretation one step further, it is conceivable to frame these and other, halakhic, controversies (related to use of new technologies on Sabbath), within the general problematization of labor in the age of Karl Marx (as alluded to above).[122]

One of the changes heralded by the new Yeshiva, again setting the stage for twentieth-century developments, was its turn to the broader public, as in the book of popular penitential *tiqqunim*, entitled *Benayau ben Yehoyada* (see 2 Samuel 23, 20; composed by Dweck and R. Eliyahu Ya'akov Legimi). As noted by Giller, this work received the stamp of approval from Hasidim and other Ashkenazi figures in Jerusalem, again a cross-denominational phenomenon that was to expand in the next century, just like Dweck's ties with Hasidic mystics (the Komarno school) and zealots (R. Tzevi Hirsch Shapira).[123] Dweck's arrival in Jerusalem was part of a wider process of ingathering of kabbalists to Palestine, as described above. This fiercely independent writer destabilized the existing hegemony not only at the institutional level. While still committed (like virtually all Sephardic kabbalists of the century) to Rashash's innovative three-dimensional and relativistic methodologies, Dweck integrated him into a wider scholastic project of close

[120] Compare to Garb, 'Shamanism', esp. 183–184.

[121] Giller, *Shalom Shar'abi*, 72–73; Morgenstern, *Yam ha-Hokhma-2008*, 218–234. Kook's permit was initially opposed, but then supported, by the above-mentioned R. Shmuel of Salant.

[122] On the 'ideology of work' amongst students of the Vilna Gaon in Palestine, see Morgenstern, *Hastening Redemption*, 158–159, 163–164 (and 195).

[123] Giller, *Shalom Shar'abi*, 9–10; Meir, *Kabbalistic Circles*, 61–63.

readings of the Lurianic corpus itself. Especially in his commentary on Zemach's *Otzrot Hayyim*, he draws on Rashash's glosses on Luria and the embellishments of his followers in systematically critiquing alternative resolutions (particularly Ramaz's commentary), as well as citing an array of sources, not all available to us and including Eastern European writers.

Another influential immigrant was Dweck's student R. Ya'aqov Hayyim Sofer (1870?–1939) of Baghdad and later (1904) Jerusalem. His multivolume *Kaf ha-Hayyim* (Scale of Life), still a mainstay for Sephardic jurists, integrates Lurianic and Rashashian Kabbalah (including *kavvanot* and notions based on the theory of *gilgul*) into the minute details of the halakhic process. Generally speaking, the Baghdad center intensified the ideology of loyalty to the Rashashian approach. This is most evident in R. Yosef Hayyim of Baghdad (1835–1909), who visited the land of Israel in 1869 (also meeting the above-mentioned Mani). His *Da'at u-Tvuna* (see Proverbs 2, 6), which represents a wave of popular summaries of Kabbalah that can also be found in Eastern Europe around the turn of the century. While adducing quite a few Zoharic and Italian texts, this work firmly rests on the (by now canonical) triad of Luria (in Vital's transmission), Rashash and de la Rossa, (with typical *patriotisme local*, R. Yosef Hayyim takes care to stress that Rashash came from Yemen to Jerusalem via Baghdad. . .).[124]

R. Yosef Hayyim, one of the most prominent communal leaders and legal figures of the century, merged a popular version of Kabbalah with *Musar*, Halakha, customs and biblical exegesis in his *Ben Ish Hay* (see 2 Samuel, 23, 20), a collection of weekly sermons that was studied on a daily basis well into the twentieth century. In a sense, R. Yosef Hayyim, who responded to modern technology and communications, can be seen as a transregional Sephardic authority. Yet, due to Baghdad's pivotal role in transglobal communications, he was also exposed to Hasidic texts and those of the circle of R. Eliyahu of Vilna (including *Sefer ha-Brit*).[125] Like Rashash's letters to the sages of Tunis, his *Rav Pe'alim* (see 2 Samuel, 23, 20) *responsa* engaged the sages of Vilna and (as well as expatriates from 'our city') on a variety of questions of practice of *kavvanot* (including the question of performance by women) and interfaces of Kabbalah and Halakha. In doing so, he continued a transregional pattern in Rashashian Kabbalah (beginning with the founder's missives to the kabbalists of Tunis, through Bakher's interchange with those of Damascus). An indication of his particular indebtedness to the

[124] Yosef Hayyim of Baghdad, *Da'at u-Tvuna*, 4B.
[125] For the quotes from Lithuanian authors, see ibid., 25A–26A. On technology and communications, see Tzoref, 'The Flâneur in Baghdad'.

kabbalistic center in Jerusalem can be found in his emphasis here on the custom of the *Beit El* Yeshiva. This work was later joined by the less venerated *Sh'aarei Rahamim* (Gates of Mercy) by R. Rahamim David Sarim. Joining the immigration to Jerusalem, R. Hayyim Yosef's close student, R. Salman Eliyahu (1879–1941), was directed by him to find a teacher who could reconcile the Rashashian innovations with the Lurianic canon (thus refuting the critiques of R. Shlomo Molkho the second). For Eliyahu this person was to be Dweck.[126] The former's multivolume *Kerem Shlomo* (vineyard of Solomon) has become a mainstay for students of the Lurianic classic *Derekh 'Etz Hayyim* (printed and distributed, alongside Rashash's *Nahar Shalom*, in Jerusalem in 1910).

As we have already seen, North Africa was not overtaken by the Rashashian hegemony and thus continues to display a greater diversity of Sephardic centers, inclinations and developments. This period saw the continued spread of liturgical-ritual practices, one of the most noteworthy being *tiqqunim* through ritual reading of Zoharic passages (a practice extremely common in North Africa), in accordance to the limbs of the body. This can be found in *Shi'ur Qomah*, by R. Yosef Qorqus of Gibraltar (d. 1800), and in a Rashashian *tiqqun* designed to stop the spread of the plague.[127] Clearly, the most striking figures of the century operated in Morocco. R. Ya'akov Abuhazeira of Tafilalt (1806–1880), who synthesized Kabbalah and *Musar* in an extremely popular (to this day) set of commentaries on the Bible, founded a dynasty also remarkable for its composition of songs and poems. His theoretical contribution here is his emphasis on the theurgical construction of the *Shekhina* (interestingly reminiscent of the discourse of the Luzzatto circle), accompanied by emphatic participation in her pain. While the extent to which he was exposed to Rashashian Kabbalah is unclear, his position on *kavvanot* was certainly independent from it (following rather the system of Hai Ricci).[128] This literature was joined by translation of Safedian *Musar* into Arabic, especially in the scholastic center of Djerba, Tunisia, that deserves more research.[129] In expression of the deepening of earlier processes of globalization, these included tales of the Eastern European Hasidim, perhaps imported by an emissary from the Hasidic center in Tiberias.[130]

126 Yosef Hayyim of Bagdhad, *Da'at u-Tvuna*, unpaginated introduction (as well as Meir, 'Toward the Popularization of Kabbalah', also containing important comments on Ya'aqov Hayyim Sofer).

127 Hallamish, *The Kabbalah in North Africa*, 149.

128 Mopsik, *Les grands textes*, 618–620.

129 This corpus will be addressed through a research project headed by Patrick Koch.

130 Hallamish, *The Kabbalah in North Africa*, 119–120.

The magical predilection of North African Kabbalah had manifold striking expressions. Rabbi Makhluf Amsalem (1837–1928) of Fez, Morocco, added study of alchemical texts in Arabic to his early knowledge of Kabbalah. The next stage in his career was attracting the attention of Sultan Hassan I (1857–1894), who sought to enlist the art of alchemy in resisting the encroachments of the colonial powers (his fervent wish being to turn the Christians into fish and throw them in the sea). Hassan annexed Amsalem's collection in his central library of alchemical texts, while later granting him a laboratory in the royal palace.[131] However, the most colorful and mysterious figure was the legendary R. Ya'akov Wazana, who was bound by his Arab and Berber mentors to observe Islamic prayer rites in return for secrets of their magical trade, had a family in the demonic realm and met an untimely death as result of falling foul of that world.[132]

Finally, we should consider the influence of Rashashian Kabbalah on the Ashkenazi world, reaching back to ties forged in the previous century and expanding dramatically at the beginning of the next one. The most striking example of this trend is *Tal Orot* (see Isaiah 26, 19), by the Rumanian halakhist R. Yaakov Meir Spielmann (1813–1888). R. Spielmann testifies that

> I did not come but to the edge [of the divine wisdom] until I journeyed to the countries of the West, and there I found the works of R. Shmuel Vital . . . And the works of the holy R. Shalom Shar'abi. And I found favor by a student of one of his students . . . And thereby came to understand like a drop in the ocean this sweet delightful beloved holy wisdom.[133]

However, this encounter in Tunis (joined by his travels in Turkey) was only the catalyst for a wider synthesis, including Habad Hasidism (based on his travels deep into Russia), and his early studies with Eichenstein. Together with his indebtedness to the works of R. Menahem 'Azzariya of Fano, Del Medigo, Luzzatto and other Italian kabbalists, Spielmann's writing represents almost the entire gamut of modern Kabbalah.[134] In particular, his ability to join East, West and North expresses processes of globalization and greatly enhanced possibilities of transportation and communication to which he explicitly responded in his works (also in a messianic vein).

However, Spielmann was also an important theoretical innovator, setting forth the following hologramic and fractal theory: drawing on the monistic

[131] Fenton, 'Rabbi Makhluf Amsalem'. [132] Bilu, *Without Bounds*.

[133] Spielmann, *Tal Orot*, adduced and translated in Giller, *Shalom Shar'abi*, 91.

[134] Although he mentions the Gaon of Vilna, he himself did not address this school (although a commentary on *Tal Orot* drew some parallels and his colleague the Malbim was strongly influenced by *Sefer ha-Brit*).

potential that some readers may have already sensed in Rashash's system, he constructs a system in which each of its part is reflected in all of the others, so that each minute detail repeats the entire structure:

> As in the simile of the tree, whose trunk includes it all, and then branches into several limbs, and from the large branches smaller ones, and from the smaller ones some twigs, and from there some leaves, and at times we speak of the totality of the tree, or its trunk, and at times of a large branch that include all below that.[135]

The latter part of this statement, employed so as to resolve manifold contradictions found in the variants of the Lurianic corpus and in its commentaries, clearly exhibits the relativistic approach of Rashash. More generally, his painstaking didactic efforts were designed at guiding his readers beyond the morass of questions and complications created by the Lurianic and Rashashian corpora. In other words, together with R. Yosef Hayyim in the East, Spielmann spearheaded the late-century effort to synthesize and render accessible the now-stabilized kabbalistic canon. Spielmann's more senior (and generally better known) colleague and rival in Bucharest, R. Meir Leibush Wisser (1809–1879, known as the Malbim) helped popularize kabbalistic themes such as *tzimtzum* through their insertion in the central genre of biblical exegesis. Although the Malbim shared Spielmann's hostility to the *Haskala*, his voluminous and highly influential works reflect far great exposure to contemporary science, philosophy and even contemporary disciplines such as Egyptology.

KABBALAH, GLOBALIZATION AND CULTURE

The arrival of the *Haskala* in Eastern Europe in the first part of the century was accompanied by the expansion of Emden's critiques of the *Zohar* by figures such as Itzhak Baer Levisnon (in 1828), as well as a new genre of joined antikabbalistic and anti-Hasidic satire.[136] The classical example of this type of discourse is *Megale Tmirin* (Revealer of Secrets, printed in 1819) by the influential Galician educator Yosef Perl (1773–1839), who focused his ire on his personal nemesis, Eichenstein, who represented the twin evils, as it were.[137] An interesting twist of the complex history of the relationship of *Haskala* and Kabbalah is the claim first presented by Scholem, namely that amongst the proponents of *Haskala* and reform, as well as Jewish

[135] Spielmann, *Tal Orot*, 162. [136] Huss, *The Zohar*, 277–280.
[137] Meir, *Imagined Hasidism*, esp. 122–151.

participants in nationalist and revolutionary movements in Central and Eastern Europe (especially Poland), one can find followers of the Sabbatean and Frankist movements.[138] Generally speaking, such avenues of exploration confound identification of Enlightenment and secularization, as argued eloquently in the writing of Peter Gay.[139]

Following the ebb of the Enlightenment, toward mid-century, more positive evaluations of Kabbalah amongst nontraditional scholars came to the fore. One expression of this trend was the revival of the notion of ancient strata contained within the *Zohar*, especially in scholarly circles in France (not erstwhile a center of discourse on Kabbalah). Most notable here were Meir Heinrich Landauer's work in the 1830s and the leading academic philosopher Adolphe Franck's oft-translated *La Kabbale ou la philosophie religieuse des Hèbreux* (in 1843, which not only demotes Luria's works in order to favor the *Zohar*, but associates this book with a perennial, universal form of knowledge). This approach was continued by the Orientalist Solomon Munk (1803–1867, holding a prestigious chair at the Collège de France in Paris) who presented the ancient origins of the Kabbalah as a bridge between East and West.[140] Concomitantly, a sanguine evaluation of Hasidism, described both in terms of ancient sources and of religious renewal, can be found in the conciliatory series *Shalom al-Israel* (Peace on Israel; see Psalms 128, 6), by the Russian *Haskala* poet Lazar (Eliezer Tzevi) Zweifel (1815–1888). These books occasioned a sharp polemic on the part of proponents of hard-line *Haskala* and even fell afoul of the Russian governmental censors, who perceived Hasidism as retarding the modernization of Jewry.

The Orthodox response to the *Haskala* in Germany was epitomized by the leading rabbinic figure R. Samson Raphael Hirsch (1808–1888).[141] His ambivalent, yet generally positive attitude toward Kabbalah was most vividly expressed in his most popular work, *The Nineteen Letters*:

> A form of learning came into existence which is an invaluable repository of the spirit of the Bible and the Talmud, but which unfortunately has been misunderstood... Practical Judaism, which comprehended in its purity, would perhaps have been impregnated with the spiritual, became in it,

[138] Scholem, *Major Trends*, 304, 320; Scholem, *The Messianic Idea*, 137–141. Compare to Duker, 'Polish Frankism's Duration'.

[139] Gay, *The Enlightenment*.

[140] Huss, *The Zohar*, 285–286, 295–296; Hanegraaff, 'The Beginnings of Occultist Kabbalah'.

[141] The term Orthodox is appropriate for this movement, as it itself espoused this identity as early as 1854, though Hirsch himself was well aware of its external origin.

> through misconception, a magical mechanism, a means of influencing or resisting theosophic worlds and anti-worlds.[142]

His grandson R. Itzhak Breuer (1883–1946) employed Kantian philosophy as a weapon in defense of Torah, yet moves beyond this thought, incorporating the critique (informed by Far Eastern mysticism) of Arthur Schopenhauer (1788–1860). Breuer's reworking of the latter's doctrine of the primacy of will over reason includes the notion of the contraction of the will, probably again related to the Lurianic theme of *tzimtzum*. This adoption of kabbalistic metaphysics leads into a far more receptive approach to this lore, including its psychology, ascription of cosmic portent to human action, as well as its divinization of the Hebrew language and Jewish nationhood.[143] This modernistic movement, despite its proliferation well beyond Germany, was to peter out by the mid-twentieth century, yet nonetheless requires further study as a fertile meeting ground of Kabbalah and German thought.

Both sanguine and choleric stances toward Kabbalah can be discerned amongst the proto-academic origins of today's Jewish Studies: Adolf Yellinek (1821–1893), the chief rabbi of Vienna, while eventually abstaining from the ancient strata theory (and predating a major view in modern scholarship in identifying de Leon as the author of the *Zohar*), generally viewed Kabbalah positively, investing considerable funds, not to mention intellectual efforts, in collecting manuscripts. Through this vital groundwork, he pioneered the rigorous study of R. Avraham Abulafia, commencing a process that led to his rehabilitation toward the end of the next century. Significantly, George Y. Kohler has contextualized these projects as 'intended to spur a fresh appreciation of Kabbalah as an original school of Jewish thought that could foster a new Jewish self-confidence within the realm of modernity'.[144]

His view can be dramatically contrasted with that of the major German Jewish historian Heinrich Graetz (1817–1891), who contributed the first comprehensive survey of the history of Kabbalah. The latter, in the seventh volume of his *Geschichte der Juden*, virulently blamed Kabbalah for what he described as Jewish superstition as well as 'coarse' sexual language, inter alia describing the *Zohar* in terms of forgery. As for Lurianic Kabbalah, he

[142] Hirsch, *The Nineteen Letters*, 122.

[143] Mittleman, *Between Kant and Kabbalah*, esp. 31, 57–58, 63–72, 113–123, 169–174 (and see 8 for similar approaches amongst his contemporaries, one of whom, Nehemiah Nobel, was to significantly influence the more famous Franz Rosenzweig).

[144] Kohler, *Kabbalah Research*, 103.

deemed it to be a further, 'imbecilic' degeneration.[145] His academic adversary Abraham Geiger (1810–1874, one of the founding figures of the Reform movement) also wrote in his multivolume *Das Judethum und seine Geshichte* (translated as *Judaism and Its History*) that the advent of the Kabbalah ended free thought (echoing the earlier views of Shadal).[146]

However, even these acerbic pronouncements do not add up to the Scholemian image of hostility to Kabbalah in *Wissenschaft des Judentums* (Science of Judaism or scholarly study of Judaism).[147] More generally speaking, these early endeavors, later joined by the massive oeuvre of the painstaking philologist Morris Steinschneider (1816–1907), marked the beginning of the relocation of nontraditional Kabbalah study to the Humboltian University. Steinschneider's many pioneering contributions include his comments on Christian influences on the *Zohar*.[148] The research-based University, holding sway until its near-completed replacement (by the market or corporate University) in the later part of the twentieth century, can be seen as a profound expression of the scientific spirit of the long nineteenth century, that as we have seen had substantial impact on kabbalists. This process was to greatly accelerate in the next century.

An interesting example of a traditional writer immersed in Kabbalah yet responding to academic study of religion (including a critique of his compatriot Shadal) is R. Eliyahu Benamozegh (1823–1900), of Moroccan descent, who wrote in his native Italian and in French as well as Hebrew. Benamozegh presented the Torah and especially the Kabbalah (as its soul and source), as the source of a universal template of religion. His claims were informed by the contemporary move toward comparative study of myth and religion, including East Asian faiths (itself a core expression of the philological ethos of the research University).[149] His attempts to rebut the critiques of the *Zohar*'s antiquity should be seen within the context of his wider concern with ancient religion. At the same time, Benamozegh drew on contemporary philosophical sources, such as German idealism, in

145 Myers, 'Philosophy and Kabbalah' (also discussing the revival of theories as to the antiquity of the *Zohar* on the part of Graetz's Romanian student Moshe Gaster); Kohler, *Kabbalah Research*, esp. 197–198, 201, 205 (although this writer generally attempts to mitigate the vehemence of Graetz's hostility toward Kabbalah).

146 Huss, *The Zohar*, 286–287.

147 Scholem, *The Messianic Idea*, 308–310. Note there the contrast to Zionist scholarship, described as a 'breath of fresh air'.

148 Busi, 'Steinschneider and the Irrational'. For an overview of the early history of Kabbalah scholarship see Idel, *New Perspectives*, 6–14.

149 Boulouque, 'Elia Benamozegh'; Holzman, 'Universalism and Nationality', esp. 111–114.

buttressing the strong claims of kabbalistic theurgical discourse.[150] This very openness to non-Jewish sources led the rabbis of Aleppo to ban and burn his commentary on the Torah in 1865.

It was the Romantic Movement that opposed and to some extent replaced the hegemony of the Enlightenment. The German philosopher Franz Joseph Molitor (1779–1860), devoted several volumes to the Kabbalah already toward the mid-century (unlike many writers, then and today, he studied texts in the original Hebrew or Aramaic). Molitor combined the by now familiar theme of Kabbalah as an ancient wisdom with a typically nineteenth-century historiosophical account of its organic development through the historical process: 'a real growth and development from within ... like a tree'.[151] This writer corresponded with the leading Romantic philosopher Friedrich Wilhelm Joseph Schelling (1775–1854) who probably also accessed kabbalistic ideas through other sources, such as Boheme and Oetinger. Cristoph Schulte has argued that the notion of *tzimtzum* is central for Schelling's notion of the contraction of the ideal within the real. One should add that beyond the trope of *tzimtzum*, it is very much in keeping with the radical thrust of kabbalistic theurgy that this process, à la Schelling, not only enables the formation of life and time, but is also, as Schulte well put it, theogonic, or part of God's own coming into being.[152] Likewise, Paul Franks has speculated that a complex mediation of the 'logic of *tzimtzum*' (as a moderation of force) informed notions of the coexistence of the infinite and the finite in the writings of Johann Gottlieb Fichte (1762–1814).[153] In the literary realm, there are suggestions that the poet and visionary painter William Blake (1757–1827), who epitomizes the Romantic critique of Enlightenment, was influenced by kabbalistic imagery (via Boehme and Swedenborg).[154] However, Ockham's razor cuts in the direction of assuming that such similarities have more to do with his direct, autodidactic and

[150] Franks, 'Rabbinic Idealism', also addressing the wider issue of the interrelationship of Kabbalah and German idealism.

[151] Translated in Mertens, 'This Still Remarkable Book', 170 (and compare to 172–174).

[152] Schulte, 'Ẓimẓum in the Works of Schelling', and more generally Schulte, *Zimzum: Gott und Weltursprung*; Goodman-Thau, Mattenklott and Schulte (eds.), *Kabbala und die Literatur der Romantik*.

[153] Franks, 'Fichte's Kabbalistic Realism'. Ingenious though his argument is, it makes several strong claims as to the centrality of *tzimtzum* in Lurianic doctrine as well as its Christian reception. For example, the notion of *tzimtzum* as moderation of force appears in texts that I seriously doubt that any nineteenth-century Christian reader saw, such as Irgas' *Shomer Emunim* and works from Luzzatto's circle that were printed only at the end of the century.

[154] Alitzer, *The New Apocalypse*, esp. 15–19, 81, pointing at a near-direct reference to *Adam Qadmon*.

idiosyncratic relationship with biblical imagery, such as the Chariot of Ezekiel.[155] One methodological inference here is that the endless search for influences should not occlude the possibility of individual innovation, which at times takes curious paths.

Schelling's erstwhile roommate and protagonist George Wilhelm Friedrich Hegel (1770–1831) adduced some kabbalistic terms and ideas (mediated to some extent through Boehme, the 'mighty spirit'), especially in his later *Lectures on the History of Philosophy* (*Vorlesungen über die Geschichte der Philosophie*).[156]. It must be emphasized that as in the other cases discussed just now, the body of writing that mostly affected Hegel was the modern, Lurianic one. The most interesting item of absorption of modern Kabbalah is Hegel's direct reference to R. Avraham deHerrera, whose 'enigmatic' yet 'universal' thought he compares, like Kabbalah in general, to the first-century Philo of Alexandria, who is actually arousing interest in current Kabbalah scholarship as a possible early parallel).[157] However, what is far more evident is the influence of Hegel on the origins of University-based research on Kabbalah, most notably that of Gershom Scholem.[158] If, as Randal Collins has persuasively argued, German idealism is the ideology of the new model of the research University, one can again discern here an unfolding affinity between modern Kabbalah, its research and the general late modern setting.[159] Jewish adherents of Hegel and Romanticism, most prominently the influential Galician writer Nahman Krochmal (1785–1840) and his circle, returned this shifting of Kabbalah into mainstream discourse to its Jewish context. In his 1851 *More Nevukhei ha-Dor* (Guide to the Perplexed of the Generation), Kromchal joined the description of Kabbalah as an (albeit deteriorated) form of an ancient wisdom (originating in the Orient), describing the doctrine of the *sefirot* as 'the primary roots of the philosophy of Israel'.[160] Such Jewish Romantics writers especially admired the *Zohar*'s literary or poetic merits, a trend that continues to this day.

The post-Enlightenment era was also characterized by the burgeoning of esotericism and secret societies. One clear example is that of the Freemasons (one of whose lodges was led by Franz Joseph Molitor for a brief period).

155 Ackroyd, *Blake*, esp. 13–17, 23–25, 94.
156 Magee, *Hegel and the Hermetic Tradition* (the quote is on 157).
157 Hegel, *Lectures on the History of Philosophy*, vol. II, 395–396.
158 Idel, 'Unio Mystica as a Criterion'. Ironically, discussions of the influence of Kabbalah on Hegel usually rely on Scholem, whose Hegelian descriptions are then read back into the sources that supposedly informed Hegel's doctrine. . .
159 Collins, *The Sociology of Philosophies*, 638–660.
160 *More Nevukhei ha-Dor*, translated and discussed in Greenberg, *Modern Jewish Thinkers*, 116.

Initially operating within the framework of the Enlightenment (and thus open to Jewish membership), the movement gradually gravitated in more mystical directions. Its focus on the symbolism of building fomented interest in kabbalistic templar imagery, especially around the pillars *Yachin* and *Boaz* (usually associated with the *Sefirot Netzah* and *Hod*).[161] Conspiracy theories surrounding this connection joined with suspicions of Kabbalah as an anti-Christian plot (hence the word 'cabal' for conspiracy in European languages) within anti-Semitism, a powerful political and cultural force by the end of the century (and likewise representing retreat from the egalitarian aspirations of the Enlightenment).[162] The bonds between Freemasonry and Kabbalah were not restricted to Western Europe. Konstantin Burmistrov has pointed at both the significant role played by the freemasons in the later Romanov period as well as the influence of Kabbalah on such secret societies. It is especially notable that unlike most kabbalistic Christians, figures such as Burmistrov had access to original and specialized texts in Hebrew (besides, inter alia, translations of Molitor's works). In particular, they were interested in Lurianic themes, and especially that of *Adam Qadmon*, representing the Masonic vision of the original unity of mankind (which requires reconstruction).[163] Seen as a whole, these diverse manifestations point at the increasing naturalization of Kabbalah as a legitimate and rather influential part of the cultural scene. This multifaceted phenomenon should probably not be encapsulated under the otherwise useful rubric of Western esotericism.

In the overall process of incorporation of Kabbalah in scholarship and in spiritual life in general, Europe was rapidly joined by America. While the American Reform movement, taking roots in mid-century, shared the *Haskala*'s hostility to Kabbalah, the Jewish Theological Seminary in New York (founded in 1886), the intellectual center of what was later known as Conservative Judaism, was to be led (from 1902) by the Moravian-born Solomon Schechter (1815–1915), who wrote of Safedian Kabbalah with great sympathy, drawing on his Hasidic background (of which he wrote with more reserve). One of the most striking and enduring developments in American religious history was the 1830 inception of the Mormon religion (The Church of Jesus Christ of Latter-Day Saints), starting with its founder Joseph Smith

[161] Katz, *Jews and Freemasons*, as well as the earlier history of templar imagery in Freemasonry discussed in Schuchard, *Restoring the Temple of Vision*, esp. 404–406, 732.

[162] For now see Wasserstrom, 'The Great Goal of the Political Will'; Schuchard, *Restoring the Temple of Vision*, esp. 529, 652, 720.

[163] Burmistrov, 'Kabbalah and Secret Societies'.

(1805–1844) and continued by his successor Brigham Young (1801–1877). While the exact nature of kabbalistic influence on these figures is both complex and contested, it appears that Zoharic and other ideas, mediated not only by Christian sources but also through a European Jewish convert, Alexander Neibaur (1808–1883), informed radical notions such as the divinity of Adam (as in *Adam Qadmon*) and the plural nature of the divine realm (as in the *Sefirot*).[164] The religious ferment reflected in Mormonism was part of a wider American (and to some extent global) phenomenon known as the great awakenings. Looking beyond the United States, one should note kabbalistic elements in the syncretistic Orisha worship in Trinidad (though its exact provenance is cloudy).[165]

Beyond the American context, Mormonism was one of the New Religions forming during the course of the century (and becoming far more common during the next century). Another was the *Bābi-Bahā'i* faith, founded (in two stages) around the same time as Mormonism.[166] Here too we can find speculation, requiring further study, as to the influence of Kabbalah. Specifically, Moshe Sharon, who noted several intriguing similarities between these two new religions, has also pointed at parallels between views of the magical power of letters in the writings of the founding figure of this global religion, 'Ali Muhammad Shirāzi, the *Bāb* (1819–1850 Gate) and kabbalistic notions.[167] In other words, just as modern Kabbalah had the capacity to instigate mass socio-spiritual movements in the Jewish world, it was also able to influence new religious formations outside it, as we shall see further.

The esoteric moved further into the public domain as a result of the mystical-magical revival of the fin de siècle. As Alex Owen has perceptively contextualized it, occultism (a term largely overlapping with esotericism) resonated with threads in post-Enlightenment, Romantic cultivation of interiority, along with fin-de-siècle ambiguity regarding the spiritual and the secular (hence the attempt to retain scientific rhetoric, also characteristic of many forms of kabbalistic discourse in the following century).[168] A pivotal moment here was the formation of the Theosophical Society in London in 1875, headed by the Russian émigré Helena Petrovna Blavatsky, 1831–1891 (who absorbed kabbalistic ideas via Knorr's seventeenth-century writings),

[164] Owens, 'Joseph Smith and Kabbalah' (cf. Quinn, *Early Mormonism*, esp. 296).
[165] Houk, 'The Role of Kabbalah'.
[166] I cannot enter here the complex question of the relationship between the two stages.
[167] Sharon, 'New Religions'.
[168] Owen, *The Place of Enchantment*, esp. 114–147, as well as Thurschwell, *Literature, Technology and Magical Thinking*.

though this is far from a central facet in her eclectic mélange of sources.[169] Kabbalistic Christianity played a major role in the discourse and practices of the Hermetic Order of the Golden Dawn, one of several splinter groups breaking off (in 1888) from the schism-ridden Society. Aleister Crowley (1875–1947), a rather sinister figure who broke off in turn from the order in 1907, was especially attracted to the clairvoyant (as in his development of the practice of Tarot cards) and magical applications of kabbalistic lore (mostly within a sexual context). This interest co-existed with anti-Semitic tendencies.[170]

As part of the intensive interchange between English and French occultism, figures such as the American-born Arthur Edward Waite (1857–1942), who predictably also broke off from the Order of the Golden Dawn, engaged in sharp debate with French mystical-magical writers such as Eliphas Lévi Zahed (Alphonse-Louis Constant, 1810–1875), who vastly influenced Crowley (who saw himself as the reincarnation of Lévi). Both Waite and Lévi especially emphasized the *Zohar* (just like their academic counterparts, such as Franck). However, Lévi added a specifically nineteenth-century contextualization to Franck's claims as to the universality of kabbalistic-Zoharic wisdom, in claiming, as a revolutionary thinker, that 'it alone reconciles . . . power with liberty, science with mystery'.[171]

A striking example of the steady penetration of Kabbalah into mainstream Western European culture (also reflecting the intensification of what came to be known as the 'Jewish problem') can be found in the literary form most frequently associated with the nineteenth century: the novel. While one could adduce more esoteric cases, it is more effective to utilize a mainstream example:[172] the philo-semitic (in her later career) and proto-Zionist George

169 Scholem, *Major Trends*, 398–399, n. 2, Cf. Hanegraaff, *New Age Religion*, 453 (and 396).

170 On Tarot and Kabbalah, see Farley, *A Cultural History of Tarot*, esp. 113–117, 135–136. On the influence of the Kabbalah on perceptions of sexuality (and gender equality) in this order, see Owen, *The Place of Enchantment*, 110 (and compare to Hannegraaff, 'Mysteries of Sex', on Waite). On Crowley's anti-Semitism, see 194.

171 Hanegraaff, 'The Beginnings of Occultist Kabbalah' (the translation and quote is from 120). On the Waite–Lévi dispute see 122, as well as McIntosh, *Lévi*, 142, 144. On Lévi, Crowley and the Theosophists, see Kilcher, 'Verhüllung und Entheüllung', 353–362.

172 E.g. the novelist Edward Bulwer-Lytton, an admirer of Lévi's. A more famous earlier (1818) example is that of Mary Shelley's *Frankenstein; or, The Modern Prometheus*, possibly influenced by the legend of the *Golem*, or artificial anthropoid created through magical applications of linguistic techniques derived from Kabbalah (see for now Gelbin, 'Was Frankenstein's Monster Jewish?', which sadly ignores central studies of the Golem and its reception, e.g. the work of Idel. However, the article contributes by placing the nineteenth-century revival of the legend within extra-Jewish circles in the context of representations of Kabbalah in anti-Semitism).

Eliot (Mary Ann Evans, 1819–1880) cast a kabbalist, Ezra Mordecai Cohen, as a mentor figure for Daniel Deronda, the hero of the novel by that name. Amongst other kabbalistic references, we find the following: 'In the doctrine of the Cabbala, souls are born again and again in new bodies until they are perfected and purified . . . it is the lingering imperfection of the souls already born into the mortal region that hinders the birth of new souls and the preparation of the messianic time.'[173] It is interesting that the doctrine of 'new souls' accompanying the advent of the renewal in the messianic period was developed intensely by nineteenth-century kabbalists such as Haver (and then by twentieth-century writers).[174] This Western cultural fascination with kabbalistic psychology continues to be in evidence.

In various senses, Zionism, besides being a sustained attempt to resolve the 'Jewish problem', began as a fin-de-siècle movement. Seemingly a secularizing force (turning its back on traditional, 'exile-based' writing such as Kabbalah), the Romantic aspects of Zionism were there from the outset, soon lending themselves to incorporation of mystical and Hasidic themes by prominent figures such as the pioneer-writer Aharon David Gordon (1856–1922).[175] An earlier example for this nexus is the highly romanticized portrayal of Hasidism in the writings of the early Zionist activist Aharon Marcus (1843–1916). More generally, although the nineteenth century was characterized by a certain decline of Kabbalah (echoed in the relative ideational hiatus of Hasidism), the diverse and substantial forces arrayed against secularization (with globalization accelerating both processes equally) explain how it bounced back with greater vigor in the next century.[176]

KABBALAH AT THE TURN OF THE CENTURY

While in the first parts of the nineteenth century Kabbalah was still largely clustered around three main schools (those founded by the Besht, R. Eliyahu of Vilna and Rashash), its global spread and internal diffusion created a far

[173] Eliot, *Daniel Deronda*, 161 (and 169, 183 for an experience of the 'new self'); Nurbhai and Newton, *George Eliot, Judaism and the Novels*, esp. 44–52 (on notions and images of the soul, and see also 135–147), 89 (for the image of the vessel, not sufficiently developed in these authors' analysis, and see also 98),

[174] Shilo, 'Rabbi Yizhak Isaac Haver's Influence'.

[175] See generally Neumann, *Land and Desire*.

[176] An unstudied (and partly unprinted) corpus that should be factored in assessments of the place of Kabbalah in early nineteenth-century Hasidism is that of R. Ya'akov Tzevi Yalish of Dinov (1777–1824), who significantly influenced later writers (such as R. Shlomo Elyashiv). For now, see Idel, *The Privileged Divine Feminine*, 149–150.

more complex array by the end of the century. On the one hand, one can speak of shifting patterns of controversy: the chasm between Hasidim and *mitnagdim* was largely bridged, also in the face of the shared foe of secularization. On the other hand, the Hasidic movement witnessed fierce controversies (only the more ideationally motivated of which were discussed here) and even bans (as in the cases of Bratzlav and Psischa). It is intriguing that the Psischa fashion of constant rebellion and splitting is mirrored in the history of the Theosophical school. This structural parallel may point at the role of the period itself in fomenting comparable tensions in widely disparate contexts. Even the Rashashian school, despite the unswerving dedication to its founder, disputed the authoritative version of his teachings and the very method by which it can be established. Predictably, this strong canonization entailed in the oft-reiterated (also through accounts of dream communications) sense of absolute authority of Luria (purely according to Vital's transmission) and of Rashash, encountered the resistance of tendencies toward independent thinking. These were expressed, albeit entirely within the system, by the philological genius of figures such as the Yare. While the authority of R. Eliyahu of Vilna reigned supreme within Lithuanian culture (which transcended mere geography, as in the case of South Africa), the *Musar* movement and the Lithuanian Yeshiva world in general subtly displaced his kabbalistic-messianic concerns in their overt discourse and curricular practices.[177]

However, supported by the ever-increasing availability of printed books, there were also strong efforts toward synthesis. At the turn of the century, Spielmann's *Tal Orot* was joined by the merger of Italian Kabbalah, that of R. Eliyahu of Vilna and Hasidism in R. Shmuel ben Qalonimus Landau's *Binyan Ariel* (The Building of Ariel, 1906). While Sabbatean Kabbalah was no longer operative by the beginning of the century, its end witnessed a remarkable rehabilitation of the semi-Sabbatean teachings of the circle of Luzzatto (again assisted by a wave of printing). The attempt to summarize the complexity of kabbalistic doctrine accessible can be discerned in both Christian (as in the writings of Molitor or Waite's *The Doctrine and Literature of the Kabala*, concluded in 1899) and Jewish circles, as far afield as Baghdad (the above-mentioned *Da'at u Tvuna*). The sheer mass of kabbalistic writing, the elaboration of its practice (especially in the Rashashian tradition but also in the Hasidic school of Ziditchov-Komarno and in works such as *Or ha-Ganuz la-Tzadiqqim*, light concealed for the righteous, by

177 Lithuanian immigrants published works by R. Itzhak Haver in Johannesburg around the mid-century.

R. Aharon ha-Kohen of Zelichov) and its institutionalization in massive, well-organized Hasidic courts and Sephardic Yeshivas, clearly established the Kabbalah as a well-defined, confident discipline. In broader terms, medieval Kabbalah was that of teachers and disciples, the sixteenth century witnessed the rise of circles, the seventeenth and eighteenth centuries were the age of movements and in the nineteenth century the Kabbalah bifurcated into a forbiddingly difficult discipline and a cultural force (a split that would grow steadily wider in the course of next century). The disciplinary sense was accompanied with a clear sense of the history, uniqueness and destiny of Kabbalah. One clear expression of this self-perception is the work *Ha-Hakdama ve Ha-Petikha* (The Introduction and The Opening, to the main work of his father) by R. Gershon Hanokh Leiner. Here is his précis of the history of modern Kabbalah, focusing on the complex and tension-fraught relationships between canonization, interpretation, diffusion and innovation:

> The language of the Ari was only understood by his disciple [Vital] because he taught in a very abbreviated fashion and only spent a very short time with him. In this short time, however, he transmitted all the secrets . . . . In later generations his [Luria's] teachings were made more accessible and all who wanted could engage with them and understand them. However, everyone who wholeheartedly strove to understand his teaching [comprehensively] and construct a worldview on its foundations found it very difficult. There are numerous attributes given to one thing and several things labeled with many attributes, until one who reads them without a deep understanding [of the entire system] will find many contradictions. This is especially true if one wants to build on these principles [*hadesh be-da'ato*] . . . .
>
> His teachings began spreading to many countries, each country copied and understood them in their own way.[178]

And, as expected, Leiner then leads his account toward the revelatory message of Besht and his Hasidic movement:

'The gates of wisdom, understanding, and knowledge, were opened for him. Using them, he began to explicate the "unblemished esoteric Torah" compelling himself to explain the concealed wisdom in them, reaching to the outer limits of one's ability to understand in those days.' And then, through a highly creative rendering of the chain of Lublin, to R. Mordekhai Yosef, the

[178] Translated and discussed in Magid, *Hasidism on the Margin*, 15 (I myself would substitute 'innovate' for 'build on').

founder of his own school, embedding a subtle critique of other variants of Hasidism:

> And his [the Besht's] many students . . . in all the known places where Israel are scattered . . . took ways in the Torah of God, each one according to his aspect . . . Yet even though they greatly told and interpreted according to their holy way, due to lack of comprehension of their words . . . their opponents found room to untruthfully interpret their sayings . . . and our teacher R. Itzhak of Lublin . . . raised many famous holy righteous students . . . and the chosen of his students who came after our teacher in Lublin was R. Simkha Bunim of Psischa . . . And the exalted of the students of our teacher R. Simha Bunim was . . . R. Mordekhai Yosef . . . he was the special one . . . and the time came and the spirit of God began to move him in the year 5600 [1840] . . . and he was the first, who opened the gate, and began to . . . teach how all the words of Torah that on the surface appear to be high and exalted and beyond human grasp, actually are relevant to each individual.[179]

Given the sheer scope of kabbalistic writing, as implied in this very text, one can wonder if there is one factor or predilection that bridges the various divides and streams of the century, even in a rudimentary fashion. The best candidate, also alluded to just now, would appear to be messianism: even if one does not accept specific claims promoted by Morgenstern, it is hard to deny the clear intensification of messianic discourse in virtually every stream of nineteenth-century Kabbalah (setting the stage for a further intensification in the long twentieth century), including independent figures whose *Sitz im Leben* is unknown. One such unstudied figure operating (at the earliest) around the end of the previous century and whose works are barely accessible in libraries, is R. Yosef Tzevi Hirsch of Kaminka (Galicia).[180] In his collections *Rimonei Zahav* (Pomegranates of Gold, printed 1783) and *Meshivat Nefesh* (see Psalms 19, 8, printed in 1786), he responds to what he describes (critically) as popular interest in Kabbalah, offering a basic presentation of its principles (generally following the Lurianic system). However, his main endeavor (intermixed with high-level halakhic discourse) was to fulfill what he describes as a commandment to calculate the end of days,

179 Ibid., 16; Leiner, *Ha-Hakdama ve Ha-Petikha*, 55–7, 68, 71. One can mention here the parallel discussions of the history of Kabbalah by another member of this school, R. Zadok ha-Kohen of Lublin.

180 According to a reliable testimony that I have heard, his commentary on tractate Berakhot is extant only in a private collection.

mentioning dates such as 1790, 1795, 1840 and 1848, as well as, predictably, discussing the two Messiahs.[181]

In these terms, it is not surprising that the rudimentary origins of Jewish mysticism on the Atlantic seaboard in the late eighteenth century, including dialogue with Protestant writers, are intermingled with messianic aspirations (as posited by Laura Arnold Leibman). This association becomes far stronger in a new religion such as Mormonism.[182] It is fitting that messianism lies close to the core of the development of Kabbalah in a globalized century that witnessed the development of the secular messianism of Marx, the potentially messianic vision of evolution in the case of Darwin, as well as poetic visions of redemption, as in the case of Ralph Waldo Emerson (1803–1882) and the American Transcendentalists (explicitly influenced by figures such as Boehme and Swedenborg).[183] The above-noted Bulwer-Lytton was but one of a series of utopian novelists, the most famous of whom being Samuel Butler (*Erewhon*,1872).[184]

It would be tempting to view contention with secularization as another common denominator, also of Jewish and Christian Kabbalah. However, one must point at major divides in the scope of secularization, not only between Europe and the Near East, but also along the timeline of the century. Hasidism was much stronger in the mid-century than at its end, when secular forces (now including Zionism and the Socialist General Jewish Labor Bund) were on the offensive in terms of lifestyle and habitus as well as ideology. Around this time, ideas of secular origin, such as Zionism, penetrated into the heart of Hasidism.[185] Figures such as the Malbim and Breuer mediated Kabbalah and post-Kantian philosophy, beginning (this trend would accelerate in the next century) to bridge a gap that opened (as we have seen) already at the beginning of the modern period. Concomitantly, we increasingly find works devoted largely to a counteroffensive against 'heresy'.[186] The kabbalistic-ideological motivation for *humrot*

181 See e.g. his *Meshivat Nefesh*, 3, 7, 11; *Rimonei Zahav*, 13–14, 31, 39 (the pagination is that of the Otzar ha-Hokhma database, as none is found in the printed book).

182 Arnold Leibman, *Messianism, Secrecy and Mysticism*, esp. 211–216. This direction will be developed much further in a study in preparation by Brian Ogren on Kabbalah in colonial America.

183 Versluis, *The Esoteric Origins*, esp. 127–128, 139–144, 167–168.

184 The messianic potential of evolutionary theory was globally developed over the next century by figures such as Sri Aurobindo, Teilhard de Chardin and R. Avraham Itzhak ha-Kohen Kook.

185 Biale et al (eds.), *Hasidism: A New History*, 544–545.

186 Sagiv, *Dynasty*, 75, 292–296 (on R. David of Talne [1808–1882]); Feiner, 'Sola Fide!'. One should also note Spielmann's *Nahlat Ya'akov* and our discussion of R. Itzhak Haver above.

(stringencies) in Halakha, one of the most potent forces in traditional Judaism to this day, can be largely ascribed to this countermove.[187]

Looking now beyond the Jewish world, one can point at the transformation of Kabbalah from a largely European and elite phenomenon, known as Christian Kabbalah (again, better as kabbalistic Christianity), to a far more diffuse and ecumenical cultural force, incorporating new religions, literary adaptations, quasi-scientific discourses and secret societies or sects. In many ways, this realignment, reframing kabbalistic ideas in a much wider spiritual context (to some extent bridging the religious-secular divide) presaged the New Age movement, which is still with us. All of these were facilitated by globalization and imperial expansion, as well as the popularization of reading and knowledge (epitomized by the novel). The positioning of Kabbalah within a dialogue bridging East and West (clearly evident in the offshoots of the Theosophical Society) was to be far more pronounced in the next century, but should not be missed earlier: one clear indication here is the repeated description of Kabbalah as the recovered or preserved wisdom of the Orient, intriguingly paralleled by the onset of the proliferation of Rashashian Kabbalah in Eastern Europe.[188] Here again, the external, geopolitical process is mirrored in the internal kabbalistic discourse, as in the interest in world history. The latter is most strikingly apparent in the disturbing geopolitical visions (including portents of the destruction of much of European Jewry) of the last major German kabbalist, Elhanan Hillel Wechsler (1843–1894).[189]

[187] Brown, 'Stringency'. However, some roots can be found already in the seventeenth century (see Garb, *Modern Kabbalah*, 30, n. 3).

[188] Besides already-mentioned cases, we have the citations of texts by Bakher amongst writers of the Munkats dynasty (already in the nineteenth century). See Ehrenfeld, *Yira'ukha im-Shemesh*, 197.

[189] Horwitz, 'The Mystical Visions'.

6

Destruction and Triumph

The Twentieth Century

This is, after all, the twentieth century
I would never have known if you hadn't told me
(Chaim Potok, *The Book of Lights*)

OVERVIEW

The long twentieth century (including the first two decades of the twenty-first century) is, at least from a quantitative point of view, the apex of kabbalistic life and writing. At first blush, this is surprising, as this was the century that witnessed not only the decimation of the Hasidic and other kabbalistic centers in almost all of Europe during the Holocaust but also the forced displacement, and (in Israel) semiforced partial secularization of all of the Sephardic communities of the Near East and North Africa. Not to mention even more intensive processes of secularization, forced (in the Soviet Union), and voluntary (in North America and the remnants of Jewish communities in Western Europe). Actually, highly disruptive processes can be traced already to World War I.[1] However, one should immediately mention three countering factors: First, the renaissance of kabbalistic life in Central and Eastern Europe (centered on metropolises such as Warsaw), was powerful enough to have more than residual effects even after the Holocaust. Concomitantly, even prior to World War II, and especially in its aftermath, the emergence of the vibrant centers in Ottoman and mandatory Palestine (later the state of Israel) and (to a far lesser extent) in the

[1] On the effect of the war on the Lithuanian Yeshiva world (which I shall argue was one site of kabbalistic creativity), see Klibansky, *The Golden Age*, 76–116.

United States galvanized kabbalistic creativity. Finally, the Israeli center was reinforced by the forced relocation of the Sephardic kabbalists, in spite of the shocks of banishment and acculturation.

This grand scheme covers the geographical (or geopolitical), and thus quantitative, dimension of twentieth-century Kabbalah. However, it does not do justice to its qualitative dimension (often overlooked by approaches of a more sociological nature). These two domains actually conjoin in the fostering of new syntheses and dialogues by the contact situations (to use the felicitous phrase coined by Manuel De Landa) enabled, within the new centers, by the ingathering of mystics from a variety of locales and regional cultures.[2] These were joined by the response of the late modern kabbalists to the selfsame political and cultural upheavals. This was far from a one-way street, as we have already observed the increasing influence of Kabbalah on the emerging globalized culture. As a result, kabbalistic ideas and approaches play an increasing role in processes such as the move of national-religious Zionism toward the center of Israeli political and cultural life as well as the self-titled Jewish renewal in the United States. However, they are also prominent in wider sea changes such as so-called postmodernism and the New Age. It is at times forgotten, that the academic study of Kabbalah, as expressed in this volume, had a major part here. It should be stressed that here University writing shall be read, in context, as part of the history of recent Kabbalah (matching the numerous cases of kabbalists with academic background to be addressed here), rather than in its own terms. Ironically it is only in the twenty-first century that twentieth-century Kabbalah has become a significant concern of academe. One should partly attribute this striking discrepancy between context and content to the general premodern bias (described in the introduction chapter).[3]

Guided by this overview, we shall begin with the Kabbalah of the Land of Israel (or Palestine), facilitated and responding to the Zionist era (which officially commenced in Basel in 1897, but actually had earlier, though debated, beginnings). In tandem, the last days of European Kabbalah shall be described in all of its scope and resilience (further in the chapter we shall revisit its residual presence). Within this discussion, a special place shall be granted to the Hasidic and neo-Hasidic revival. Taking up our narrative after World War II, we shall follow the formation of the new centers of Kabbalah in Israel and North America and their contribution to the new global

[2] De Landa, *One Thousand Years*, 194.

[3] At present we only have a history of Israeli scholarship up to 2010 (Gam Hacohen, *Kabbalah Research in Israel*).

mysticism. The chapter shall conclude with an attempt to capture the present state of Kabbalah, especially as expressed in the vigorous self-assertion of the *Haredi* (God-fearing, so-called Ultra-Orthodox) worlds.

THE KABBALAH OF THE LAND OF ISRAEL

One natural location for the late nineteenth-century and early twentieth-century process of deliberate, ideological immigration to Ottoman Palestine, largely under the auspices of the new Zionist movement, was the country's only and rudimentary port, Jaffa. Extending this 'new' *yishuv* (settlement) was its neighbor (founded in 1909) Tel Aviv, perhaps the central symbol of secularization in Israel, and thus the counterpart of the 'old' *yishuv* of Jerusalem. It is not entirely surprising that the Jewish community of Jaffa was led successively in those years by two modern kabbalists, one less-known, the other of far greater fame.

The first of these, R. Naftali Hertz ha-Levi (1852–1902), was an innovative representative of the school of R. Eliyahu of Vilna. For a start, Hertz went beyond his teacher Kahana in strongly merging R. Eliyahu's Kabbalah with that of Luzzatto. Furthermore, he displayed a strong interest in interpreting the Kabbalah in light of the new wave of scientific discoveries, especially electro-magnetism, chemistry and psychology.[4] In 1904 he was succeeded by a young Latvian Rabbi, R. Avraham Itzhak Ha-Kohen Kook (1865–1935). As shown by Yehuda Mirsky, Kook's immigration, explicitly motivated by his growing sympathy with the fledgling Zionist movement, was accompanied by an intensification of the mystical dimension of his writing.[5] This process was reflected in an attempt to incorporate Hasidic sources (which Hertz shunned) in his repertoire. Despite the differences between the two Jaffa rabbis, they shared a formative interlocutor, the (then) Lithuanian kabbalist R. Shlomo Haikel Elyashiv (1841–1926), who shall be discussed in the next section.

Kook's Zionist orientation suitably expressed itself in the concept of 'The Torah of the Land of Israel', which he understood as a renewal of Jewish thought and literature (including poetics), with Kabbalah at its center. For him, secularization, especially in its Zionist variants, was a stimulant for this

4 Garb, *Modern Kabbalah*, 79–80.

5 Mirsky, *Rav Kook*, esp. 58–64, 94–119. My reading of Mirsky's theses also rests on his rich doctoral dissertation, much of which did not make its way into his book. The best of the massive Israeli scholarship on Kook extant in English is Schwartz, *The Religious Genius*. A massive study of Kook's kabbalistic sources can be found in Avivi, *The Kabbalah of Rabbi A. I Kook*.

Figure 2 House of R. Avraham Itzhaq Kook in Jerusalem (now a museum devoted to his heritage). CC BY-SA 4.0. Source: Available at https://commons.wikimedia.org/wiki/File:House_of_Rav_Kook_in_Jerusalem,_Israel.jpg

process, rather than a deviation to be merely abhorred. In Kook's dialectical thinking (loosely inspired by the Hebrew and Yiddish reception of Hegel), such paradoxes were created, guided and resolved by the same divine redemptive imperative that presided over the physical rebuilding of the land. Only recent publications enable differentiating Kook's own diary writing from more systematic editing of followers. It is through the diaries that one can best observe the intensive visionary and mystical life that he led, in often fraught contrast to his more reserved public roles. However, at times the mystical seeped into his public discourse, arousing the ire of the old *yishuv*. The most striking instance is that of his insistence (in face of opposition on part of his chief editor, his son R. Tzi Yehuda ha-Kohen Kook, 1891–1982), in keeping the following inflammatory passage in his most widely read collection *Orot* (Lights):

> Physical fitness, as practiced by Jewish youngsters in the Land of Israel in order to strengthen their bodies to be stalwart children of the nation, refines the spiritual power of the supreme *tzaddiqim* who are immersed in the unification of the Sacred Names... and neither manifestation of light can exist without the other... therefore the youngsters should

> practice sports in order to strengthen their body and spirit for the might of the nation as a whole. This holy work uplifts the *Shekhina* higher and higher, like its exaltation through the songs and praises, composed by King David in his book of Psalms . . . And one should not be taken aback if there are drawbacks [e.g. games held on the Sabbath] in the lifestyle of those engaged in bodily empowerment and all the physical strengthening of Israel, because even the appearance of the Holy Spirit needs to be refined from the admixture of impurity which clings to it, and it constantly becomes more pure, holy and refined.[6]

This passage gives a flavor of Kook's poetic style, which he envisaged as part of the dual process of revival and 'sanctification' of the new Hebrew writing accompanying Zionism. It also captures his sense of the return to the Land as an occasion for somatic, as well as psychic renewal. Kook's love affair with the Land of Israel was interrupted by his forced exile during World War I, which he envisioned as a further sign of the redemptive process, especially in view of the 1917 Balfour declaration on the Jewish 'national home' in Palestine (a diplomatic feat that he himself contributed to in his temporary rabbinical role in London). Fortuitously, this displacement enabled his encounter with his second editor, R. David Kohen (1887–1972), known as 'the Nazarite', due to his highly rare assumption of the biblical option of consecration to divine service through abstaining from wine and haircuts (to which he added vegetarianism, extended periods of complete silence and later also vision quests in the Judean desert). Kohen brought to this emerging circle his in-depth knowledge of both classical and modern philosophy in the original, which (as he himself ruefully noted, as we shall now see) Kook elder and junior both lacked. It is well worth quoting Kohen's dramatic description of this fateful encounter:

> After immersion in the waters of the Rhine . . . full of doubt and anticipation, I made my way to the rabbi [Kook] . . . I came to him, finding him studying *Halakha* with his son [Zvi Yehuda]. The conversation turned to Greek wisdom [philosophy] and literature, which did not satisfy a soul which knows it from its primary sources. I stayed over with them.
>
> On my bed my heart did not rest, the fate of my life hung in the scales. And then early in the morning I heard the sound of pacing, the blessings of dawn, the *'aqeda* [binding of Isaac] prayer, with supernal song and tune . . . and I hearkened, and lo, I was changed and turned into a different man

6 Kook, *Orot*, 80 (the translation adapts and merges those found in Garb, *The Chosen*, 42; Garb, 'Rabbi Kook', 10).

> [I Samuel 10, 6]. After the prayer, I hurried to announce by letter, that more than I had prayed for did I find, I found myself a teacher.[7]

Before considering the implications of this encounter for Kohen's own trajectory, one should pause to note the centrality of the *'aqeda* biblical verses, describing the binding of Isaac by Abraham, for the meditative prayer of Itzhak Avraham Kook, as we can observe in his commentary on the prayer book, *'Olat Re'iya* (burnt offering on the occasion of arriving at the temple).[8] Kohen's mention of his hearing Kook's prayer without seeing him is pivotal. His own thought, as expressed in his fittingly entitled magnum opus *Qol ha-Nevu'a* (The Voice of Prophecy) centered on the superiority of auditory Hebrew thought to ocular-centric thought, beginning with Greece. This would not be the last time that kabbalistic writing presaged both Catholic critical theology and so-called postmodern theory.[9] Kohen's reclusive and ascetic lifestyle, focused on the quest for auditory prophetic revelation (in response to what he perceived as Kook's achievement of visual revelation), ensured that he was to be sidelined in the later transformation of the circle into a full-fledged political movement.

The institutional power of the Kook circle was cemented when its leader became the first Ashkenazi Chief Rabbi of mandatory, postwar Palestine in 1921. Another focal event was the establishment of the so-called central World Yeshiva, with Kook at its head, in 1923. These events, alongside many others (such as his speech at the festive opening of the Hebrew University, in 1925), demonstrate how Kook and his followers both benefited from and expressed the accelerated modernization of Jewish Palestine. At the same time, the move to Jerusalem, despite some opposition, was facilitated by Kook's skill in developing strong ties with the old *yishuv*. A major example is that of his third major student, the ascetic R. Yaakov Moshe Harlap (1882–1951). Harlap's major theoretical contribution was an unprecedented divinization of the Land of Israel: 'In days to come, *Eretz Israel* shall be revealed in its aspect of Infinity, and shall soar higher and higher . . . Although this refers to the future, even now, in spiritual terms, it is expanding infinitely.'[10]

[7] Editor's introduction to Kook, *Orot ha-Qodesh*, vol. I, 17–18.

[8] *Re'iya* is often used as an acronym for Avraham Itzhak Ha-Kohen. On the binding of Isaac in Hasidism, see Gellman, *Abraham! Abraham!*, esp. 13–25, 57–63, 77–89.

[9] See e.g. Levin, *The Listening Self*. English-language writing on Kohen is lacking. See for now Bitty, *The Mystical Philosopher*.

[10] Harlap, *Ma'ayanei ha-Yeshu'a*, translated and discussed in Garb, *The Chosen*, 62.

Kook also developed close relations with the first Ashkenazi kabbalistic Yeshiva, *Sha'ar ha-Shamayim* (The Gate of Heaven, founded in 1906) that – just like Kook's own Yeshiva – is still highly influential in Jerusalem. Indeed, its first president, R. Hayyim Yehuda Leib Auerbach (1883–1954), just like the above-mentioned R. Elyashiv, was the grandfather of one of the late twentieth-century leaders of the *Haredim* of Jerusalem. As Jonatan Meir has shown at length, this was but one of a set of new kabbalistic Yeshivas, active in printing of key texts, communal outreach and original writing,. The first of these was *Rehovot na-Nahar* (whose genesis has already been described). Although both Yeshivas participated in the printing of the prayer-book containing Rashashian *kavvanot*, Dweck expressed reservations as to its distribution, including the concern that it might reach the recently (1894) established National Library.[11]

While Meir has foregrounded the public performance of verbal rites of rectification (especially of sexual sin), one should also note that a prominent immigrant from the Allepo center, R. Itzhaq Alafiya (1878–1955) promoted *ta'anit dibbur* ('speaking fasts', or periods of silence). This earlier custom also gained popularity in North Africa, including the establishment of fraternities dedicated to penitential silence.[12] However, the most striking project (supported by Kook himself) essayed by the growing world of Jerusalemite kabbalists was the quest for the lost Ten Tribes in the Far East, spearheaded by the prolific writer R. Shimeon Zvi Horowitz of Lida (1869–1946), one of the leaders of *Sha'ar ha-Shamayim*.[13] We have here yet another expression of the opportunities provided by late modern globalization.

On the regional level, Kook was prominent in formulating the widespread condemnatory rabbinical response to the antikabbalistic writing of R. Qihya Kafih (1850–1932), founder of the rationalistic circle in Yemen known as *Dor De'a* (generation of wisdom). Kafih's critique was guided by a purist conception of the original Yemenite way, purged of foreign influences. In this sense, his movement should be regarded as part of the self-assertion of regional Jewish identities.[14] Besides reviving doubts (starting in 1913) as to the authenticity of the *Zohar*, Kafih accused Lurianic Kabbalah of ascribing

11 Meir, *Kabbalistic Circles*, esp. 64–84, 140–148. One should mention that Meir, 'Lights and Vessels', has critiqued the notion of the 'Kook circle'. I have rather espoused the approach of Uriel Barak (in English, see 'Can Amalek Be Redeemed?').

12 Hallamish, *Kabbalah in North Africa*, 150.

13 Meir, *Kabbalistic Circles*, 96–134. For a global history of the myth of the lost tribes, see Ben-Dor Benite, *The Ten Lost Tribes*.

14 Yaakov, *God Came from Yemen*, 256–288.

divinity to the *partzuf* of *Ze'ir Anpin*. It must be said that though the strong focus on this aspect is typically found in Sabbatean circles (and amongst those suspected of Sabbateanism), it made its way into entirely normative twentieth-century works, including those of Elyashiv.[15]

In the very years (1921) that Kook seated himself in Jerusalem, he was joined there by a Polish kabbalist who was to become his friend and protégée – R. Yehuda Leib Ashlag (1885–1955). Though the latter's early training is somewhat nebulous, we know that he was a student of several Hasidic *rebbes* (especially the kabbalistically inclined R. Yehosu'a Asher Rabinovitz of Porisov, d. 1938), yet he repeatedly quotes Hertz's supercommentaries on the Vilna Gaon's commentary on the prayer-book.[16] Unlike Kook, Ashlag soon found himself in conflict with the kabbalistic Yeshivas, mainly as result of his open critique of the hallowed tradition of Rashash. Placing little store by merely following the internal intricacies of the Lurianic system, Ashlag opted for a rereading of its meaning, combining sociopolitical thought, scientific imagery and psychology. The source of confidence for this consciously revolutionary move was his self-perception as an *'ibbur*, or partial reincarnation of Luria himself.[17]

At the core of this innovative system, also inspired by autodidactic study of modern European philosophy, lies the tension between the egotistic *ratzon le-qabel* (will to receive) and the altruistic *ratzon le-hashpi'a* (will to bestow/influence). The drama of personal as well as collective history is that of the transformation of the first psychic drive into the second. Following Luzzatto, Ashlag found a place for receiving in order to cooperate with God's own desire to give, thus innately transforming passive reception into active bestowing, and thus emulating the divine imperative to give.[18] Let us see how Ashlag reinterpreted the concept of *tzimtzum* in these terms: the contraction, which for him took place in the *Malkhut* of *Ein-Sof*, was a diminution of the desire to receive (predictably associated with *Malkhut*, traditionally depicted as the receiving aspect). In a typically dialectical manner, this self-limitation was motivated by a desire to increase the will to bestow, thus enabling the process of divine emanation and eventually creation as the ultimate form of giving.[19] In other words, the Lurianic notion of withdrawal paving the way for the world is reinterpreted in terms of social psychology, rather than cosmology.

15 Darmon, *L'Esprit de la Kabbale*, 42.
16 On Ashlag's early years, see Meir, 'New Discoveries'.
17 Ashlag, *Igrot ha-Sulam*, 271–272.
18 Garb, *The Chosen*, 53–54, 56.
19 Ashlag, *Talmud 'Eser Sefirot*, vol. I, 4–5, 18.

As he saw his vision as encompassing 'The entire human species together: Black as white as yellow without any initial difference', and following on from his valorization of altruism, Ashlag admired the Socialist wing of Zionism rather than its nationalistic aspirations.[20] In fact, he went so far as to adjure David Ben-Gurion (1886–1973), Israel's first prime minister, to ally himself with the Soviet bloc, rather than reorienting westwards (as Ben-Gurion eventually moved in the 1950s). However, in his posthumously published *Writings of the Last Generation*, Ashlag predicted that Socialist Zionism, epitomized by the kibbutz movement, would not survive as a vital force without the aid of Kabbalah, as the ultimate form of science (and thus of 'scientific socialism'). For him, humanity's innate egotistic tendency cannot be assuaged by mere political devices, but rather: 'Religion is the only basis sure to raise the level of the collective to the moral level of "working according to the ability and receiving according to the need [the known Marxist formula]"'. Thus, he proposed 'a collective religion of all of the nations that will come within the framework of Communism'.[21]

Like Kook, Ashlag soon found himself at the hub of a kind of mystical fellowship. Newly published and annotated material affords us a peek into his daily psychological work with his students (which is reminiscent of that of his Armenian contemporary George Ivanovich Gurdjieff [1872?–1949], in Russia and later in France). One of the closest of these, R. Moshe Barukh Lemberger, reports the following entry from January 26, 1940: 'Before the class he [Ashlag] spoke specifically and personally about me, why am I not satisfied?' Ashlag went on to say: 'For one needs to know that just as we see that the time is difficult in the material [divine] guidance of the world, so it is with the spiritual guidance . . . so why am I complaining so much? For there are thousands of people without even a roof over their heads.' Two days later, Ashlag called him in and announced that Lemberger had reached the state in which he cannot deceive himself anymore, so that he has to strengthen himself to receive 'real lights'. Ashlag returned to the effect of the world war on spiritual development on April 12, speaking in a less personal manner. After explaining the kabbalistic significance of the aerial battle between England and Germany, he stated: 'During wartime it is harder for the worker for God, for in peacetime the vessel and time to conquer the Other Side is the work of self-sacrifice (and great effort), but during war self-sacrifice is not exceptional, so that one needs miracles and great merit.'[22]

20 Ashlag, *Ma'amrei ha-Sulam*, 31.
21 Ashlag, *The Writings of the Last Generation*, 30, 71 (and 58, 108).
22 Gotlieb, *Hashem Sima'kha Sham'ati*, 157–158, 192.

Besides his interpretation of Luria (found mostly in his *Talmud 'Eser Sefirot*), Ashlag composed a massive translation of and commentary on the *Zohar*, entitled *ha-Sulam* (The Ladder). Rather than being an attempt to follow the *Zohar*'s plain sense, *ha-Sulam* performs a double rendering, first into Lurianic terms and then into those of his own system. This project should be contrasted with that of another new immigrant (1933), in this case from Baghdad, R. Yehuda Moshe Petaya (1859–1942), student of R. Yosef Hayyim. While tactfully acknowledging the authority of Rashash in principle, Petaya declared his loyalty to the plain sense of Luria's writings, and followed a similar path in commenting on Luria's main Zoharic sources, the *Idrot*.[23] Petaya's magnum opus *Beit Lehem Yehuda* (Bethlehem Judea) reflects not only his exegetical skill but also his visionary life, including several mystical dreams. His method of dream interpretation, which joined his practice as an exorcist, was further developed by his son Shaul.[24] The introduction to Petaya the elder's commentary captures the last days of the Baghdadi center, against the background of the global upheaval of World War I, reflecting what one could describe as an urbanization of kabbalistic self-perception:

> For in our city Baghdad, God protect it, we had two golden cherubs [Exodus 25, 18], covering the city from within and without, and they were for us the wall and refuge in the day of rage. The first in holiness [Mishna, *Taharot* 2, 5] was the *tzaddik*, the foundation of the world, Yosef Hayyim- ... and the second in holiness, the Rabbi and Gaon Shimeon Aharon ... known as Agasi [1852–1914] ... and these two righteous were alone in our city ... Protecting the town ... yet when the sins [of the public] caused the taking of the holy ark [Samuel 1, 4, 22] R. Yosef Hayyim in the year 1909 ... the city began to limp, walking on one leg, and the troubles began to arrive, for after his burial the youth of Israel for taken to the work of the army of the king of Ishmael [Ottoman forces] to be instructed in the order of war, and all of the people wailed and cried, and we were consoled with R. Shimeon Aharon ... and five years later ... he too went to his rest ... and then the last spark went out in the city ... and after the departure of R. Shimeon, early in the morning, red posters were put up on behalf of the king and his great ones ... and on the poster was drawn a red sword to signal the war between kingdoms, Constantinople and Britain.[25]

A third European figure who reached Jerusalem in the early years of the British Mandate was Gershom Gerhard Scholem (1897–1982) of Berlin.[26]

[23] Giller, *Shalom Shar'abi*, 13. [24] Bilu, 'Sigmund Freud'.
[25] Petaya, *Beit Lehem Yehuda*, vol. I, 33–34.
[26] On Scholem in the context of Israeli intellectual history, see Engel, *Gershom Scholem*. On his continued dual position in Israeli and German cultural life, see Zadoff, *From Berlin to*

Scholem, like other Zionist figures of the time (especially the poet laureate Hayyim Nahman Bialik, 1873–1934), shared the revival of interest in the *Zohar* in Israel, which can be attributed, at least in part, to its Galilean literary setting.[27] Although Scholem maintained close ties with German critical thinkers and theorists (especially Walter Benjamin), the centrality of Zionism in his worldview is apparent in his stress on the messianic dimension in Jewish mysticism (especially in his exhaustive studies of Sabbateanism). This inclination was closely related to his tendency to decipher the course of kabbalistic creativity as a response to national historical events. In the project of rendering the *Zohar* accessible, Scholem was later joined (1933), by a Hungarian immigrant with earlier roots in the anti-Zionist circles described below, who adopted the messianic name Isaiah Tishby (originally Schwartz Shandor, 1908–1992).[28] Already in 1949, the latter published the first volume of his monumental set of introductions to and translations of the Zoharic literature. Scholem was drawn into Kabbalah studies partly due to his admiration of the literary output of Martin Buber (1878–1965), who will be discussed anon in the context of prewar Hasidism. However, Scholem's formation of identity as a philological scholar, expressed in his staggering contribution to location, cataloguing, identification and publication of new texts (a facet less addressed in the remarkably profuse biographical writing on him), soon led him into conflict with Buberian romanticization.[29]

Scholem was in close contact with an Eastern European immigrant, Shmuel Yosef Agnon (1887–1970), later to be Israel's only Nobel Prize winner in literature to date (1966). As Elhanan Shilo has shown, besides his anthologizing of Hasidic stories, Agnon was in close contact with the kabbalists of the *Beit El* Yeshiva as well as R. Yehuda Brandwein of the Ashlag circle. However, Agnon, especially in his later years, could also be critical of various aspects of the Kabbalah including what he saw as the lowly literary level of the *Zohar* and its preoccupation for sexual issues. Tzahi Weiss has pointed at the closeness between the Scholemian scholarly narrative and the Agnonian

Jerusalem and Back. For the German-language perspective, see esp. Weidner, *Gershom Scholem*.

27 See Abrams, *Kabbalistic Manuscripts*, esp. 281–282, 291–292, 296–298, 325–326, 331–338; Meir, 'Hillel Zeitlin's Zohar'. One can compare this Galilean inclination to the revival of interest in Jesus in popular academic writing (especially that of Joseph Klausner, 1874–1958) and Hebrew literature (especially Uri Zvi Greenberg, as shown by Stahl, 'Uri Zvi before the Cross').

28 Tishby is the name of Elijah the prophet, psycho-pomp for many kabbalists.

29 For a sophisticated discussion, see Magid, 'Gershom Scholem's Ambivalence'.

literary narrative (one may add, as two canonical Israeli corpora), as well as Scholem's appearance as a character in at least one of Agnon's stories. At the same time, like Shilo, he emphasizes Agnon's independence from Scholem's filter in approaching the kabbalistic world.[30] In terms of economic history, one should stress that these two writers shared the support of the increasingly powerful publisher Shlomo Zalman Schocken (1877–1959), who displayed a keen interest in Kabbalah as such.

Figure 3 Uri Zvi Greenberg. Source: Wikimedia Commons. Public Domain.

Perhaps the most striking literary immigrant who shared Scholem's interest in topics such as the *Zohar* and Sabbateanism, yet was positioned on the opposite side of the political spectrum, was Uri Zvi Greenberg (1896–1981) of Lemberg, Poland. Greenberg, who formed close ties with Kook after arriving (1923) in Palestine, shared his tendency toward visions described in prophetic language, and was indeed hailed as a prophet by his most prominent followers, largely due to his chilling descriptions of the Holocaust and the wars of Israel. Here is but one example of a visionary text penned in 1936: 'I see murdered and slaughtered and fires . . . and I already see a flock of planes circling the Temple mount on a festival . . . I see masses of

[30] Shilo, *The Kabbalah*, 18–42; Weiss, *Death of the Shekhina*, esp. 73, 127–130.

celebrants.'[31] His messianic consciousness extended to explicit admiration of Shabbetai Zvi (whose gravesite in Montenegro he visited as a soldier in the Austrian army in World War I). As Baruch Falach has shown, Greenberg was part of a wider circle of right-wing intellectuals (the main organ of expression being the journal *ha-Sulam*, The Ladder), who merged kabbalistic symbolism in their vision of the restoration of the Davidic kingdom and even the temple.[32] The great majority of the circle's members participated in the underground activities of the right wing of the Zionist movement in the 1930s and 1940s (contributing to the end of British rule in Palestine). Falach's analysis underscores the poetic-messianic meaning that these writers afforded their underground activity (on its later offshoots, see anon).

These examples demonstrate the important role played by Kabbalah in the various forms of the literary and cultural ferment accompanying the steady development of sociopolitical Zionism. Like European national movements, Zionism strove to construct a cultural canon as part of its construction of national identity, focusing on nonhalakhic texts such as the *Zohar*, more suitable for secular reception. It is far from coincidental that Naphtali Hertz Imbar (1856–1909), the author of the poem *ha-Tikvah* (The Hope), later to become the anthem of the new state of Israel, displayed great interest in Kabbalah (alongside Far Eastern mysticism, a combination recurring in the course of the century).[33] The *Zohar* was also valorized by pro-Zionist writers of the late Eastern European *Haskala*, such as Sholem Yankev Abramovich (better known as Mendele Mokher Sforim, 1836–1917), who went so far as to say that 'The Zohar is sacred as Mount Sinai . . . the pillar of the fire of love that the Children of Israel saw for the first time in the darkness of the Middle Ages.'[34]

Alongside, and often in contention with, these Zionist figures, Jerusalem was also home to sharp critics of the movement. Here too, one can observe a close alliance between Sephardic and Ashkenazi figures. Amongst the former, most prominent was the reclusive veteran Safedian kabbalist and halakhist R. Shlomo Eli'ezer Alfandri (1830?–1930), erstwhile (until 1917) of Damascus. Alfandri was in close contact with the Hungarian anti-Zionist zealot R. Hayyim Eli'ezer Shapira (the Rebbe of Munkatsh, 1871–1937), as well as the Jerusalemite zealot R. Yeshi'a Asher Zelig Margaliot (1894–1967).

[31] Greenberg, *Collected Writings*, vol. III, 188–189.

[32] Falach, 'The "Sulam" Journal', esp. 157–164, 234. For Greenberg's prophetic self-consciousness, see Corb-Bonfil, *Where Words Are Silence*, 93–144.

[33] Huss, 'Forward to the East'.

[34] *Emek ha-Bakhah*, quoted and contextualized in Huss, *The Zohar*, 301–303.

These figures had close ties with the Sephardic Yeshiva world, for as we have seen, at least Dweck shared their suspicion toward secular institutions. Margaliot's highly colorful and prolific writing is replete with attacks on any contact with the 'mixed multitude', or secularists, alongside a sustained effort to strengthen the revival of the Zoharic myth, especially the cult of R. Shimeon bar Yohai and his alleged gravesite in Meron, near Safed. In this respect, he complemented the work of Shapira, who composed an extensive commentary on *Tikkunei Zohar*, entitled *Be'er Lehai Ro'i* (see Genesis 16, 14). Besides the Safedian activity, the Galilee was also home to the circle in Tiberias, including descendants of the Hasidic immigrants of the eighteenth century. One such group belonged to the dynasty of Slonim, whose *rebbe*, R. Avraham Weinberg the second (1884–1933), visited from Belorussia in 1929. The creative wave occasioned by this visit included *'Avodat Pnim* (Inner Work), by R. Aharon Yosef Luria (1894–1969), which as indicated by its title includes detailed guidance on psychological-mystical development.

From the point of view of kabbalistic circles, the most significant anti-modern figure was R. Aharon (Arale) Roth (1894–1947). Roth, who immigrated to Jerusalem in 1925 (and again in 1939), founded an elitist, highly ascetic fellowship known as *Shomer Emunim*, or Keepers of the Faith, which later splintered into several groups. Roth's thought, contained mostly in his *Shomer Emunim* (not to be confused with the earlier volume with the same title), is exceptional in its stress on the theurgical power of simple faith (in the face of both secularization and the vicissitudes of history, specifically designed to test it). In his self-consciousness, he saw himself as part of a series of *tzaddikim*, charged with reviving this faith in each generation. Indeed, enlisting the Lurianic doctrine of transmigration within his historiosophical construct, Roth envisaged the process of *tiqqun* as transgenerational and retroactive (as each individual could amend the sins of the soul-sparks incarnated in him).[35]

THE LAST DAYS OF EUROPEAN KABBALAH

Momentarily setting aside the further proliferation of Hasidism, which merits a separate discussion, European Kabbalah in the first half of the century can be divided into two unrelated developments. The first was the continued elaboration of the kabbalistic system of R. Eliyahu of Vilna, as well as its sources, within the Lithuanian Yeshiva world. This internal

[35] Greenberg, 'R. Areleh Roth's Pristine Faith'.

development, focused on greater Lithuania (with some offshoots in Poland, Russia, Germany and even England, as we shall soon see), was accompanied by the continued expansion of both Kabbalah and kabbalistic Christianity inside and outside the Jewish world. The latter, far more diffuse process took place within literary and philosophical circles and also in the psychoanalytic movement inaugurated around the beginning of the century. Alongside some less-known Russian counterparts, these writers were located in Central and Western Europe. The geographical spread of Kabbalah and the very existence of two separate processes (alongside the largely autonomous Hasidic world, to be addressed further on) conjointly exemplify the culmination of the nineteenth-century process of the diversification of Kabbalah and its move well beyond any fixed canons. In this sense, European Kabbalah matched the new forms it acquired when figures such as Kook, Ashlag and Scholem immigrated to Palestine. Indeed, these writers continued to respond to some of the European developments that we shall trace here, and encountered some of their key agents (also during visits, facilitated by the improvement of global transportation, such as the one by Weinberg described just now).

Turning first to the internal development of European Kabbalah, one should pause to note the general transition that galvanized Lithuanian discourse, rendering it a potent spiritual and intellectual force throughout the century. This small, yet highly intense and elitist scholarly community was at that time in the throes of two major religious revolutions: The first, continuing the pioneering efforts of R. Israel Salanter, was the development of several discrete schools of *Musar*, initially guided by his personal students. The second was the elaboration of *lomdut* (Talmudic analytics), assisted with conceptual and legal categories that justify its description as a form of modernization. We have seen that Salanter accorded Kabbalah a relatively minor role in his overt, public discourse, concomitantly with his stress on emotional self-awareness and self-formation. Clearly, some of his followers, in particular the notorious ascetic R. Yosef Yozel Huruwitz of Novardok (1848–1919), continued to downplay mystical pursuits and sources. Yet other students, especially R. Simkha Zissel Zusskind Ziv of Kelm (1824–1898) valorized classics of kabbalistic *Musar*, such as Cordovero's *Tomer Devora*. One of 'the *alter* (old man)' of Kelm's more independent students, R. Yeruham Leibovitz of Mir (1873–1936), developed his own school, thus joining the ranks of Salanter's direct students.[36] Leibovitz synthesized ideas drawn from medieval Jewish philosophy (especially as it is found in biblical

[36] Garb, *Yearnings of the Soul*, 67, 70–74; Pachter, 'The Musar Movement'.

exegesis, such as that of Avraham Ibn Ezra, 1089–1167), the early modern writings of R. Ya'akov Emden and kabbalistic materials, especially the corpus of Luzzatto. Here is a clear statement of his position on Kabbalah:

> Man needs to know two things: The first is that the greatest secrets, all the 'worlds' and firmaments of the books of Kabbalah, are called secrets only relative to one who does not know and apprehend them . . . for really they are simple and evident matters . . . this secret is revealed and simple for all: 'the whole earth is filled with his glory' [Isaiah 6, 3] and 'there is none besides him' [Deuteronomy 4, 25] . . . the second knowledge: that our own level is exactly the opposite, that the simplest matters are 'secrets' to us.[37]

In other words, the teachings of Kabbalah (including the immanentist and a-cosmic theology that one usually associates with the Hasidim) are not intrinsically esoteric. However, in true, self-critical *Musar* fashion, Leibovitz cautions that in the actual state of his hearers, much simpler forms of knowledge are obscured. It is clear that at least part of this expansion of *Musar* toward the metaphysical realm can be traced to his instruction of overseas students (including Americans) arriving in Lithuania for shorter periods of study. A similar experience can be found in the trajectory of another one of the *alter* of Kelm's students, R. Eliyahu Eliezer Dessler (1892–1953). After his relocation to England (1927), he began to tutor the children of leading members of the local Jewish community. The questions arising from their exposure to secular education led Dessler to engage modern science and particularly psychology. In doing so, he was assisted by his contact with Ashlag, during the latter's brief stay in London (1926–1928). Dessler's oeuvre reflects two notable expansions of the Lithuanian repertoire. Following the general approval of Luzzatto amongst the students of R. Eliyhau of Vilna, he became interested in the thought of his associate Valle, a trend that was to intensify amongst later generations of his school. More dramatically, Dessler sought to minimize the scope of the disagreement with the Hasidim (on issues such as the interpretation of *tzimtzum*), describing it as a question of focus in the ways of worship of God, rather than a dispute on metaphysics or ontology.[38]

A third kabbalistically inclined figure, who appears to be an almost entirely independent figure (rather than a follower of one of the *alters*), was R. Yosef Yehuda Leib Bloch (1860–1930), of Telz. Bloch sought to integrate the teachings of Luzzatto and medieval sources (especially

[37] Leibovitz, *Da'at Hokhma u-Mussar*, vol. IV, 300.
[38] Fraenkel, *Nefesh HaTzimtzum*, vol. II, 106–118.

Gikatila's *Sha'arei Orah*) within a stalwart ideology that could withstand the pressures of secularization in its various forms. More significantly, he mobilized the idea of parallelism between the material and supernal world to provide a metaphysical backdrop for the *lomdut* revolution. According to his teaching, Talmudic observations on human psychology (central for the legal and interpersonal issues that are found in the Talmudic tractates focused on in Lithuanian Yeshivas) reflect the rabbinic sages' precise perception of the supernal roots of human processes. Therefore, the role of the Talmudic exegete is to reconstruct this process with maximal finesse.

Furthermore, Bloch attributes modern science and technology to the partial discovery of this secret dimension of reality: 'in recent generations we have seen several new inventions that have caused a worldwide revolution by finding and inventing hidden and wonderful forces of nature... yet all that has been revealed till now is only a drop in the sea in face of the mysteries of nature that have not yet been revealed'. True to his basically conservative stance, Bloch minimizes the import of modernity by claiming that earlier generations knew many 'wonderful powers' that have been forgotten. This argument tallies with his general adjuration to trust in the power of the Talmudic sages to penetrate the inner dimension of reality. It is not surprising that Bloch concludes this particular address from 1927 (which is in turn highly representative of his thought), with a critique of the Zionists, who attempt to bring redemption on the basis of our limited present-day concepts of the term, oblivious of its hidden nature, as a reflection of God's primal thought (preexistent to the world itself).[39]

Telz was where the above-mentioned Elyashiv acquired his initial training. Indeed, Bloch recorded some of his dialogue with his elder colleague, especially pertaining to the writings of Luzzatto (toward whom Elyashiv was reserved). Elyashiv's extensive and highly erudite writing can be divided into two stages. At first, he explicitly strove to synthesize the teachings of Luria, in their various renditions, with those of R. Eliyahu of Vilna (while incorporating a surprising amount of medieval Jewish philosophy). One book from this early period (within the series *Leshem Shvo ve-Ahlama*; see Exodus 28, 19) was *Haqdamot u-She'arim* (Introductions and Gates).[40] This slim, relatively systematic volume joined other

[39] Bloch, *Shi'urei Da'at*, vol. III, 56, 65–66. The kabbalistic dimension becomes more explicit with the progression of Bloch's thought.

[40] In tracing the diachronic progression of Elyashiv's writing, mere print history is insufficient, as each volume is multilayered, containing dated and undated portions from various periods.

introductions to Kabbalah written in the Lithuanian world, such as *Klalei Hathalat Ha-Hokhma* (Principles of the Beginning of Wisdom), penned by none other than Salanter's nephew, Aryeh Leib Lipkin (1840–1902). The main difference between the two books (besides the superiority of Elyashiv's analytics and the scope of topics covered) was R. Aryeh Leib's extensive integration of Luzzatto's system.

The far lengthier work from Elyashiv's earlier period, *Drushei 'Olam ha-Tohu* (Homilies on the World of Chaos), is a dense, ambitious attempt to provide a history of evil and its defeat, from the breaking of the vessels and Adam's sin through to the postmessianic period and the resurrection. Strikingly, Elyashiv engages in repeated critiques of any attempts to blur the distinction between the sacred and the profane, although the import of redemption is the transformation of the lower worlds within the divine realm. This stance was closely related to his near espousal of Hai Ricci's literal interpretation of *tzimzum*. For Elyashiv, premature attempts at rectifying evil account for some of the cardinal failures and setbacks of human history (such as the Talmudic *pardes* tale). It is quite clear that these diatribes reflect Elyashiv's recorded debate with the above-mentioned Hertz, as well as a probable, less explicit exchange with his erstwhile study partner, R. Avraham Itzhak Kook.[41] This dialogue with kabbalists located in Palestine naturally intensified after Elyashiv's own move to Jerusalem in 1924. One should also note that Elyashiv shared Kook's propensity toward recording revelatory experiences, though as he was writing for publication, he was more reserved in describing them.

It was through a fellow-immigrant from Lithuania, R. Menahem Menkhin Halperin of Grodno (1834–1924) that Elyashiv came to possess the library of Rashashian Kabbalah. This textual encounter effected the transition to his second period. Increasingly, Elyashiv strove to balance profound reverence toward Rashash and his followers with an attempt to preserve an independent stance:

> regarding the words of the holy R. Shalom [Shar'abi] may his merit protect us, here I will state that while in truth many of the teachings from his holy words are fundamental and essential regarding the depth of *Torat ha-Ari* [Lurianic doctrine] without which it is difficult to grasp the truth; in general his approach is but one facet in *Torat ha-Ari*, and it is possible to understand them properly, in my opinion, with other approaches as well.[42]

41 Garb, 'Shamanism', 184–185.
42 Ehrenfeld, *Yira'ukha im-Shemesh*, translated and discussed in Rosenfeld, 'A Tribute'.

Finally, we are indebted to Elyashiv for preserving, in a gloss, the following tradition from Salanter (thus demonstrating that the latter was associated with Kabbalah despite claims to the contrary), on the imperative to disclose secrets in the late modern period:

> Permission has been given to all those who yearn to cling to the living God and occupy themselves with the wisdom of truth [Kabbalah] to enter... (And whoever delves deeply into it will be enlightened and find and all this was not the case prior to the year 5660 [1840]. For till then it was still obscure and sealed. And only for the chosen few, thus I have heard in the name of the Gaon, the *hasid* [in the nonsociological sense of piety], R. Israel Salanter of blessed memory.)[43]

We should turn now to the spread of Kabbalah beyond the relatively limited audience of the traditional Jewish world, providing a counterpart to the almost entirely insular Lithuanian center. One should commence with the world of German Jewry (in which Scholem grew up). The eminent neo-Kantian philosopher Hermann Cohen (1842–1918), after his turn to Jewish concerns, wondered whether the Kabbalah, for all of its complex dialectic, rests content with truth or seeks to soar above and thus displace it (and by doing so falls into illogical mysticism).[44] However, his close student Franz Rosenzweig (1886–1929) went much further in both study and integration in his complex theology. Within his view of the process leading to the messianic redemption, the medieval notion of the union of God and the *Shekhina* played a significant role. Furthermore, as Benjamin Pollock has argued, the Lurianic (and thus modern) trope of *tzimtzum*, understood as withdrawal of the divine inwards, operates on several registers in Rosenzweig's magnum opus, the *Star of Redemption* (Der Stern Der Erlösung). Besides explaining the possibility of human freedom (and thus underpinning ethics as such), *tzimtzum* is a model for similar, necessary withdrawals of the world and self (part of the triangular model of the *Star*). Furthermore, it represents the contracting force of the Jews as opposed to the expanding force of the Christians (whom Rosenzweig accorded an important role in the messianic process).[45] This consideration of Kabbalah (mediated by figures

43 Elyashiv, *Leshem Shvu ve-Ahlama: Drushi 'Olam ha-Tohu*, pt. 1, 38B.

44 Cohen, *Religion der Vernunft*, 480 (and the more prosaic translation offered in Kaplan, *The Religion of Reason*, 414).

45 Pollock, 'The Kabbalistic Problem' (a similar notion of *tzimtzum* as enabling freedom, for all of its consequences, is central in the Holocaust theology of Talmudic scholar David Weiss-Halivni, another important immigrant to America and later Israel). For an innovative discussion of Rosenzweig's incorporation of Kabbalah, see Idel, *Old Worlds, New Mirrors*, 159–167.

such as Franz Joseph Molitor) in Weimar discourses on messianism and redemption of the world in the more general sense can also be observed in the thought of Ernest Bloch (1885–1977), who belonged to Rosenzweig's circle and influenced his thought, as well as that of Walter Benjamin.[46] In this context of the Weimar cultural renaissance, one should also mention the highly innovative composer Arnold Schoenberg (1874–1951) and his 1938 composition around the *Kol Nidre* (All Vows) service of Yom-Kippur, which he began with a text, narrated by a 'Rabbi', on the Kabbalah's 'legend' of the crushing of the light into atomic sparks hidden in the world. In this scientific reinterpretation of the Lurianic theme of the breaking of the vessels, Schoenberg was probably more influenced by the new discoveries in physics than by thinkers such as del Medigo.[47]

Figure 4 Franz Kafka. Source: Available at https://commons.wikimedia.org/wiki/File:Kafka.jpg Accessed 25.4.2020. Public domain.

Another major central European Jewish cultural figure somewhat influenced by Kabbalah was Franz Kafka (1883–1924). While the cultural and literary critic George Steiner perhaps exaggerates when describing him as a

[46] Levy, 'Utopia and Reality'; Mertens, 'This Still Remarkable Book', esp. 178–179. On Rosenzweig, Benjamin, Bloch and models of messianism, see Wolfson, 'Not Yet Now'.

[47] HaCohen, *The Music Libel*, 330–339.

'modern Kabbalist', there is clear evidence of the influence of the tales of R. Nahman (as mediated by Buber) on his sense of existential searching. Likewise, his 1917–1918 Zürau aphorisms echo Hasidic teachings on divine immanence and thus the illusory nature of evil.[48]

Moving to the margins of the Jewish world, but still in Central Europe, one must consider the new psychoanalytic movement. While kabbalistic influence on Sigmund Freud belongs to the very realm of fantasies and projections explored by psychotherapists, the modest effect of Jewish (alongside many other forms of) mysticism on Carl Gustav Jung (1875–1961, who should be seen as all but a co-founder of the movement rather than as a mere disciple) is clear. The reverse influence of Jung and his disciple Erich Neumann (1905–1960), who immigrated to Israel in 1934, on scholarly and popular discourse in Kabbalah in recent decades is much clearer. In any case, one should be less concerned with Jung's relatively sparse textual borrowings mediated by kabbalistic Christian and alchemical writings, or by academic scholars such as Scholem (with whom Jung interacted somewhat in the famous Eranos conventions in Switzerland). Rather, one should focus on the following vision (from 1944), recorded in his spiritual autobiography, *Memories, Dreams, Reflections* and eerily reminiscent of the *tiqqun hazot* rite:

> Towards evening I would fall asleep, and my sleep would last until about midnight. Then I would come to myself and lie awake for about an hour, but in an utterly transformed state. It was as if I were in an ecstasy. I felt as though I were floating in space, as though I were safe in the womb of the universe – in a tremendous void, but filled with the highest possible feeling of happiness . . .
>
> Everything around me seemed enchanted. At this hour of the night the nurse brought me some food . . . For a time it seemed to me that she was an old Jewish woman. Much older than she actually was, and that she was preparing ritual kosher dishes for me. When I looked at her, she seemed to have a blue halo around her head. I myself was, so it seemed, in the Pardes Rimmonim, the garden of pomegranates, and the wedding of Tiferet with Malchuth [*Malkhut*] was taking place. Or else I was Rabbi Simon ben Jochai [Bar Yohai], whose wedding in the afterlife was being celebrated. It was the mystic marriage as it appears in the Cabalistic tradition. I cannot tell you how wonderful it was. I could only think continually: 'Now this is the garden of pomegranates! Now this is the marriage of Malcuth with

[48] Kafka, *The Zuerau Aphorisms*, no. 85 (84 in the Hofmann translation). Steiner, *After Babel*, 67; Oron, 'Kafka und Nachman Von Bratzlav'; Grözinger, *Kafka und die Kabbala*, 184–196 (and 64–79, 146–163).

Tifereth!' I do not know exactly what part I played in it. At bottom it was myself; I was the marriage . . .[49]

In other areas of Europe, one can note the still-active magical, occult groups based in England.[50] One of the more important figures who defected from the *Hermetic Order of the Golden Dawn* was the Irish poet William Butler Yeats (1865–1939), who had an early interest in Kabbalah, mediated through various sources such as the writings of Blake.[51] Yeats (like other members of the order) initially belonged to the Theosophical Society. As Huss has shown, besides numerous adherents in Europe and the United States, the Jewish theosophists also had offshoots in South Africa, Iraq and especially India, whose translation of the *Idrot* (into Judeo-Arabic), in 1887, had aroused the ire of rabbinical authorities in the Near East, including R. Eliyahu Mani. One of the issues requiring further explanation was the influence of Kabbalah of non-Jewish Indian spiritual leaders such as Sri Aurobindo Ghose (1872–1950), who became (1906) a devotee of 'the [incarnated divine] Mother', the Paris-born Rachel Mirra Alfassa (1878–1973), a disciple of Max Theon (1848–1927), a Polish-born Jew (who may well have been exposed to Hasidism) who led the *Mouvement Cosmique*.[52] Pascal Themanlys (1909–2000), son of Theon's student David Themnalys, led the Israeli group of students (known as the *Argaman* [crimson] circle, which is still active).[53]

Speaking of France, one should mention the influence of kabbalistic speculations on language on the artistic movement, inaugurated straight after World War II, known as *lettrism*, whose approach included deconstruction of words into more basic components, as well as its earlier Surrealistic antecedents (especially Antonin Artaud, 1896–1948).[54] Finally, one of the less-studied proliferations is the role of Kabbalah in the mystical-spiritual revival in Russia, which was heavily damaged, yet not entirely removed, by the Communist revolution of October 1917. As part of the mystical awakening of the 'silver age', unconventional yet influential Russian Orthodox thinkers such as the strongly Judeophilic Valdmir Sergeyevich Soloviev (1853–1900) betray substantial kabbalistic influence (again mediated

[49] Jung, *Memories, Dreams, Reflections*, 324–325.
[50] These circles were pioneers in translation of the *Zohar* into English.
[51] Goldreich, *Automatic Writing*, 355–365.
[52] Huss, 'The Sufi Society'; Huss, 'Qabbalah'. My thanks to Peter Heehs and Orit Sen-Gupta for their comments on Aurobindo. Another instance is the commentary by the later New Age guru Baghwan Shree Rajneesh (1931–1990, aka Osho) on Buber's rendition of Hasidic tales.
[53] Verman, *The History and Varieties of Jewish Meditation*, 174–176.
[54] Sjöberg, 'Writing in Secret'; Knapp, *Antonin Artaud*, esp. 27–28, 73, 96, 140.

by Knorr), especially in the former's doctrine of the divine feminine (which may well have influenced Bialik's poetics of the *Shekhina*).[55] Like Jiri Langer, Soloviev and his followers were taken by what they saw as the positive attitude of kabbalistic writings toward human sexuality.[56]

Of special interest is the doctrine of Gregory von Moebes (1868–1934), one of the more active esotericists of the last days of the Russian Empire (who was arrested in 1926 by the Soviet secret police). Von Moebes claimed that while Jewish kabbalists restricted themselves to the *Sefirot* and avoided discussing the *Ein-Sof*, the Rosicrucians discussed the structures mediating between these two aspects (somewhat similarly to Sarugian Kabbalah). This was not at all the first time that kabbalistic Christians claimed an attainment superior to that of their Jewish sources.[57] This brief survey should suffice to demonstrate the transformation of Kabbalah into a significant presence in varied cultural, spiritual, intellectual and artistic domains, throughout Europe (with branches in the colonies), and far beyond the enclosure of the traditional Jewish world.[58] Yet tragically, the heart of this flourishing creativity took place in the very centers decimated by the war initiated by the Nazis, who persecuted some of the figures mentioned above and shortly below (while others, such as Jung, came close to sympathizing with them).[59]

THE MODERNIZATION OF HASIDISM

The proliferation and popularization of Hasidic thought in the early twentieth century occupies a median position between the two cases discussed just now: traditional and nontraditional Kabbalah. On the one hand it is rooted in internal debates and interpretations couched in highly traditionalist terms. On the other hand, in metropolises such as Warsaw and Vienna, processes of modernization promoted exposure to (and at times influence on) extra-Jewish developments. With this backdrop in mind, we shall proceed from the more traditional circles, through Orthodox (at this stage

[55] Bar-Yosef, *Mysticism*, 311–329.

[56] Kornblatt, 'Russian Religious Thought', esp. 90; Rubin, *Holy Russia*, esp. 26–31, 48–51, 79–81.

[57] Burmistrov, 'Kabbalah and Secret Societies', 111–115 (see 119–121, on anti-Semitism in later groups of this nature and 122–123 on historiosophical explanations of the fall of the Empire).

[58] Here one can add *The Dybbuk* (Between Two Worlds) by S. Ansky (Sholyme Zanvyl Rapoport). This 1913 tale of exorcism, based on the author's ethnographic work, was swiftly translated into Hebrew by Bialik and received numerous theatrical and cinematic adaptations throughout the century.

[59] Psychoanalytically speaking, Jung's above-quoted vision (toward the end of the war) around his nurse as an old Jewish woman (perhaps representing the *Shekhina*) can be seen as compensating for guilt feelings around this episode.

this term becomes relevant) expositors to figures situated within the secular (e.g. Zionist) domain.

One should begin with considering the role of Kabbalah in the larger Hasidic groups, which wielded some political power in Poland in the first part of the century (especially around the formation of the *Agudat Israel*, Union of Israel, party in 1912). As we have seen R. Yehuda Leib Alter inherited the Ger dynasty, and more generally the major branch of the Kotzk tradition, from his grandfather, R. Yitzhak Meir. Alter's early writing, as exhibited in his *Sefer ha-Liqutim* (Book of Compilations) was heavily indebted to the *Zohar* and its commentaries and the Lurianic corpus (and includes a rather lengthy commentary on *Tikkunei Zohar*). However, in his later *Sfat Emet* (Language of Truth), recording sermons delivered between 1871 and 1904, Alter shifted to reworking core elements of kabbalistic thought for a wider audience in pithy, poetic statements, reflecting far less engagement with the textual tradition.[60] This discourse, more ideological than scholastic in its nature, focuses on essential Jewish identity (focused on the heart but expressed bodily in circumcision), and its relationship with sacred space (the Land of Israel, the Sabbath). The focus on the Land of Israel was not perceived as contradicting Alter's opposition to the first stirrings of Zionism (following the 1897 first Zionist conference at Basel). Actually, Alter's perception (following Maharal of Prague) of the land and people of Israel as transnatural entities fueled his opposition to secular-political return to the Holy Land.

Both Alter's stress on the Land of Israel and his effort to popularize and psychologize core kabbalistic teachings were shared by R. Shmuel Borenstein (1856–1926) of Sochathov, grandson of the *rebbe* of Kotzk. They also shared a strong emphasis on the centrality of Talmudic learning, which Borenstein saw as a route to obtaining mystical powers. However, even this moderated form of mysticism is not typical of the development of Ger and other demographically and politically prominent Hasidic dynasties, such as Vizhnitz, Zanz and Belz. Indeed, Assaf has pointed at a growing spiritual malaise amongst certain Hasidic leaders, such as Yitzhak Nahum Twersky of Shpikov (1882–1942), who led a branch of the Chernobyl dynasty. This is what he had to say of idealization of Hasidism by outsiders: 'Most of the books . . . who have begun to deal in recent years with Hasidism as a system and movement are so remote from life and reality . . . The light of Hasidism

[60] Jacobson, *Truth, Faith and Holiness*, 425–443. For an English-language compilation, see Green, *The Language of Truth* (and for new material, Reiser and Mayse, *Language of Truth*).

has dimmed . . . and it has atrophied, continually declining . . . until it is now no more than a debased coin.'[61] Thus, even if one does not concur with a general theory of the decline of Hasidic mystical energy, one can note processes of relative dekabbalization similar to those that we have encountered above amongst some of Salanter's followers. These joined the sheer impact of secularization, moving many Jews (especially immigrants to the new Jewish mega-center of New York) entirely outside the ambit of traditional Jewish learning and practice.[62]

Predictably, the main exception here was Habad-Lubavitch. The fifth *rebbe*, R. Shalom Dovber (1860–1920, Rashab), revived the complexity and profundity of his legacy, introducing extremely lengthy discussions of the higher aspects of the divine world, especially in terms of will and pleasure. His delving into the deeper, unconscious layers of the psyche can be at least partly attributed to his treatment by Sigmund Freud and his associates in 1903.[63] However, Rashab also joined Alter not only in opposition to Zionism, but also in institution-building. The most striking example was his establishment, in 1897, of *Tomkhei Temimim* (Supporters of the Pure), the first Yeshiva incorporating extensive Hasidic study in its curriculum. The period of Rashab's son and successor, R. Yosef Yitzhak (1880–1950, Rayatz) was troubled by the 1917 Russian revolution (leading to his imprisonment and exile to Siberia), ending more than a century of cooperation between Habad and the Russian Empire, and later by his narrow escape from the Nazis in 1940, which led to the relocation in America (whose profound consequences shall be described below). Thus, it is hard to say that he contributed greatly to the theoretical development of Habad doctrine. Indeed, the relative decline of spiritual intensity in Habad in the transition from the Rashab to the Rayatz led R. Avraham Dov Ber Levin (c.1862–1938), known as 'the angel', to break off and establish a mystical-ascetic fellowship, remnants of which are still active in the United States. Interestingly, Levin declared his sympathy with the breakaway Kapost branch of Habad.

However, Rayatz was a pivotal figure in the crystallization of Habad identity, interlaced with an ideology in the modern sense (just then being explicated by the sociologist Karl Mannheim), through the following literary and organizational activities: construction of an entire Hasidic

[61] Assaf, *Untold Tales*, 206–235 (the quote is from 221).

[62] I myself have heard sad accounts of kabbalistic manuscripts languishing, at best, in the homes of disinterested descendants. Thus, secularization also affected the scope of material available to us.

[63] Berke, *The Hidden Freud* (cf. Katz-Balakirsky, 'A Rabbi').

historiography (much of it of dubious accuracy), the establishment of a highly active publishing house (in 1942), the commissioning of the encyclopedic *Sefer ha-Nigunim* (The Book of Melodies), the maintenance of a Hasidic underground in the face of Communist persecution and the beginnings (with the move to North America) of a program of outreach to secular Jews, that he accorded messianic significance. One should add that the popularization of Hasidic melodies, some of which were explicitly assigned kabbalistic-meditative significance, also aroused the interest of pioneers of Jewish ethnomusicology, in Russia and later (with government support), in Israel.[64]

Of far more minor historical significance, yet of phenomenological importance, was the further development of Bratzlav Hasidism. Here one can trace two lineages, one clinging to the sacred sites of the movement in the Ukraine, and the other immigrating (like the kabbalists discussed above) to Palestine. Amongst the first branch one can mention R. Levi Itzhak Bander (1897–1989), student of R. Avraham Hazan (1849–1917), the son of R. Nahman of Tulchin. Bander, who immigrated to Israel after the war, taught the leaders of various contemporary offshoots of Bratzlav. The second branch, characterized by its espousal of old-new sacral sites in the Land of Israel, was led by R. Avraham Sternhartz (1862–1955, grandson of R. Nahman of Tsharin) and his student R. Gedalyah Aharon Qening (1921–1980), who established a group in Safed after arriving in 1935. On an ideational level, the latter's main contribution was his *Hayye ha-Nefesh* (life of the soul), a defense (mostly responding to R. Hayyim Itzkovitz's critique) of the practice and discourse of near deification of R. Nahman (which intensified during the course of the century, as one can see on screen in Gidi Dar's highly acclaimed 2004 movie *ha-Usphizin*). The bifurcation between the two branches was clearly expressed in the sharp debate around the theoretical importance (as the Communist regime rendered it all but impossible in practice) of pilgrimage to R. Nahman's gravesite in Uman, as opposed to the renewed popularity of Meron, or, alternatively, Jerusalemite sites, such as the Western Wall.[65] This seemingly minor debate reflects not only the shift from Europe to Palestine, but also the naissance of regional subidentities around the sacral sites of the Holy Land (see further in the conclusion).

[64] On Rayatz's historiography in context, see Rapoport-Albert, 'Hagiography with Footnotes'. On outreach see Greenberg, 'Redemption after Holocaust'.

[65] This topic has been partly discussed by Mark, 'Mi-Ron' (see also Meir, 'R. Nathan Sternhartz's Liqquṭei Tefilot', 83–84). There is valuable material and argumentation in internal Bratzlav sources that I am not at liberty to cite.

Generally speaking, processes of modernizing creativity were more likely to occur amongst Hasidic figures not strikingly aligned with a particular dynasty (compare to the case of Spielmann). One of these was R. Menahem Ekstein (1884–1928), a follower of the kabbalistically oriented Dzikov dynasty (a branch of Ropshitz), who operated in Hungary and later Vienna. In his well-received 1921 book *Tena'ei ha-Nefesh le-Hasagat ha-Hasidut* (Mental Conditions for Achieving Hasidism), Eckstein presents techniques of guided imagery drawn from extra-Jewish sources, such as hypnosis. Tellingly, a lengthy induction aimed at shifting the practitioner's perspective away from the ego includes visualization of 'the entire earth as if we are seeing it from a distance, with all five continents and the oceans surrounding them. We will also visualize all the nations dwelling in all parts of the world, according to their languages and borders, and the number of people of each nation and language.'[66] Here too, the effect of globalization and what was later termed 'the whole earth image' (facilitated by space travel) are apparent.

In Warsaw we had R. Qalman Qalonymus Shapira of Piaseczno (1889–1943), who attempted (like the above-mentioned Roth) to renew the format of fellowships devoted to intensive mystical practice, as outlined in his *Bnei Mahshava Tova* (Sons of Good Thought). Shapira, who shared Epstein's interest in hypnosis, records visionary trance-like states, in which he sees a burning altar while flipping somersaults.[67] Shapira's homilies, delivered in the Warsaw ghetto during the Holocaust, represent harrowing documentation of the trials of religious imagination in unimaginable adversity: after stating that often there are tribulations in which the Jews suffer, yet their purpose is to destroy the evil amongst the nations, 'as we saw in the previous war, when [the people of] Israel suffered, and later we saw that this was from heaven, in order to bring to an end the evil kingdom with the hater of Israel, the Czar', Shapira delves into the *Derekh 'Etz Hayyim*, in order to show that the root of evil, the breaking of the vessels, was also directed by the attribute of *Hesed.* Yet then, he shifts from the mode of kabbalistic-historiosophical explanation, through near despair to quietist acceptance:

> Every heart is torn to splinters . . . and especially as the tribulations persist, then even one who initially strengthened himself and the rest of Israel, also tires of strengthening himself and wearies of consoling. For even if he wishes to make an effort and say some words of consolation and encouragement, he lacks words for during the long period of tribulations he has

[66] *Tene'ai Ha-Nefesh*, translated and discussed in Reiser, *Imagery Techniques*, 272.

[67] For trance states and somersaults (including earlier research on this remarkable somatic practice), see Leshem, 'Flipping into Ecstasy'.

already said and repeated all that he could say and the words are stale and have no effect on himself or on his listeners . . . we have also to say . . . the entire world is God's, we are also not our own, but only God's, we came to the world through His will and our existence is through his will, and we will also go to the next world through his will, and what God wills is itself the good, and we are not permitted to balk . . . at his will . . . when one also lowers one's head and says 'He is God and He will do what is best in his eyes' (Samuel 1, 3, 18), then the bitter feeling of the evil and pain of the suffering is abated and weakened and one can suffer more . . . now we have the additional work of overcoming our own falling and breaking of spirit, and to be strong with God. Yet it is a very very difficult matter, for the suffering is too great to suffer . . . But when many of Israel are burnt alive for God's name and are killed and slaughtered just for being Jews, then we must at least endure this trial.[68]

A somewhat less Orthodox figure, working in Warsaw and sharing Shapira's ecstatic (his own choice of words!) tendencies, his aspirations (including repeated attempts to found a mystical fellowship) and his tragic fate was his admirer Hillel Zeitlin (1871–1942). After an early Nietzschean-period, Zeitlin became highly active in publicizing a romanticized version of Kabbalah and Hasidism in the Yiddish press, in both poetry and prose. He also visited Jerusalem in 1925 and was greatly taken by Kook, whose poetic aspirations he shared (despite a subtle critique). Like other figures with Zionist sympathies, he took part in the neo-Zoharic revival, composing lengthy texts in Zoharic Aramaic. Like Kook, Zeitlin responded to World War I and its globalizing effects with texts based on what he experienced as messages from his soul and directed at the nations of the world:

In these days of poverty and distress for many peoples, God has blessed you, you Americans, with wealth and calm and plenty. And what do you do with your wealth? You add wealth to wealth and cast your invisible rule over many nations, becoming the judges of states and peoples: who to lend to and who to cease lending to . . . and even if the sin of the workers is smaller than the sin of the plutocrats, they have also stumbled, in joining the demand to close the gates of America to strangers and 'foreigners'. For the gates of your country are closed and locked, sons of America, to the miserable myriads who ask: open gates.[69]

[68] Reiser (ed. and trans.), *Sermons*, 276–281. It is well worth seeing his discussion of *tzimtzum*, which I have skipped in my quote and translation.

[69] Zeitlin, *Sifran shel-Yehidim*, 162–163. On Zeitlin and his visions, see Meir, 'The Book of Visions'. For an English-language compilation, see Green, *Hasidic Spirituality*.

A different, activist, response to the Holocaust, renouncing former opposition to Zionism, is found in *Em HaBanim Semeha* (The Mother of the Sons Is Joyful; Psalms 113, 9), by the Slovakian R. Yissakhar Shlomo Teichthal (1885–1944). Kabbalistic ideas, in popular, sermon-style form, feature in this work prominently, as in the notion (alluded to in the title) of the Holy Land as the mother of the Jewish people. Indeed, the author's imagination of her joy in the return of her sons motivated the composition of the book.[70] The most innovative move found in this work is what Isaac Hershkovitz has aptly termed an esoteric view of redemption. According to this approach, God disguised the redemptive move of the return to the land in a secular form in order to hide it from the resistance of the Other Side (which, as Teichthal deduces from Lurianic sources, will be mitigated by the sacrificial martyrdom of the Holocaust victims).[71] This theology of the redemptive value of secular Zionism tallies with that of Kook, although in all likelihood he did not read the latter's works.

The above-mentioned Zeitlin was but one of a series of Central European intellectuals who became attracted to Hasidism. From the point of view of cultural history, the most important of these was the poet and journalist Georg Mordekhai (Jiri) Langer (1894–1943), who became for a while (1913–1918) a Hassid of R. Issakhar-Dov Rokeah the elder (1854–1926), the *rebbe* of Belz (Galicia), whom as we have seen, spearheaded the resistance to secular modernization. In other words, he was an early exemplar of the phenomenon of returnees to Orthodox Judaism, *Ba'alei Teshuva* (Repentants), which grew steadily stronger in the second half of the century.[72] His 1937 autobiographical account (translated into English as *Nine Gates to the Hasidic Mysteries*) can be seen as part of the evolving ethnography of the Hasidic world. After returning to his home town of Prague, he joined the circle of Kafka, moving to Palestine at the end of his life. Yet his greatest achievement was his 1923 *L'Erotique de la Kabbale* (The Eroticism of Kabbalah), already incorporating psychoanalytic theory and addressing a domain that moved steadily toward the center of the research agenda in the course of the century (including the question of homoeroticism).

And here we move beyond the Orthodox world, to the secular proponents of 'Neo-Hasidism'. This cultural-literary movement commenced with Yitzhak Leib Peretz (1852–1915), one of the founders of modern Yiddish literature

[70] Teichthal, *Em HaBanim*, 36.

[71] Hershkovitz, 'The Vision of Redemption', 145–149, 191. I do not entirely agree with Hershkovitz's unconsciously Straussian reading of the text.

[72] See also Ross, *A Beloved-Despised Tradition*, 85.

(who characteristically described the Hasidim as champions of the common people). Niham Ross has contextualized this trend in terms of the fin-de-siècle neo-mystical revival (especially in Eastern Europe), as well as Nietzschean vitalism.[73] Foremost amongst these cultural agents was Martin Buber (1878–1965), yet another immigrant (1938) to Jerusalem, and a professor at its Hebrew University (though not in Jewish Studies). Beginning with an interest in Christian and especially German mysticism (Meister Eckhart and Jacob Boehme), Buber incorporated Hasidism in his existential and dialogic philosophies (which do not concern us here). In this early period, Buber shared the romanticizing tendencies of figures such as Zeitlin, and in both cases, R. Nahman of Bratzlav was relocated from the near margins to the center of the Hasidic universe (as in Buber's first book, published in 1906). Buber was a pioneer of the notion that Hasidism meets 'the crisis of Western man that has become fully manifest in our [late modern] age'.[74] His reconstruction of Hasidic life, based on very little direct exposure and heavily based on reworking of the Hasidic tales compiled in the nineteenth century, foregrounds ideas such as hallowing the everyday, overcoming the separation between the holy and the profane and more generally transformative and immediate lived experience. Besides the clear influence of Christian mysticism, Buber's coining of new, quasi-kabbalistic terms reflects the powerful influence of the post-Nietzschean *Lebensphilosophie* (life philosophy) current in Germany at the time.[75] Despite the increasing distance of this construction from theosophical-theurgical (as in Lurianic), magical and ascetic elements readily found in the Hasidic library (a removal that understandably aroused the ire of Scholem), Buber's narratives have had a continued effect on both popular and academic perceptions of Kabbalah.[76] Certainly, he was a pioneer of the comparative move, drawing Kabbalah into the ambit of world mysticism. Finally, he was the first to call attention to the potential of Hasidic forms of community for the social sciences.[77]

After the Holocaust, romanticization of Hasidism (epitomized by Elie Wiesel's 1972 *Souls on Fire*, that actually follows Jacob Minkin's tellingly titled *The Romance of Hasidism*, published in 1935), became part of the

[73] Ibid., 64–65, 95–107, 491–507. Nietzsche and his Hebrew-writing followers also significantly influenced Kook.

[74] Buber, *Hasidism and Modern Man*, 27.

[75] From a large literature, see Urban, *Aesthetics of Renewal*, esp. 77–107.

[76] Katz, *Post-Holocaust Dialogues*, 52–93.

[77] Mendes-Flohr, *From Mysticism to Dialogue*, esp. 115–126. For a contemporary representative of this move (though with far more recourse to textual scholarship), see Wexler, *Mystical Sociology*.

cultural project of placing the Holocaust (alongside nostalgia for the decimated world of Eastern European Jewry) in the forefront of American Jewish identity.[78] This process, for which literature was a major agent, was increasingly institutionalized both in academic structures and in museum exhibitions. To these English-language endeavors one should add the Yiddish discourse on what the Hasidim themselves term the *khurbn* (destruction), rather than the Holocaust. As Justin Jaron Lewis has shown, the very choice to use Yiddish (and its indigenous terms) is an act of defiance, contrasting strongly with the supplanting of this culture by what (following the French philosopher Jean Baudrillard) one could describe as its English-language simulation. Despite this divergence, one can deduce from Lewis' own findings that the Yiddish writers and their English-language counterparts have in common an attempt, clearly influenced by the Holocaust, to present the Hasidic masters as fallible, human, individuals, rather than wonder-workers.[79]

Likewise, in Israel, figures such as the educator Yosef Shechter (1901–1994, who also founded a fellowship, as it were), cultivated what they perceived as universalistic elements of Hasidism (again compared to Far Eastern mysticism) as a cure for the ills of alienated consumer society. In this move they were joined by Scholem's rebellious student, the short-lived Yosef Weiss (1918–1969), who offered an existential interpretation on Hasidism and did much to call attention to the writings of R. Nahman. It is to these two post-Holocaust centers, both continuing certain elements of European Kabbalah and adding new variations in response to the new global reality, that we shall now turn.

THE NEW CENTERS OF KABBALAH

The Holocaust decimated the great majority of the European centers described just now. As noted above, its traumatic effect on the worlds of Kabbalah was soon joined by the forced relocation of the communities of the Near East and North Africa, who encountered militant socialism upon arrival in the new state of Israel. Counter to common wisdom and its assumptions, apart from episodes such as the employment of magical

[78] Heinze, *Jews and the American Soul*, 330–339. Here one should mention the descriptions of Hasidic and kabbalistic figures and beliefs in the works of Nobel laureate Isaac Bashevis Singer (1902–1991), and especially his portrayal of Sabbateanism in his 1955 novel *Satan in Goray*.

[79] Lewis, 'Miracles and Martyrdom', 231–232, 238–241.

techniques in face of the swift advance of the German forces led by Erwin Rommel toward Palestine in 1942, kabbalists as such did not greatly respond to the annihilation of European Jewry and the resultant theological challenges.[80] Rather, the focus was on rebuilding, both in Israel and in North America, where several Hasidic leaders took refuge. Geopolitically, this shift in location and culture ended a long period of activity within imperial settings (including mandatory Palestine), and repositioned Kabbalah in the 'marketplace of ideas' characteristic of liberal democracies.

It is thus most effective to consider the two centers in tandem, while highlighting the bifurcation between them. Only then one may focus on the Sephardic stream and the Kook circle that both operated almost entirely in Hebrew and in Israel. One clear example of dialogue across continents and between streams is that of the small coterie of Lithuanian kabbalists. The above-mentioned Dessler arrived in the new Haredi town of Bnei Brak in the year (1948) of Israel's declaration of independence. After his early death, his approach was developed by R. Hayyim Freidlander (1923–1986), who later, like his teacher, was appointed as *masgiah* (spiritual director) in the flagship Yeshiva Ponevezh. In his multivolume *Siftei Hayyim* (Lips of Life), R. Freidlander especially drew on the thought of Maharal and of Luzzatto (whose manuscripts he published in scholarly editions).

This process, of transformation of *Musar* into more abstract, theological, at times ideological discourse, can be observed in the case of R. Yitzhak Hutner (1906–1980), a prominent graduate of Slovodka Yeshiva (a not very kabbalistic yet highly psychological *Musar* flagship), who had also learnt with Kook during his prewar stays in Palestine, relocating in New York in 1934. While Hutner was also greatly indebted to Maharal, he subtly camouflaged kabbalistic teachings (especially drawn from the writings of R. Eliyahu of Vilna) in his meticulously crafted discourses. He also was in dialogue with Hasidic thinkers, incorporating inter alia the teachings of the Izbiche-Radzin school. Upon his immigration to Israel in 1970, Hutner had a transformative effect on two figures: R. Shlomo Wolbe (1914–2005), a student of R. Yeruham Leibovitz of Mir, was amongst the many graduates of this Yeshiva who survived the Holocaust, and arrived in Israel in 1947. Soon becoming a prominent teacher of *Musar*, he shifted to a far greater involvement with Kabbalah upon becoming Hutner's student. A similar process can be

[80] Harari, 'Three Charms for Killing Hitler'. On the kabbalistic-Hasidic response to the Holocaust, unearthing rather rare texts, see Greenberg, 'Menahem Mendel Schneersohn's Response' (including an important note on the Schneerson-Wiesel dialogue); Greenberg, 'Hasidic Thought and the Holocaust'.

observed in the case of the younger R. Moshe Shapira (1935–2017), a leading student in the Hebron (relocated to Jerusalem after the 1929 massacre) Yeshiva, which had largely transplanted the Slovodka school to Palestine already in 1924. Shapira, who spent two years (1979–1981) in the United States, developed and popularized Hutner's method of concealing kabbalistic ideas in exoteric garb, this garment becoming thinner toward the end of his life.

R. Yosef Baer Halevi Soloveitchik (1903–1993), a friend of Hutner's (from their prewar Berlin period), with far more extensive secular-philosophical education, established himself as a major authority in Boston and in New York (Yeshiva University). This complex thinker seemingly upheld Halakhic Man (also the title of his main book), as opposed to *homo religious*, including the mystics. Yet in some of his writings one can discern an attempt to synthesize a philosophical version of Lithuanian texts such as *Nefesh ha-Hayyim* and the doctrine of Habad. However, this indebtedness to Kabbalah cannot be observed amongst his many successors in leadership of what came to be known as Modern Orthodoxy, neither in North America nor in Israel. In this respect, these followers reflect the general renitence toward overt kabbalistic exposition in the Lithuanian world. Certainly, towering scholar-leaders such as R. Avraham Yesha'ya Karelitz (1878–1953, known by the title of his works, *Hazon Ish*, One Man's Vision) in Bnei Brak (from 1933) and R. Aharon Kotler (1891–1962) in the United States did not encourage venturing far beyond the Talmudic curriculum (the former even critiqued *Musar*, while greatly respecting its proponents, up to and including Wolbe). In the conclusion to this chapter, we shall examine an even more pronounced example, that of R. Eli'ezer Menahem Man Shach (c.1898–2011), who among other things curtailed the activity of Wolbe, Shapira and another kabbalistically inclined teacher, R. Shimshon David Pinkus (1944–2011).

This guarded approach should be contrasted with the freer development of kabbalistic lore and practice in the postwar Hasidic world. The most prominent of American kabbalists was R. Menahem Mendel Schneerson (1902–1994), son-in-law and successor (1951) of R. Yosef Yitzhak Schneerson, who was in close dialogue with both Hutner and Soloveitchik, was the son of a highly learned kabbalist, R. Levi Yitzhak Schneerson (1878–1944).[81] Public attention (including that of some academics) has focused on his messianic

[81] On Habad's influence on Soloveitchik, see Wolfson, 'Eternal Duration'. For some earlier American developments, see Meir, 'The Beginnings of Kabbalah in America'; Margolin: 'The Directives of Rav Ashlag'.

self-perception (which was more openly voiced in his last years), practically expressed in his massive outreach programs and perhaps also in his hawkish political stance (commenting on the Israeli context, in close communication with leading diplomatic and military figures). Yet Wolfson has exposed the profundity and dialectical nature of his mystical teaching and its contribution to more universal themes (indeed Schneerson, who studied engineering at the Sorbonne before the war, was exceptional in the degree of his interest in the non-Jewish world).

Wolfson's discussion of Schneerson's perception of America is especially pertinent for the thrust of this section. As he puts it, again in dialectical terms: 'In the nonlocalized space of the messianic ideal, America occupies a special place.' As a result, while Schneerson joined the general twentieth-century revival of concern with the restoration of the temple (see also below), for him its location was to be the Habad headquarters in New York. Now adducing Schneerson himself (in a 1982 letter to President Ronald Reagan): 'More than ever before the civilized world of today will look to the United States of America for guidance as behooves the world's foremost Super Power – not merely in the ordinary sense of this term, but, even more importantly, as a moral and spiritual Super Power.' This locution expresses not only Schneerson's preoccupation of the theme of power (expressed inter alia in the militaristic trappings of his organization and court ritual), but more importantly, his conviction that spiritual values must perforce be clearly expressed in the material realm.[82]

Thus, a significant way of presenting his vast corpus, proposed by Reuven Hacohen Oria, is that Schneerson greatly developed Habad's a-cosmic inclination, leading toward a theology of manifestation of the *'atzmut* (essence or self-being) of the divine precisely and deliberately in the material world. On the one hand, this leads to a radical reinterpretation of traditional religious categories, especially in blurring normative distinctions between the sacred and the secular, miracle and nature, the Land of Israel and the Diaspora and even Jew and non-Jew.[83] In this sense, Schneerson was surprisingly close to Kook. On the other hand, his sense of personal messianic destiny (as the *tzaddik* who embodies *'atzmut*) led him to vigorously deny that his period (prior to his open royal manifestation) was already the

[82] Wolfson, *Open Secret*, 226, 134, 228. On the 'super' theme in American mystical culture, see Kripal, *Mutants and Mystics*, esp. 5 (see also 9, 142–147, 211, 352 n. 28, on the influence of Kabbalah on this popular cultural discourse).

[83] Hacohen Oria, 'The Messianic and Mystical Consciousness'.

beginning of redemption.[84] Here is a highly illustrative quote, describing the messianic state in surprisingly quotidian terms: 'That even when walking in the streets, or sitting at home, and even sleeping, they [the Jews] will announce and cry out: "There is none besides Him" (Deuteronomy 4, 35).'[85] As in discussions of the subway and motorway found in his writings (and those of his predecessor), the attention to movement in the street reflects the challenges of the new metropolitan environment.

One of the now-blurred categories was gender: Schneerson vigorously promoted women's learning of Hasidism, as well as their active participation in outreach, radicalizing pioneering steps taken already by his predecessor while ascribing them messianic portent. As Rapoport-Albert has put it, underlining his innovation relative to previous generations of kabbalists, 'he was the first to incorporate, and even privilege women in the enterprise of hallowing the mundane'.[86] At the same time, dialectically, the very claim that the universal is most apparent in the particular, reasserts the potency of classical Jewish language and identity (it is not coincidental that Schneerson waged a fierce campaign against any deviation from Orthodox mores in Israel's so-called who is a Jew legislation).[87] Though it is more of anthropological interest, one cannot avoid mentioning that many of Schneerson's followers not only believed in his posthumous existence (and eventual return in the flesh as resurrected Messiah), but experienced visions and other communications from him.[88]

However one chooses to interpret Schneerson's vision, one thing should be clear: this is a consistent response to secularization, as well as the return of the Jews to concrete history, not only in the State of Israel, but also, or perhaps even especially, in their dramatic financial and political success in the North American democratic setting.[89] A very different response can be found in the theology of R. Yoel Teitelbaum (1887–1979), the *rebbe* of Satmar, staunch leader of the anti-Zionism of Hungarian Orthodoxy, who survived a Nazi concentration camp and arrived in New York in 1946. For Teitelbaum, Israel and its military successes (such as the 1967 Six-Day War, which Schneerson described as a miracle), as well as the revival of the

84 On Schneerson and Kook, see Schwartz, *Habad's Thought*, 357–367. It should be noted that Kook himself referred more frequently to the end of the exile than to the beginning of redemption, the term favored by his followers.

85 Schneerson, *Torat Menahem 1952*, 318.

86 Rapoport-Albert, *Women and the Messianic Heresy*, 272–273, n. 39 (and the contextualization in Loewenthal, 'Women and the Dialectic of Spirituality').

87 Wolfson, *Open Secret*, esp. 257–264.

88 Bilu, *'With Us More Than Ever Before'*.

89 Feldman, *Lubavitchers as Citizens*.

Hebrew language in everyday usage, were all manifestations of the tempting yet illusory power of the Other Side. As Sorotzkin has shown, for Teitelbaum the presence of evil in the Zionist process lies precisely in the illusory seduction itself, as in what he saw as falsification of Halakha for religious-Zionist purposes. In other words, he perceived the Zionist movement and any Orthodox collaboration with it as an 'enclothing' of evil within the realm of sanctity, theurgically damaging the domain of holiness.[90] Although this ideology necessarily leads to the establishment of an enclave culture, Shaul Magid has pointed out that Satmar has used the tools of liberal democracy (much as Schneerson operated the American political and financial system to further his outreach programs) in order to sustain its separate towns (and highly parochial educational system).[91]

Another major American figure, extending the reach of Kabbalah beyond the Orthodox world (in America Orthodoxy is an explicit institutional category), was Avraham Yehosua Heschel (1907–1972), namesake and scion of the esteemed Hasidic leader, the *rebbe* of Apt. Heschel immigrated to New York, after doctoral studies in Germany, in 1940. While operating within the Conservative movement (and active for extra-Jewish causes such as the civil rights movement), he was similar to the staunchly Orthodox Soloveitchik not only in his early philosophical training, but also in writing mainly in English. His strongly Hasidic interpretation of Judaism focused on what one could term emotional theurgy, or the pathos of God's need for man. The move beyond Orthodoxy, yet within the orbit of Hasidic thought, is most evident in his rereading of revelation as an interpretative experience, following R. Menahem Mendel of Riminov. Heschel also extended the comparativist tendency of Neo-Hasidism (as in already-mentioned discussion of the Kotzker *rebbe* and Kierkegaard).

A less-known figure of substantial phenomenological portent was R. Aharon Rokeach of Belz (1880–1957), who narrowly escaped the Nazis and moved to Tel Aviv and then Jerusalem in 1944. As Ido Harari has argued, he was seen as chosen to carry the suffering of the Jewish people, especially around the Holocaust (as manifested in the burning alive of his son by the Nazis in July 1941). Harari relates this perception to his intensely ascetic regimen (one daily meal at most and constant ritual handwashing).[92] A fifth and final post-Holocaust Hasidic leader, who expressed a relatively more less positive attitude to the spread of Kabbalah (similar to that of Lithuanian figures noted above), was R. Yequtiel Yehuda Halberstam of Sanz

[90] Sorotzkin, *Orthodoxy*, 374–386. [91] Magid, 'America Is No Different'.

[92] Harari, 'The Tzaddikate of Suffering', esp. 530, 547–548.

(1904–1994), who led a community in Hungary, survived Auschwitz and immigrated in 1960 after a period in the United States. Halberstam gave the *Zohar* a major role in halakhic decision-making, while fully co-opting the authority of the Kabbalah within legalistic rationale and process. Thus, he was sternly opposed to rejected widespread study of Kabbalah, an attitude upheld by his heir, R. Tzevi Elimelekh Halberstam of Netanya (northern Israel).[93] Generally speaking, the ex-European world was split between the sociological-institutional imperative to rebuild the Haredi world, refounded on a relatively uniform and simple ideological identity and more adventurous spiritual explorations. This ultimately creative tension can explain the successful development of this community (which wielded considerable political clout since the 1977 shift to right-wing dominance in Israel, led by the traditionally oriented Menachem Begin) better than some of the less ideationally attuned proposals aired in academic writing.[94]

The renewed vigor and sway of the Haredi world in the third quarter of the century largely overlapped with the resurgence of the Kook circle as a cultural and political force. The circle vigorously responded first to the 1967 Six-Day War, then to the initial military setbacks (and subsequent minor territorial withdrawals) of the 1973 October (Yom Kippur) War and then to the 1977 elections and their aftermath. A major institutional mechanism here was the promotion of settlement in the territories (especially the West Bank, or Judea and Samaria), occupied in 1967. The spiritual authority for this movement, that became known as *Gush Emunim* (the Bloc of the Faithful), was the above-mentioned R. Zvi Yehuda Kook. In tandem with the growing politicization of the circle (and hence favoring nationalistic elements over mystical themes, which are both more universal and more individualistic), R. Zvi Yehuda marginalized the study of Kabbalah, especially Hasidism and even (on the exoteric level) the mystical portions of his father's writings. Such pursuits were subsumed under the new rubric of studies of *emuna* (faith, echoing the name of the political branch). Amongst the key texts in this revised curriculum were the works of Maharal.

As the alliance with the new political regime (led by Prime Minister Menahem Begin, the erstwhile leader of the right-wing underground) cooled (especially after the 1978–1979 peace agreements with Egypt, leading to further territorial withdrawals), the Kook circle was split into two wings.

93 Granot, 'The Revival of Hasidism', 196–218; Garb, 'Towards the Study', 127–129.

94 See e.g. the massive volume: Brown and Leon (eds.), *The Gdoilim*. In the one entry (by Samuel Heilman) on a kabbalistic writer (Schneerson), Kabbalah (or any other theological corpus for that matter) is barely mentioned.

The more activist of these responded to disappointment of messianic hopes, amongst other steps, through the so-called Jewish underground. During 1980–1984, this loose network, enjoying considerable public support (and hence rapidly pardoned), planned (and at times executed) terror attacks against the Palestinians in the West Bank, the most daring of which was the plot to blow up the mosques on the Temple Mount. The more ideologically oriented wing of this much-publicized group combined a strong messianic reading of the writings of R. Kook the elder with the radically messianic corpus (largely published by Yehuda Etzion, b. 1951) of Shabbtai Ben Dov (1924–1978), a prominent member of the *Sulam* circle (see above), who actually critiqued the other-worldly tendency of kabbalistic theurgy. Another prominent figure here was Yeshu'a ben Sussan (1945–2018), a highly esteemed student of the Sephardic kabbalists of Jerusalem.[95] Toward the end of the chapter, we shall address another kabbalistic figure, to whom these activists, antinomian in the political, and at times in the religious sense, gravitated after a similar setback, the 2005 disengagement from the Gaza Strip.

The second wing of the Kook circle, known as *mamlakhti* (statist), strongly condemned the underground, as well as any violent rhetoric or civil unrest around the withdrawals. Drawing on the younger Kook's sanctification of state symbols as expressions of the redemptive process, these ideologues saw the study of faith (while steering away from open study of the Kabbalah) as a bastion for staunch belief in this process, for all of its dialectical setbacks. In the reading of such figures, most prominently R. Zvi Israel Tau (b. 1937), R. Eliyhau of Vilna and both Kook rabbis had predicted, in semiprophetic vein, the winding course of the path toward national restoration, which for them was primarily educational, internal, soul-centered and spiritual, in the sense of 'uplifting the spirit of the nation'.[96] Hence, for example, they sharply opposed any attempt to approach the Temple site.

The politicization, statist co-option and nationalization of Israeli Kabbalah extended well beyond traditional circles: this process extended to nationalist critiques of the writings of Scholem (who was associated with the radical left) by Barukh Kurzweil (1907–1972), a professor of literature in

95 Falach, 'The "Sulam" Journal', 264–268 (also on Ben-Dov's critiques of Scholem's writing); Garb, *The Chosen*, 93–95.

96 Tau, *Le-Emunat 'Itenu*, e.g. vol. II, 257 (and compare to the discussion in vol. VIII, 186–190, of uplifting the spirit through the study of faith, while concealing the soul-level, namely the explicit teachings of Kabbalah).

the new (since 1955) religious-Zionist Bar-Ilan University and a close friend of Uri Zvi Greenberg (who was joined in this critique by nonkabbalistic right-wing thinkers, some of whom were academics).[97] Indeed, prominent members of the Israeli political establishment were involved in Kabbalah research. For example, Israel's third education minister, Ben Zion Dinur (1884–1973), propagated a strong messianic interpretation of Hasidism and other forms of Jewish mysticism, casting them as predecessors of Zionism. Likewise, Israel's second president, Yitzhak Ben-Zvi (1884–1963), was keenly interested in the legend of the lost tribes, while the third president, Zalman Shazar (1889–1974), reinforced the Scholemian focus on Sabbateanism. This ideological tendency has persisted in later generations of Kabbalah scholarship.[98] To these trends, one should add the steadily increasing presence of mystical themes in Israeli literature, especially in the poetry of Zelda Schneurson Mishkovsky (1914–1984), who frequently corresponded with her cousin R. Menahem Mendel Schneerson.[99] One of Zelda's younger associates was the controversial Yona Wallach (1944–1985), whose strongly erotic poetry was partly based on her mystical experiences occasioned by being experimentally treated with LSD at a psychiatric hospital. One example of the interplay of Kabbalah, gender and messianism in her avant-garde writing can be seen in these lines (in my translation):

> A man is not a man
> a woman not a woman
> making love
> exposing breasts
> without a *partzuf*
> sex or face
> like in Kabbalah
> in black magic
> losing the
> face . . .[100]
> and one may preserve
> the emotional
> virginity
> until the coming of the Messiah
> and he will come

97 Myers, 'The Scholem-Kurzweil Debate'.

98 Ben-Dor Benite, *The Ten Lost Tribes*, 220–225: Idel, 'Messianic Scholars'.

99 Rechnitzer, 'To See God in His Beauty'; Weiss, 'Listening to the Silent Crying of the Shekhina'.

100 Compare to the quote from R. Nahman of Bratzlav in Chapter 5.

> the woman will be a woman
> the man a man
> . . .[101]

As can be gleaned from the preceding discussion, at this point it is hard to disentangle Israeli Kabbalah from the vibrant and tense sociopolitical and cultural developments in the country (though it should not be reduced to these). This observation extends to economics, as the steady increase of government funding for Yeshivas and 'Torah culture' (joined by private donations, though to a lesser extent than in the United States) supported numerous institutions, publication houses, musical performances (focused on *nigunim*) and lecture series including kabbalistic elements. All this also holds true for the Sephardic world. The political dimension can be located in statements by the following scholarly figures. First and foremost, we have R. Ovadiya Hadaya (1889–1984), who succeeded his father R. Shalom (1862–1945, student of R. Yitzhak Alafiya) in leadership of the *Beit El* Yeshiva (following its uprooting from its centuries-long site in the 1948 Israeli-Arab War). Writing also as a halakhic authority, Hadaya strongly opposed any withdrawal from the occupied territories, describing such moves as follows:

> And if, God forbid, we return even one foot, by doing so we grant control to the husks and Other Side, and the *Shekhina*, whose horn has been uplifted from dust [by the miraculous results of the war]. If heaven forbid we again give any control to the Other Side, will return to be lowly and captive amongst the husks . . . for if we give a bit of control to the Other Side, it will continue to expand foot by foot and conquer all of holiness.[102]

Yet his main contribution to kabbalistic writing was his extensive *responsa* (especially in answer to queries from Tunisian kabbalists), expressing the ongoing process of drawing together regional traditions in a cross-Sephardic dialogue.

A second figure with considerable institutional clout (including an extensive publishing project, inserting numerous unnoticed glosses of his own in canonical texts) was R. Mordekahi 'Attiya the elder (1898–1978), who emigrated in 1936 from Mexico City and established the *Ha-Hayyim ve ha-Shalom* (Life and Peace) Yeshiva in Jerusalem in 1967.[103] 'Attiya, who was in close contact with the younger Kook, strongly upheld immigration to

101 Wallach, *Forms*, 22–23. Like much of Israeli poetry, these lines have been set to music.
102 Hadaya, *Yaskil 'Avdi*, vol. VIII, 81. The term 'not one foot' was a slogan of the Greater Israel movement, of which Agnon and of course Greenberg were members.
103 Turgeman, *Miqpahat Sefarim*.

the Land of Israel, explicitly presenting it as part of the redemptive process (see below on the present generation of this school). However, both politically and culturally, the Sephardic world was dominated by less scholastic and more magically oriented figures, such as the *baba sali* (praying father), R. Israel Abu-Hazeria (1889–1984), grandson of the legendary '*ribi* (rabbi) Yaakov'. The *baba sali*'s support was highly valuable for the *Agudat Israel* party in election seasons. A similar venerable sage was R. Yitzhak Kaduri (1898–2006), who gravitated in the 1980s to the new *Shas* (Sephardi Torah Guardians) party, and gave even more crucial support to the 1996 electoral victory of Benyamin Netanyahu.[104] Beyond specific figures, the cult of the saints, as in visits to their gravesites and belief in their paranormal powers, greatly enhanced the popular appeal of Sephardic kabbalists, just like their Safedian predecessors.[105] This was not without its hazards, as in the case of the *baba sali*'s grandson, R. Eli'ezer Abuhazeira (1948–2011), who was stabbed to death by a disgruntled supplicant.

If one should attempt to locate the most obvious common denominator of the American and Israeli centers, I believe that it is the renewed popularity of the *Zohar*, read without Lurianic or post-Lurianic mediation (thus continuing the less traditional developments discussed above). In Israel, we have in this period the highly visible popularizations of R. Daniel Parish (1935–2005) of *Sha'ar ha-Shamayim* Yeshiva and of R. Hayyim David ha-Levi (1924–1988, the chief rabbi of Tel Aviv).[106] In the United States, besides works geared at an academic audience, we have the highly successful Pritzker translation (led by Daniel Matt), demonstrating the increasing role played by private donors in American Jewish Studies. As we shall see in the next section, this pan-Zoharic tendency accelerated as the Kabbalah became part of the New Age spiritual supermarket. In a sense the mystique of the often enigmatic text of the *Zohar*, and its literary framework, rendered it as popular amongst twentieth-century non-Jewish seekers as amongst sixteenth-century kabbalistic Christians. Also, ironically, its pseudo-Aramaic equalizes non-Jews (or most American Jews, who do not read, at least fluently, in Hebrew) and most Israelis, who are equally puzzled by Aramaic.[107]

[104] Paradoxically, the main spiritual leader of the party, R. 'Ovadya Yosef (1920–2013), was rather critical of public study of the Kabbalah and granted it limited place in halakhic jurisdiction. See further on this knotty issue in the conclusion.

[105] Bilu, *The Saint's Impresarios*.

[106] Meir, 'The Revealed and the Revealed within the Concealed', 222–231. One must stress that Parish's translation, though striving for the plain meaning of the text, is nonetheless Lurianic.

[107] As anyone who has taught *Zohar* to first-year students in Israeli universities can testify.

Yet beforehand, one should briefly consider the slowly but steadily recovering European Kabbalah. Here the main center was France, where the highly influential philosopher Emanuel Levinas (1906–1995) and the rabbi-academic Andre Neher (1914–1988) successfully mediated the Kabbalah for highly educated, yet not traditionally erudite, audiences. While Neher focused on Maharal, Levinas engaged *Nefesh ha-Hayyim*.[108] One popular teacher emerging from this loose circle was the Algerian-born R. Léon Ashkenazi (1922–1996, aka Manitou), who immigrated to Israel from Paris after the Six-Day War and merged with the nationalist agenda of the Kook circle, while also expressing the influence of Ashlag. A slightly similar case is that of Jean-Paul Sartre's erstwhile secretary, the Egyptian-born Benny Lévy (aka Pierre Victor, 1945–2003), who returned to traditional observance and identity, immigrated to Jerusalem in 1997 and became one of the closest followers of R. Moshe Shapira. One should of course note the influential role of academic scholarship. Here one should note especially Georges Vajda (1908–1981) and Charles Mopsik (1956–2003). Besides drawing Kabbalah into dialogue with gender, comparative religion and body theory, Mopsik excelled in translations of the *Zohar* and other key texts (for Mopsik's successor, Julien Darmon, see the introduction chapter). German scholarship is spearheaded by what has been quite accurately described as the school of Peter Schäfer (b. 1943), which is largely philological and focused on antiquity and the medieval period (and thus of less pertinence for modern Kabbalah). The expectable interest of Italian scholarship (which is similar to the German center in its mostly philological and premodern agenda) in kabbalistic Christianity and Renaissance was at least partly addressed in Chapter 2. Generally speaking, these centers do not share the French, Israeli and American interest in joining the wider cultural conversation.[109] The fall of the Soviet Union and dissolution of the Eastern bloc, after 1989, has led to a new wave of interest in Kabbalah in Eastern Europe, which has not yet drawn the attention of the English-speaking world (mostly for linguistic reasons).

KABBALAH IN POSTWAR GLOBAL MYSTICISM

To a far greater extent than in the prewar period, Kabbalah became a significant player in the global mystical resurgence that was in full gear by the 1960s and continued without much letup till now (usually under the

[108] Del Nevo, 'The Kabbalistic Heart of Levinas'. [109] See below on England.

rubric of New Age). Here, naturally, the American center played a greater role, the new hegemony of English being a major factor here: while figures such as Heschel, Hutner, Schneerson and Soloveitchik conducted much of their discourse in Yiddish, the writers that we shall survey now, even if they personally spoke and read this language (over time less so), taught and wrote in English. This simple fact, in and of itself, determined a far lesser degree of adherence to the modern textual and interpretative tradition and a far greater affinity with the general mystical setting. Actually, even the more globalized, or 'discontinuous' forms of Kabbalah in Israel, in the second part of the century, were either established or heavily influenced by Anglophone figures, for which Hebrew was but one of several languages (again, mostly English) in which their teachings were propagated.

One of the pioneers amongst this new generation of writers was Mattiyahu Glazerson (b. 1937), who initially operated in South Africa as part of the *ba'alei teshuva* movement. Indeed, discontinuity is embedded in the very identity of the *ba'al teshuva* (even when, as we shall soon see, it is denied). Hebrew was an explicit and central theme in his writing, yet not as a self-evident, native speech, but rather as part of an attempt to capture the allegiance of those who grew up distant from it. Glazerson's propagandistic argument was that Hebrew is the root of all other languages. His explicit contention with the rival allure of Far Eastern religions is apparent in his writing on meditation and related issues.[110] This discourse of rivalry continued in the more sophisticated writing (borrowing heavily, yet not openly, from academic scholarship) of R. Aryeh Kaplan (1934–1983), an American *ba'al teshuva* who initially trained as a physicist, and unlike others of his ilk made a sustained effort to translate and annotate core kabbalistic texts. As Tomer Persico has argued, Kaplan sought to provide Jews interested in Far Eastern religions with an alternative history of Jewish religiosity, with meditative practice at its heart. As he correctly claims, Kaplan is but one example of the transformation of meditation into a keyword of kabbalistic discourse in the second part of the century.[111] Besides his meditative interest, Glazerson later joined nonkabbalistic writers in using codes in an attempt to discover hidden messages in the Bible. This method of skipping letters (e.g. forming a word by choosing every forty-ninth letter in a biblical portion), used somewhat already in medieval Kabbalah, was rendered much easier by computers. It joined the popular postwar cultural and popular scientific

[110] Glazerson, *The Grandeur of Judaism and the East.*

[111] Persico, *The Jewish Meditative Tradition*, 290–320.

theme of codes, also reflecting the discovery of the genetic code, to later surface in contemporary Haredi Kabbalah (see below).

These interests in mathematical codes, in the superior metaphysical dimensions of the Hebrew language, in rivalry with the Far Eastern faiths and in scientific parallels with kabbalistic themes, were all greatly developed by another American *ba'al teshuva* with a scientific background, R. Itzhak Ginsburgh (b. 1944). Ginsburgh, who like Kaplan was greatly attracted by the writings of Abulafia, gravitated into the Hasidic world, declaring his allegiance to Habad. After his 1965 immigration, he increasingly moved toward nationalistic expressions and political involvement, going far beyond the Kook circle (some of the more activist members of which transferred their allegiance to him) in declaring the innate superiority of the Jewish people and in calling for the restoration of the Israelite kingdom (as a prerequisite to the rebuilding of the Temple). However, besides the international scope of Ginsburgh's activity (and his *Kabbalah and Meditation for the Nations* book), one should not let the intensive involvement with Israeli activism (starting with the classes that he delivered to the members of the Jewish Underground when they were still jailed, and including his own period of administrative detention in 1996) occlude the role of the marketplace in the formation of his discourse.[112] Like Glazerson, Ginsburgh especially focuses on themes such as sexuality and marriage, whose appeal is obvious, as well as promoting discs containing his original musical compositions, and even kabbalistic jewelry. Indeed, a kabbalistic model for business corporations is an important theme of his writing.

The absorption of Kabbalah by the global marketplace is even more starkly evident in certain branches of the Ashlag circle (ironically so in view of the founder's socialist doctrine). The more continuous amongst these was *Bnei Barukh* (the sons of Barukh), a fellowship established in 1991 by Michael Laitman (b. 1946), an immigrant from Russia and a student of R. Barukh Ashlag (1907–1991), the elder son of Ashlag the senior.[113] Working initially with the numerous immigrants arriving in Israel in the 1990s after the collapse of the Soviet Union, Laitman rapidly developed a multilingual, international, technologically based network. On the one hand, Laitman's teaching takes the form of commentary on the writings of Ashlag (which again are in turn commentaries on the *Zohar* and Lurianic works). However,

112 For Ginsburgh's kabbalistic defense of an even more extreme act of Jewish terror, Baruch Goldstein's 1994 Hebron massacre, see Seeman, 'Violence', 1017–1028.

113 One of Barukh's better-known students is Avichai Mandelblit (b. 1963), Israel's current attorney-general.

the larger background of kabbalistic literature is almost entirely occluded in favor of a strong, strident ideology, holding that Ashlag's teachings are the cure to the economic, political and ecological upheavals of the turn of the century. Here too, the trope of Kabbalah as science is prominent, and rests on Laitman's early training in cybernetics.

This discontinuous tendency is far more pronounced in the case of the Kabbalah Center, founded in 1969 by Philip (Shraga) Berg (1929–2013), who studied briefly with R. Yehuda Brandwein (1903–1969), rabbi of the General Organization of Workers in Israel (and as such a partisan of the socialist teachings of his teacher Ashlag).[114] Berg's move away from the languages of Kabbalah (including the claim that one does not need to read Hebrew or Aramaic in order to obtain the spiritual benefit of the *Zohar* through 'scanning' it, itself a technological term) is but part of his distance from the orbit of the tradition, as reflected not only in strong merchandising (assisted by the enlistment of media celebrities, most prominently Madonna, or Louise Ciccone), but also in the strong presence of Christian themes in his writings and those of his followers.[115] Thus, Véronique Altglas is correct in placing this particular group within the context of the transnational New Age setting (as in her fruitful comparison of the center to Siddha Yoga and Sivananda), rather than that of Kabbalah, at least in the forms described in this volume.[116]

The cases of Madonna and the music of Ginsburgh, seemingly belonging to radically different locales and cultures, reflect the transformation of Kabbalah into a prominent feature in the artistic and literary scene (together with claims to it being a science).[117] This process extends beyond the Jewish world, as evidenced in the centrality of Abulafia's doctrine in semiotician Umberto Eco's 1988 novel *Foucault's Pendulum*. Indeed, the popularity of Abulafia's language theory, also in cinema (as in the 2005 *Bee Season*, directed by Scott McGehee, based on the 2000 novel by Myla Goldberg) reflects not only the move of this erstwhile semimarginal kabbalist (whose books were first printed as late as the 1980s) into the foreground, but also the

[114] For the history of the Center in America, see Myers, *Kabbalah and the Spiritual Quest*. The Center is a prime example of the effect of globalization. Thus, it has a strong presence (together with other, Abulafian forms of Kabbalah) in Latin America and Scandinavia (otherwise very rarely a location of European Kabbalah).

[115] Meir, 'The Revealed and the Revealed within the Concealed', 180–182, 186–187. It is interesting to speculate whether the name Madonna itself galvanized this process.

[116] Altglas, *From Yoga to Kabbalah*.

[117] On the more popular level, one should note the presence of kabbalistic themes in the genre of fantasy, whose popularity is ever increasing.

influence of academic writers such as Gershom Scholem and Moshe Idel (b. 1947).[118] This more highbrow presence of Kabbalah can be noted worldwide, ranging from the works of Jorge Luis Borges to Israeli writers such as Hayyim Be'er (b. 1945), who tellingly sends a Hasidic *rebbe* to Tibet in his 2010 novel *El Makom Sheharuakh Holekh* (Back from Heavenly Lack), which replays the inter-Hasidic drama surrounding the Napoleonic Wars.[119] The transdenominational reach of Kabbalah, extended by academe as a universalistic life form, is exemplified in the substantial influence of Scholem's studies on contemporary Christian theologians such as Jurgen Moltmann (b. 1926, who was also heavily influenced by Ernst Bloch).[120]

Despite forays into theatre, the visual arts and other media, the main cultural conduit for modern Kabbalah and especially Hasidism remained music. Here the key figure was Berlin-born Shlomo Carlebach (1925–1994) yet another Habad-trained outreach agent within the *ba'alei teshuva* movement. Carlebach almost single-handedly transformed Hasidic *nigunim* into a worldwide musical genre (collaborating amongst others with Nina Simone), later joined (mostly in Israel) by the revival of Middle Eastern *baqashot* and other devotional songs. On the textual level, he contributed, alongside with academic scholars (including Aviva Gottlieb Zornberg, b. 1944, who upon leaving academe became one of the most successful of a new generation of women teaching Hasidism) to the awakening of popular interest in the hitherto marginal Izbiche-Radzin teachings. However, Carlebach's reputation was somewhat marred by alleged sexual scandals, also haunting other kabbalists and Hasidic teachers (those convicted being Ezra Sheinberg of Safed and the veteran Bratzlav teacher Eliezer Berland), and similar to problems of this nature accompanying the passage of Far Eastern traditions to the West.

Carlebach was joined in moving out of Habad into the 1960s countercultural scene, by Polish-born R. Zalman Schachter-Shalomi (1924–2014), who went far in incorporating Kabbalah into the transdenominational mystical culture, in close dialogue with the ecological movement. His work in the Buddhist Naropa University can be seen as an institutional manifestation of the transcendence of parochial Jewish identity, as championed by his student Shaul Magid (b. 1958). As Magid shows, the former expanded the idea (especially developed in modern Kabbalah) of converts as Jewish souls in non-Jewish bodies toward the notion of 'psycho-semites', who are

118 For an interesting example of the global influence of Scholem in unexpected avenues (in Latin America), see Brown, 'Aryan Kabbalah'.

119 Mualem, 'Borges and Kabbalistic Infinity'.

120 Moltmann, *The Crucified God*, xi; Moltmann, *The Coming of God*, esp. 37–38, 65.

'Jewish already', not requiring the mere formality of conversion.[121] The significance of this move is highlighted if one compares it to the drifting of Carlebach from the rather universalist House of Love and Prayer (founded in San Francisco in 1968) toward the Israeli right wing, symbolized by his dance with Begin in a rally held in a West Bank settlement during the tense and pivotal 1981 election campaign.

Magid, a leading American scholar and publicist, exemplifies the migration of students or descendants (see below) of kabbalistic figures into the academic world, at times also as public intellectuals. This was also the case with another student of Schachter-Shalomi, Arthur Green (b. 1941), who plays an important role in the above-mentioned Jewish Renewal movement, which has since established tentative footholds in Israel.[122] Green's transformation of R. Nahman of Bratzlav into a cultural hero was joined, in America, by his Bratzlav contemporaries in the East Coast of the United States. These include Polish-born R. Zvi Aryeh Rosenfeld (1922–1978), who collaborated with Aryeh Kaplan on translation projects (and managed to renew the pilgrimage to Uman in the Soviet period) and R. Gedalya Fleer (b. 1940), who was actually arrested by the Soviet authorities in 1962 (and later immigrated to Israel). A very different (as seen in Green's 1997 attack on his first major book) test case is that of scholar, artist and poet Elliot Wolfson (b. 1956), who greatly facilitated the dialogue of Kabbalah scholarship with the broader worlds of religious studies, gender theory, philosophy and poetics.[123] Wolfson's numerous comparisons with Buddhist thought have furthered the comparative move, again facilitating the shift of Kabbalah into the global mystical library (assisted by translation projects such as the Paulist Press' *Classics of World Spirituality* series, in which Green played a major role). Wolfson's mystical poetics is substantially influenced by Leonard Norman (Eli'ezer) Cohen (1934–2016), whose spiritual seeking drew on Buddhism and on to a lesser extent on Kabbalah. In many ways, Cohen can be seen as an icon of the mystical-artistic synthesis in North America.[124]

KABBALAH IN THE EARLY TWENTY-FIRST CENTURY

While the later part of the twentieth century was characterized, as we have just seen, by the exploitation (also in the economic sense) of the possibilities

[121] Magid, *American Post-Judaism*, 52–54 (and 127–130).
[122] Werczberger, *Jews in the Age of Authenticity*.
[123] For an influential evaluation, see Kripal, *Roads of Excess*, 258–298.
[124] Wolfson, 'New Jerusalem Glowing'.

opened up by the loosening of the constraints of continuity with the textual tradition, a reverse trend developed in the first two decades of the next century. The ever-confident entrenchment of the political and demographic power of the *Haredim* created a relatively insulated envelope obviating the need to greatly address or respond to the world beyond its confines. This internal discourse unfolded into numerous subidentities, interlinked in complex networks. Linguistically, there is a certain return to Yiddish and generally close reading and interpretation of core modern texts reigns, accompanied by careful attention to methodology. From an institutional point of view, the maturation and expansion (also into New York and Paris, as well as of course several Israeli centers) of the kabbalistic Yeshiva world led to the emergence of a new set of leaders, whose own students are just now coming into their own. In all cases, information technology plays a major role, enabling new syntheses, yet in some cases there is staunch ideological resistance to the Internet (associated with the Other Side).

The primary textual layer of the new *Haredi* Kabbalah is the array of editions of and commentaries on the Lurianic corpus, accompanied by an invigorated ideological discourse on its superiority and on the primacy of the Vitalian transmission. Most prominent here is R. Ya'akov Moshe Hillel (b. 1945), a *ba'al teshuva* originating in the unique community of Cochin, India, and head of the *Hevrat Ahavat Shalom* (Society of Love of Peace) Yeshiva, founded in Jerusalem around 1972.[125] Part of his massive publication endeavor (supported by highly successful fundraising, assisted by translations into other languages, a rare phenomenon in this Sephardic world) is the publication of the original *'Etz Hayyim* penned by Vital. This project is accompanied by extensive philological-historical discussion, partly in imitation of the equally massive project conducted by Avivi in the academic setting. The Lurianic ideology is accompanied by the glorification of the teachings of Rashash, accompanied by extensive writings on *kavvanot* and (also through *responsa*) on the interrelationship of Halakha and Kabbalah. Here we can discern the focus on praxis that characterizes much of *Haredi* Kabbalah (as opposed to the more metaphysical and psychological concerns discussed in the previous section). An even greater predilection for close, conjoint reading of the Lurianic corpus and its Rashashian elaborations, alongside with constant and explicit attempts to establish the Halakha of *kavvanot*, can be found in a rival, influential school, that of R. Mordekhai 'Attiya the younger (grandson of the founder of the above-mentioned

[125] Meir, 'The Boundaries of Kabbalah'.

Yeshiva, now renamed *'Ateret Mordekhai*, The Crown of Mordekhai). Similar moves, also accompanied by an effort to publish new manuscripts, can be found in the circles of R. Benayahu Shmu'eli, the head of the *Nahar Shalom* Yeshiva and R. David Batzri (b. 1941), head of *Yeshivat ha-Shalom* (who is more famous for a public exorcism and for homophobic and racist statements). Indeed, the *Haredi* world has currently all but overtaken academic scholarship in the publication of manuscripts (certainly in terms of quantity).[126]

Within the Ashkenazi world, the figure most similar to Hillel in ideological purism was R. Eliyahu Israel Weintraub (1932–2010), a student of Hutner who took up his interest in Izbiche-Radzin Hasidism (as well as studying with Schneerson).[127] The progressive publication of his lecture notes and correspondence reveals the scope and intensity of his teaching, 'below the radar' of the official Lithuanian attitude toward Torah study. His staunchly anti-Zionist theology (drawing on Hutner's historiosophy) is based on the portrayal of the greater part of the contemporary world as 'anti-human', even lacking the divine image.[128] Yet his major project, continuing amongst his students, is that of close reading of the works of R. Eliyahu of Vilna (and of his student Izcovitz). Besides this project of Weintraub's, one should note another non-Rashashian project, the massive publication of the works of Luzzatto and his close associate Vallee, by the above-mentioned Freidlander's student, the American-born R. Yosef Spinner, who later joined the *Sha'ar ha-Shamayim* Yeshiva.

The triumph of Rashashian Kabbalah is well apparent in the intense preoccupation of some Ashkenazi kabbalists with deciphering its core text, *Nahar Shalom*, and its own main commentary, de la Rossa's *Torat Hakham*. This project is most developed in the Yeshiva of this name, founded in 2002 in Jerusalem by R. Yitzhak Meir Morgenstern (b. 1967), originally of London. The massive and dense writings of Morgenstern's student, R. Shmu'el Ehrenfeld, again reflect the keen interest in philological-historical issues. However, R. Morgenstern's main contribution is the synthesis (reminiscent of that of Spielmann) between Rashash (and of course Luria) and Hasidic thought (especially that of Bratzlav and Habad, including R. Aharon

[126] Abrams, *Kabbalistic Manuscripts*, 33–34 (regarding Germany and Italy as exceptions to the decline of academic manuscript work), 47–48, 51–52, 60–61, 63–64, 68.

[127] It is perhaps no coincidence that R. Michael Borenstein, the heir of Hutner's above-mentioned close student R. Moshe Shapira, is a senior student of Hillel's.

[128] Garb, 'Mystical and Spiritual Discourse', 26–28.

Horowitz).[129] Indeed, one of Morgenstern's teachers, the American-born (1950) R. Moshe Schatz, closely follows Spielmann's *Tal Orot*, as well as reviving interest in the works of Elyashiv. Besides his evident interest in current theory in physics, Schatz is rather unique in synthesizing Lurianic and post-Lurianic teachings with medieval Kabbalah (especially the teachings of R. 'Azriel of Gerona, described as the foundation of the Lurianic doctrine).[130]

Morgenstern's horizons are equally broad, extending to a rare openness to the teachings of Ashlag in the massive volumes of his *Yam ha-Hokhma* (The Sea of Wisdom). However, his flexibility stops somewhat short of acceptance of alternative medicine, which is usually critiqued in the halakhic sections of these works. This very engagement reflects the increasing interest in the Far East (fueled by *ba'alei teshuva*) amongst *Haredi* kabbalists. The more lenient approach toward alternative medicine (and generally toward the unique concerns of *ba'alei teshuva*) is supported by the mystical charisma of the *rebbe* of Amshinov, R. Ya'akov Arye Milikovsky (b. 1947), who is the mentor of some of the new generation of Hasidic spiritual directors. These forays outside the mainstream (including subterranean interest in Sabbateanism) reflect not only the complex situation of *Haredi* enclave culture, but also the ongoing dialectic of canonization, decanonization and recanonization that we have followed throughout the history of modern Kabbalah.[131]

Figures such as Avivi being almost the exception that proves the rule, the Religious Zionist Yeshiva world has played a relatively minor role in the development of Kabbalah studies. The most notable trend here is the further proliferation and elaboration of Zohar study, assisted by cultural figures such as the leading scholar and translator Yehuda Liebes (b. 1947), and the scholar, activist and poet (also as a young follower of the poetess Zelda) Haviva Pedaya (b. 1957, great-granddaughter of the above-mentioned R. Yehuda Petaya).[132] Here final comments on the role of academic scholarship in the grand scheme of things are due. Despite a certain Cross-Atlantic

[129] In this context, one should mention another important Bratzlav kabbalist, R. Ya'akov Meir Schechter of the *Sha'ar ha-Shamayim* Yeshiva (where Morgenstern and some of his associates also studied).

[130] Schatz, *Tarshish, Shoham ve Yashfe*, esp. 11 (and Garb, *Yearnings of the Soul*, 43, 45, 117–124; Garb, 'Mystical and Spiritual Discourse', 19–26, also addressing R. Yitzhak Moshe Erlanger, another figure displaying keen interest in medieval Kabbalah). For the innovations of R. Itamar Schwartz, an erstwhile student of Morgenstern, see Wolfson, 'Building a Sanctuary of the Heart'.

[131] On reading of Sabbatean texts in the Haredi world, see Barnai, *Sabbateanism*, 139–140 (supported by my own fieldwork observations).

[132] One should also note the poetry of scholar Asi Farber-Ginat.

split, the connection between the two main centers of Kabbalah study is institutionalized in the voluminous multilingual publications of Cherub Press, based in California yet headed by an American academic operating in Israel, Wolfson's student Daniel Abrams (b. 1965), who was also very close to the late Charles Mopsik. Second, the influence of woman academics (including Ada Rapoport-Albert, of the relatively less voluble English center) is echoed in the new phenomenon of women mystics operating around the modern Orthodox/Religious Zionist world (yet with some influence in non-Orthodox circles), such as the Moroccan-born University graduate Yemima Avital (1929–1999, although her connection to the Kabbalah in the textual sense is questionable).[133] The participation of women in various worlds of kabbalistic learning and practice (including filmmaking, as in the case of Rama Burshtein, b. 1967, a follower of Bratzlav), is one of the most striking changes in the course of the history of Kabbalah as such.

CONCLUSION

The twentieth century, with its extensive documentation (including, especially after the war, audio-video recordings, and now ever enhanced by the Internet), greatly facilitates tracing lines of influence and processes of circle-formation. It can be posited that technology was and is (to an increasing extent), a powerful aid for connectivity amongst kabbalists, in face of dispersion and state-directed persecution. In this and other senses, with all due caution, one can expand our earlier suggestions as to the similarity with such processes in the previous golden age – the sixteenth century. One clear common denominator is the intense preoccupation, intra-kabbalistic, academic and mass-marketed, with the *Zohar*. In both cases, this predilection was related to the spread of the Kabbalah beyond traditional circles and even beyond the Jewish world (which evoked anxieties in both periods). In both periods, the Zoharic revival was associated with messianic and national discourses (partly but not entirely related to relocation of kabbalists to the Land of Israel, and especially the Galilee). Another one was the migration of previously neglected corpora (Abulafia in both cases, and Bratzlav in the twentieth-century case) from the margins to the center.[134] Notwithstanding these processes, the twentieth century (following on late nineteenth-century processes, likewise linked to migration) has established the supremacy of eighteenth-century canons. One of these, the Rashashian, holds sway inside

[133] Kauffman, 'The Yemima Method'. See also above on Aviva Gottlieb Zornberg.

[134] Meilicke, 'Abulafianism'.

the kabbalistic world, and another, Hasidism, facilitates ever-growing fertilization of other cultural domains. As part of the process of canonization, ideologues such as Hillel have combated the proliferation of magical forms of Kabbalah.

However, as in the case of the sixteenth century, the intensive proliferation of Kabbalah in the long twentieth century is not merely a matter of adulation. We have seen how writers and thinkers ranging from Agnon to Ben-Dov critiqued the Kabbalah and expressed impatience with its otherworldly aspirations, which were perceived as inimical to the process of Jewish modernization, especially in its Zionist form. Despite the constant removal of limitations on the study of Kabbalah in the Lithuanian *Haredi* world, the surprising claim by the above-mentioned R. Eli'ezer Shach, namely that one cannot fulfill the formal obligation of Torah study through learning Kabbalah, is still a looming presence.[135] While in the sixteenth century, one of the major halakhic figures (R. Yosef Karo) was himself a kabbalist, in the twentieth century leading halakhists, such as R. Israel Meir Kagan of Radin (1839–1933, better known as the author of *Hafetz Hayyim*, Seeker of Life), or the above-mentioned R. 'Ovadiya Yosef, restricted the impact of Kabbalah on jurisprudence.[136] We have also noticed sharp critiques of the prevalent tendency to openly propagate the Kabbalah, voiced by leaders in various streams covered here. These reservations on the part of otherwise sympathetic readers, all sharing the modern consensus as to the sanctity of the Kabbalah, can be contrasted to strident rationalistic critiques, ranging from Kafih (see above), to the left-wing scientist and public intellectual Yesh'ayahu Leibowitz (1903–1994). However, Leibowitz was, at least to date, probably the last influential ideological opponent of the Kabbalah. Like ideology, the figure of the public intellectual is a cardinal facet of the intertwined cultural and political dimensions of the twentieth century (as well as the end of the nineteenth century). So it is not surprising that important public intellectuals and *hommes (femmes) de lettres* (some of whom, most prominently Scholem and his conversation partner Hannah Arendt, were academics), granted the Kabbalah diverse, yet substantial roles in their discourse, enhancing the citation of kabbalistic ideas throughout the humanities. This tendency is a clear reflection of the fact that the Kabbalah not only remarkably flourished in the long twentieth century, but also actually had an indelible impress on its rich tapestry.

[135] Shach, *'Avi 'Ezri*, vol. I, unpaginated introduction to fourth edition (this ruling has a rather obscure earlier source).

[136] Brown, 'Kabbalah in the Rulings of the Hafetz Hayyim'.

7

Recurrent Themes

Gender, Messianism and Experience?

> Revolutionary and new departures of kabbalism are thus separated by veritable caesuras.
>
> (R. J. Zvi Werblowsky)

In the face of the staggering diversity of the schools and corpora of modern Kabbalah, over the centuries and across continents, the question arising now is whether there is a central axis around which one can organize this vast material? Failing that, are there recurrent themes and topics around which the various trends and centers coalesce to some extent? A subsidiary, yet vital, question emerging from this investigation is the extent to which such themes continue those of medieval Kabbalah, with which we commenced.

The major existing proposal within the framework of the autonomy of modern Kabbalah (as opposed to the panoramic approach of Idel and several of his students, which blurs the distinction from earlier periods) remains that of Gershom Scholem. As we have seen, working from the assumption that Lurianic doctrine was 'completely new', breaking with its medieval predecessors, Scholem then posited that Sabbateanism drew this teaching into history, that Hasidism neutralized this move, but not before it fueled secularization and the Enlightenment.[1] Scholem himself, who famously critiqued the *Haskala*, is then the true 'last phase' in this history, as part of the Zionist movement, to some extent applying Sabbatean messianism and religious 'anarchism' in this sociopolitical context.[2]

[1] Scholem, *Major Trends*, 287 (and compare 244–245). This general correlation has been recently strengthened, in a nuanced manner, in a study in progress by Menachem Lorberbaum.

[2] Mendes-Flohr, *Divided Passions*, 400 (and 348–349).

While the survey in this volume has largely affirmed the autonomy of modern Kabbalah and the centrality of Luria, later chapters have demoted Sabbateanism (at best a movement with a rough century of continuous history) from its dominance over early modernity, and also placed Hasidism (still going strong, but after only two and a half centuries, mostly in Eastern and Central Europe) in wider perspective for later modernity. Therefore, irrespective of its current anchorage in the shifting sands of academic fashion, Scholem's eloquent narrative cannot guide us here. Once this edifice has been chipped at (though by no means shattered), one should quest for an alternative, preferably reframing the terms in which the question is couched. Here the following observation is pertinent: the great majority of academic writing is concerned with content, while process has been largely neglected (two exceptions being the works belonging to Idel's sociological phase around the turn of the twentieth century and the observations of Philip Wexler, coming from sociological meta-theory and social psychology).[3] Therefore, it is to process that we shall now turn. In other words, this chapter shall deal far less with the complex, controversial issue of conceptual ruptures versus continuities and rather with social structures, organization and diffusion of knowledge, cultivated psychological states, transformed views of gender and sexuality, innovative regimes of ritual and daily life, self-perception of the Kabbalah as a discipline or literary genre and kinds of reciprocal impact with a gamut of extrakabbalistic worlds.[4]

In these terms, one should first turn to the question of continuity (or its absence) in the sense of institutions and teacher–disciple transmission. Here a simple fact must be noted: for all of its diversity and inner ruptures, the Hasidic world is continuous, also in the sense of familial descent, from its somewhat nebulous beginnings in the mid-eighteenth century till this day. As for its opponents, one can trace a large degree of institutional continuity from the Volozhin Yeshiva, founded already in 1802 by R. Hayyim Itzcovitz, to the present-day extensive 'Lithuanian' network. However, despite the kabbalistic engagement of numerous figures, from R. Eliyahu the Gaon of Vilna to R. Eliyahu Weintraub (who consciously modeled himself on the founder figure), this lore was never a component in curriculum or official discourse. However, one cannot ignore the direct teacher–disciple chain from R. Eliyahu to, say, R. Shlomo Wolbe, my own first teacher. Taking the road not often taken eastwards and southwards, one can invite visitors to Jerusalem, the present-day capital of continuous Kabbalah, to observe the

[3] Wexler, *Mystical Sociology*, esp. 56–69.

[4] For a recent study of the first mentioned kind, see Idel, 'The Mud and the Water'.

Beit El Yeshiva, for all its dislocations and changes in orientation nonetheless the institution led by Rashash in the eighteenth century. These empirical observations place Yeshivas as the institutional heart of Kabbalah as a discipline (a gauntlet presently taken up only by Meir), raising a further question of comparison between the age of the kabbalistic Yeshiva and the overlapping Yeshiva revolution in Lithuania (alongside the largely imitative inception of the Hasidic Yeshiva). Here fieldwork, despite its hazard of anachronistic projection, can be valuable. For if a large swath of modern Kabbalah reaches into the present, the history of the present is rendered unavoidable.

In other words, at least since high kabbalistic modernity, one can speak of continuity in these social terms. It is in this framework that one should reject the centrality of Sabbateanism in understanding modern Kabbalah, due to its limited durability. It may be paradoxical and then again not so, that the continuities of mid to late modernity parallel the transformation of Kabbalah into a global cultural force that does not necessarily even overlap with the Jewish world (not to mention the orthodoxy alleged to have formed in this very period). Looking ahead both to our subsequent discussion of periods inside modern Kabbalah and the issue of future research, one should foreground the following guiding question: to what extent do the canons of high-late kabbalistic modernity relate to those of earlier modernity? And how do these relate to both the extra-kabbalistic world and options that fell down along the wayside, such as Sabbateanism? Answering these queries should afford some further insight as to our opening question of the autonomy of modern Kabbalah.

One can very well contend that the one factor that both unifies and uniquely identifies all of the three streams mentioned is their adherence to Safedian, and mostly Lurianic Kabbalah. The shared commitment to authority and to a given textual corpus overrides major conceptual differences (as around the *tzimtzum* issue or around the question of purist loyalty to Vital). Yet here one should point at a major difference, almost entirely overlooked in present research: Rashashian Kabbalah is joined by independent figures in its incredibly intensive dedication to close, page-by-page commentary on the Lurianic corpus, accompanied by remarkable philological efforts, upholding a vibrant manuscript culture. For these purposes, Zoharic commentary filtered through the Lurianic grid is part and parcel of the same exegetical project. Here Hasidism is closer to the rejected Sabbatean option in its moving away not so much from the Lurianic doctrine itself but from the detailed practice of *kavvanot* and the close study of the 'writings' (as the Hasidim often generally termed the Lurianic works, many of which did not reach Eastern Europe before the mid-nineteenth century). Hence it is clear why Hasidism, up to very recently, did not maintain a kabbalistic Yeshiva culture. The circle of R. Eliyahu of Vilna occupies a median position, relying on the Yeshiva-style training of its members to produce some exceptional commentaries (and super-commentaries, such as the recently released exegesis on Elyashiv's *Leshem Shvo ve-Ahlama* penned by Weintraub and his close disciples). However, Itzcovitz's dual move – the simplification of *kavvanot* and documented suspicion as to the textual veracity of most Lurianic works (itself a sign of philological alertness) greatly constricted these endeavors. These kabbalists were thus closer to their Eastern European rivals in being more concerned with adding new layers of meaning to Luria's images and terms than in delving, in the Sephardic fashion, into their minute details.[5] Though Itzcovitz himself kept it at a remove, the quasi-Sabbatean corpus of the Luzzatto circle (perhaps joining other covert Sabbatean influences) is most at home in the 'Lithuanian' stream. To the differences between Europe and the Near East in textual culture, one should add more extrinsic factors such as the far greater scope of print (joined and fueled by the demographic explosion) in the former, alongside with the role of vernaculization, in the form of (albeit mostly oral and mostly Hasidic) discourse in Yiddish (kabbalistic writing in Ladino is mostly confined to the Sabbatean movement).[6]

Yet in the face of this spectrum, a marked degree of continuity is assured by the constant return to the Lurianic corpus (in this hermeneutical sense greatly eclipsing its Cordoverian rival, which enjoyed far fewer commentaries).[7] Well outside the world of kabbalistic Yeshivas, and in little or no dialogue with its Sephardic mainstay, one should note the emergence of two new, twentieth-century canons – those of Ashlag and Kook. Both underwent the same process of grudged uncovering of manuscripts, editing and commentary as Luria's works did. One needs to be alert for the formation of further exemplars (as above on Elyashiv). All of these relatively continuous forms of discourse can be clearly differentiated not only from Kabbalah's reverberations outside the traditional Jewish world (including most

[5] Here one can fruitfully compare to the Lithuanian move away from detailed discussion of halakhic observance toward new conceptualizations of Talmudic thinking and logic (the *lomdut* revolution). Amongst Sephardic-style writers, one can include European journeyers to the east, such as Hai Ricci and his commentator Spielmann.

[6] Reiser and Mayse, *Language of Truth*; Lehmann, *Ladino Rabbinic Literature*, 57–58. As we have seen, twentieth-century discontinuous Kabbalah witnessed marked linguistic diversification.

[7] And the same holds true for its more rudimentary system of *kavvanot*.

academic writing), but also from the residual yet potent presence of ecstatic Kabbalah, representing a throwback to pre-Lurianic worlds. In recent decades, the latter (present also in the kabbalistic branch of the Kook circle) is enjoying some revival even in solid kabbalistic Yeshivas such as *Sha'ar ha-Shamayim*.

However, it cannot be denied that kabbalistic Christianity, which began, inter alia, as a form of Christian-Jewish polemic and by late modernity became part of a far more ecumenical movement (known today best as 'spiritual but not religious') is another constant of modern Kabbalah, with its own institutionalization in secret societies and sects. As part of the wider, cultural (rather than disciplinary) kabbalistic watershed, it resembles much of academic study of Kabbalah in several ways, including a greater interest in the *Zohar* (and hence the Sefirotic system) than in Luria, the near total absence of page-by-page commentary as well as a careful avoidance of *kavvanot*, in sharp distinction from the liturgical turn in mainstream modern Kabbalah, which included massive publication of prayer-books.[8]

The predilection for summary, as opposed to close reading, often led to a shared interest in a rather constricted, often medieval, set of themes: infinity, theosophy, sexuality and gender, and psychology.[9] This correlation is logical, due to the central role played by German idealism in the European reception of Kabbalah and the now rapidly dismantling Humboltian University. The clear influence of Hegel on Scholem as well as more traditional figures such Kook (and his student R. David Kohen) speaks for itself here. Academic research, as a form of discontinuous Kabbalah, has certainly contributed to its global reception. Yet this was a two-way street, starting with the first University-educated kabbalists such as di-Herera and Valle, and reaching to the marked impact of Henry Corbin (1903–1978) the renowned scholar of

[8] Idel, 'The Liturgical Turn'. It remains to be seen whether the admirable efforts of younger scholars (such as Assaf Tamari and Uri Safrai, following on Kallus, 'The Theurgy of Prayer') in analyzing Lurianic practice will draw academia closer to investigation of the Lurianic system and thus to the world of continuous Kabbalah. On the *Zohar* in kabbalistic Christianity, see Secret, *Zôhar*.

[9] It is not coincidental that a major institutional embodiment of the move of kabbalistic Christianity into a wider cultural frame was the Theosophical Society, while the term theosophy was central for both Scholem and Idel. When considering the role of Christianity itself, one must consider the strong academic stress on Christian influence on Kabbalah, first in Israel (esp. Liebes) and more recently in the United States (esp. Magid). This Eurocentric discussion is at great remove from the concerns of the Sephardic world (see below on Anidjar's critique, which could have well factored in the stark neglect of modern Sephardic Kabbalah in academic teaching as well as research).

both Islamic thought and Western Esotericism on several contemporary researchers (Elqayam, Garb and Wolfson).

This being said, as part of the process of professionalization, these long-term continuities described above enabled major branches of modern Kabbalah to disconnect from extra-Jewish intellectual concerns.[10] Furthermore, especially in the case of Rashashian Kabbalah and its environs, the strong commitment of medieval kabbalists to couch their innovations as commentary on the Bible or rabbinic corpus was released, as the proof-texts became increasingly those of Luria, then of Rashash, and now of his own super-commentaries. Here the following observation by Randal Collins captures the gist of this argument: 'Factions which keep their identities during many generations of argument become locked into a long dance step with one another; increasingly impervious to outside influences and turned inward upon their mutually constituted argumentative identities, they drive the collective conscience of the intellectual attention space repeatedly to new heights of abstract self-reflection.'[11] This considered, one should exercise caution as to sweeping claims of continuity with premodern sources. As a whole, modern kabbalists tend to address other modern kabbalists and this tendency is markedly on the increase, even as the academic habitus (even in undergraduate training) may still privilege the hallowed earlier periods. Complementing this process, one must point at the modern decline of entire medieval genres, such as cosmological commentaries on the Deed of Creation and the Deed of the Chariot (of Ezekiel), angelological lists (petering out after the sixteenth century) and commentaries on the ten *sefirot* (one of Scholem's early bibliographical projects).

Concomitantly, in examining Kabbalah after the Renaissance the proper domain of comparative study is less that of examining engagements with other religions (though discontinuous twentieth-century Kabbalah affords the fascinating discovery of the Far East), but rather looking into similarities in processes of modernization, true to the focus here on process rather than

[10] Tworek, *Eternity Now*, has shown that even when an earlier figure such as R. Shneur Zalman of Liadi resorts to philosophy (which he usually demonizes), it is that of the medievals rather than any current concern. Even the modern kabbalistic engagement with Greek thought (e.g. Maharal) no longer rested on any exposure to the original (or even its Arabic translations), and should be opposed to the revival of the classics in Renaissance thought, and in modern England and Germany (on the return to Greece in secular modern Judaism, see Shavit, *Judaism*, 317–416). Two exceptions are Horowitz's *Sefer ha-Brit* and the writings of R. David Kohen.

[11] Collins, *The Sociology of Philosophies*, 818.

content.[12] One obvious candidate for such a controlled comparison is that of the Jesuits, as an entirely modern, highly scholastic mystical movement. This would be less a case of influence (as suggested by Weinstein) but rather of structural similarities in responses to shared contexts.[13] Likewise, it would not be unfruitful to compare the role of the Catholic spiritual director to that of the *tzaddik* in some branches of Hasidism.[14] This study should be regional in its orientation, taking into account divergent paces and paths of modernity.[15] Regional distinctions somewhat overlap with the internal terms Sephardic and Ashkenazic, as utilized here throughout. Generally speaking, while in early modern Kabbalah the Spanish diaspora dominated, the weight of demography and especially the proliferation of Hasidism (as well as the success of Ashkenazi, often Hasidic, immigrants to the United States and of their descendants), shifted the balance to some extent (although the contemporary kabbalistic Yeshiva world is in thrall to Rashashian, and thus Sephardic discourse).

This focus, accompanied with attention to the role of custom and language (as above on Yiddish), can blend with examination of long-term continuities in specific locales. For example, it is intriguing that the Hasidic imagination returned to the medieval Hasidim (Pietists in scholarly parlance) of Germany.[16] It is also not coincidental that kabbalists and *Musar* teachers in contemporary Israel or North America still term themselves 'Lithuanians'. As for the Middle East, one may reread the text on Baghdad adduced in Chapter 6 from this perspective.[17]

SOME SHARED THEMES

Current Kabbalah research is typified by a shift away from Scholemian historical narrative (which was the genre adopted in this book, while

[12] For an example of such a venture, see Hervieu-Léger, 'Multiple Religious Modernities' (who focuses on the question of subjectivity). An interesting example of the possibilities afforded by exposure to Asian religion is the learned comparison of Abulafian and Yogic techniques (a direction first broached by Scholem), in Sen-Gupta, 'Abraham Abulafia'.

[13] Weinstein, *Kabbalah and Jewish Modernity*, 98–99, 134–135.

[14] Sluhovsky, *Becoming a New Self*, 44–52. Compare to Schachter-Shalomi, *Spiritual Intimacy*.

[15] One example could be the interaction between readsorption of the *conversos*, a process that affected early modern Kabbalah in many ways, and the culture of port Jews (a topic now enjoying innovative scholarly examination).

[16] The question of the relationship between medieval German and modern Eastern European Hasidism was first raised in Scholem, *Major Trends*, 118. For a recent case study, see Kahana, 'Sources of Knowledge'. For an attempt to stem the tide of the regional turn, see Rosman, *How Jewish Is Jewish History?*, 97–104.

[17] An unmined treasury of material on Baghdad and its kabbalists is Sabbath, *Yeshivot Baghdad*.

embodying the impossible aspiration toward comprehensiveness, as opposed to Scholem's 'major trends' mode) toward thematic, sometimes described as phenomenological investigation. Actually, in direct dialogue with fields such as religious studies, Scholem himself went along that path in his lectures at the Eranos conferences (attended by Corbin and Jung). The most divisive of these thematic discussions is that of gender. While dwelling on explicit sexual imagery differentiates much of scholarly writing from more reticent continuous forms of Kabbalah (though not from Sabbatean texts), one can find claims as to female equality (or even superiority) in both genres.[18] The connection between sexuality and nationalism (addressed most profoundly by George Mosse) can be noted here. The concern with gender often accompanies Zionist preoccupations in the often insular Israeli academic writing, and the indeed overall tendency of modern Kabbalah is toward intensification of particularistic identities (alongside the above-described retreat into intra-Jewish discourse). As found in medieval sources, the image of the covenant (usually reified in the *sefira* of *yesod*) closely links these two concerns.

Apologetic accounts of kabbalistic views on gender often occlude or sideline the striking (in comparison with other mystical cultures) absence of women in modern Kabbalah, nearly as total as in its premodern forms (Yiddish culture providing the most notable exceptions, as discussed in Chapter 4). Put bluntly, all of the texts surveyed in this volume were written by men, were intended for a male audience and indeed were almost entirely read by men. In Chapter 1 the dampening effect of menstrual impurity was mentioned as a possible cause. However, one can ask, more simply, if the situation was any different in other traditional forms of Jewish scholarship, such as philosophy or Talmudics. The limitation (originating already in Talmudic sources), of the supreme commandment of Torah study by women surely had a decisive effect. Likewise for the restriction of time-bound positive commandments (a large portion of those relevant in absence of the Temple and its rites) to men (coupled with the typically halakhic claim that performance out of duty is superior to action without obligation). This is especially true for modern Kabbalah, with its massive emphasis on the *kavvanot* of prayer and other such rites.

A closely related theme is that of messianism.[19] While the Scholemian account renders its propagation or neutralization the centerpiece of modern

[18] The writings of Nir Mennusi and Sara Y. Schneider, both students of Ginsburgh, have made their way into academic bibliographies.

[19] The relationship of messianism and sexuality deserves a separate study. See for now Idel, *Messianic Mystics*, esp. 143; Wolfson, 'The Engenderment of Messianic Politics'.

Kabbalah, alternative approaches (most notably that of Idel) point at the diverse nature of trends covered by this rubric, as well as ebbs and flows in the intensity of acute, activist or apocalyptic forms of redemptive outlooks. Nonetheless, the findings marshaled here would advocate a certain revival of the Scholemian account. Already in Talmudic literature one may find deliberations on the dependency of redemption on repentance. While the dominance of *teshuva* in different periods and comparison to medieval models require further study, the studies of scholars such as Jacob Elbaum have shown how this theme often cross-pollinated *Musar*, frequently interwoven with concern with sexual sins, known as 'blemish of the covenant' (and thus joining the national-sexual nexus).[20] Following the more psychological turn of Hasidism, more rarified discourses emerged, such as Kook's *Orot ha-Teshuva* (Lights of Repentance), a gem of mystical writing enjoying numerous commentaries, in both Israel and the United States.

A close competitor to messianism, especially in recent scholarship, is that of experience, itself one of the key words of late modernity, expressing broader processes of internalization and enhancement of subjectivity.[21] Once again, this concern bridges scholarly writers and many kabbbalistic authors, especially Hasidim and those joining later with the New Age. Here one can discern two major variants: On the one hand we have a continued concern with visionary experience, from Safed through Hasidism (especially Komarno, but also Bratzlav) and several Rashashian figures to contemporary writers, both traditional and academic, such as Morgenstern and Wolfson (also in his artwork).[22] One can subdivide here into anthropomorphic representations (continuing the *Idrot*) and more abstract, geometrical designs, incorporating the input of figures such as R. David ben Yehuda ha-Hasid (who was probably influenced by the an-iconic tendencies of the Islamic world).

On the other hand, building on the continued influence of Abulafian Kabbalah, one has a strong emphasis on auditory reception, through Habad to late modern writers (again both kabbalists and researchers) such as R. David Kohen and Idel. The latter cluster of techniques and experiences merges with more impersonal emphases on language. Here one must note that intensive engagement with the names of God (especially the

[20] Elbaum, *Repentance*.

[21] For the methodology of keywords in the history of culture, see Williams, *Keywords*.

[22] For a Bratzlav statement on the absolute centrality of anthropomorphic imagery in Kabbalah, earlier and that of 'these generations', see Sternhartz, *Liqqutei Halakhot*, vol. II, Laws of Minha Prayer, 7, 22, fol. 206A.

Tetragrammaton) joins virtually all streams of modern Kabbalah, from Safed through Rashash to the somewhat misleadingly named imagism. The late modern (and accelerating) blend of the Rashashian tradition with Hasidism is based on the shared interest in this theme, which also extends to theological renderings of Hasidic mysticism for wider audiences (as in the case of Green).[23] This mystique of Hebrew persists either in spite of, or dialectically because of (as in the fascination with the Hebrew language in kabbalistic Christianity and its later deriviations), the relative diminishing in the centrality of Hebrew in twentieth-century Kabbalah. Actually, this is a truly panoramic theme, continuing not only medieval Kabbalah but also the writings of late antiquity.[24] Furthermore, this is the most promising candidate for global comparative study, embracing parallels with Vedic culture and Japanese Buddhism.[25] Here one can also find the most overlap with the world of magic. Most studies in this vast domain (such as the remarkably detailed works of Gideon Bohak) still focus on the medieval and late antique periods (and indeed much continuity can be noted, as is typical for magical practice), so that Jewish Studies lacks endeavors such as Leigh Wilson's examination of the intertwining of magic and modernism, or Simon During's bold thesis as to the influence of magic (in secular forms) on modern culture.[26]

THREE PERIODS OF KABBALISTIC MODERNITY

Despite a certain unity of themes and processes (which should always be examined in tandem), it is still more productive to parse modern Kabbalah not only into centuries but also phases, for all the attendant risk of assuming linear progression. These were named throughout this volume as early, high and late modernity. Ruderman has already eloquently responded to doubts as to the utility of the term early modern for Jewish culture, and much of his argumentation is relevant for (and at times rests on) Kabbalah. The challenge to religious authority posed by Sabbateanism blended with a more general religious crisis, ranging from the Reformation through the general crisis of the seventeenth century to very early forms of secularization (as in Spinoza's Amsterdam). Representing the shift of Kabbalah from the very

[23] Green, *Seek My Face, Speak My Name*.

[24] For late antiquity, see e.g. Janowitz, *The Poetics of Ascent*.

[25] See for now Holdredge, *Veda and Torah*.

[26] Wilson, *Modernism and Magic* (and compare to Styers, *Making Magic*, esp. 12–14); During, *Modern Enchantment*. For exceptions in the Jewish context, see e.g. Harari, 'Jewish Incantation Texts'; Harari, 'Wonders and Sorceries'.

early modern (but not medieval) age of circles to the time of movements, Sabbateanism quite clearly sets apart the second half of the early modern period, perhaps ending in early Hasidism (which took the shift toward social movements one step further). Going back to the beginnings of modern Kabbalah, its partial break with its medieval predecessor can be seen as a foretelling of this crisis of authority.

Once Hasidism and post-Sabbatean corpora like those of the Luzzatto circle and Hai Ricci were absorbed within the kabbalistic mainstream, one can discern a successful resolution of the crisis of authority, through the high modern canons of the eighteenth century, all resting solidly on the sanctified Lurianic corpus. Thus, this was the time of the breakthrough of Lurianic Kabbalah toward printing and extensive commentary (see below). Here we can also observe the beginning of the move of Kabbalah further outward from a form of Christian thought toward full-fledged participation in the cultural and philosophical life of Europe. Notwithstanding the regional gap between this European context and the Middle East, the commonality is the successful stabilization and proliferation of Kabbalah, resting on but reaching beyond the elitist concerns of Lurianism. Here the steady expansion of Kabbalah beyond the traditional and even beyond the Jewish world dovetailed with the internal drive to freer propagation of this lore in late modern kabbalistic circles, ranging from Komarno to Elyashiv.

The romance (now in the context of Romanticism) between Kabbalah and general philosophical-literary culture signifies the late modern rapprochement between Kabbalah and philosophy. Here one may join another common denominator of late modernity: non-Sabbatean and often sublimated messianism.[27] This type of thought easily bridges Kabbalah and German Jewish philosophy (as demonstrated by Rosenzweig and Bloch).[28] Although the relationship between modernization as a process and modernism as a literary-philosophical trend is both complex and contested, one can risk simplification and assert that modernism is the cultural stance of late modernity. Having done so, one can bring the study of Kabbalah in this period (especially, but not only, in its extra-Jewish forms) into engagement with the array of studies of modernism as a mystical, esoteric or occult set of images and tropes (according to the nomenclature espoused by various

27 Sublimation is itself very much a late modern term, often associated with modernism, to which we shall soon turn. There is room for a study dedicated to kabbalistic forms of sublimation (and also sublimation or *aufheben* in the Hegelian sense). For now see Idel, *Hasidism*, 62.

28 For an overview see Bouretz, 'Messianism'.

researchers).[29] From the bewildering range of definitions of modernism, one may select two that are pertinent for the development of late modern Kabbalah: ontological uncertainty, a doubt-ridden state that captures much of the writing of figures such as R. Nahman of Bratzlav and Leiner, and the resort to spiritual alternatives to mainstream modernity in pursuit of revitalization, an aspiration best expressed in the writings of Kook.[30]

The final and most striking characteristic of late modern Kabbalah, which after all was the main focus of this volume, is the triumph of globalization. Here one remarkable unresearched text is *Mesharim Magid* by the late twentieth-century Australian kabbalist R. Yitzhak Tzevi Bernfeld (c.1916–1998), who traveled to sites such as the Galápagos Islands, in order to perform the appropriate 'rectifications'. Here is an appetizer:

> At midnight in the town of Pago Pago in the remote island of Samoa in the great ocean of the United States . . . 5727 (1967), it [the *magid* or revelatory entity] appeared to me as a child of around twelve, after [I performed] the [midnight] *tiqqun* of Rachel and Leah . . . he came to me while I was in a pool of tears over being in this remote island, and he comforted me with glad face and said to me: 'Happy are you and it shall be well for you [Psalms 128, 2], for from the day that God created heaven and earth, no man like you made a blessing with *kavvana* on this island, which is full of the sons of Ham, son of Noah, and by reciting the midnight prayer that numerically equals *Het Mem* [The letters of Ham] you rectified some of them, and were it not for the powers of Lilith wandering around the place [due to the sexual sins of the inhabitants] I would allow you to stay in it.'[31]

AREAS FOR FUTURE RESEARCH

Besides a daunting mass of unresearched (and even unstudied) works such as the one just cited, the preceding chapters can furnish decades of further work on genres, figures, processes, themes, trends and contexts. Yet the most glaring lacuna, alluded to above, is that of page-by-page commentary on Luria (or the *Zohar* mediated via Luria). This rapidly expanding literature ranges from the Italian school of Ramaz through the vast Rashashian corpus

[29] Besides the studies cited in Chapter 5, see Talar (ed.), *Modernists and Mystics*; Eburey, *Modernism and Cosmology*.

[30] For ontological uncertainty, see Foley, *Haunting Modernisms*, 21–25. For doubt and modern Kabbalah, see Garb, 'Doubt and Certainty'. On modernism and revitalization I was advised by Gooding-Williams, *Zarathustra*, dealing with a figure (Nietzsche) who clearly influenced Kook, Zeitlin and other modernist kabbalists.

[31] Abuhatzera (ed.), *Liqqutei Mesharim Magid*, 71.

(and its independent tributaries, such as the works of R. Shlomo Kohen and R. Yehuda Petaya) to the relatively new genre of Hasidic commentary (as in *Netiv Hayyim* by Morgenstern, building on the heritage of Komarno, itself enjoying a renaissance now). In this ever-expanding genre, one may find, inter alia, super-commentaries on nineteenth-century works such as the writings of Sasson. On R. Ya'akov Tzemakh's edition *Otzrot Hayyim* alone one can already find entire shelves of commentaries, mostly Sephardic and Lithuanian. Not only is there no academic parallel to Shamma Freidman's *Talmud ha-Igud* project or Jacob Bildstein's close commentary on Maimonides, we do not even possess a bibliographical overview of this literature or a discussion of major divergences and variants. Similarly, there has been no attempt to encapsulate the modern kabbalistic exegesis of the Bible (Valle alone providing several dozens of volumes), tractate *Avot* of the Mishna or the *Aggada* (e.g. the fantastic tales of Rabba bar Rav Hanna in tractate *Baba Batra*). Unlike the commentary on Luria, these subgenres largely continue and expand medieval projects. Indeed, the major continuity between medieval and modern Kabbalah lies in the shared reservoir of earlier and binding sources (here one should note the continued practice of commenting on *Sefer Yetzira*, as in the circle of R. Eliyahu of Vilna).

A final, though mostly late modern, topic is the role of technology – both in facilitating the propagation of Kabbalah and as a theme in kabbalistic discourse. In other words, the unity of content and process is most apparent here. Already amongst nineteenth-century writers such as Sternhartz, Safrin and Spielmann one may find numerous images relating to new developments such as the railways, telegraphs and other 'machines'. And here is an early twentieth-century (1925) description (penned by Kook's student Harlap) of the role of kabbalistic theurgists:

> I am now . . . with our teacher the Gaon of Israel and its holiness [Kook] . . . It is impossible to transmit the impressions . . . but I will venture one simile . . . a large machine supports some markets and maybe also some large towns, and in one of the small corners one or two people [i.e. Kook and himself] open the motor and close it, and quietly and calmly and unfailingly do their work . . . and no one knows of them, know and understand this.[32]

In recent years, the shift from print to audiovisual and digital media has both greatly facilitated the spread of Kabbalah in all levels of profundity (pioneered by Habad) as well as evoking discourses centered on

[32] Harlap, *Mikhtavei Marom*, 67.

demonization of the Internet (as in the equation of Google with the apocalyptic archenemy of Gog, as described in the book of Ezekiel). Thus, appreciating the increasing role of the intrinsically accelerating phenomenon of technology in Kabbalah (affording fruitful comparison with other mystical systems) requires a far finer resolution than our tripartite periodization. Also regional differences can be very meaningful in both the adoption of technology and its interpretation in kabbalistic terms (see above on print).

CODA

It is perhaps fitting that we began this chapter with Scholem, who more than any one person represents the academization of Kabbalah in late modernity. In recent years, we have increasingly witnessed a certain blurring of the distinction (also in the terms developed by the French sociologist Pierre Bourdieu) between research and the amplification of kabbalistic themes in general culture (especially the New Age movement). This process partly accounts for the accelerating quantitative increase and successful reception of books on Kabbalah (at a monthly rate this decade). While much of this writing returns to known, often medieval corpora such as the *Zohar*, one can note the breaking of new, philologically based ground in the study of central yet unresearched early modern kabbalists (such as R. Menahem ʻAzzariya of Fano or Hai Ricci).[33] Ironically, the decline of government funding for the humanities worldwide has fueled this process, as competition for dwindling scholarships and positions (coupled with the financial pressure on Universities to increase the number of doctorates produced in their 'teaching machine') exacerbate the 'publish or perish' routine.[34] However, in a more positive vein, one should marvel at the intrinsic dynamism of the Scholemian school, which has been able to successfully reinvent itself over three further generations (also enriched by the input of figures held at a distance by Scholem, especially Alexander Altmann and their own disciples).

Concomitantly, the basic groundwork of manuscript publication has largely shifted to the Yeshiva world, whose scholars are also increasingly

[33] One should add that the recent shift to the *Idrot* in Zoharic research provides a welcome bridge with modern Kabbalah, which (starting with Luria) largely focused on this Zoharic layer.

[34] See Spivak, *Teaching Machine*. Her postcolonial reflections (esp. 56–64, 278–280) are relevant for indigenous forms of knowledge, the less addressed of whom are Middle Eastern (see Anidjar, 'Jewish Mysticism' and cf. Idel, 'Orienting'). For the delicate interplay of indigenous and imported concepts of spirituality, see Van der Veer, *The Modern Spirit of Asia*.

engaged in detailed historical investigation (as in the case of Avish Schor, who figured prominently in earlier chapters). Indeed, the very potential for discovery of new manuscripts (still a frequent and exciting event) relies largely on private holdings in the *Haredi* (or semi-*Haredi*) worlds.[35] In true dialectical fashion (an approach famously espoused by Scholem), this dual process both deepens and mitigates the tensions between continuous, globalized and discontinuous, parochial and exegetical forms of Kabbalah. These shifts of symbolic capital and emotional energy may well be of portent for the unfolding of the history of modern Kabbalah over the course of the present century.[36]

[35] Known examples include parts of the corpora of Ashlag, Elyashiv, Hutner, Kohen, Kook and Weintraub.

[36] For these terms, with application to academic life, see Collins, *The Sociology of Philosophies*, 28–40.

APPENDIX

Timeline[1]

Major events in general and Jewish modernity	Main events in the history of modern Kabbalah
1453 The Fall of Constantinople to the Ottoman Empire and the end of the Byzantine Empire.	c.1480 R. Meir ibn Gabbai born in Spain.
c.1455 Printing of the Gutenberg Bible.	c.1480 R. David ibn Zimra born in Spain.
1478 Establishment of the Spanish Inquisition.	c.1485 R. Shimeon ibn Lavi born in Spain.
1492 The Alhambra Decree orders the expulsion of the Jews from Castile and Aragon.	1486 Pico della Mirandola publishes his *900 Theses*.
1492 Christopher Columbus lands in the Americas.	1488 R. Yosef Karo born in Spain.
1494–1559 The Italian Wars.	c.1500 R. Shlomo ha-Levi Alqabetz born in Salonika.
1501 King Alexander of Poland readmits Jews to the Grand Duchy of Lithuania.	c.1513 R. Abraham ben Eli'ezer ha-Levi arrives in Jerusalem.
1516 Ghetto of Venice established.	1517 Johann Reuchlin's *De Arte Cabalistica* published in Haguenau.
1517 Martin Luther publishes his *95 Theses*.	c.1520 R. Yehuda Loew, Maharal of Prague, is born.
1517 The Ottoman Empire conquers Palestine.	1522 R. Moshe Cordovero is born, and soon after arrives in Safed.
1520–1566 Reign of the Ottoman Emperor Suleiman the Magnificent.	1534 R. Itzhak Luria born in Egypt.
1529 The Ottoman armies are defeated at the Siege of Vienna.	c.1535 R. Shlomo Alqabetz and R. Yosef Karo arrive in Safed.
1540 The foundation of the Jesuit Order.	1542 R. Hayyim Vital born in Safed.
1542 Establishment of the Roman Inquisition.	c.1548 R. Yosef ibn Sayyah arrives in Jerusalem.
1545–1563 The Council of Trent.	1548 R. Menahem 'Azaria da Fano born in Bologna.
	1558–1560 Printing of the *Zohar* in Mantua and Cremona.

[1] A few of the events listed here are drawn from the timeline (naturally with a rather different focus) found in Arnold-Leibman, *Messianism, Secrecy and Mysticism*, xxi–xxviii.

(cont.)

Major events in general and Jewish modernity	Main events in the history of modern Kabbalah
1553 Burning of the Talmud in Rome.	1561 Printing of R. Yosef Gikatilla's *Sh'arei Orah* in Mantua.
1580 First session of the Council of Four Lands in Lublin, Poland.	1565 R. Sabbetai Sheftel Horowitz born in Prague.
1593 Pope Clement VIII expels the Jews from the Papal states.	1565 R. Yosef Karo's *Sulkhan 'Arukh* printed in Venice.
1598 The Edict of Nantes ends the French Wars of Religion.	1567 R. Meir ibn Gabbai's *'Avodat ha-Qodesh* published in Venice.
1618–1648 The Thirty Years' War.	c.1570 R. Itzhak Luria arrives in Safed.
1648 The Peace Treaties of Westphalia.	c.1570 R. Yosef ibn Tavul arrives in Safed.
1648 The Chmielnicki uprising and massacres of Jews in the Polish-Lithuanian commonwealth.	1562 R. Abraham Kohen de Herrera born to a *converso* family.
1660 Royal Society of London for the Improvement of Natural Knowledge founded.	c.1583 Lurianic manuscripts begin to circulate in Italy.
1683 The Ottoman armies are defeated in the second Siege of Vienna.	1592 R. Moshe Cordovero's *Pardes Rimonim* is published in Cracow.
1701 Kingdom of Prussia declared under King Frederick I.	1598 R. Shmuel Vital born in Damascus.
1712 First steam engine is commercialized.	1618 R. Ya'akov Tzemach arrives in Palestine.
1740 Frederick the Great comes to power in Prussia.	c.1620 R. Moshe Zacuto born in Amsterdam.
1772–1795 The Partitions of Poland.	c.1624 R. Meir Poppers born in Cracow.
1776 The United States' Declaration of Independence.	1626 Shabbetai Tzevi born in Smyrna.
1782 Austrian Emperor Joseph II issues his edict of tolerance.	1627 Abraham Miguel Cardozo born in Spain.
1789 Declaration of the Rights of Man and of the Citizen and the beginning of the French Revolution.	1643/4 Nathan Ashkenazi of Gaza born in Jerusalem.
1801 Formation of the United Kingdom.	1648 R. Naftali Bakrakh's *'Emeq ha-Melekh* published in Amsterdam.
1803–1815 The Napoleonic Wars.	1648 R. Yesh'ayahu Horowitz's *Shnei Luhot ha-Brit* published in Amsterdam.
1804 Napoleon crowns himself Emperor of the French.	1665 Shabbetai Tzevi proclaimed Messiah by his followers.
1804 Austrian Empire founded by Francis I.	1666 Shabbetai Tzevi converts to Islam.
1806 Treaty of Pressburg and the end of the Holy Roman Empire.	1677–1684 Knorr von Rosenroth's *Kabbala Denudata* published in Sulzbach.
1812 Prussia's Edict of Emancipation grants citizenship to Jews.	1690 R. Yonatan Eybeschütz born in Cracow.
1815 The Congress of Vienna redraws the European map.	1696 R. Hayyim ben 'Attar born in Morocco.
1821 The Odessa pogroms.	1698 R. Jacob Emden born in Altona.
1829 First electric motor built.	1698 R. Moshe Graf's *Va-Yakhel Moshe* published in Dessau.
1831 France invades and occupies Algeria.	c.1699 R. Israel Ba'al Shem Tov born in Podolia.
1837–1901 The Victorian era.	1707 R. Moshe Hayyim Luzzatto born in Padua.
1840 The Damascus blood libel.	

(cont.)

Major events in general and Jewish modernity	Main events in the history of modern Kabbalah
1848 The Communist Manifesto published.	1704 R. Dov Baer Freidman, the Maggid of Mezeritch, born in Lokachi.
1848 Revolutions of 1848 in Europe, the 'Spring of Nations'.	1720 R. Eliyahu Kremer (Zalmanovitch), the Vilna Gaon, born in Sialiec (Belarus).
1858–1947 Following the Indian Rebellion of 1857 the British Empire assumes control of India.	1720 R. Shalom Shar'abi born in Yemen.
1859 Charles Darwin publishes *On the Origin of Species*.	1726 Yaakov Frank born in the Polish-Lithuanian commonwealth.
1861–1865 The American Civil War.	1730 R. Moshe Hayyim Luzzatto's first ban and later excommunication.
1863 Abraham Lincoln issues the Emancipation Proclamation.	1736 R. Yosef Irgas' *Shomer Emunim* published in Amsterdam.
1863–1865 Polish uprising against the Russian Empire.	1737 The *Beit El* Yeshiva founded in Jerusalem.
1869 First transcontinental railroad completed in United States.	1742 R. Immanuel Hai Ricci's *Mishnat Hasidim* published in Amsterdam.
1869 The Suez Canal opens, linking the Mediterranean to the Red Sea.	1749 R. Hayyim Itzkovitz born in Volozhin.
1870–1871 The Franco-Prussian War.	1751 R. Shalom Shar'abi becomes dean of the *Beit El* Yeshiva.
1881 'Storms in the South' pogroms in the Russian Empire.	1756 The Brody Ban on the popular study of Kabbalah.
1881 First electrical power plant and grid in Britain.	1772 The bans of excommunication against the Hasidim.
1882 The British invasion and occupation of Egypt.	1782 R. Meir Poppers' edition of R. Hayyim Vital's *Derekh 'Etz Hayyim* published in Koretz.
1884–1885 The Berlin Conference and the start of the European 'scramble for Africa'.	1802 The Volozhin Yeshiva, 'mother' of Lithuanian Yeshivas, is founded.
1894–1906 Dreyfus Affair in France.	1803 R. Yaakov Kopel Lipshitz's *Sha'arei Gan Eden* published in Koretz.
1897 The First World Zionist Congress held at Basel.	1808 R. Nahman of Bratzlav's *Liqqutei Moharan* published in Ostroh, Ukraine.
1903 First controlled flight of the Wright Brothers.	c.1821 The Great Wedding in Ustila, and the 'trial' of the Psischa Hasidim.
1905 Albert Einstein's formulation of relativity.	1841 R. Shlomo Haikel Elyashiv born in Siauliai, Lithuania.
1908 Young Turk Revolution in the Ottoman Empire.	1865 R. Abraham Itzhak Kook born in Griva, Latvia.
1913 Ford Motor Company introduces the first moving assembly line.	1876–1883 R. Ya'akov Meir Spielmann's *Tal Orot* published in Lemberg.
1914–1918 World War I.	1871 Hillel Zeitlin born in Mogilev Governorate (Belarus).
1915 Armenian genocide in the Ottoman Empire.	1878 Martin Buber born in Vienna.
1916–1918 The Great Arab Revolt.	1885 R. Yehuda Leib Ashlag born in Lodz.
1917 October Revolution in Russia.	1890 R. Hayyim Shaul ha-Kohen Dweck arrives in Jerusalem.
1917 The Balfour Declaration, announcing support for the establishment of a 'national home for the Jewish people' in Palestine.	1896 *Rehovot ha-Nahar* Yeshiva breaks away from *Beit El* Yeshiva.

(cont.)

Major events in general and Jewish modernity	Main events in the history of modern Kabbalah
1918 The Partition of the Ottoman Empire.	1897 Gershom (Gerhard) Scholem born in Berlin.
1918 The British occupy Palestine.	1897 *Tomkehi Temimim*, the first Hasidic (Habad) Yeshiva, founded in Lubavitch, Russia.
1919 Treaty of Versailles.	1902 R. Menahem Mendel Schneerson born in Nikolayev, Ukraine.
1919 The establishment of the Weimar Republic.	1906 *Sha'ar ha-Shamayim*, the first Ashkenazi kabbalistic Yeshiva, founded in Jerusalem.
1919 League of Nations founded in Paris.	1921 R. Kook becomes the first Ashkenazi Chief Rabbi of mandatory Palestine.
1920 Mandatory Palestine established.	1941 Gershom Scholem's *Major Trends in Jewish Mysticism* published in New York.
1922–1925 Benito Mussolini rises to power in Italy.	1946 R. Yoel Teitelbaum, the Satmar *rebbe*, arrives in New York.
1922 The Union of Soviet Socialist Republics (USSR) is formed.	1951 R. Menahem Mendel Schneerson becomes the (last) Rebbe of Habad.
1923 Kemal Atatürk becomes the first president of the newly established Republic of Turkey.	1968 R. Shlomo Carlebach founds House of Love and Prayer in San Francisco.
1927 Joseph Stalin becomes leader of the Soviet Union.	1993 Charles Mopsik's *Les grands textes de le Cabale* published in Paris.
1929 Arab riots in Palestine.	c.1972 R. Ya'akov Hillel founds *Hevrat Ahavat Shalom* Yeshiva in Jerusalem.
1933 Adolf Hitler becomes Chancellor of Germany.	1974 R. Zvi Yehuda Kook involved in formation of *Gush Emunim* settlement movement.
1935 Enactment of the Nuremberg racial laws.	c.1991 foundation of *Bnei Barukh* Ashalgian fellowship.
1936–1939 The Spanish Civil War.	
1936–1939 Arab revolt in Palestine.	
1937 Japanese invasion of China, and the beginning of World War II in the Far East.	
1938 Anschluss unifies Germany and Austria; Munich Agreement hands Czechoslovakia to Nazi Germany; Kristallnacht.	
1939–1945 World War II; the Holocaust.	
1945 United Nations founded. Nuremberg trials for war criminals begin.	
1947 United Nations Partition Plan for Palestine. The Israeli War of Independence begins.	
1947 Independence of India and Pakistan after partition.	
1948 Israeli Declaration of Independence.	
1950 Beginning of Tibetan Diaspora after Communist Chinese takeover.	
1952 First detonation of thermonuclear weapon.	
1959–1975 Vietnam War.	
1961 Berlin Crisis.	
1962 Cuban missile crisis.	
1967 The Six-Day War.	

(cont.)

Major events in general and Jewish modernity	Main events in the history of modern Kabbalah
1968 Worldwide protests, especially in Czechoslovakia and France.	
1971 Switzerland joins the rest of Europe in recognizing women's suffrage.	
1973 The October/Yom Kippur War.	
1977 Likud Party led by Menachem Begin wins Israeli elections.	
1978–1979 Israeli-Egyptian peace accords.	
1982 The First Lebanon War.	
1989 Dismantling of Berlin Wall.	
1991 Dissolution of Soviet Union.	
c.1991 The Internet goes online.	
1993 End of apartheid regime in South Africa.	
1993 Israeli-Palestinian Oslo Accords.	
1993 Maastricht Treaty establishes European Union.	
1996 First electoral victory of Benjamin Netanyahu.	
2001 Terrorist attack on Twin Towers in New York.	

Glossary

Aggada nonlegal portions of the Talmuds
Ashkenazim Jews of Western, central and Eastern Europe
'assiya making, lowest of the four worlds
atzilut emanation, highest and divine of the four worlds
'ayin nothingness, as a cosmic state prior to emanation and as a mystical aspiration (especially in Hasidism)
beri'a creation, second of the four worlds
Bina understanding, the third of the *sefirot*
birur sifting of the divine sparks prior to uplifting them
Da'at knowledge, if listed as one of the *sefirot*, it is the third (instead of Keter)
devequt adherence to God, usually emotional
Ein Sof infinite divine reality
gematria numerological method based on the numerical value of Hebrew words
gilgul transmigration of souls
Halakha Jewish religious law
hanhagot literary genre designed for molding everyday conduct
Hasidism Eastern European mystical movement founded in the eighteenth century
Hasidut Ashkenaz German Jewish Pietistic movement in the twelfth and thirteenth centuries
heikhalot (lit. chambers). A corpus of late antique Jewish mystical writings heavily edited in the medieval period
Hokhma wisdom, the second of the *sefirot*
kavvanot meditative intentions of the prayers

middot divine (as in *middot* of mercy) or human emotional qualities. Often the subject of *Musar* discourse
Mishna Jewish legal code, edited in the second and third centuries. The basis of the Talmuds
mitzvot the commandments and prohibitions of the Law
mohin intelligences, the higher *sefirot* in the Lurianic system
Musar medieval and modern literature on self-perfection
partzufim facial countenances, which in modern Kabbalah often reorganize the system of the *sefirot*
pshat plain sense of the text
qelipot husks or demonic layers
rebbe Hasidic master
sefirot ten emanations or potencies making up the basic structure of the supernal realm
Sephardim Jews of the Near East, North Africa and Balkans
Shekhina immanent divine presence, usually feminine and associated with the lowest of the *sefirot*
shemtitot cosmic cycles patterned on the Biblical Sabbatical Law
shevira primordial calamity of the breaking of vessels containing the light of the *sefirot*
teshuva repentance, but also self-transformation
tiqqun cosmic rectification
tzaddik righteous, could be a divine aspect or a human leader
tzelem anthropomorphic divine image
tzimtzum primordial contraction or withdrawal of the infinite light
Yetzira formation. Third of the four worlds
Yihudim mental Unifications of divine names
yishuv settlement, generally refers to the phases of Jewish presence in the land of Israel prior to the state
yovlim cosmic cycles patterned on the Biblical Jubilee law
zivug intercourse between the male and female aspects of the divine

Bibliography

SOURCES

Abuhatzera, Ran (ed.), *Liqqutei Mesharim Magid*, 2nd ed. Afula, 2015.

Alqabetz, Shlomo, *Brit Halevi (Commentary on the Passover Hagada)*. Lemberg, 1863.

Ashkenazi, Tzevi Hirsch, *Hakham Tzevi Responsa*. Debriziner, 1942.

Ashlag, Yehuda Leib, *Igrot ha-Sulam (Letters)*. Bnei Brak, 2014.

Ma'amrei ha-Sulam. Bnei Brak, 2017.

Talmud 'Eser Sefirot, 7 vols. Jerusalem, 1970, vol. I.

The Writings of the Last Generation and the Nation, C. Ratz (trans.). Toronto: Laitman Kabbalah Publishers, 2015.

Avraham Dov of Ovruch, *Bat 'Ayin*, 2 vols. New York, 2014, vol. II.

Azikri, El'azar, *Sefer ha-Haredim ha-Shalem*. Jerusalem, 1990.

Bakrakh, Naftali, *'Emeq ha-Melekh*, Bnei Brak, 1973 (reprint of Amsterdam, 1648).

Ben Israel, Menashe, *Nishmat Hayyim*. Jerusalem, 1998 (reprint of Leipzig, 1862).

Bloch, Yehuda Leib, *Shi'urei Da'at (Lectures on Musar)*, 3 vols. Tel Aviv, 1953, vol. III.

Buber, Martin, *Hasidism and Modern Man*. New York: Horizon Press, 1958.

Chavel, Charles (H. Dov) (ed.), *Kitvei ha-Ramban*, 2 vols. Jerusalem: Mossad ha-Rav Kook, 1964, vol. II.

Chriqui, Mordekhai (ed.), *The Letters of Ramhal and His Generation*. Jerusalem, 2001.

Cohen, Hermann, *Religion der Vernunft: Aus den Quellen des Judentums*. Frankfurt am Main: Verlag, 1929 (trans. by S. Kaplan as *The Religion of Reason*, New York: Fredrick Unger, 1972).

Cordovero, Moshe, *The Palm Tree of Deborah*, L. Jacobs (ed. and trans.). London: Vallentine, Mitchell, 1960.
Pardes Rimonim. Jerusalem, 1962.
Shi'ur Qoma. Warsaw, 1883.
Da Fano, Menahem 'Azzariya, *Kanfei Yonah*. Jerusalem, 1998.
Pelah ha-Rimmon (with *'Asis Rimonim*). Jerusalem, 2000.
Da Vidas, Eliyahu, *Reshit Hokhma*. Warsaw, 1875.
De Hererra, Avraham Kohen, *Gate of Heaven*, K. Krabbenhoft (trans.). Leiden: Brill, 2002.
De la Rossa, Hayyim, *Torat Hakham*. Jerusalem, 1999.
De Modena, Yehuda Arye, *Ari Nohem*. Jerusalem, 1929.
Del Medigo, Yosef, *Mezaref la-Hokhma*, Warsaw, 1890.
Shever Yosef (printed with other writings), Basiliah, 1629.
Doron, Erez Moshe, *The Warriors of Transcendence*, R. Misk (trans.). Mevo Horon, 2008.
Ehrenfeld, Shmu'el, *Yira'ukha im-Shemesh*. Jerusalem, 2012.
Eliot, George, *Daniel Deronda*. New York: Harper & Brothers, 1876.
Elyashiv, Shlomo, *Leshem Shvu ve-Ahlama: Drushi 'Olam ha-Tohu*. Jerusalem, 1976.
Emden, Ya'akov, *Mitpahat Sefarim*. Lvov, 1870.
Fischel, Eli'ezer of Strizov, *Olam Hafukh*. Jerusalem, 2006.
Fraenkel, Avinoam, *Nefesh ha-Tzimtzum: Understanding Nefesh haChaim through the Key Concept of Tzimtzum and Related Writings*, 2 vols. Jerusalem: Urim, 2015.
Frankel, Elimelekh E. (ed.), *Imrei Pinhas*, 2 vols. Bnei Brak, 2003, vol. I.
Ginsburgh, Itzhak, *Kabbalah and Meditation for the Nations*, M. Genuth (ed.). Jerusalem, 2011.
Glazerson, Mattityahu, *The Grandeur of Judaism and the East: Judaism and Meditation*. Johannesburg: Himelsein-Glazerson, 1981.
Gotlieb, Avraham Mordekhai, *Hashem Sima'kha Sham'ati (Talks on the True Worship of God Recorded by the Loyal Students)*. Qiriat Ye'arim, 2009.
Grade, Hayyim, *The Yeshiva: Masters and Disciples*, C. Leviant (trans.), 2 vols. Indianapolis: Bobbs-Merrill, 1977, vol. II.
Greenberg, Uri Zvi, *Collected Writings*, 19 vols. Jerusalem: Bialik Institute, 1991, vol. III. [Hebrew]
Hadaya, 'Ovadya, *Yaskil 'Avdi*, 8 vols. Jerusalem, 1983, vol. VIII.
Hai Ricci, Immanuel, *Yosher Levav*. Safed, 2010.
Ha-Kohen, Nathan Net'a (ed.), *Mayim Rabim: Sayings of R. Yehiel Mikhel of Zlotshov*. Warsaw, 1899.
Halberstam, Hayyim of Zanz, *Divrei Hayyim*, 3 vols. New York, 2003, vol. II.
Harlap, Ya'akov Moshe, *Mikhtavei Marom*. Jerusalem, 1988.
Haver, Itzhak, *Pithei She'arim*. Tel Aviv, 1995.

Hegel, Georg Wilhelm Friedrich, *Lectures on the History of Philosophy: Plato and the Platonists*, E. S. Haldane and F. H. Simpson (trans.), 3 vols. Lincoln: University of Nebraska Press, 1995.

Hemdat Yamim, 3 vols. Bnei Brak, 2011, vol. I.

Hillel, Ya'akov Moshe, *Ahavat Shalom*. Jerusalem, 2002.

Hirsch, Samson Raphael, *The Nineteen Letters*, B. Drachman (trans.). New York: Feldheim, 1969.

Horowitz, Eli'ezer (ed.), *Torat ha-Maggid mi-Zlotchov*. Jerusalem, 1999.

Horowitz, Sabbetai Sheftel, *Shef'a Tal*. Jerusalem, 1971.

Irgas, Yosef, *Shomer Emunim*. Jerusalem, 1965.

Itamari, Eliyahu, *Shevet Musar*. Petrakov, 1889.

Itzkovitz, Itzhak (of Volozhin), *Milei de-Avot*. Vilna, 1888.

Jung, Carl Gustav, *Memories, Dreams, Reflections*, Aniela Jaffé (ed.) and R. and C. Winston (trans.). London: Fontana, 1983.

Kafka, Franz, *The Zuerau Aphorisms*, M. Hofman (trans.). London: Harvill Secker, 2006.

Kaplan, Avraham Eliyahu, *Selected Writings*. Jerusalem, 2006. [Hebrew]

Koidanover, Tzevi Hirsch, *Qav ha-Yashar*, Jerusalem, 1982.

Kook, Avraham Itzhaq, *Orot*. Jerusalem: Mossad ha-Rav Kook, 1985.

Orot ha-Qodesh, 4 vols. Jerusalem: Mossad ha-Rav Kook, 1963, vol. I.

Kremer, Eliyahu (the Gaon of Vilna), *Commentary on Sifra de-Tzniuta*. Bnei Brak, 1983.

Leibovitz, Yeruham, *Da'at Hokhma u-Mussar* (Hever Ma'amarim), 6 vols. New York, 1967, vol. IV.

Leiner, Gershon Hanokh, *Ha-Hakdama ve Ha-Petikha*. Bnei Brak, 1996.

Leiner, Yosef Mordekhai, *Mei ha-Siloach*, 2 vols. Beni Brak, 1995.

Loew, Yehuda (Maharal), *Derekh Hayyim*. Bnei Brak, 1980.

Netzah Israel. Bnei Brak, 1980.

Tiferet Yisrael. Bnei Brak, 1980.

Luzzatto, Moshe Hayyim, *The Knowing Heart* (*Da'ath Tevunoth*), S. Silverstein (trans). New York: Feldheim, 1982.

The Path of the Upright (*Mesilat Yesharim*), S. Silverstein (trans.). New York: Feldheim, 1980.

Matt, Daniel (trans. and commentary), *The Zohar: Pritzker Edition*, 12 vols. Stanford University Press, 2014, vol. VIII.

Meizels, Uziel, *Tiferet 'Uziel*. Warsaw, 1863.

Miller, Chaim (trans.), *The Practical Tanya, Part One: The Book for Inbetweeners*. New York: Kol Menachem, 2016.

Molkho, Shlomo, *Shemen Zayyit Zakh*. Jerusalem, 2002.

Morgenstern, Itzhak Meir, *Yam ha-Hokhma-2008*. Jerusalem, 2008.

Yam ha-Hokhma-2010. Jerusalem, 2010.

Petaya, Yehuda, *Beit Lehem Yehuda*, 4 vols. Jerusalem, 2008, vol. I.

Potok, Chaim, *The Chosen*. London: Penguin Books, 1970.
Rapoport, Shlomo, *Markevet ha-Mishne*. Frankfurt, 1751.
Safrin, Yitzhak Eizek, *Sulkhan ha-Tahor*. New York, 2009.
Schatz, Moshe, *Tarshish, Shoham ve Yashfe*. Jerusalem, 2018.
Schneerson, Menahem Mendel. *Torat Menahem 1952*. New York, 1995.
Schneerson, Shlomo Zalman, *Magen Avot*. Berditchev, 1902.
Shach, Eli'ezer Menachem, *'Avi 'Ezri* (on Maimonides' Code of Law). Bnei Brak, 1995.
Spielmann, Ya'akov Meir, *Tal Orot*. Jerusalem, 2015.
Sternhartz, Nathan, *Liqqutei Halakhot*, 8 vols. Jerusalem, 1999, vol. II.
Tau, Zvi Israel, *Le-Emunat 'Itenu*, 13 vols. Jerusalem, 1995, vol. II; Jerusalem 2008, vol. VIII.
Teichthal, Yissakhar Shlomo, *Em HaBanim Semeha: Restoration of Zion as a Response during the Holocaust*, P. Schindler (trans.), Hoboken, NJ: Ktav Publishing House, 1999.
Torim, Menahem Mendel (of Riminov) and others, *Ilana de-Haye*. Pitrikov, 1914.
Turgeman, Ohad (ed.), *Ginzei ha-Rav Ferira*. Jerusalem, 2016.
Miqpahat Sefarim, 4th ed. Jerusalem, n.d.
Tzemach, Yaakov, *Tiferet Adam*. Bnei Brak, 1982.
Vital, Hayyim, *Derekh Etz Hayyim*, Meir Poppers (ed.). Jerusalem, 2013.
Liqqutei Torah. Jerusalem, 1972 (reprint of Vilna, 1880).
Sha'ar ha-Gilgulim. Jerusalem, 1981.
Sha'ar Ruah ha-Qodesh, 3 vols. Jerusalem, 1999, vol. I.
Wallach, Yona, *Forms* (Poems). Tel Aviv: Ha-Kibbutz ha-Meuchad, 1985. [Hebrew]
Yosef Hayyim of Baghdad, *Da'at u-Tvuna*, Jerusalem, 1911.
Yosef Tzevi Hirsch of Kaminka, *Meshivat Nefesh*. Lemberg, 1786.
Rimonei Zahav. Lemberg, 1783.
Zeitlin, Hillel, *Sifran shel-Yehidim*. Jerusalem: Mossad ha-Rav Kook, 1979.

STUDIES

Abrams, Daniel (ed.), *The Book Bahir: An Edition Based on the Earliest Manuscripts*. Los Angeles: Cherub Press, 1994.
The Female Body of God in Kabbalistic Literature: Embodied Forms of Love and Sexuality in the Divine Feminine. Jerusalem: Magnes Press, 2004. [Hebrew]
'From Germany to Spain: Numerology as a Mystical Technique', *Journal of Jewish Studies* 47 (1996), 85–101.
Kabbalistic Manuscripts and Textual Theory (2nd ed.). Los Angeles: Cherub Press, 2013.

'"A Light of Her Own": Minor Kabbalistic Traditions on the Ontology of the Divine Feminine', *Kabbalah: Journal for the Study of Jewish Mystical Texts* 15 (2006), 20–23.

Sefer Hibbur 'Amudei Sheva': by R. Aaron Zelig ben Moshe, Cracow 1675: A Chapter in the History of Textual Criticism to the Editio Princeps of the Book of the Zohar, Cremona 1558. Los Angeles: Cherub Press, 2017.

Ackroyd, Peter, *Blake*. London: Minerva, 1995.

Afterman, Adam, *'And They shall be as One Flesh': The Language of Mystical Union in Judaism*. Leiden: Brill, 2016.

Akerman-Hjren, Susanna, 'De Sapientia Salomonis: Emanuel Swedenborg and the Kabbalah' in Peter J. Forshaw (ed.), *Lux in Tenebris: The Visual and the Symbolic in Western Esotericism*. Leiden: Brill, 2017, 206–219.

Alitzer, Thomas J. *The New Apocalypse: The Radical Christian Vision of William Blake*. Aurora, CO: The Davies Group, 2000.

Altglas, Véronique, *From Yoga to Kabbalah: Religious Exoticism and the Logics of Bricolage*. Oxford University Press, 2014.

Altmann, Alexander, 'Eternality of Punishment: A Theological Controversy within the Amsterdam Rabbinate in the Thirties of the Seventeenth Century', *Proceedings of the American Academy for Jewish Research* 40 (1972), 1–88.

'Lurianic Kabbalah in a Platonic Key: Abraham Cohen Herrera's *Puerto del Cielo*', in Isadore Twersky and Bernard Septimus (eds.), *Jewish Thought in the Seventeenth Century*. Cambridge, MA: Harvard University Press, 1987, 1–37.

Studies in Jewish Philosophy and Mysticism. Ithaca, NY: Cornell University Press, 1969.

Altshuler, Mor, *The Life of Rabbi Yosef Karo*. Tel Aviv University Press, 2016. [Hebrew]

The Messianic Secret of Hasidism, J. Linsider (trans.). Leiden: Brill, 2006.

Anidjar, Gil, 'Jewish Mysticism Alterable and Unalterable: On Orienting Kabbalah Studies and the "*Zohar* of Christian Spain"' *Jewish Social Studies* 3 (1996), 89–157.

Aptekman, Marina, *"Jacob's Ladder": Kabbalistic Allegory in Russian Literature*. Boston: Academic Studies Press, 2011.

Arnold Leibman, Laura, *Messianism, Secrecy and Mysticism: A New Interpretation of Early American Jewish Life*. London: Vallentine Mitchell, 2012.

Assaf, David, *Beguiled by Knowledge: An Anatomy of a Hasidic Controversy*. Haifa University Press, 2012 [Hebrew]

Bratzlav: An Annotated Bibliography. Jerusalem: The Zalman Shazar Center, 2000. [Hebrew]

"Polish Hasidism" or "Hasidism in Poland": On the Problem of Hasidic Geography', *Gal Ed – On the History of the Jews in Poland* 14 (1995), 197–206. [Hebrew]

The Regal Way: The Life and Times of R. Israel of Ruzhin, D. Louvish (trans.). Stanford University Press, 2002.

Untold Tales of the Hasidim: Crisis and Discontent in the History of Hasidism, D. Ordan (trans). Waltham, MA: Brandeis University Press, 2010.

'From Volhynia to Safed: Rabbi Abraham Dov of Ovruch as a Hasidic Leader in the First Half of the Nineteenth Century', *Shalem: Studies in the History of the Jews in Eretz Israel* 6 (1992), 223–279. [Hebrew]

Avivi, Yosef, *Kabbala Luriana*, 3 vols. Jerusalem: Yad Ben Zvi, 2010. [Hebrew]

The Kabbalah of R. Eliyahu of Vilnah (The Gaon of Vilna). Jerusalem: Kerem Eliyahu Institute, 1993. [Hebrew]

The Kabbalah of Rabbi A. I Kook, 4 vols. Jerusalem: Yad Ben Zvi, 2018. [Hebrew]

Qitzur Seffer (!) ha-'Asilut. Jerusalem: Yad Ben Zvi, 2010.

Barak, Uriel, 'Can Amalek Be Redeemed? A Comparative Study of the Views of Rabbi Avraham Itzhak HaCohen Kook and Rabbi Yaakov Moshe Harlap', *Da'at* 73 (2012), XXIX–LXIX.

Bar-Asher, Avishai, *Journeys of the Soul: Concepts and Imageries of Paradise in Medieval Kabbalah*. Jerusalem: Magnes Press, 2019.

'Penance and Fasting in the Writings of Rabbi Moses De Leon and the Zoharic Polemic with Contemporary Christian Monasticism', *Kabbalah: Journal for the Study of Jewish Mystical Texts* 25 (2011), 293–319. [Hebrew]

Bar-Levav, Avriel, 'Death and the (Blurred) Boundaries of Magic: Strategies of Coexistence', *Kabbalah: Journal for the Study of Jewish Mystical Texts* 7 (2002), 51–64.

'Ritualisation of Jewish Life and Death in the Early Modern Period', *Leo Baeck Institute Year Book* 47 (2002), 69–82.

'"When I Was Alive": Jewish Ethical Wills as Egodocuments', in Rudolf Dekker (ed.), *Egodocuments and History: Autobiographical Writing in Its Social Context since the Middle Ages*. Rotterdam: Erasmus University, 2002, 45–59.

Barnai, Yaakov, 'Christian Messianism and the Portuguese Marranos: The Emergence of Sabbateanism in Smyrna', *Jewish History* 7 (1993), 119–126.

'On the History of the Sabbatian Movement and Its Place in the Life of the Jews in the Ottoman Empire', *Pe'amim: Studies in Oriental Jewry* 3 (1980), 59–71.

Sabbateanism: Social Perspectives. Jerusalem: The Zalman Shazar Center, 2000.

Bartal, Israel, 'Messianic Expectations and Their Place in History', in Richard I. Cohen (ed.), *Vision and Conflict in the Holy Land*. New York: St. Martin's Press, 1985, 171–181.

'Messianism and Nationalism: Liberal Optimism versus Orthodox Anxiety', *Jewish History* 20 (2006), 5–17.

Bar-Yosef, Hamutal, *Mysticism in XX Century Hebrew Literature*. Boston: Academic Studies Press, 2010.

Barzilay, Isaac, *Yosef Shlomo Delmedigo (Yashar of Candia): His Life, Work and Times*. Leiden: Brill, 1974.

Baumgarten, Eliezer, 'Comments on R. Naftali Bachrach's Usage of Pre-Lurianic Sources', *AJS Review* 37 (2013), 1–23. [Hebrew]

Baumgarten, Jean, *La Naissance du Hasidsme: Mystique, rituel, société (XVIIIe–XIXe siècle)*. Paris: Albin Michel, 2006.

'Quelques échos de Shabbetaï Tsevi dans la littérature yiddish ancienne (XVIIe–XVIIIe siècle)', *Revue des Etudes Juives* 171 (2012), 149–172.

'Yiddish Ethical Texts and the Diffusion of the Kabbalah in the 17th and 18th Centuries', *Bulletin du Centre de Recherche Français de Jérusalem* 18 (2007), 73–91.

Beck, Ulrich, *A God of One's Own*. Cambridge University Press, 2010.

Beltrán, Miquel, *The Influence of Abraham Cohen de Herrera's Kabbalah on Spinoza's Metaphysics*. Brill: Leiden, 2016.

Benarroch, Jonathan M., 'God and His Son: Christian Affinities in the Shaping of the Sava and Yanuqa Figures in the Zohar', *The Jewish Quarterly Review* 107 (2017), 38–65.

'"The Mystery of Unity": Poetic and Mystical Aspects of a Unique Zoharic Shema Mystery', *AJS Review* 37 (2013), 231–256.

Sava and Yenuqa: God, the Son, and the Messiah in Zoharic Narratives. Jerusalem: Magnes Press, 2018. [Hebrew]

Benayahu, Meir, 'Devotion Practices of the Kabbalists of Safed at Meron', *Sefunot* 6 (1962), 169–179. [Hebrew]

'The Fellowship Charters of the Kabbalists of Jerusalem', *Assufot* 9 (1995), 9–127 [Hebrew]

Ben-Dor Benite, Zvi, *The Ten Lost Tribes: A Global History*. Oxford University Press, 2009.

Benin, Stephen D., *The Footprints of God: Divine Accommodation in Jewish and Christian Thought*. Albany: SUNY Press, 1993.

Benmelech, Moti, 'History, Politics and Messianism: David Ha-Reuveni's Origin and Mission', *AJS Review* 35 (2011), 35–60.

Ben Sasson, Hillel, *YHWH: The Meaning and Significance of God's Name in Biblical, Rabbinic and Medieval Jewish Thought*. Jerusalem: Magnes Press, 2019.

Ben Shalom, Ram, *The Jews of Provence and Languedoc: Renaissance in the Shadow of the Church*. Raanana: Open University of Israel Press, 2017. [Hebrew]

Ben-Shlomo, Joseph, *The Mystical Theology of Moses Cordovero*. Jerusalem: Bialik Institute, 1965. [Hebrew]

Berke, Joseph H., *The Hidden Freud: His Hassidic Roots*. London: Karnac Books, 2015.

Betz, Otto, *Licht vom unerschaffnen Lichte: Die Kabbalistische Lehrtafel der Prinzessin Antonia*. Tübingen: Verlag Werner Grimm, 2013.

Biale, David, Assaf, David, Brown, Benjamin et al. (eds.), *Hasidism: A New History*, Princeton University Press, 2017.

Bilu, Yoram, 'Dybbuk and Maggid: Two Cultural Patterns of Altered Consciousness in Judaism', *AJS Review* 21 (1996), 341–366.

The Saints Impresarios: Dreamers, Healers, and Holy Men in Israel's Urban Periphery, H. Watzman (trans.). Brighton, MA: Academic Studies Press, 2010.

'Sigmund Freud and Rabbi Yehudah: On a Jewish Mystical Tradition of "Psychoanalytic" Dream Interpretation', *The Journal of Psychological Anthropology* 2 (1979), 443–463.

Without Bounds: The Life and Death of Rabbi Ya'aqov Wazana. Detroit: Wayne State University Press, 2017.

'With Us More than Ever Before': Making the Absent Rebbe Present in Messianic Chabad. Raanana: Open University of Israel Press, 2016. [Hebrew]

Bitty, Yehuda, *The Mystical Philosopher: Studies in Qol Ha-Nevu'ah*. Tel Aviv: Ha-Kibbutz Hameuchad, 2016. [Hebrew]

Bohak, Gideon, *Ancient Jewish Magic: A History*. Cambridge University Press, 2008.

Bolzoni, Lina, 'Giulio Camillo's Memory Theatre and the Kabbalah', in Ilana Zinguer, Abraham Melamed and Zur Shalev (eds.), *Hebraic Aspects of the Renaissance: Sources and Encounters*. Leiden: Brill, 14–26.

Bonfil, Robert (Reuven), 'Halakhah, Kabbalah and Society: Some Insights into Rabbi Menahem Azariah of Fano's Inner World', in Isadore Twersky and Bernard Septimus (eds.), *Jewish Thought in the Seventeenth Century*. Cambridge, MA: Harvard University Press, 1987, 39–61.

Boss, Gerrit, 'Hayyim Vital's Practical Kabbalah and Alchemy: A 17th Century Book of Secrets', *The Journal of Jewish Thought and Philosophy* 4 (1994), 55–112.

Boulouque, Clémence, 'Elia Benamozegh (1823–1900): Kabbalah, Tradition and the Challenges of Interfaith Encounters', unpublished Ph.D. dissertation, New York University, 2014.

Bouretz, Pierre, 'Messianism in Modern Jewish Philosophy', in Michael L. Morgan and Peter E. Gordon (eds.), *The Cambridge Companion to Modern Jewish Philosophy*. Cambridge University Press, 170–191.

Bregman, Dvora, 'Moses Zacuto: Poet of Kabbalah', in Ilana Zinguer, Abraham Melamed and Zur Shalev (eds.), *Hebraic Aspects of the Renaissance: Sources and Encounters*. Leiden: Brill, 2011, 170–181.

Brill, Alan, 'The Spiritual World of a Master of Awe: Divine Vitality, Theosis, and Healing in the "Degel Mahaneh Ephraim"', *Jewish Studies Quarterly* 8 (2001), 27–65.

Thinking God: The Mysticism of Rabbi Zadok of Lublin. New York: Yeshiva University Press, 2002.

Brody, Seth, 'Open to Me the Gates of Righteousness: The Pursuit of Holiness and Non-duality in Early Hasidic Teachings', *The Jewish Quarterly Review* 89 (1998), 3–44.

Brown, Benjamin, 'Kabbalah in the Rulings of the Hafetz Hayyim', *Jerusalem Studies in Jewish Thought* 23 (2013), 485–542. [Hebrew]

"Like a Ship on a Stormy Sea": The Story of Karlin Hasidism. Jerusalem: The Zalman Shazar Center, 2018. [Hebrew]

The Lithuanian Musar Movement: Personalities and Ideas. Tel Aviv: The Ministry of Defense, 2014. [Hebrew]

'Stringency: Five Modern-Era Types', *Dine Israel* 20–21 (2001), 123–237. [Hebrew].

'Substitutes for Mysticism: A General Model for the Theological Development of Hasidism in the Nineteenth Century', *History of Religions* 56 (2017), 247–288.

'The Two Faces of Religious Radicalism: Orthodox Zealotry and Holy Sinning in Nineteenth-Century Hasidism in Hungary and Galicia', *The Journal of Religion* 56 (2013), 341–374.

Brown, Benjamin and Leon, Nissim (eds.), *The Gdoilim: Leaders Who Shaped Haredi Jewry*. Jerusalem: Magnes Press, 2017. [Hebrew]

Brown, Jeremy, 'From Nacionalista Anti-Kabbalistic Polemic to Aryan Kabbalah in the Southern Cone', *The Journal of Religion* 99 (2019), 341–360.

Burmistrov, Konstantin, 'Kabbalah and Secret Societies in Russia (Eighteenth to Twentieth Centuries)', in Boaz Huss (ed.), *Kabbalah and Modernity: Interpretations, Transformations, Adaptations*. Leiden: Brill, 2010, 97–130.

Busi, Giulio, 'Francesco Zorzi – A Methodical Dreamer', in Joseph Dan (ed.), *The Christian Kabbalah: Jewish Mystical Books and Their Christian Interpreters*. Cambridge, MA: Harvard College Library, 1997, 97–126.

La Qabbalah Visiva. Torino: Eimaudi, 2005.

'Steinschneider and the Irrational: A Bibliographical Struggle against the Kabbalah', in Reimund Leicht and Gad Freudental (eds.), *Studies on Steinschenider: Moritz Steinschneider and the Emergence of the Science of Judaism in Nineteenth-Century Germany*. Leiden: Brill, 2011, 213–231.

Bynum, Caroline, *Holy Feast and Holy Fast: The Religious Significance of Food to Medieval Women*. Berkeley: University of California Press, 1988.

Calhoun, Craig, 'New Social Movements of the Early Nineteenth Century', *Social Science History*, 17 (1993), 385–427.

Campanini, Saverio, 'A Neglected Source Concerning Asher Lemmlein and Paride da Ceresara: Agostino Giustiniani', *European Journal of Jewish Studies* 2 (2008), 89–110.

Campbell, Ted A., *The Religion of the Heart: A Study of European Religious Life in the Seventeenth and Eighteenth Centuries*. Eugene, OR: Wipf and Stock, 2000.

Carlebach, Elisheva, *Divided Souls: Converts from Judaism in Germany, 1500–1750*. New Haven, CT: Yale University Press, 2001.

The Pursuit of Heresy: Rabbi Moses Hagiz and the Sabbatian Controversies. New York: Columbia University Press, 1990.

Chajes, Joseph H., 'Accounting for the Self: Preliminary Generic-Historical Reflections on Early Modern Jewish Egodocuments', *The Jewish Quarterly Review* 95 (2005), 1–15.

'Kabbalah and the Diagrammatic Phase in the Scientific Revolution', in Richard I. Cohen et al. (eds.), *Jewish Culture in Early Modern Europe: Essays in Honor of David B. Ruderman*. University of Pittsburg Press, 2014, 109–123.

'Too Holy to Print: Taboo Anxiety and the Publishing of Practical Hebrew Esoterica', *Jewish History* 26 (2002), 247–262.

Between Worlds: Dybbuks, Exorcists and Early Modern Judaism. Philadelphia: University of Pennsylvania Press, 2003.

Chayes, Evelien, 'Visitatori libertine del Ghetto: Ismael Boulliau e Charles de Valliquierville', in Giuseppe Veltri and Evelien Chayes (eds.), *Olre le Mura del Ghetto: Accademie, Scetticismo e Tolleranza Nella Venezia Barroca, Studi e Documenti d'Archivio*. Palermo: New Digital Frontiers, 2016, 121–146.

Collins, Randall, *The Sociology of Philosophies: A Global Theory of Intellectual Change*. Cambridge, MA: Harvard University Press, 1988.

Copenhaver, Brian and Kokin, Daniel, 'Egidio da Viterbo's Book: On Hebrew Letters: Christian Kabbalah in Papal Rome', *Renaissance Quarterly* 67 (2014), 1–42.

Corb-Bonfil, Aliza, *Where Words Are Silence*. Tel Aviv: Hakibbutz Hameuchad, 2011. [Hebrew]

Coudert, Alison P., *The Impact of the Kabbalah in the Seventeenth Century: The Life and Thought of Francis Mercury Van Helmont (1614–1698)*. Leiden: Brill, 1999.

'Kabbalistic Messianism versus Kabbalistic Enlightenment', in Matt Goldish and Richard H. Popkin (eds.), *Millennialism and Messianism in Early Modern European Culture, Part I: Jewish Messianism in the Early Modern World*. New York: Springer, 2001, 107–124.

Leibniz and the Kabbalah. Dordrecht & Boston: Kluwer, 1995.

Dan, Joseph (ed.), *The Early Kabbalah*, R. Kiener (trans.). New York: Paulist Press, 1986.

'The Emergence of Messianic Mythology in 13th Century Kabbalah in Spain', in Róbert Dán (ed.), *Occident and Orient: A Tribute to the Memory of A. Scheiber*. Leiden: Brill, 1988, 57–68.

History of Jewish Mysticism. Vol. VII: Early Kabbalistic Circles, 2012. *Vol. VIII: The Gerona Circle of Kabbalists*, 2012. *Vol. IX: The Middle Ages*. 2013. Jerusalem: Zalman Shazar Center. [Hebrew]

'"No Evil Descends from Heaven" – Sixteenth Century Jewish Concepts of Evil', in Bernard Cooperman (ed.), *Jewish Thought in the Sixteenth Century*. Cambridge, MA: Harvard University Press, 1983, 89–105.

Darmon, Julien, *L'Esprit de la Kabbale*. Paris: Éditions Albin Michel, 2017.

Dauber, Jonathan, *The Knowledge of God and the Development of Early Kabbalah*. Leiden: Brill, 2012.

David, Abraham, 'The Lutheran Reformation in Sixteenth-Century Jewish Historiography', *Jewish Studies Quarterly* 10 (2003), 124–139.

Davies, Owen, *The Haunted: A Social History of Ghosts*. New York: Palgrave Macmillan, 2007.

De Certeau, Michel, *The Mystic Fable: The Sixteenth and Seventeenth Centuries*, M. B. Smith (trans.), 2 vols. Chicago University Press, 1992, vol. I.

De Landa, Manuel, *One Thousand Years of Non-linear History*. New York: Swerve, 1997.

De León-Jones, Karen, 'John Dee and the Kabbalah', in Stephen Clucas (ed.) *John Dee: Interdisciplinary Studies in English Renaissance Thought*. Dordrecht: Springer, 2006, 143–158.

Del Nevo, Matthew, 'The Kabbalistic Heart of Levinas', *Culture, Theory and Critique* 52 (2011), 183–198.

Dresner, Samuel, *The Zaddik: The Doctrine of the Zaddik according to the Writings of Rabbi Yaacov Yosef of Polnoy*. New York: Aberlard-Schuman, 1960.

Duker, Abraham G., 'Polish Frankism's Duration: From Cabbalistic Judaism to Roman Catholicism and from Jewishness to Polishness: A Preliminary Investigation', *Jewish Social Studies* 25 (1963), 287–333.

During, Simon, *Modern Enchantment: The Cultural Power of Secular Magic*. Cambridge, MA: Harvard University Press, 2002.

Dweck, Yaacob, *The Scandal of Kabbalah: Leon Modena, Jewish Mysticism, Early Modern Venice*. Princeton University Press, 2011.

Dynner, Glenn, *Men of Silk: The Hasidic Conquest of Polish Jewish Society*. Oxford University Press, 2006.

Ebstein, Michael and Weiss, Tzahi, '"A Drama in Heaven": Emanation on the Left in Kabbalah and a Parallel Cosmogonic Myth in Ismāʿīlī Literature', *History of Religions* 55 (2015), 148–171.

Eburey, Kathrine, *Modernism and Cosmology: Absurd Lights*. New York: Palgrave Macmillan, 2014.

Elbaum, Jacob, 'Aspects of Hebrew Ethical Literature in Sixteenth-Century Poland', in Bernard Cooperman (ed.), *Jewish Thought in the Sixteenth Century*, Cambridge, MA: Harvard University Press, 1983, 146–166.

Openness and Insularity: Late Sixteenth Century Jewish Literature in Poland and Ashkenaz. Jerusalem: Magnes Press, 1990. [Hebrew]

Repentance and Self-Flagellation in the Writings of the Sages of Germany and Poland, 1348–1648. Jerusalem: Magnes Press, 1992. [Hebrew]

Elior, Rachel, *Israel Ba'al Shem Tov and His Contemporaries: Kabbalists, Sabbatians, Hasidim and Mitnaggedim*, 2 vols. Jerusalem: Carmel Press 2014. [Hebrew]

Jacob Frank's Book of the Words of the Lord: Mystical Automythography, Religious Nihilism and the Messianic Vision of Freedom as a Realization of Myth and Metaphor. Leuven: Peeters, 2019.

'Joseph Karo and R. Israel Ba'al Shem Tov – Mystical Metamorphosis, Kabbalistic Inspiration and Spiritual Internalization', *Tarbiz: A Quarterly for Jewish Studies* 65 (1996), 671–709. [Hebrew]

'Messianic Expectations and Spiritualization of Religious Life in the Sixteenth Century', *Revue des etudes juives* CXLV (1986), 35–49.

'The Paradigms of "Yesh" and "Ayin" in Hasidic Thought', in Ada Rapaport-Albert (ed.), *Hasidism Reappraised: The Social Functions of Mystical Ideals in Judaism*. Oxford: The Littman Library of Jewish Civilization, 1996, 168–179.

The Paradoxical Ascent to God: The Kabbalistic Theosophy of Habad. Albany, NY: SUNY Press, 1992.

'R. Nathan Adler and the Frankfurt Pietists: Pietist Groups in Eastern and Central Europe during the 18th Century', in Karl E. Grözinger (ed.), *Judische Kultur in Frankfurt am Main, von den Anfangen bis zur Gegenwart*. Wiesbaden: Harrassowitz Verlag, 1997, 135–177.

Elqayam, Abraham (Avi), 'The Horizon of Reason: The Divine Madness of Sabbatai Sevi', *Kabbalah: Journal for the Study of Jewish Mystical Texts* 9 (2003), 7–61.

'Liberating Nudity in Sabbateanism – Between the Messiah and His Prophet', *Kabbalah: Journal for the Study of Jewish Mystical Texts* 34 (2016), 185–251. [Hebrew]

'Nudity in Safed in the 16th Century: Between Hasidism and Deviance', *Kabbalah: Journal for the Study of Jewish Mystical Texts* 30 (2013), 303–320.

Elstein, Yoav, *The Ecstatic Story in Hasidic Literature*. Ramat Gan: Bar-Ilan University Press, 1998. [Hebrew]

Engel, Amir, *Gershom Scholem: An Intellectual Biography*. The University of Chicago Press, 2017.

Esdaile, Charles, *Napoleon's Wars: An International History*. London: Penguin Books, 2009.

Etkes, Immanuel, *The Besht: Magician, Mystic, and Leader*, S. Sternberg (trans.). Waltham, MA: Brandeis University Press, 2004.

The Gaon of Vilna: The Man and His Image, J. M. Green (trans.). Berkeley: The University of California Press, 2002.

Rabbi Israel Salanter and the Mussar Movement: Seeking the Torah of Truth, J. Chipman (trans.). Philadelphia and Jerusalem: The Jewish Publication Society, 1993.

Rabbi Shneur Zalman of Liady: The Origins of Chabad Hasidism, J. M. Green (trans.). Waltham, MA: Brandeis University Press, 2014.

'The Vilna Gaon and His Disciples as the First Zionists: The Metamorphoses of a Myth', *Zion* 80 (2015), 69–114.

Faierstein, Morris A., *All Is in the Hands of Heaven: The Teachings of Rabbi Mordecai Joseph Leiner of Izbica*. Hoboken, NJ: Ktav Publishing House, 1989.

Jewish Customs of Kabbalistic Origin: Their History and Practice. Boston: Academic Studies Press, 2003.

Jewish Mystical Autobiographies: Book of Visions and Book of Secrets. Mahwah, NJ: Paulist Press, 1999.

'Kabbalah and Early Modern Yiddish Literature Prior to 1648', *Revue des études juives* 168 (2009), 507–520.

'The Possession of Rabbi Hayyim Vital by Jesus of Nazareth', *Kabbalah: Journal for the Study of Jewish Mystical Texts* 37 (2017), 29–36.

Falach, Baruch, 'The "Sulam" Journal: Between Poetry and Politics', unpublished Ph.D. dissertation, Bar-Ilan University, 2010.

Faye Koren, Sharon, *Forsaken: The Menstruant in Medieval Jewish Mysticism*. Waltham, MA: Brandeis University Press, 2011.

Farber-Ginat, Asi, '"Husk Precedes Fruit": On the Origins of Metaphysical Evil in Early Kabbalistic Thought', *Eshel Beer-Sheva* 4 (1996), 118–142. [Hebrew]

Farley, Helen, *A Cultural History of Tarot: From Entertainment to Esotericism*. London: I. B. Tauris, 2009.

Fehér, Ferenc (ed.), *The French Revolution and the Birth of Modernity*. Berkeley: The University of California Press, 1990.

Feiner, Shmuel. *The Origins of Jewish Secularization in Eighteenth-Century Europe*, C. Naor (trans.). Philadelphia: University of Pennsylvania Press, 2010.

'Sola Fide! The Polemic of Rabbi Nathan of Nemirov against Atheism and Haskalah', *Jerusalem Studies in Jewish Thought* 15 (1999), 89–124. [Hebrew]

Feldman, Jan, *Lubavitchers as Citizens: Paradox of Liberal Democracy*. Ithaca, NY: Cornell University Press, 2003.

Fenton, Paul B., 'Abraham Maimonides (1187–1237): Founding a Mystical Dynasty', in Moshe Idel and Mortimer Ostow (eds.), *Jewish Mystical Leaders and Leadership in the 13th Century*. Northvale, NJ and Jerusalem, 1998, 127–154.

'The Banished Brother: Islam in Jewish Thought and Faith', in Alon Goshen-Gottstein and Eugene Korn (eds.), *Jewish Theology and World Religions*. Oxford: Littman Library of Jewish Civilization, 2012, 235–261.

'Influences soufies sur le dévéloppement de la Qabbale à Safed: le cas de la visitation des tombes', in Paul B. Fenton and Roland Goetschel (eds.), *Expérience et écriture mystiques dans les religions du livre*. Leiden: Brill, 2000, 163–190.

'Rabbi Makhluf Amsalem – A Moroccan Alchemist and Kabbalist', *Pe'amim* 55 (1993), 92–123. [Hebrew]

'The Ritual Visualization of the Saint in Jewish and Muslim Mysticism', in Alexandra Cuffel and Nikolas Jaspert (eds.), *Entangled Hagiographies of the Religious Other*. Cambridge Scholars Publishing, 2019, 193–231.

'Shabbatay Sebi and His Muslim Contemporary Muhamad An-Nizai', in David R. Blumenthal (ed.), *Approaches to Judaism in Medieval Times*, vol. 3, Atlanta, GA: Scholars Press, 1988, 81–88.

Fine, Lawrence, *Physician of the Soul, Healer of the Cosmos: Isaac Luria and His Kabbalistic Fellowship*. Stanford University Press, 2003.

Safed Spirituality: Rules of Mystical Piety, the Beginning of Wisdom. New York: Paulist Press, 1984.

Fishbane, Eitan P., 'A Chariot for the Shekhinah: Identity and the Ideal Life in Sixteenth-Century Kabbalah', *Journal of Religious Ethics* 37 (2009), 385–418.

As Light before Dawn: The Inner World of a Medieval Kabbalist. Stanford University Press, 2009.

Fishbane, Elisha, *Judaism, Sufism, and the Pietists of Medieval Egypt: A Study of Abraham Maimonides and His Circle*. Oxford University Press, 2015.

Fishbane, Michael, *Biblical Myth and Rabbinic Myth-Making*. Oxford University Press, 2003.

The Exegetical Imagination: On Jewish Thought and Theology. Cambridge, MA: Harvard University Press, 1998.

The Kiss of God: Spiritual and Mystical Death in Judaism. Seattle: University of Washington Press, 1996.

Fishman, Talya, 'The Penitential System of Hasidei Ashkenaz and the Problem of Cultural Boundaries', *The Journal of Jewish Thought and Philosophy* 8 (1999), 201–229.

Shaking the Pillars of Exile: 'Voice of a Fool', an Early Modern Jewish Critique of Rabbinic Culture. Stanford University Press, 1997.

Flatto, Sharon, *The Kabbalistic Culture of Eighteenth-Century Prague: Ezekiel Landau and His Contemporaries*. Oxford: The Littman Library of Jewish Civilization, 2010.

Foley, Matt, *Haunting Modernisms: Ghostly Aesthetics, Mourning and Spectral Resistance Fantasies in Literary Modernism*. Cham: Springer International, 2017.

Forster, Eckhart, *The Twenty-Five Years of Philosophy: A Systematic Reconstruction*. Cambridge, MA: Harvard University Press, 2012.

Foucault, Michel, *Madness and Civilization: A History of Insanity in the Age of Reason*. R. Howard (trans.), London: Tavistock Publications, 1982.

Foxbrunner, Ronald, *Habad: The Hasidism of R. Shneur Zalman of Lyady*. Tuscaloosa: University of Alabama Press, 1992.

Fram, Edward, 'German Pietism and Sixteenth- and Early Seventeenth-Century Polish Rabbinic Culture', *The Jewish Quarterly Review* 96 (2006), 50–59.

Franks, Paul, 'Fichte's Kabbalistic Realism: Summons as *zimzum*', in G. Gottlieb (ed.), *Fichte's Foundations of Natural Right*. Cambridge University Press, 2016, 92–116.

'Rabbinic Idealism and Kabbalistic Realism: Jewish Dimensions of Idealism and Idealist Dimensions of Judaism', in Nicholas Adams (ed.), *The Impact of Idealism: The Legacy of Post-Kantian German Thought*. Cambridge University Press, 2013, 219–245.

Freudenthal, Gad, 'The Kabbalist R. Jacob ben Sheshet of Girona: The Ambivalences of a Moderate Critique of Science ca. 1240', *Girona Judaica* 5 (2011), 287–301.

Freudenthal, Gideon, *No Religion without Idolatry: Mendelssohn's Jewish Enlightenment*. Notre Dame University Press, 2012.

Funkenstein, Amos, '*Imitatio Dei* Umusag Hatzimtzum Bemishnat Chabad', in Shmuel Yeivin (ed.), *Studies in Jewish History Presented to Professor Raphael Mahler on His Seventy-Fifth Birthday*. Tel Aviv: Sifriat Poalim, 1974, 83–88.

'Nahmanides' Symbological Reading of History', in Joseph Dan and Frank Talmage (eds.), *Studies in Jewish Mysticism*. Cambridge, MA: Association of Jewish Studies, 1988, 129–150.

Gam Hacohen, Moran, *Kabbalah Research in Israel: Historiography, Ideology and the Struggle for Cultural Capital*. Tel Aviv: Resling, 2016. [Hebrew]

Garb, Jonathan, *The Chosen Will Become Herds: Studies in Twentieth Century Kabbalah*, Y. Berkovitz-Murciano (trans.). New Haven, CT: Yale University Press, 2009.

'The Cult of the Saints in Lurianic Kabbalah', *The Jewish Quarterly Review* 98 (2008), 203–229.

'Doubt and Certainty in Early Modern Kabbalah', in Giuseppe Veltri (ed.), *Yearbook of the Maimonides Center for Advanced Studies*. Berlin: De Gruyter, 2017, 239–246.

'The Kabbalah of Rabbi Joseph ibn Sayyah as a Source for the Understanding of Safedian Kabbalah', *Kabbalah: Journal for the Study of Jewish Mystical Texts* 4 (1999), 255–313.

Kabbalist in the Heart of the Storm: R. Moshe Hayyim Luzzatto. Tel Aviv University Press, 2014. [Hebrew]

Manifestations of Power in Jewish Mysticism: From Rabbinic Literature to Safedian Kabbalah. Jerusalem: Magnes Press, 2004. [Hebrew]

Modern Kabbalah as an Autonomous Domain of Research. Los Angeles: Cherub Press, 2016. [Hebrew]

'Mystical and Spiritual Discourse in the Contemporary Ashkenazi Haredi Worlds', *Journal of Modern Jewish Studies* 9 (2010), 29–48.

'Rabbi Kook: Working Out as Divine Work', in George Eisen et al. (eds.), *Sport and Physical Education in Jewish History*. Netanya: Wingate Institute, 2003, 7–14.

'A Renewed Study of the Self-image of R. Moshe David Valle, As Reflected in His Biblical Exegesis', *Tarbiz: A Quarterly for Jewish Studies* 69 (2011), 265–306. [Hebrew]

Shamanic Trance in Modern Kabbalah. The University of Chicago Press, 2011.

'Shamanism and the Hidden History of Modern Kabbalah', in April DeConick and Grant Adamson (eds.), *Histories of the Hidden God*. Sheffield: Equinox, 2013, 175–192.

'Shame as an Existential Emotion in Modern Kabbalah', *Jewish Social Studies* 21 (2015), 83–116.

'Towards the Study of the Spiritual-Mystical Renaissance in the Contemporary Ashkenazi Haredi World in Israel', in Boaz Huss (ed.), *Kabbalah and Contemporary Spiritual Revival*. Beer Sheva: Ben Gurion University of the Negev Press, 2011, 117–140.

Yearnings of the Soul: Psychological Thought in Modern Kabbalah. University of Chicago Press, 2015.

Gay, Peter, *The Enlightenment: An Interpretation, Vol. I: The Rise of Modern Paganism*. New York: Alfred A. Knopf, 1966.

Gelbin, Cathy, 'Was Frankenstein's Monster Jewish?', *Publications of the English Goethe Society* 82 (2013), 16–25.

Gellman, Jerome Y., *Abraham! Abraham! Kierkegaard and the Hasidim on the Binding of Isaac*. Abingdon: Routledge, 2003.

'Hasidic Existentialism?', in Yaakov Elman and Jeffrey Gurock (eds.), *Hazon Nahum: Studies in Jewish Law, Thought, and History Presented to Dr. Norman Lamm on His Seventieth Birthday*. New York: Yeshiva University Press, 1997, 397–405.

Gellman, Uriel, *The Emergence of Hasidism in Poland*. Jerusalem: The Zalman Shazar Center, 2018 [Hebrew]

'The Great Wedding in Uścilug: The Making of a Hasidic Myth', *Tarbiz: A Quarterly for Jewish Studies* 80 (2013), 567–594. [Hebrew]

Giller, Pinchas, *The Enlightened Will Shine: Symbolization and Theurgy in the Later Strata of the Zohar*. Albany, NY: SUNY Press, 1993.

Kabbalah – A Guide for the Perplexed. New York: Continuum, 2012.

Reading the Zohar: The Sacred Text of the Kabbalah. New York: Oxford University Press, 2001.

'Recovering the Sanctity of the Galilee: The Veneration of Gravesites in Classical Kabbalah', *Journal of Jewish Thought and Philosophy* 4 (1994), 147–169.

Shalom Shar'abi and the Kabbalists of Beit El. New York: Oxford University Press, 2008.

Ginsburg, Elliot K., *The Sabbath in the Classical Kabbalah* (2nd ed.). Oxford: The Littman Library of Jewish Civilization, 2008.

Goetschel, Ronald, *Meir ibn Gabbay: Le discours de la Kabbale Espagnole*, Leuven: Peeters, 1981.

Goldberg, Hillel, *Israel Salanter: Text, Structure, Idea: The Ethics and Theology of an Early Psychologist of the Unconscious*. New York: Ktav Publishing House, 1982.

Goldish, Matt, *Judaism in the Theology of Sir Isaac Newton*. Dordrecht: Kluwer Academic, 1998.

The Sabbatean Prophets. Cambridge, MA: Harvard University Press, 2004.

'The Spirit of the Eighteenth Century in the Anti-Sabbatean Polemics of Hakham David Nieto', in Jeremy D. Popkin (ed.), *The Legacies of Richard Popkin*. Lexington, KY: Springer, 2008, 229–243.

Goldreich, Amos, *Automatic Writing in Zoharic Literature and Modernism*. Los Angeles: Cherub Press, 2010. [Hebrew]

'Investigations of the Self-Perception of the Author of Tikkunei Zohar', in Michael Oron and Amos Goldreich (eds.), *Mass'uot: Studies in Kabbalistic Literature and Jewish Philosophy in the Memory of Prof. Ephraim Gottlieb*. Jerusalem: Bialik Institute, 1994, 459–496. [Hebrew]

Gondos, Andrea, *Kabbalah in Print: The Study and Popularization of Jewish Mysticism in Early Modernity*. Albany: SUNY Press (2021).

Gooding-Williams, Robert, *Zarathustra's Dionysian Modernism*. Stanford University Press, 2001.

Goodman-Thau, Eveline, Mattenklott, Gert and Schulte, Christoph (eds.), *Kabbala und die Literatur der Romantik: Zwischen Magie und Trope*. Berlin: De Gruyter, 2012 (reprint).

Granot, Tamir, 'The Revival of Hasidism after the Holocaust: The Ideological, Halachic and Social Doctrine of the Admor R. Yequtiel Yehuda Halberstam of Sanz-Klausenber', unpublished Ph.D. dissertation, Bar-Ilan University, 2008.

Green, Arthur, 'Early Hasidism: Some Old/New Questions', in Ada Rapaport-Albert (ed.), *Hasidism Reappraised: The Social Functions of Mystical Ideals in Judaism*. Oxford: The Littman Library of Jewish Civilization, 1996, 441–446.

Hasidic Spirituality for a New Era: The Religious Writings of Hillel Zeitlin. New York: Paulist Press, 2012.

Keter: The Crown of God in Early Jewish Mysticism. Princeton University Press, 1997.

The Language of Truth: The Torah Commentary of the Sefat Emet. Pennsylvania: The Jewish Publication Society, 2012.

Seek My Face, Speak My Name: A Jewish Mystical Theology. Woodstock, VT: Jewish Lights, 2003.

'Sekhinah, the Virgin Mary and the Song of Songs: Reflections of a Kabbalistic Symbol in Its Historical Context', *AJS Review* 26 (2002), 1–52.

Tormented Master: The Life and Spiritual Quest of Rabbi Nahman of Bratslav. Woodstock, VT: Jewish Lights, 1992 (reprint).

(trans. and intro.), *Upright Practices, The Light of the Eyes by Menahem Nahum of Chernobyl*. London: SPCK, 1982.

Green, Arthur, Leader, Ebn, Evan Mayse, Ariel and Rose, Or N. (eds.), *Speaking Torah: Spiritual Teaching from around the Maggid's Table*, 2 vols. Woodstock, VT: Jewish Lights, 2013.

Greenberg, Gershon, 'Hasidic Thought and the Holocaust (1933–1947): Optimism and Activism', *Jewish History* 27 (2013), 353–375.

'Menahem Mendel Schneersohn's Response to the Holocaust', *Modern Judaism: A Journal of Jewish Ideas and Experience* 34 (2014), 86–122.

Modern Jewish Thinkers: From Mendelssohn to Rosenzweig. Brighton, MA: Academic Studies Press, 2011.

'R. Arele Roth's Pristine Faith', *Journal of Modern Jewish Studies* 14 (2015), 72–88.

'Redemption after Holocaust according to Mahane Israel-Lubavitch 1940–1945', *Modern Judaism: A Journal of Jewish Ideas and Experience* 12 (1992), 61–84.

Gries, Zeev, *The Book in Early Hasidism: Genres, Authors, Scribes, Managing Editors*. Tel Aviv: Hakibbutz Hameuchad, 1992. [Hebrew]

The Book in the Jewish World, 1700–1900. Oxford: Littman Library of Jewish Civilization, 2007.

Conduct Literature (Regimen Vitae) – Its History and Place in the Life of Beshtian Hasidim. Jerusalem: Bialik Institute, 1990. [Hebrew]

The Hebrew Book: An Outline of Its History. Jerusalem: Bialik Institute, 2015. [Hebrew]

Grözinger, Karl Erich, *Kafka und die Kabbala: Das Jüdische im Werk und denken von Franz Kafka*. Berlin: Philo, 2003.

Grunwald, Nohem (ed.), *Ha-Rav: On the Book Tanya, the Doctrine of Habad, the Way, Conduct and Students of R. Shneur Zalman of Liadi*. New Jersey: Makhon ha-Rav, 2015.

Hacohen Oria, Reuven, 'The Messianic and Mystical Consciousness of the Rebbe, R. Menachem Mendel Schneerson (1902–1994)', unpublished Ph. D. dissertation, Bar-Ilan University, 2016.

HaCohen, Ruth, *The Music Libel against the Jews*. New Haven, CT: Yale University Press, 2013.

Halbertal, Moshe, *By Way of Truth: Nahmanides and the Creation of Tradition*. Jerusalem: Shalom Hartman Institute, 2006. [Hebrew]

Concealment and Revelation: Esotericism in Jewish Thought and Its Philosophical Implication, J. Feldman (trans.). Princeton University Press, 2007.

Hallamish, Moshe, *An Introduction to the Kabbalah*, R. Bar-Ilan and O. Wiskind-Elper (trans.). Albany, NY: SUNY Press, 1999.

Kabbalah in Liturgy, Halakhah and Customs. Ramat Gan: Bar-Ilan University Press, 2000. [Hebrew]

The Kabbalah in North Africa: A Historical and Cultural Survey. Tel Aviv: Ha-Kibbutz Ha-Meuḥad, 2001. [Hebrew]

Kabbalistic Customs of Shabbat. Orhot: Jerusalem, 2006. [Hebrew]

Halperin, Dalia-Ruth, 'The Sarajevo Haggadah Creation Cycle and the Nahmanides School of Theosophical Kabbalah', *Studies in Iconography* 35 (2014), 165–186.

Halpern, David (ed.), *Abraham Miguel Cardozo: Selected Writings*. New York: Paulist Press, 2001.

Hames, Harvey, *The Art of Conversion: Christianity and Kabbalah in the Thirteenth Century*. Leiden: Brill, 2000.

Like Angels on Jacob's Ladder: Abraham Abulafia, The Franciscans and Joachimism. Albany, NY: SUNY Press, 2007.

'A Seal within a Seal: The Imprint of Sufism in Abraham Abulafia's Teachings', *Medieval Encounters* 12 (2006), 153–172.

Hanegraaff, Wouter J., 'The Beginnings of Occultist Kabbalah: Adolphe Franck and Eliphas Lévi', in Boaz Huss (ed.), *Kabbalah and Modernity: Interpretations, Transformations, Adaptations*. Leiden: Brill, 2010, 107–128.

'Mysteries of Sex in the House of the Hidden Light: Arthur Edward Waite and the Kabbalah', *Kabbalah: Journal for the Study of Jewish Mystical Texts* 40 (2018), 163–182.

New Age Religion and Western Culture: Esotericism in the Mirror of Secular Thought. Leiden: Brill, 1996.

Haran, Raya, 'Olam Hafuch (An Inverted World): The Radical Concept of the World in the Teaching of R. Zevi Hirsch of Zhidachov', *Tarbiz: A Quarterly for Jewish Studies* 71 (2002), 537–564. [Hebrew]

Harari, Ido, 'The Tzaddikate of Suffering: R. Aharon of Belz, Der Belzer Rov', in Benjamin Brown and Nissim Leon (eds.), *The Gdoilim*, Jerusalem: Magnes Press, 2017, 520–549. [Hebrew]

Harari, Yuval, 'Jewish Incantation Texts from Modern Times: From the Muslim Sphere to Israel', *Pe'amim* 110 (2007), 55–78. [Hebrew]

'Three Charms for Killing Hitler: Practical Kabbalah in WW2', *Aries: Journal for the Study of Western Esotericism* 17 (2017), 171–214.

'Wonders and Sorceries in Yeruham: A Magical-Political Rashomon', *Jerusalem Studies in Jewish Folklore* 31 (2018), 69–91. [Hebrew]

Harkness, Deborah E., *John Dee's Conversations with Angels: Cabala, Alchemy and the End of Nature*. Cambridge University Press, 1999.

Harvey, Warren Z., 'What Did the Rymanover Really Say about the Alpeh of Anokhy', *Kabbalah* 34 (2016), 297–314.

Hecker, Joel, *Mystical Bodies, Mystical Meals: Eating and Embodiment in Medieval Kabbalah*. Detroit: Wayne University Press, 2005.

Heelas, Paul and Woodhead, Linda, *The Spiritual Revolution: Why Religion Is Giving Way to Spirituality*. Oxford: Wiley Blackwell, 2005.

Heinze, Andrew, *Jews and the American Soul: Human Nature in the Twentieth Century*. Princeton University Press, 2004.

Heller Wilensky, Sarah, 'Messianism, Eschatology and Utopia in the Philosophical-Mystical Stream of Thirteenth Century Kabbalah', in Zvi Baras (ed.), *Messianism and Eschatology: A Collection of Essays*, Jerusalem: Shazar Center, 1983, 221–238. [Hebrew]

Hellner-Eshed, Melila, *A River Flows from Eden: The Language of Mystical Experience in the Zohar*. Stanford University Press, 2009.

Seekers of the Face: The Secrets of the Idra-Rabba (Great Assembly) of the Zohar. Rishon Lezion: Miskal, 2017. [Hebrew]

Hershkovitz, Isaac, 'Reevaluating Kol ha-Tor', *Da'at* 79–80 (2015), 163–182. [Hebrew]

'The Vision of Redemption in Rabbi Yissakhar Shlomo Teichtal's Writings: Changes in His Messianic Approach during the Holocaust', unpublished Ph.D. dissertation, Bar-Ilan University, 2009.

Hervieu-Léger, Danièle, 'Multiple Religious Modernities', in Eliezer Ben-Rafael and Yitzhak Sternberg (eds.), *Comparing Modernities: Pluralism versus Homogenity, Essays in Homage to Shmuel n. Eisenstadt*. Leiden: Brill, 2005, 327–338.

Herzog, Frederick, *European Pietism Reviewed*. Eugene, OR: Pickwick Publications, 2003.

Heschel, Abraham Joshua, *A Passion for Truth*. New York: Farrar, Strauss and Giroux, 1973.

Hisdai, Yaakov, 'Eved haShem (Servant of the Lord) in Early Hasidism', *Zion* 47 (1982), 253–292. [Hebrew]

Holdrege, Barbara, *Veda and Torah: Transcending the Textuality of Scripture*. Albany: SUNY Press, 1996.

Holzman, Gitit, 'Universalism and Nationality in Judaism and the Relationship between Jews and Non-Jews in the Thought of Rabbi Eliyahu Benamozegh', *Pe'amim* 74 (1998), 104–130. [Hebrew]

Horowitz, Elliott, 'Coffee, Coffeehouses and the Nocturnal Rituals of Early Modern Jewry', *AJS Review* 14 (1989), 17–46.

'Notes on the Attitude of Moshe De Trani toward Pietist Circles in Safed', *Shalem* 5 (1987), 273–284. [Hebrew]

Horwitz, Rivka, 'The Mystical Visions of Rabbi Hyle Wechsler in the 19th Century', in Karl E. Grözinger and Joseph Dan (eds.), *Mysticism, Magic and Kabbalah in Ashkenazi Judaism*. Berlin: Walter de Gruyter, 1995, 257–274.

Houk, James, 'The Role of Kabbalah in the Afro-American Religious Complex in Trinidad', *Caribbean Quarterly* 39 (1993), 42–55.

Hundert, Gershon, *Jews in Poland-Lithuania in the Eighteenth Century: A Genealogy of Modernity*. Berkeley: University of California Press, 2004.

Huss, Boaz, 'Forward to the East: Napthali Hertz Imber's Perception of Kabbalah', *Journal of Modern Jewish Studies* 12 (2013), 398–418.

'Mysticism versus Philosophy in Kabbalistic Literature', *Micrologus* 9 (2001), 125–135.

'Qabbalah: The Theo-Sophia of the Jews: Jewish Theosophists and Their Perceptions of Kabbalah', in Julie Chajes and Boaz Huss (eds.), *Theosophical Appropriations: Esotericism, Kabbalah and the Transformation of Traditions*. Beer Sheva: Ben Gurion University Press, 2016, 137–166.

The Question about the Existence of Jewish Mysticism: The Genealogy of Jewish Mysticism and the Theologies of Kabbalah Research. Jerusalem and Tel Aviv: Van Leer Institute Press and Hakkibutz Hameuchad Publishing House, 2016. [Hebrew]

Sockets of Fine Gold: The Kabbalah of Rabbi Shim'on Ibn Lavi. Jerusalem: Magnes Press 2000. [Hebrew]

'The Sufi Society from America: Kabbalah and Theosophy in Puna in the Late 19th Century', in Boaz Huss (ed.), *Kabbalah and Modernity: Interpretations, Transformations, Adaptations*. Leiden: Brill, 2010, 167–193.

The Zohar: Reception and Impact, Y. Nave (trans.). Oxford: The Littman Library of Jewish Civilization, 2016.

Idel, Moshe, *Absorbing Perfections: Kabbalah and Interpretation*. New Haven, CT: Yale University Press, 2002.

Ascensions on High in Jewish Mysticism: Pillars, Lines, Ladders. Budapest: Central European University Press, 2005.

Ben: Sonship and Jewish Mysticism. London: Continuum, 2007.

'Conceptualizations of *tzimtzum* in Baroque Italian Kabbalah', in Michael Zank and Ingrid Anderson (eds.), *The Value of the Particular: Lessons from Judaism and the Modern Jewish Experience*. Leiden: Brill, 2015, 28–54.

'Divine Attributes and Sefirot in Jewish Theology', in Sara O. Heller-Wilensky and Moshe Idel (eds.), *Studies in Jewish Thought*. Jerusalem: Magnes Press, 1989, 87–111. [Hebrew]

'Early Hasidism and Altaic Tribes: Between Europe and Asia', *Kabbalah: Journal for the Study of Jewish Mystical Texts* 39 (2017), 7–51.

Enchanted Chains: Techniques and Rituals in Jewish Mysticism. Los Angeles: Cherub Press, 2005.

'Enoch and Elijah: Some Remarks on Apotheosis, Theophany and Jewish Mysticism', in Graham Allen and Roy Sellars (eds.), *The Salt Companion to Harold Bloom*. Cambridge University Press, 2007, 347–376.

Golem: Jewish Magical and Mystical Traditions on the Artificial Anthropoid. Albany: SUNY Press, 1990.

Hasidism: Between Ecstasy and Magic. Albany: SUNY Press, 1995.

'The Image of Man above the Sefirot: R. David ben Yehuda he-Hasid's Theosophy of Ten Supernal "Sahsahot" and Its Reverberations', *Kabbalah* 20 (2009), 181–212.

'Israel Ba'al Shem Tov "In the State of Walachia": Widening the Besht's Cultural Panorama', in Glenn Dynner (ed.) *Holy Dissent: Jewish and Christian Mystics in Eastern Europe*. Detroit: Wayne State University Press, 2011, 71–85.

'Italy in Safed: Safed in Italy: Toward an Interactive History of Sixteenth-Century Kabbalah', in David B. Ruderman and Giuseppe Veltri (eds.), *Cultural Intermediaries: Jewish Intellectuals in Early Modern Italy*. Philadelphia: University of Pennsylvania Press, 2004, 239–269.

'On Jerusalem as a Feminine and Sexual Hypostatis: From Late Antiquity Sources to Medieval Kabbalah', in Mihail Neamtu and Bogdan Tataru-Czaban (eds.), *Memory, Humanity, and Meaning: Selected Essays in Honor of Andrey Plesus' Sixtieth Anniversary*. Florida: Zeta Books, 2009, 65–110.

'The Kabbalah in Byzantium: Preliminary Remarks', in Robert Bonfil et al. (eds.), *Jews in Byzantium: Dialectics of Minority and Majority Cultures*. Leiden: Brill, 2012, 659–708.

Kabbalah and Eros. New Haven, CT: Yale University Press, 2005.

Kabbalah in Italy, 1280–1510. New Haven, CT: Yale University Press, 2011.

'The Kabbalah in Morocco: A Survey', in Vivian B. Mann (ed.), *Morocco: Jews and Art in a Muslim Land*. New York: Merell, 2000, 105–192.

Kabbalah: New Perspectives. New Haven, CT: Yale University Press, 1988.

Les Kabbalistes de la nuit, O. Sedeyn (trans.). Paris: Éditions Allia, 2003.

Language, Torah and Hermeneutics in Abraham Abulafia, M. Kallus (trans.). Albany: SUNY Press, 1988.

'The Liturgical Turn: From the Kabbalistic Traditions of Spain, to the Kabbalistic Traditions of Safed, to the Beginnings of Hasidism', in Uri Erlich (ed.), *Jewish Prayer: New Perspectives*. Beer Sheva: Ben Gurion University Press, 2016, 9–50.

Il male primoridale nella Qabbalah. Milan: Adelphi Edizioni, 2013.

Messianic Mystics. New Haven, CT: Yale University Press, 1998.

'Messianic Scholars: On Early Israeli Scholarship, Politics and Messianism', *Modern Judaism: A Journal of Jewish Ideas and Experience* 32 (2012), 22–53.

'On Mobility, Individuals and Groups: Prolegomenon for a Sociological Approach to Sixteenth-Century Kabbalah', *Kabbalah* 3 (1998), 145–173.

'The Mud and the Water: Towards the History of a Simile in Kabbalah', *Zutot: Perspectives on Jewish Culture* 14 (2017), 64–72.

The Mystical Experience in Abraham Abulafia, J. Chipman (trans.). Albany: SUNY Press, 1988.

'On Nehemia ben Shlomo the Prophet of Erfurt and R. Itzhak Luria Ashkenazi (Ha'ari)', in Jonathan Garb, Ronit Meroz and Maren R. Niehoff (eds.), *And This Is for Yehuda: Essays Presented in Honor of Professor Yehuda Liebes' Sixty-Fifth Anniversary*. Jerusalem: Bialik Institute, 2012, 326–343. [Hebrew]

Old Worlds, New Mirrors: On Jewish Mysticism and Twentieth-Century Jewish Thought. Philadelphia: University of Pennsylvania Press, 2010.

'Orienting, Orientalizing or Disorienting the Study of Kabbalah: "An Almost Absolutely Unique" Case of Occidentalism', *Kabbalah: Journal for the Study of Jewish Mystical Texts* 2 (1997), 13–48.

'Printing Kabbalah in Sixteenth Century Italy', in Richard I. Cohen et al. (eds.), *Jewish Culture in Early Modern Europe: Essays in Honor of David B. Ruderman*. University of Pittsburg Press, 2014, 85–96.

The Privileged Divine Feminine in Kabbalah. Berlin: Walter de Gruyter, 2019.

'On Prophecy and Early Hasidism', in Moshe Sharon (ed.), *Studies in Modern Religions, Religious Movements and the Babi-Bahai Faiths*. Leiden: Brill, 2004, 41–75.

'On Rabbi Zvi Hirsh Koidanover's Sefer Qav ha-Yashar', in Karl E. Grözinger (ed.), *Jüdische Kultur in Frankfurt am Main: von den Anfangen bis zur Gegenwart*. Wiesbaden: Harrassowitz Verlag, 1997, 123–133.

'Revelation and the "Crisis of Tradition" in Kabbalah: 1475–1575', in Andreas Kilcher (ed.), *Constructing Tradition: Means and Myths of Transmission in Western Esotericism*. Leiden: Brill, 2010, 253–292.

'R. Nehemia ben Shlomo the Prophet on the Star of David and the Name Taftafia: From Jewish Magic to Practical and Theoretical Kabbalah', in Avraham Reiner et al. (eds.), *Ta Shma: Studies in Judaica in Memory of Israel M. Ta-Shma*, 2 vols. Alon Shevut: Tevunot Press, 1–76, vol. II. [Hebrew]

'R. Yehudah Ḥallewa and His "Zafenat Pa'aneaḥ"', *Shalem* 4 (1984), 119–148. [Hebrew]

'Some Forlorn Writings of a Forgotten Ashkenazi Prophet: R. Nehemia ben Shlomo ha-Navi', *The Jewish Quarterly Review* 95 (2005), 183–196.

Studies in Ecstatic Kabbalah. Albany: SUNY Press, 1988.

'Ta'anug: Erotic Delights from Kabbalah to Hasidism', in Woulter J. Hanegraaff and Jeffrey J. Kripal (eds.), *Hidden Intercourse: Eros and Sexuality in the History of Western Esotericism*. Leiden: Brill, 2008, 111–152.

'*Torah Hadashah* – Messiah and the New Torah in Jewish Mysticism and Modern Scholarship', *Kabbalah: Journal for the Study of Jewish Mystical Texts* 21 (2010), 55–107.

'Unio Mystica as a Criterion: Some Observations on Hegelian Phenomenologies of Judaism', *Journal for the Study of Religions and Ideologies* 1 (2002), 19–41.

Idel, Moshe, and Mottolese, Maurizio (eds.), *Le porte della giustizia Sa'are Sedeq, Nathan Ben Sa'adyah Har'ar*. Milan: Adelphi, 2001.

Israeli, Oded, 'Honoring Father and Mother in Early Kabbalah: From Mythos to Ethos', *The Jewish Quarterly Review* 99 (2009), 396–415.

Temple Portals: Studies in Aggadah and Midrash in the Zohar, L. Keren (trans.). Berlin and Jerusalem: de Gruyter and Magnes Press, 2016.

Izmirlieva, Valentina, *All the Names of the Lord: Lists, Mysticism, and Magic*. The University of Chicago Press, 2008.

Jacobs, Louis (ed. and trans.), *Jewish Ethics, Philosophy and Mysticism* (Vol. II of The Chain of Tradition series). New York: Berhman House, 1969.

Jacobson, Yoram, *Along the Paths of Exile and Redemption: The Doctrine of Redemption of Rabbi Mordecai Dato*. Jerusalem: Bialik Institute, 1986. [Hebrew]

'The Aspect of the Feminine in Lurianic Kabbalah', in Joseph Dan and Peter Schäfer (eds.), *Gershom Scholem's "Major Trends in Jewish Mysticism", 50 Years After*. Tübingen: J. C. B. Mohr, 1993, 239–255.

Truth, Faith and Holiness: Studies in Kabbalah and Hasidism. Tel Aviv: Idra Publishing, 2018. [Hebrew]

Janowitz, Naomi, *The Poetics of Ascent: Theories of Language in a Rabbinic Ascent Text*. Albany: SUNY Press, 1988.

Kadari, Yoed, *Cordovero's Angels: Between Theoretical and Practical Kabbalah*. Los Angeles: Cherub Press (in press). [Hebrew]

Kaennel, Lucie, 'Protestantisme et cabale', in Pierre Gisel and Lucie Kaennel (eds.), *Réceptions de la cabale*. Paris: Édition de l'éclat, 2007, 185–210.

Kahana, Maoz, 'Cosmos and Nomos: Sacred Space and Legal Action from R. Yosef Qaro to Shabbetai Şevi', *Il Prezente: Journal for Sephardic Studies* 10 (2016), 147–153.

'An Esoteric Path to Modernity: Jacob Emden's Alchemical Quest', *Journal of Modern Jewish Studies* 12 (2013), 253–275.

From the Noda BeYehuda to the Chatam Sofer: Halakha and Thought in Their Historical Moment. Jerusalem: The Zalman Shazar Center, 2015. [Hebrew]

'Sources of Knowledge and Time Oscillations: R' Yehuda Ha-Chassid's Testament in the Modern Era', in Howard Kreisel, Boaz Huss and Uri

Erlich (eds.), *Spiritual Authority: Struggles over Cultural Power in Jewish Thought*. Beer Sheva: Ben Gurion University Press, 2010, 223–262.

Kahana, Maoz and Mayse, Ariel Evan. 'Hasidic Halakha: Reappraising the Interface of Spirit and Law', *AJS Review* 41 (2017), 375–408.

Kallus, Menachem, 'The Theurgy of Prayer in the Lurianic Kabbalah', unpublished Ph.D. dissertation, Hebrew University of Jerusalem, 2002.

'The Relation of the Ba'al Shem Tov to the Practice of Lurianic Kavvanot in Light of His Comments on the Siddur Rashkov', *Kabbalah: Journal for the Study of Jewish Mystical Texts* 2 (1997), 151–167.

Kaplan, Lawrence, 'Rabbi Mordekhai Jaffe and the Evolution of Jewish Culture in Poland in the Sixteenth Century', in Bernard Cooperman (ed.), *Jewish Thought in the Sixteenth Century*, Cambridge, MA: Harvard University Press, 1983, 266–282.

Katz, Jacob, *Exclusiveness and Tolerance: Studies in Jewish-Gentile Relations in Medieval and Modern Times*. London: Oxford University Press, 1961.

Halakhah and Kabbalah: Studies in the History of Jewish Religion, Its Various Faces and Social Relevance. Jerusalem: Magnes Press, 1984. [Hebrew]

Jews and Freemasons in Europe, 1723–1939, L. Oschry (trans.). Cambridge, MA: Harvard University Press, 1970.

'Post-Zoharic Relations between Halakhah and Kabbalah', in Bernard Cooperman (ed.), *Jewish Thought in the Sixteenth Century*. Cambridge, MA: Harvard University Press, 1983, 283–307.

Tradition and Crisis: Jewish Society at the End of the Middle Ages, B. Cooperman (trans.). Syracuse University Press, 2000.

Katz, Steven T., *Post-Holocaust Dialogues: Critical Studies in Modern Jewish Thought*. New York University Press, 1984.

Katz-Balakirsky, Maya, 'A Rabbi, a Priest and a Psychoanalyst: Religion in the Early Psychoanalytic Case History', *Contemporary Jewry* 31 (2011), 3–24.

Kauffman, Tsipi, *"In All Your Ways Know Him": The Concept of God and Avodah be-Gashmiyut in the Early Stages of Hasidism*. Ramat Gan: Bar-Ilan University Press, 2009. [Hebrew]

'The Yemima Method as a Contemporary-Hasidic-Female Movement', *Modern Judaism: A Journal of Jewish Ideas and Experience* 32 (2012), 195–215.

Kiener, Ronald, 'The Image of Islam in the Zohar', *Jerusalem Studies in Jewish Thought* 8 (1989), 43–65.

'The Status of Astrology in the Early Kabbalah: From the "Sefer Yesira" to "the Zohar"', *Jerusalem Studies in Jewish Thought* 6 (1987), 1–42.

Kilcher, Andreas, 'Verhüllung und Enthüllung des Geheimnisses: Die Kabbala Denudata im Okkultismus der Modernein', *Morgen-Glantz* 16 (2006), 343–383.

Kimelman, Reuven, *The Mystical Meaning of Lekhah Dodi and Kabbalat Shabbat*. Jerusalem: Magnes Press, 2002.
Klibansky, Ben-Tsiyon, *The Golden Age of The Lithuanian Yeshivot in Eastern Europe*. Jerusalem: The Zalman Shazar Center, 2014. [Hebrew]
Knapp, Bettina, *Antonin Artaud: Man of Vision*. New York: David Lewis, 1969.
Koch, Patrick B., *Human Self Perfection: A Re-assessment of Kabbalistic Musar-Literature of Sixteenth-Century Safed*. Los Angeles: Cherub Press, 2015.
Kohler, George Y., *Kabbalah Research in the Wissenschaft des Judentums (1820–1880)*. Berlin: De Gruyter, 2019.
Kokin, Daniel S., 'Entering the Labyrinth: On the Hebraic and Kabbalistic Universe of Egidio Da Viterbo', in Ilana Zinguer, Abraham Melamed and Zur Shalev (eds.), *Hebraic Aspects of the Renaissance*. Leiden: Brill, 2011, 27–42.
Kornblatt, Judith, 'Russian Religious Thought and the Jewish Kabbala', in Bernice Rosenthal (ed.), *The Occult in Russian and Soviet Culture*. Ithaca, NY: Cornell University Press, 1997, 75–95.
Krabbenhoft, Kenneth, 'Syncretism and Millennium in Herrera's Kabbalah', in Matt Goldish and Richard H. Popkin (eds.), *Millennialism and Messianism in Early Modern European Culture, Part I: Jewish Messianism in the Early Modern World*. New York: Springer, 2001, 65–76.
Krassen, Miles (ed. and trans.), *Isaiah Horowitz: The Generations of Adam*, Mahwah, NJ: Paulist Press, 1996.
Uniter of Heaven and Earth: Rabbi Meshullam Feibush Heller of Zbarazh and the Rise of Hasidism in Eastern Galicia. Albany: SUNY Press, 1998.
Kriegel, Maurice, 'Theologian of Revolution or Adventurer? A Reassessment of Jacob Frank', *Sefarad* 72 (2012), 491–498.
Krinis, Ehud, 'Cyclical Time in the Ismāʿīlī Circle of Ikhwān al-ṣafāʾ (Tenth Century) and in Early Jewish Kabbalists Circles (Thirteenth and Fourteenth Centuries)', *Studia Islamica* 3 (2016), 20–108.
Kripal, Jeffrey, *Mutants and Mystics: Science Fiction, Superhero Comics and the Paranormal*. The University of Chicago Press, 2011.
Roads of Excess, Palaces of Wisdom: Eroticism and Reflexivity in the Study of Mysticism. The University of Chicago Press, 2001.
Kuhn, Thomas, *The Structure of Scientific Revolutions*, 3rd ed. The University of Chicago Press, 1996.
Lachter, Hartley, *Kabbalistic Revolution: Reimagining Judaism in Medieval Spain*. New Brunswick, NJ: Rutgers University Press, 2014.
Lehmann, Matthias B., *Ladino Rabbinic Literature and Ottoman Sephardic Culture*. Bloomington: Indiana University Press, 2005.
Lehrich, Christopher I., *The Language of Demons and Angels: Cornelius Agrippa's Occult Philosophy*. Leiden: Brill, 2003.

Leiman, Sid Z., 'Rabbi Jonathan Eibeschuetz's Attitude toward the Frankists', *Polin* 15 (2002), 145–151.

'When a Rabbi Is Accused of Heresy: The Stance of the Gaon of Vilna in the Emden-Eibeschuetz Affair', in Ezra Fleischer et al. (eds.), *Mea Shearim: Studies in Medieval Jewish Spiritual Life in Memory of Isadore Twersky*. Jerusalem: Magnes Press, 2011, 251–263.

Lelli, Fabrizio, 'Poetry, Myth, and Kabbala: Jewish and Christian Intellectual Encounters in Late Medieval Italy', *Conversations* 13 (2012), 53–67.

'Prisca Philosophia and Docta Religio: The Boundaries of Rational Knowledge in Jewish and Christian Humanist Thought', *The Jewish Quarterly Review* 91 (2000), 53–100.

Leshem, Zvi, 'Flipping into Ecstasy: Toward a Synacopal Understanding of Mystical Hasidic Somersaults', *Studia Judiaca* 17 (2004), 157–183.

Levin, David Michael, *The Listening Self: Personal Growth, Social Change and the Closure of Metaphysics*. London: Routledge, 1989.

Levine, Hillel, 'Frankism as Worldly Messianism', in Joseph Dan and Peter Schäfer (eds.), *Gershom Scholem's "Major Trends in Jewish Mysticism", 50 Years After*. Tübingen: J. C. B. Mohr, 1993, 283–300.

'"Should Napoleon Be Victorious": Politics and Spirituality in Early Modern Jewish Messianism', *Jerusalem Studies in Jewish Thought* 16–17 (2001), lxv–lxxxiii.

Levy, Ze'ev, 'Utopia and Reality in the Philosophy of Ernst Bloch', *Utopian Studies* 1 (1990), 3–12.

Lewis, Justin Jaron, 'Miracles and Martyrdom: The Theology of a Yiddish-Language Memorial Book of Hasidic Tales in the Context of Earlier Hasidic Historiography', *Jewish Studies: An Internet Journal* 6 (2007), 229–249.

Liebes, Eti, 'The Novelty in Hasidism according to R. Barukh of Kossow', *Da'at* 45 (2000), 75–90 [Hebrew].

Liebes, Yehuda, *Ars Poetica in Sefer Yetsira*. Tel Aviv: Schocken, 2000. [Hebrew]

The Cult of the Dawn: The Attitude of the Zohar towards Idolatry. Jerusalem: Carmel Publishing, 2011. [Hebrew]

'Mysticism and Reality: Towards a Portrait of the Martyr and Kabbalist R. Samson Ostropoler', in Isadore Twersky and Bernard Septimus (eds.), *Jewish Thought in the Seventeenth Century*, Cambridge, MA: Harvard University Press, 1987, 221–256.

'Myth vs. Symbol in the Zohar and Lurianic Kabbalah', in Laurence Fine (ed.), *Essential Papers on Kabbalah*. New York University Press, 1995, 212–242.

'New Directions in the Study of Kabbalah', *Pe'amim: Studies in Oriental Jewry* 50 (1992), 150–170. [Hebrew]

On Sabbateaism and Its Kabbalah: Collected Essays, 2nd revised ed. Jerusalem: Bialik Institute, 2007.

Studies in Jewish Myth and Jewish Messianism, B. Stein (trans.). Albany: SUNY Press, 1993.

Studies in the Zohar, A. Schwartz et al. (trans.). Albany: SUNY Press, 1993.

'Toward a Study of the Author of "Emek Ha-Melekh": His Personality, Writings, and Kabbalah', *Jerusalem Studies in Jewish Thought* 11 (1993), 101–137.

The Zevi and the Gaon: From Sabbatai Zevi to the Gaon of Vilna. Tel Aviv: Idra Press, 2017 [Hebrew].

Liwer, Amira, 'Oral Torah in the Writings of R. Zadok ha-Kohen of Lublin', unpublished Ph.D. dissertation, Hebrew University of Jerusalem, 2006. [Hebrew]

Loewenthal, Naftali, *Communicating the Infinite: The Emergence of the Habad School*. The University of Chicago Press, 1990.

'Early Hasidic Teachings: Esoteric Mysticism or a Medium of Communal Leadership', *Journal of Jewish Studies* 37, 1 (1986), 58–75.

'Women and the Dialectic of Spirituality in Hasidism', in Immanuel Etkes et al. (eds.), *Within Hasidic Circles: Studies in Hasidic in Memory of Mordecai Wilensky*. Jerusalem: Bialik Institute 1999, 9–65.

Lorberbaum, Yair, *In God's Image: Myth, Theology and Law in Classical Judaism*. Cambridge University Press, 2015.

Lurie, Ilia, *The Lubavitch Wars: Chabad Hasidism in Tsarist Russia*. Jerusalem: The Zalman Shazar Center, 2018. [Hebrew]

Maciejko, Pawel, 'The Jews' Entry into the Public Sphere: The Emden-Eibeschütz Controversy Reconsidered', *Simon-Dubnow-Institute Yearbook* 6 (2007), 135–154.

The Mixed Multitude: Jacob Frank and the Frankist Movement 1755–1816. Philadelphia: University of Pennsylvania Press, 2011.

R. Jonathan Eibeschütz: And I Came This Day unto the Fountain, 2nd revised ed. Los Angeles: Cherub Press, 2016. [Hebrew and English]

Sabbatian Heresy: Writings on Mysticism, Messianism and the Origins of European Modernity. Waltham, MA: Brandeis University Press, 2017.

Magee, Glenn Alexander, *Hegel and the Hermetic Tradition*. Ithaca, NY: Cornell University Press, 2001.

Magid, Shaul, '"America Is No Different": "America Is Different": Is There an American Jewish Fundamentalism? Part Two: American Satmar', in David Harrington and Simon A. Wood (eds.), *Fundamentalism: Perspectives on a Contested History*. Chapel Hill: University of South Carolina, 2014, 92–107.

American Post-Judaism: Identity and Renewal in a Post-ethnic Society. Bloomington: Indiana University Press, 2013.

'Conjugal Union, Mourning and *Talmud Torah* in R. Isaac Luria's *Tikkun Hatzot*', *Da'at* 36 (1996), xvii–xlv.

'Deconstructing the Mystical: The Anti-Mystical Kabbalism in Rabbi Hayyim of Volozhin's Nefesh ha-Hayyim', *Journal of Jewish Thought and Philosophy* 9 (2000), 21–67.

'Early Hasidism and the Metaphysics of Malkhut in Yaakov (Lifhitz) Koppel's *Shaarei Gan Eden*', *Kabbalah: Journal for the Study of Jewish Mystical Texts* 27 (2012), 245–268.

'Gershom Scholem's Ambivalence toward Mystical Experience and His Critique of Martin Buber in Light of Hans Jonas and Martin Heidegger', *Journal of Jewish Thought and Philosophy* 4 (1995), 245–269.

Hasidism Incarnate: Hasidism, Christianity and the Construction of Modern Judaism. Stanford University Press, 2014.

Hasidism on the Margin: Reconciliation, Antinomianism, and Messianism in Izbica/Radzin Hasidism. Madison: University of Wisconsin Press, 2003.

From Metaphysics to Midrash: Myth, History, and the Interpretation of Scripture in Lurianic Kabbalah. Bloomington: Indiana University Press, 2008.

'"A Thread of Blue": Rabbi Gershon Henoch Leiner of Radzyn and His Search for Continuity in Response to Modernity', *Polin* 11 (1998), 31–52.

Manor, Dan, 'R. Hayyim ben Attar in Ḥasidic Tradition', *Pe'amim* 20 (1984), 88–110. [Hebrew]

Margolin, Ron, 'The Directives of Rav Ashlag in the Matter of the Dissemination of Kabbalah in English in the United States', *Kabbalah: Journal for the Study of Jewish Mystical Texts* 37 (2017), 197–213.

The Human Temple: Religious Interiorization and the Structuring of Inner Life in Early Hasidism. Jerusalem: Magnes, 2005. [Hebrew]

The Phenomenology of Inner Religious Life and Its Manifestation in Jewish Sources (from the Bible to Hasidic Texts). Ramat Gan and Jerusalem: Bar-Ilan University and Shalom Hartman Institute, 2011. [Hebrew]

Mark, Zvi, (ed.) *The Complete Stories of Rabbi Nacham of Bratslav*. Jerusalem: Bialik Institute, 2014. [Hebrew]

Mark, Zvi, (ed.) '"Mi-Ron": The Secret Story of the Meeting between Rabbi Nachman of Breslov and Rabbi Shimon Bar Yochai', in Yehuda Liebes, Jonatan Benarroch and Melila Hellner-Eshed (eds.), *The Zoharic Story*, 2 vols. Jerusalem: Ben Zvi Institute, 709–763, vol. II [Hebrew]

Mysticism and Madness: The Religious Thought of Rabbi Nachman of Bratslav, Y. D. Shulman (trans.). London: Continuum, 2009.

Revelation and Rectification in the Revealed and Hidden Writings of R. Nahman of Bratslav. Jerusalem: Magnes Press, 2011. [Hebrew]

The Scroll of Secrets: The Hidden Messianic Vision of R. Nachman of Breslav. Brighton, MA: Academic Studies Press, 2010.

'"The Son of David Will Not Come Until the Sovereignty of Aram (Alexander, King of Russia) Rules Over the Entire World for Nine Months":

Messianic Hopes in Gur Hasidism', *Tarbiz: A Quarterly for Jewish Studies* 77 (2008), 295–324. [Hebrew]

Matt, Daniel, '"Ayin": The Concept of Nothingness in Jewish Mysticism', in Robert K. C. Forman (ed.), *The Problem of Pure Consciousness*. New York: Oxford University Press, 1990, 121–159.

'David ben Yehudah Hehasid and His "Book of Mirrors"', *Hebrew Union College Annual* 51 (1980), 129–172.

The Essential Kabbalah: The Heart of Jewish Mysticism. San Francisco: Harper, 1995.

'"Matnita Dilan": A Technique of Innovation in the Zohar', *Jerusalem Studies in Jewish Thought* 3 (1989), 123–145.

'The Mystic and the Mitzvot', in Arthur Green (ed.), *Jewish Spirituality: From the Bible through the Middle Ages*. New York: Crossroads Press, 1986, 367–404.

Mayse, Ariel Evan, *Speaking Infinities: God and Language in the Teachings of Rabbi Dov Ber of Mezritsh*. Philadelphia: Pennsylvania University Press, 2020.

McGinn, Bernard, 'The Language of Love in Jewish and Christian Mysticism', in Steven T. Katz (ed.), *Mysticism and Language*. New York: Oxford University Press, 202–235.

McIntosh, Christopher, *Eliphas Lévi and the French Occult Revival*. Albany: SUNY Press, 2011.

Meilicke, Christine A., 'Abulafianism among the Counterculture Kabbalists', *Jewish Studies Quarterly* 9 (2002), 71–101.

Meir, Jonatan, 'The Beginnings of Kabbalah in America: The Unpublished Manuscripts of R. Levi Isaac Krakovsky', *Aries: Journal for the Study of Western Esotericism* 13 (2013), 237–268.

'*The Book of Visions*: Hillel Zeitlin's Mystical Diary in Light of Unpublished Correspondence', *Alei Sefer* 21 (2010), 149–171. [Hebrew]

'The Boundaries of Kabbalah: R. Yaakov Moshe Hillel and the Kabbalah in Jerusalem', in Boaz Huss (ed.), *Kabbalah and Contemporary Spiritual Revival*. Beer Sheva: Ben Gurion University of the Negev Press, 2011, 161–180.

'Hillel Zeitlin's Zohar: The History of a Translation and Commentary Project', *Kabbalah* 10 (2004), 119–157. [Hebrew]

Imagined Hasidism: The Anti-Hasidic Satire of Joseph Perl. Jerusalem: Bialik Institute, 2013. [Hebrew]

Kabbalistic Circles in Jerusalem (1896–1948), A. Aronsky (trans.). Leiden: Brill, 2016.

'"Lights and Vessels": A New Inquiry into the Circle of Rabbi Kook and the Editors of His Works', *Kabbalah: Journal for the Study of Jewish Mystical Texts* 13 (2005), 163–247. [Hebrew]

'New Discoveries Concerning R. Judah Leib Ashlag', *Kabbalah: Journal for the Study of Jewish Mystical Texts* 20 (2009), 345–368. [Hebrew]

'The Revealed and the Revealed within the Concealed: On the Opposition to the "Followers" of Rabbi Yehudah Ashlag and the Dissemination of Esoteric Literature', *Kabbalah: Journal for the Study of Jewish Mystical Texts* 16 (2007), 151–258. [Hebrew]

'R. Nathan Sternhartz's Liqquṭei Tefilot and the Formation of Bratslav Hasidism', *Journal of Jewish Thought and Philosophy* 24 (2016), 60–94.

'Toward the Popularization of Kabbalah: R. Yosef Hayyim of Baghdad and the Kabbalists of Jerusalem', *Modern Judaism: A Journal of Jewish Ideas and Experience* 33 (2013), 147–172.

Melamed, Itzhak, 'Salomon Maimon and the Rise of Spinozism in German Idealism', *Journal of the History of Philosophy* 42 (2004), 67–96.

'Spinozism, Acosmism and Hasidism: A Closed Circle', in Amit Kravitz and Jörg Noller (eds.), *The Concept of Judaism in German Idealism*. Berlin: Suhrkamp Verlag, 2018, 75–85.

Mendes-Flohr, Paul, *Divided Passions: Jewish Intellectuals and the Experience of Modernity*. Detroit: Wayne State University Press, 1981.

From Mysticism to Dialogue: Martin Buber's Transformation of German Social Thought. Detroit: Wayne State University Press, 1989.

Meroz, Ronit, 'An Anonymous Commentary on Idra Raba by a Member of the Saruq School', *Jerusalem Studies in Jewish Thought* 12 (1996), 307–378. [Hebrew]

'Contrasting Opinions among the Founders of Saruq's School', in Paul B. Fenton and Roland Goetschel (eds.), *Expérience, écriture et théologie dans le judaïsme et les religions du livre*. Paris: Université de Paris-Sorbonne, 2000, 191–202.

'Faithful Transmission versus Innovation: Luria and His Disciples', in Joseph Dan and Peter Schäfer (eds.), *Gershom Scholem's "Major Trends in Jewish Mysticism", 50 Years After*. Tübingen: J. C. B. Mohr, 1993, 257–276.

'Inter-religious Polemics, Messianism and Revelation in the Short Version of Sefer Yezirah', *Da'at* 81 (2016), 1–37. [Hebrew]

'A Journey of Initiation in the Babylonian Layer of *Sefer ha-Bahir*', *Studia Hebraica* 7 (2007), 17–33.

'R. Yisrael Sarug – Luria's Disciple: A Research Controversy Reconsidered', *Da'at* 28 (1992), 41–50. [Hebrew]

'The Saruq School of Kabbalists: A New Historical Interpretation', *Shalem* 7 (2001), 151–193. [Hebrew]

The Spiritual Biography of Rabbi Simeon bar Yochay: An Analysis of the Zohar's Textual Components. Jerusalem: The Bialik Institute, 2018. [Hebrew]

Mertens, Bram, 'This Still Remarkable Book: Franz Joseph Molitor's Judeo-Christian Synthesis', *Journal of Modern Jewish Studies* 1 (2002), 167–181.

Mikaberidze, Alexander, *The Napoleonic Wars: A Global History*. London: Oxford University Press, 2018.
Mirsky, Yehuda, *Rav Kook: Mystic in a Time of Revolution*. New Haven, CT and London: Yale University Press, 2014.
Mittleman, Alan L., *Between Kant and Kabbalah: An Introduction to Isaac Breuer's Philosophy of Judaism*. Albany: SUNY Press, 1990.
Moltmann, Jurgen, *The Coming of God: Christian Eschatology*, M. Kohl (trans.). London: SCM Press, 1996.
The Crucified God: The Cross of Christ as the Foundation and Criticism of Christian Theology. Minneapolis: Fortress Press, 1991.
Mopsik, Charles, *Les grands textes de le cabale: Les rites qui font Dieu*. Paris: Verdier, 1993.
'Union and Unity in Kabbalah', in Hananya Goodman (ed.), *Between Jerusalem and Benares: Comparative Studies in Judaism and Hinduism*. Albany: SUNY Press, 1994, 223–242.
Morgenstern, Arie, *Hastening Redemption: Messianism and the Resettlement of the Land of Israel*, J. Linsider (trans.). New York: Oxford University Press, 2006.
Mysticism and Messianism from Luzzatto to the Vilna Gaon. Jerusalem: Keter, 1999. [Hebrew]
'Between the Sons and the Disciples: The Struggle over the Vilna Gaon's Heritage and over the Ideological Issue of Torah versus the Land of Israel', *Da'at* 53 (2004), 83–124.
Morlok, Elke, 'The Kabbalistic "Teaching Panel" of Princess Antonia: Divine Knowledge for Both Experts and Laity', *Church History and Religious Culture* 98 (2018), 56–90.
Rabbi Joseph Gikatilla's Hermeneutics. Tübingen: Mohr Siebeck, 2011.
'Zwischen Ekstase und Gottesfurcht: Wein in der Kabbala und im Chassidismus', in Andreas Lehnardt (ed.), *Wein und Judentum*. Berlin: Neofelis Verlag, 2014, 121–150.
Moseson, Chaim Elly, 'From Spoken Word to the Discourse of the Academy: Reading the Sources for the Teachings of the Besht', unpublished Ph.D. dissertation, Boston University, 2017.
Mottolese, Maurizio, *Analogy in Midrash and Kabbalah: Interpretive Projections of the Sanctuary and Ritual*. Los Angeles: Cherub Press, 2007.
Bodily Rituals in Jewish Mysticism: The Intensification of Cultic Hand Gestures by Medieval Kabbalists. Los Angeles: Cherub Press, 2016.
Mualem, Shlomy, 'Borges and Kabbalistic Infinity: *Ein Sof* and The Holy Book', in Richard Walsh and Jay Twomey (eds.), *Borges and the Bible*. Sheffield: Sheffield-Phoenix Press, 2015, 81–98.
Myers, David N., 'Philosophy and Kabbalah in *Wissenschaft des Judentums*: Rethinking the Narrative of Neglect', *Studia Judaica* 16 (2008), 56–71.
'The Scholem-Kurzweil Debate', *Modern Judaism: A Journal of Jewish Ideas and Experience* 6 (1986), 261–286.

Myers, Jody, *Kabbalah and the Spiritual Quest: The Kabbalah Center in America*. London: Praeger, 2007.
Nabbaro, Assaf, '"Tikkun": From Lurianic Kabbalah to Popular Culture', unpublished Ph.D. dissertation, Ben Gurion University, 2006.
Nadler, Alan, *The Faith of the Mitnagdim: Rabbinic Responses to Hasidic Rapture*. Baltimore: Johns Hopkins University Press, 1997.
'Holy Kugel: The Sanctification of Ashkenazic Ethnic Foods in Hasidism', *Studies in Jewish Civilization* 15 (2005), 193–214.
Necker, Gerold, *Humanistische Kabbala im Barock: Leben und Werk des Abraham Cohen de Herrera*. Berlin: De Gruyter, 2011.
Neumann, Boaz, *Land and Desire in Early Zionism*. Tel Aviv: 'Am Oved, 2009. [Hebrew]
Nurbhai, Saleel and Newton, Kenneth M., *George Eliot, Judaism and the Novels: Jewish Myth and Mysticism*. New York: Palgrave Macmillan, 2002.
Ogren, Brian (ed.), *Before and After: On Time and Eternity in Jewish Esotericism and Mysticism*. Leiden: Brill, 2015.
The Beginning of the World in Renaissance Jewish Thought: ma'Aseh Bereshit in Italian Jewish Philosophy and Kabbalah, 1492–1535. Leiden: Brill, 2016.
Renaissance and Rebirth: Reincarnation in Early Modern Italian Kabbalah. Leiden: Brill, 2009.
Oron, Michal, 'Kafka und Nachman Von Bratzlav: Erzählen Zwischen Traum und Erwartung', in Karl E. Gözinger, Stéphane Mosès and Hans D. Zimmerman (eds.), *Franz Kafka und das Judentum*. Frankfurt: Athenäum, 1987, 113–121.
Samuel Falk: The Ba'al Shem of London. Jerusalem: Bialik Institute, 2002.
Osterhammel, Jürgen, *The Nineteenth Century: A Global History*, P. Camiller (trans.). Princeton University Press, 2015.
Owen, Alex, *The Place of Enchantment: British Occultism and the Culture of the Modern*. The University of Chicago Press, 2004.
Owens, Lance S., 'Joseph Smith and Kabbalah: The Occult Connection', *Dialogue: A Journal of Mormon Thought* 27 (1994), 117–194.
Pachter, Mordechai (ed.), *Mili de-Shemaya* (by E. Azikri), Tel Aviv University Press, 1991.
'The Musar Movement and the Kabbalah', in David Assaf and Ada Rapoport-Albert (eds.), *Let the Old Make Way for the New*. Jerusalem: Zalman Shazar Center for Jewish History, 2009, vol. 1, 223–250. [Hebrew]
Roots of Faith and Dvekut: Studies in the History of Kabbalistic Ideas. Los Angeles: Cherub Press, 2004.
Paluch, Agata, *Megalle 'Amuqot – The Enoch-Metatron Tradition in the Kabbalah of Nathan Neta Shapira of Kraków (1585–1633)*. Los Angeles: Cherub Press, 2014.

Patai, Raphael, *The Jewish Alchemists: A History and Sourcebook*. Princeton University Press, 1994.

Pedaya, Haviva, 'The Besht, R. Jacob Joseph of Polonoy, and the Maggid of Mezeritch: Basic Lines for a Religious-Typological Approach', *Da'at* 45 (2000), 25–73.

'The Development of the Social-Religious-Economic Model in Hasidism: The Pidyon, the Group, and the Pilgrimage', in David Assaf (ed.), *Zaddik and Devotees: Historical and Sociological Aspects of Hasidism*. Jerusalem: Zalman Shazar Center for Jewish History, 2001, 343–397. [Hebrew]

Expanses: An Essay on the Theological and Political Unconscious. Tel Aviv: Hakkibutz Hameuchad, 2011. [Hebrew]

Kabbalah and Psychoanalysis: An Inner Journey Following the (!) Jewish Mysticism. Tel Aviv: Miskal, 2015. [Hebrew]

Nahmanides: Cyclical Time and Holy Text, Tel Aviv: 'Am 'Oved, 2003. [Hebrew]

Name and Sanctuary in the Teaching of R. Isaac the Blind: A Comparative Study in the Writings of the Earliest Kabbalists. Jerusalem: Magnes Press, 2001. [Hebrew]

'Text and Its Performance in the Poetry of R. Israel Najjara: Banishing Sleep as a Practice of Exile in the Nocturnal Space', in Haviva Pedaya (ed.), *The Piyyut as a Cultural Prism: New Approaches*. Jerusalem: Van Leer Institute; Tel Aviv: Hakibbutz Hameuchad, 2012, 29–67. [Hebrew]

'Two Types of Ecstatic Experience in Hasidism', *Da'at* 55 (2005), 73–108. [Hebrew]

Vision and Speech: Models of Revelatory Experience in Jewish Mysticism. Los Angeles: Cherub Press, 2002.

Walking through Trauma: Rituals of Movement in Jewish Myth, Mysticism and History. Tel Aviv: Resling, 2011. [Hebrew]

Persico, Tomer, *The Jewish Meditative Tradition*. Tel Aviv University Press, 2016. [Hebrew]

Piekraz, Menahem Mendel, *Beginning of Hasidism: Ideological Trends in Derush and Mussar Literature*. Jerusalem: Bialik Institute, 1978. [Hebrew]

Ideological Trends of Hasidism in Poland during the Interwar Period and the Holocaust. Jerusalem: Bialik Institute, 1990. [Hebrew]

Studies in Braslav Hasidism, 2nd ed. Jerusalem: Bialik Institute, 1995. [Hebrew]

Polen, Nehemia, 'The Hasidic Derashah as Illuminate Exegesis', in Michael Zank and Ingrid Anderson (eds.), *The Value of the Particular: Lessons from Judaism and the Modern Jewish Experience*. Leiden: Brill, 2015, 55–70.

Pollock, Benjamin, 'The Kabbalist Problem Is Not Specifically Theological: Franz Rosenzweig on Tsimtsum', www.academia.edu/31780256/The_Kabbalistic_Problem_is_not_Specifically_Theological_Franz_Rosenzweig_on_Tsimtsum.docx.

Popkin, Richard, 'Jewish-Christian Relations in the Sixteenth and Seventeenth Centuries: The Conception of the Messiah', *Jewish History* 6 (1992), 163–177.

'Some Aspects of Jewish-Christian Theological Interchanges in Holland and England 1640–1700', in Johannes van den Berg and Ernestine van der Wall (eds.), *Jewish-Christian Relations in the Seventeenth Century: Studies and Documents*. Dordrecht: Kluwer Academic Publishers, 1988, 3–32.

Porat, Oded, '"A Peace without Interruption": Renewed Speculation in *Sefer Brit ha-Menuha*', *Kabbalah: Journal for the Study of Jewish Mystical Texts* 25 (2011), 223–292. [Hebrew]

Sefer Brit Menuha (Book of Covenant of Serenity): Critical Edition and Prefaces. Jerusalem: Magnes Press, 2016. [Hebrew]

The Works of Iyyun: Critical Editions. Los Angeles: Cherub Press, 2013. [Hebrew]

Putzu, Vadim, 'Bottled Poetry, Quencher of Hopes: Wine as a Symbol and as an Instrument in Safedian Kabbalah and Beyond', unpublished Ph.D. dissertation, Hebrew Union College, 2014.

Quinn, Michael, *Early Mormonism and the Magic World Views*. Salt Lake City: Signature Books, 1998.

Rapoport-Albert, Ada, 'Hagiography with Footnotes: The Writing of History in Hasidism', in Ada Rapoport-Albert and Jacob Neusner (eds.), *Essays in Jewish Historiography*. Gainsville: University of South Florida Press, 1988, 119–159.

'Hasidism after 1772: Structural Continuity and Change', in Ada Rapaport-Albert (ed.), *Hasidism Reappraised: The Social Functions of Mystical Ideals in Judaism*. Oxford: The Littman Library of Jewish Civilization, 1996, 76–140.

Women and the Messianic Heresy of Sabbatai Zevi, 1666–1816. Oxford: Littman Library of Jewish Civilization, 2015.

Ravitzky, Aviezer, *Maimonidean Essays: Society, Philosophy and Nature in Maimonides and His Disciples*. Tel Aviv: Schocken Publishing House, 2006. [Hebrew]

Raviv, Zohar. *Decoding the Dogma within the Enigma: The Life, Works, Mystical Piety and Systematic Thought of Rabbi Moses Cordoeiro (Aka Cordovero; Safed, Israel, 1522–1570)*. Saarbrücken: Verlag, 2008.

Rebiger, Bill, 'Zur Redaktionsgeschichte des "Sefer Razi'el ha-Mal'akh"', *Frankfurter Judaistische Beiträge* 32 (2005), 1–22.

Rechnitzer, Haim O., '"To See God in His Beauty": Avraham Chalfi and the Mystical Quest for the Evasive God', *Journal of Modern Jewish Studies* 10 (2011), 383–400.

Regev, Shaul, 'Practices and Rituals Constituted by Rabbi Yosef Hayim ("Ben Ish Hai") in Babel: Between Halakah and Kabbalah', *Da'at* (2016), 516–541. [Hebrew]

Reiner, Elchanan, 'The Attitude of Ashkenazi Society to the New Science in the Sixteenth Centuries', *Science in Context* 10 (1997), 589–603.

'Wealth, Social Position and the Study of Torah: The Status of the *Kloiz* in Eastern European Jewish Society in the Early Modern Period', *Zion* 58 (1993), 287–328. [Hebrew]

Reiser, Daniel, *Imagery Techniques in Modern Jewish Mysticism*. Berlin: Walter de Gruyter, 2018.

(ed. and trans.) *Sermons from the Years of Rage: The Sermons of the Piaseczno Rebbe from the Warsaw Ghetto, 1939–1942*. Jerusalem: Herzog Academic College, 2017. [Hebrew]

Reiser, Daniel and Mayse, Ariel, *Language of Truth in Mother Tongue: The Yiddish Sermons of Rabbi Yehudah Aryeh Leib Alter*. Jerusalem: Magnes Press (in press).

Robinson, Ira, 'Messianic Prayer Vigils in Jerusalem in the Early Sixteenth Century', *The Jewish Quarterly Review* 72 (1981), 32–42.

Rosen, Michael, *The Quest for Authenticity: The Thought of Reb Simhah Bunim*. Jerusalem: Urim Publications, 2008.

Rosenfeld, Joey, 'A Tribute to Rav Shlomo Elyashiv, Author of Leshem Shevo v-Achloma: On His Ninetieth Yahrzeit', http://seforim.blogspot.co.il/2016/03/a-tribute-to-rav-shlomo-elyashiv-author.html.

Rosman, Moshe (Murray J.), *The Founder of Hasidism: A Quest for the Historical Ba'al Shem Tov*. Berkeley: University of California Press, 1996.

'Hasidism as a Modern Phenomenon: The Paradox of Modernization without Secularization', *Simon Dubnow Yearbook Institute* 6 (2007), 215–224.

How Jewish Is Jewish History? Oxford: Littman Library of Jewish Civilization, 2007.

Ross, Niham, *A Beloved-Despised Tradition: Modern Jewish Identity and Neo-Hasidic Writing at the Beginning of the Twentieth Century*. Beer Sheva: Ben Gurion University Press, 2010. [Hebrew]

Rubin, Dominic, *Holy Russia, Sacred Israel: Jewish-Christian Encounters in Russian Religious Thought*. Brighton, MA: Academic Studies Press, 2010.

Ruderman, David, *A Best-Selling Hebrew Book of the Modern Era: The Book of the Covenant of Pinhas Hurwitz and Its Remarkable Legacy*. Seattle: University of Washington Press, 2014.

Early Modern Jewry: A New Cultural History. Princeton University Press, 2010.

Jewish Thought and Scientific Discovery in Early Modern Europe. New Haven, CT: Yale University Press, 1995.

Kabbalah, Magic and Science: The Cultural Universe of a Sixteenth-Century Jewish Physician. Cambridge, MA: Harvard University Press, 1988.

(ed. and trans.) *A Valley of Vision: The Heavenly Journey of Abraham ben Hananiah Yagel*. Philadelphia: University of Pennsylvania Press, 1990.

Sabbath, Moshe. *Yeshivot Baghdad*, 3 vols. Jerusalem: Makhon Ohel David Sasson, 2019.

Sack, Bracha (ed.), *The Fourth Fountain of the Book "Elimah"*. Beer Sheva: Ben Gurion University Press, 2009. [Hebrew]

'The Influence of Rabbi Moshe Cordovero on Hasidism', *Eshel Beer-Sheva* 3 (1986), 229–246. [Hebrew]

The Kabbalah of R. Moshe Cordovero. Beer Sheva: Ben Gurion University Press, 1995. [Hebrew]

Shomer ha-Pardes: The Kabbalist Rabbi Shabbetai Sheftel Horowitz of Prague. Beer Sheva: Ben Gurion University Press, 2002. [Hebrew].

Solomon Had a Vineyard: God, the Torah and Israel in R. Shlomo Halevi Alkabetz's Writings. Beer Sheva: Ben Gurion University Press, 2018. [Hebrew]

Sacks-Shmueli, Leore, 'A Castilian Debate about the Aims and Limits of Theurgic Practice: Rationalizing Incest in the Zohar, the Writing of R. Joseph Hamadan and R. Moses De León', in Jeremy Brown (ed.), *Accounting for the Commandments in Medieval Judaism*. Leiden: Brill (in press).

Safrai, Uri, '"Give Strength to God": The Daily Prayer Intentions ('Kavanot') according to R. Isaac Luria', unpublished Ph.D. dissertation. Beer Sheva: Ben Gurion University, 2011.

Sagerman, Robert, *The Serpent Kills or the Serpent Gives Life: The Kabbalist Abraham Abulafia's Response to Christianity*. Leiden: Brill, 2011.

Sagiv, Gadi, 'Dazzling Blue: Color Symbolism, Kabbalistic Myth, and the Evil Eye in Judaism', *Numen* 64 (2017), 183–208.

Dynasty: The Chernobyl Hasidic Dynasty and Its Place in the History of Hasidism. Jerusalem: The Zalman Shazar Center for Jewish History, 2004. [Hebrew]

'*Yenuka*: On Child Leaders in Hasidism', *Zion* 76 (2011), 139–178. [Hebrew]

Salmon, Yosef, 'The Precursors of Ultra-Orthodoxy in Galicia and Hungary: Rabbi Menachem Mendel Torem of Rymanów and His Disciples', *Modern Judaism: A Journal of Jewish Ideas and Experience* 36 (2016), 115–143.

Samet, Moshe, *Chapters in the History of Orthodoxy*. Jerusalem: Carmel, 2005. [Hebrew]

Schachter-Shalomi, Zalman, *Spiritual Intimacy: A Study of Counseling in Hasidism*. Northvale, NJ: Jason Aronson, 1991.

Schacter, Jacob J., 'Rabbi Jacob Emden: Life and Major Works', unpublished Ph.D. dissertation, Harvard University, 1988.

'Rabbi Jacob Emden, Sabbatianism, and Frankism: Attitudes towards Christianity in the Eighteenth Century', in Elisheva Carlebach and Jacob J. Schacter (eds.), *New Perspectives on Jewish-Christian Relations*. Leiden: Brill, 2012, 359–396.

Schäfer, Peter. *Mirror of His Beauty: Feminine Images of God from the Bible to the Early Kabbalah*. Princeton University Press, 2004.

The Origins of Jewish Mysticism. Princeton University Press, 2011.

Schatz-Uffenheimer, Rivka, *Hasidism as Mysticism: Quietistic Elements in Eighteenth Century Hasidic Thought*, J. Chipman (trans.). Jerusalem: Magnes Press, 1993.

The Messianic Idea from the Expulsion from Spain. Jerusalem: Magnes Press, 2005. [Hebrew]

Schmidt-Biggemann, Wilhelm, *Geschichte der Christlichen Kabbalah*, 4 vols. Stuttgart-Bad Canstatt: Fromann-Holzboog, 2012–2014.

'Political Theology in Renaissance Christian Kabbalah: Petrus Galatinus and Guillaume Postel', *Hebraic Political Studies* 1 (2006), 286–309.

Scholem, Gershom, *Kabbalah*. New York: Dorset Press, 1987.

On the Kabbalah and Its Symbolism, R. Manheim (trans.). New York: Schocken Books, 1974.

Lurianic Kabbalah: Collected Studies by Gershom Scholem, Daniel Abrams (ed.). Los Angeles: Cherub, 2008.

Major Trends in Jewish Mysticism. New York: Schocken, 1961.

The Messianic Idea and Other Essays on Jewish Spirituality. New York: Schocken, 1971.

On the Mystical Shape of the Godhead, J. Neugroschel (trans). New York: Schocken Books, 1991.

Origins of the Kabbalah, A. Arkush (trans.). Princeton University Press, 1990.

Sabbatai Sevi the Mystical Messiah (1626–1676), R. J. Werblowsky (trans.). Princeton University Press, 1975.

Studies and Texts Concerning the History of Sabbeatianism and Its Metamorphoses. Jerusalem: Bialik Institute, 1974. [Hebrew]

Schor, Avraham A., *Studies in the Doctrine and History of Karlin-Stolin*. Jerusalem: Makhon Beit Aharon ve-Yisrael, 2018. [Hebrew]

Schuchard, Keith Marsha, *Emanuel Swedenborg: Secret Agent on Earth and in Heaven: Jacobites, Jews and Freemasons in Early Modern Sweden*. Leiden: Brill, 2012.

Restoring the Temple of Vision: Kabbalistic Freemasonry and Stuart Culture. Leiden: Brill, 2002.

Schulte, Christoph, *Die Jüdische Aufklärung: Philosophie, Religion, Geschichte*. Munich: Beck Verlag, 2002.

Zimzum: Gott und Weltursprung. Frankfurt am Main: Jüdischer Verlag, 2014.

'Ẓimẓum in the Works of Schelling', *Iyun: The Jerusalem Philosophical Quarterly* 41 (1992), 21–40.

Schwartz, Dov, *Habad's Thought from Beginning to End*. Ramat Gan: Bar-Ilan University Press, 2010. [Hebrew]

The Religious Genius in Rabbi Kook's Thought, E. Levin (trans.). Boston: Academic Studies Press, 2014.
Schwartz, Michael, *Astral Magic in Medieval Jewish Thought*. Ramat Gan: Bar-Ilan University Press, 1999. [Hebrew]
Schwartz, Yossi, 'On Rabbinic Atheism: Caramuel's Critique of Cabala', in Petr Dvořak and Jacob Schmutz (eds.), *Juan Caramuel Lobkowitz: The Last Scholastic Polymath*. Prague: Filosofia, 2008, 129–145.
Secret, François, *Zôhar chez les kabbalistes chrétiens de la Renaissance*. Paris: Mouton, 1964.
Seeman, Don, 'Violence, Ethics and Divine Honor in Modern Jewish Thought', *Journal of the American Academy of Religion* 73 (2005), 1015–1048.
Segal, Avraham, *The Path of Worship: Topics in the Hasidic Kabbalah of Rabbi Tzvi Hirsch of Zydachov*. Jerusalem, 2011. [Hebrew]
Segol, Marla, *Word and Image in Medieval Kabbalah: The Texts, Commentaries and Diagrams of the Sefer Yetsirah*. New York: Palgrave Macmillan, 2012.
Sen-Gupta, Orit, 'Abraham Abulafia: A Jewish Yogi', www.academia.edu/31841362/Abraham_Abulafia_A_Jewish_Yogi.
Seroussi, Edwin, 'Judeo-Islamic Sacred Soundscapes: The "Maqamization" of Eastern Sephardic Jewish Liturgy', in Bernard D. Cooperman and Zvi Zohar (eds.), *Jews and Muslims in the Islamic World*. Bethesda: University of Maryland Press, 2013, 279–302.
'Music', in Marcin Wodziński (ed.), *Studying Hasidism: Sources, Methods, Perspectives*. New Brunswick, NJ: Rutgers University Press, 2019, 197–230.
Sharon, Avital, 'The Hida's Kaballah in His Halachic Writings', unpublished Ph.D. dissertation, The Hebrew University, 2014.
Sharon, Moshe, 'New Religions and Religious Movements: The Common Heritage', in Moshe Sharon (ed.), *Studies in Modern Religions, Religious Movements and the Bābi-Bahā'i Faiths*. Leiden: Brill, 2004, 5–36.
Sharot, Stephen. *Messianism, Mysticism and Magic: A Sociological Analysis of Jewish and Religious Movements*. Chapel Hill: University of North Carolina Press, 1982.
Shavit, Yaacov, *Judaism in the Greek Mirror and the Emergence of the Modern Hellenized Jew*. Tel Aviv: Am Oved, 1992. [Hebrew]
Shilo, Elchanan, *The Kabbalah in the Works of S.Y. Agnon*. Ramat Gan: Bar-Ilan University Press, 2011. [Hebrew]
'Rabbi Yizhak Isaac Haver's Influence on Rabbi Kook's Interpretation of the *Kabbalah*', *Da'at* 79 (2015), 89–111. [Hebrew]
Shokek, Shimeon, 'The Relationship between Sefer ha-Yashar and the Gerona Circle', *Jerusalem Studies in Jewish Thought* 6 (1987), 337–366. [Hebrew]
Shuchat, Raphael, 'The Theory of the General and the Specific in the Thought of R. Itzhak Kahana', *Da'at* 79–80 (2015), 119–135. [Hebrew]

A World Hidden in the Dimensions of Time: The Theory of Redemption of the G'aon of Vilna, Its Sources and Influence on Later Generations. Ramat Gan: Bar-Ilan University Press, 2008 [Hebrew].

Silber, Michael K., 'A Hebrew Heart Beats in Hungary: Akiva Yosef Schlesinger—Ultra-Orthodoxy and Early Jewish Nationalism', in Avi Saguy and Dov Schwartz (eds.), *Mea Shnot Tziyonut Datit* [A Century of Religious Zionism], 3 vols. Ramat Gan: Bar-Ilan University Press, 2003, vol. I, 225–254. [Hebrew]

Sisman, Cengiz, *The Burden of Silence: Sabbatai Sevi and the Evolution of the Ottoman-Turkish Dönmes.* Oxford University Press, 2015.

Sjöberg, Sami, 'Writing in Secret: Kabbalistic Language, Mysticism and Messianic Teleology in Lettrism', *Neohelicon* 39 (2012), 305–319.

Skopcol, Theda, *States and Social Revolutions: A Comparative Analysis of France, Russia and China* (37th ed.). Cambridge University Press, 2015.

Slezkine, Yuri, *The Jewish Century.* Princeton University Press, 2006.

Sluhovsky, Moshe, *Becoming a New Self: Practices of Belief in Early Modern Catholicism.* The University of Chicago Press, 2017.

Sobol, Neta, *Transgression of the Torah and the Rectification of God: The Theosophy of Idra Rabba in the Zohar and Its Unique Status in Thirteenth-Century Kabbalah.* Los Angeles: Cherub Press, 2017. [Hebrew]

Soloveitchik, Haym, 'Pietists and Kibbitzers', *The Jewish Quarterly Review* 96 (2006), 60–64.

Sommer, Benjamin, *Revelation and Authority: Sinai in Jewish Scripture and Tradition.* New Haven, CT: Yale University Press, 2015.

Sorotzkin, David, *Orthodoxy and Modern Disciplination: The Production of the Jewish Tradition in Europe in Modern Times.* Tel Aviv: Hakibbutz Hameuchad, 2011. [Hebrew]

Spivak, Gayatri C., *Outside in the Teaching Machine.* New York: Routledge, 1993.

Stahl, Neta, 'Uri Zvi before the Cross: The Figure of Jesus in the Poetry of Uri Zvi Greenberg', *Religion and Literature* 40 (2008), 49–80.

Stampfer, Shaul, 'How and Why Did Hasidism Spread', *Jewish History* 27 (2013), 201–219.

Steadman, John, 'Adam and the Prophesied Redeemer ("Paradise Lost", XII, 359–623)', *Studies in Philology* 56 (1959), 214–225.

Steinbock, Anthony J., *Phenomenology and Mysticism: The Verticality of Religious Experience.* Bloomington: Indiana University Press, 2007.

Steiner, George, *After Babel: Aspects of Language and Translation.* New York: Oxford University Press, 1975.

Stern, Eliyahu, *The Genius: Elijah of Vilna and the Making of Modern Judaism.* New Haven, CT: Yale University Press, 2013.

Jewish Materialism: The Intellectual Revolution of the 1870's. Yale University Press, 2018.

Stroumsa, Guy, 'A Zoroastrian Origin to the Sefirot?', *Irano-Judaica* 3 (1994), 17–33.

Styers, Randall, *Making Magic: Religion, Magic and Science in the Modern World*. Oxford University Press, 2004.

Talar, Charles T. J. (ed.), *Modernists and Mystics*, Washington, DC: Catholic University of America Press, 2009.

Tamar, David, *Eshkolot Tamar: Studies of the History of Safed and Its Sages and the Luminaries of Later Generations*, M. Riegler (ed.). Jerusalem: Rubin Mass, 2002 [Hebrew].

Tamari, Assaf, 'The Body Discourse of Lurianic Kabbalah', unpublished Ph.D. dissertation, Ben Gurion University, 2016.

Teller, Adam, 'Hasidism and the Challenge of Geography: The Polish Background to the Spread of the Hasidic Movement', *AJS Review* 30 (1996), 1–29.

Thon, Johannes, 'The Power of (Hebrew) Language: Grammar, Kabbalah, Magic and the Emerging Protestant Identity', *European Journal of Jewish Studies* 6 (2012), 105–122.

Thurschwell, Pamela, *Literature, Technology and Magical Thinking 1880–1920*. Cambridge University Press, 2004.

Tirosh-Samuelson, Hava, *Between Worlds: The Life and Thought of Rabbi David ben Judah Messer Leon*. Albany: SUNY Press, 1991.

'Kabbalah and Science in the Middle Ages: Preliminary Remarks', in Gad Freudenthal (ed.), *Science in Medieval Jewish Cultures*. New York: Cambridge University Press, 2011, 476–510.

'Philosophy and Kabbalah: 1200–1600', in Daniel H. Frank and Oliver Leaman (eds.), *The Cambridge Companion of Medieval Jewish Philosophy*. Cambridge University Press, 2003, 218–257.

Tishby, Isaiah, *The Doctrine of Evil in Lurianic Kabbalah*. Jerusalem: Schocken, 1942. [Hebrew]

'Gnostic Doctrines in 16th Century Jewish Mysticism', *Journal of Jewish Studies* 6 (1955), 146–152.

Messianic Mysticism: Moses Hayim Luzzatto and the Padua School, M. Hoffman (trans.). Oxford: Littman Library of Jewish Civilization, 2008.

Paths of Faith and Heresy: Essays in Kabbalah and Sabbateanism. Jerusalem: Magnes Press, 1994. [Hebrew]

Studies in Kabbalah and Its Branches, 3 vols. Jerusalem: Magnes Press, 1993. [Hebrew]

The Wisdom of the Zohar: An Anthology of Texts, D. Goldstein (trans.), 2 vols. Oxford: The Littman Library of Jewish Civilization, 1989.

Tobi, Yosef, 'Two Poems on Sabbatean Events in Yemen – A Sabbatean Poem by R. Shlom Shabbazi and a Poem by R. Sa'adia Demarmari', *Pe'amim* 44 (1990), 53–64.

Tourov, Igor, 'Hasidism and Christianity of the Eastern Territory of the Polish-Lithuanian Commonwealth: Possible Contacts and Mutual Influences', *Kabbalah: Journal for the Study of Jewish Mystical Texts* 10 (2004), 73–105.

Tuchman, Barbara, *Bible and Sword: England and Palestine from the Bronze Age to Balfour*. New York: Ballantine Books, 1984.

Twersky, Isadore, 'Law and Spirituality: A Case Study in R. Yair Hayyim Bacharach', in Isadore Twersky and Bernard Septimus (eds.), *Jewish Thought in the Seventeenth Century*. Cambridge, MA: Harvard University Press, 1987, 447–467.

'Talmudists, Philosophers, Kabbalists: The Quest for Spirituality in the Sixteenth Century', in Bernard Cooperman (ed.), *Jewish Thought in the Sixteenth Century*. Cambridge, MA: Harvard University Press, 1983, 431–457.

Tworek, Wojciech, *Eternity Now: Rabbi Shneur Zalman of Liady and Temporality*. Albany: SUNY Press, 2019.

Tzfatman, Sara, *Jewish Exorcism in Early Modern Ashkenaz*. Jerusalem: Magnes Press, 2015. [Hebrew]

Tzoref, Avi-Ram, 'The Flâneur in Baghdad: The Wandering Experience in One of R. Yosef Haim's Talmudic Exegeses', *Theory and Criticism* 48 (2017), 105–126. [Hebrew]

Urban, Martina, *Aesthetics of Renewal: Martin Buber's Early Representation of Hasidism as Kulturkritik*. The University of Chicago Press, 2008.

Vajda, Georges, 'Un Chapitre de l'histoire du conflit entre la Kabbale et la Philosophie: la Polemique anti-intellectualiste de Joseph b. Shalom Ashkenazi', *Archives d'histoire doctrinale et littéraire du Moyen Age* 23 (1956), 45–127.

'Passages anti-chrétiens dans "Kaf ha-qetoret"', *Revue de l'historie des religions* 197 (1980), 45–58.

Valabregue-Perry, Sandra, *Concealed and Revealed: 'Ein Sof' in Theosophic Kabbalah*. Los Angeles: Cherub Press, 2010. [Hebrew]

Van der Haven, Alexander, *From Lowly Metaphor to Divine Flesh: Sarah the Ashkenazi, Sabbatai Tsevi's Messianic Queen and the Sabbatian Movement*. Amsterdam: Menasseh ben Israel Institut, 2012.

Van der Heide, Albert, 'PARDES: Methodological Reflections on the Theory of the Four Senses', *Journal of Jewish Studies* 34 (1983), 147–159.

Van der Veer, Peter, *The Modern Spirit of Asia: The Spiritual and the Secular in China and India*. Princeton University Press, 2014.

Verman, Mark, 'The Development of Yihudim in Spanish Kabbalah', *Jerusalem Studies in Jewish Thought* 3 (1989), 25–41.

The History and Varieties of Jewish Meditation. Northvale, NJ and London: Jason Aronson, 1996.

Versluis, Arthur, *The Esoteric Origins of the American Renaissance*. Oxford University Press, 2001.

Wasserstrom, Steven, 'The Great Goal of the Political Will: Ernst Jünger and the Cabala of Enmity', in Boaz Huss (ed.), *Kabbalah and Modernity: Interpretations, Transformations, Adaptations*. Leiden: Brill, 2010, 403–437.

Weidner, Daniel, *Gershom Scholem: Politisches, Esoterisches und Historiographisches*. Munich: Wilhelm Fink Verlag, 2003.

Weinstein, Roni, 'Jewish Modern Law and Legalism in a Global Age: The Case of Rabbi Joseph Karo', *Modern Intellectual History* (2018), 1–18. doi:10.1017/S1479244318000264.

Juvenile Sexuality, Kabbalah, and Catholic Religiosity among Jewish Italian Communities. "Glory of Youth" by Pinhas Baruch b. Pelatya Monselice (Ferrara, XVII Century). Leiden: Brill, 2008.

Kabbalah and Jewish Modernity. Oxford: Littman Library of Jewish Civilization, 2016.

'The Rise of the Body in Early Modern Jewish Society: The Italian Case Study', in Maria Diemling and Giuseppe Veltri (eds.), *The Jewish Body: Corporeality, Society, and Identity in the Renaissance and Early Modern Period*. Leiden: Brill, 2009, 15–55.

Weisler, Chava, 'Woman as High Priest: A Kabbalistic Prayer in Yiddish for Lighting Sabbath Candles', in Lawrence Fine (ed.), *Essential Papers on Kabbalah*. New York University Press, 1995, 525–546.

Weiss, Joseph G., *Studies in Braslav Hasidism*, 3rd ed. Jerusalem: Bialik Press, 2016 [Hebrew].

Studies in Eastern European Jewish Mysticism and Hasidism, D. Goldstein (ed.). London: The Littman Library of Jewish Civilization, 1997.

Weiss, Judith, *On the Conciliation of Nature and Grace: A Latin Translation and Commentary on the Zohar by Guillaume Postel (1510–1581)*. Jerusalem: Magnes Press, 2017. [Latin and Hebrew]

A Kabbalistic Christian Messiah in the Renaissance: Guillaume Postel and the Book of the Zohar. Tel Aviv: Hakibbutz Hameuchad Publishing House, 2016. [Hebrew]

Ta'am ha-Te'Amim by Guillaume Postel (1510–1581): Introduction and an Annotated Edition. Jerusalem: Magnes Press, 2018. [Hebrew]

'Two Zoharic Versions of the Legend "The Tana and the Deadman"', *Tarbiz: A Quarterly for Jewish Studies* 78 (2009), 521–554. [Hebrew]

Weiss, Tzahi, *Cutting the Shoots: The Worship of the Shekhinah in the World of Early Kabbalistic Literature*. Jerusalem: Magnes Press, 2015. [Hebrew]

Death of the Shekhinah: Readings in Four Agnon Stories and in Their Sources. Ramat Gan: Bar-Ilan University Press, 2009. [Hebrew]

'Listening to the Silent Crying of the Shekhinah: Mysticism in Modern Hebrew Literature – Between Textual Influence and Mythical Narrative', in Avi Elkayam and Shlomy Mualem (eds.), *Kabbalah, Mysticism and*

Poetry: The Journey to the End of Vision. Magnes Press: Jerusalem, 2015, 527–546. [Hebrew]

Werblowsky, Raphael Jehudah Z., 'A Collection of Prayers and Devotional Compositions by Solomon Alkabets', *Sefunot* 6 (1962), 135–182. [Hebrew]

Joseph Karo: Lawyer and Mystic. Philadelphia: The Jewish Publication Society, 1962.

'Milton and the Conjectura Cabbalistica', *Journal of the Warburg and Courtauld Institutes* 18 (1955), 90–113.

Werczberger, Rachel, *Jews in the Age of Authenticity: Jewish Spiritual Renewal in Israel*. New York: Peter Lang Publishing, 2017.

Wexler, Philip, *Mystical Sociology: Toward Cosmic Social Theory*. New York: Peter Lang Publishing, 2013.

Wilensky, Mordechai L., 'Hasidic-Mitnaggedic Polemics in the Jewish Communities of Eastern Europe: The Hostile Phase', in Gershon Hundert (ed.), *Essential Papers on Hasidism: Origins to Present*. New York University Press, 1991, 244–271.

Williams, Raymond, *Keywords: A Vocabulary of Culture and Society*, revised ed. New York: Oxford University Press, 1983.

Marxism and Literature. Glasgow: Oxford University Press, 1977.

Wilson, Leigh, *Modernism and Magic: Experiments with Spiritualism, Theosophy and the Occult*. Edinburgh University Press, 2013.

Wineman, Aryeh, *The Hasidic Parable*. Philadelphia: The Jewish Publication Society, 2011.

Wirshubsky, Chaim, *Between the Lines: Kabbalah, Christian Kabbalah and Sabbatianism*, Moshe Idel (ed.). Jerusalem: Magnes Press, 1990. [Hebrew]

Wiskind-Elper, Ora, *Tradition and Fantasy in the Tales of R. Nahman of Bratslav*. Albany: SUNY Press, 1998.

Wisdom of the Heart: The Teachings of Rabbi Ya'akov of Izbica-Radzyn. Philadelphia: The Jewish Publication Society, 2010.

Wodziński, Marcin, *Hasidism and Politics: The Kingdom of Poland, 1815–1864*. Portland, OR: Littman Library of Jewish Civilization, 2013.

Wodziński, Marcin and Gellman, Uriel, 'Toward a New Geography of Hasidism', *Jewish History* 27 (2013), 171–199.

Wolfson, Elliot R., *Abraham Abulafia, Kabbalist and Prophet: Hermeneutics, Theosophy, and Theurgy*. Los Angeles: Cherub Press, 2000.

Along the Path: Studies in Kabbalistic Myth, Symbolism, and Hermeneutics. Albany: SUNY Press, 1995.

'Beyond the Spoken Word: Oral Tradition and Written Transmission in Medieval Jewish Mysticism', in Yaakov Elman and Israel Gershony (eds.), *Transmitting Jewish Traditions: Orality, Textuality, and Cultural Diffusion*. New Haven, CT: Yale University Press, 2000, 166–224.

'Building a Sanctuary of the Heart: The Kabbalistic-Pietistic Teachings of Itamar Schwartz', in Boaz Huss (ed.), *Kabbalah and Contemporary*

Spiritual Revival. Beer Sheva: Ben Gurion University of the Negev Press, 2011, 141–162.

Circle in the Square: Studies in the Use of Gender in Kabbalistic Symbolism. Albany: SUNY Press, 1995.

'Circumcision, Vision of God, and Textual Interpretation: From Midrashic Trope to Mystical Symbol', *History of Religions* 27 (1987), 189–215.

'Constructions of the Feminine in the Messianic Theosophy of Abraham Cardoso with an Annotated Edition of *Derush ha-Shekinha*', *Kabbalah: Journal for the Study of Jewish Mystical Texts* 3 (1998), 11–143.

'Divine Suffering and the Hermeneutics of Reading: Philosophical Reflections on Lurianic Mythology', in Robert Gibbs and Elliot R. Wolfson (eds.), *Suffering Religion*. London: Routledge, 2002, 101–162.

A Dream Interpreted within a Dream: Oneiropoiesis and the Prism of Imagination. New York: Zone Books, 2011.

'The Engenderment of Messianic Politics: The Symbolic Significance of Sabbatai Sevi's Coronation', in Peter Schäfer and Mark Cohen (eds.), *Toward the Millennium: Messianic Expectations from the Bible to Waco.* Leiden: Brill, 1998, 203–258.

'Eternal Duration and Temporal Compresence: The Influence of Habad on R. Joseph B. Soloveitchik', in Michael Zank and Ingrid Anderson (eds.), *The Value of the Particular: Lessons from Judaism and the Modern Jewish Experience*. Leiden: Brill, 2015, 195–238.

'The Holy Kabbalah of Changes: Jacob Böhme and Jewish Esotericism', *Aries: Journal for the Study of Western Esotericism* 18 (2018), 21–53.

'Iconicity of the Text: Reification of Torah and the Idolatrous Impulse of Zoharic Kabbalah', in Hava Tirosh-Samuelson and Aaron Hughes (eds.), *Elliot R. Wolfson: Poetic Thinking*. Leiden: Brill, 2015, 69–96.

'Immanuel Frommann's Commentary on Luke and the Christianizing of Kabbalah: Some Sabbatian and Hasidic Affinities', in Glenn Dynner (ed.), *Holy Dissent: Jewish and Christian Mystics in Eastern Europe*. Detroit: Wayne State University Press, 2011.

Language, Eros, Being: Kabbalistic Hermeneutics and Poetic Imagination. New York: Fordham University Press, 2005.

'Language, Secrecy and the Mysteries of Law: Theurgy and the Christian Kabbalah of Johannes Reuchlin', *Kabbalah: Journal for the Study of Jewish Mystical Texts* 13 (2005), 7–41.

Luminal Darkness: Imaginal Gleanings from Zoharic Literature. Oxford: One World Publications, 2007.

'Messianism in the Christian Kabbalah of Johann Kemper', in Matt Goldish and Richard H. Popkin (eds.), *Millenarianism and Messianism in Early Modern European Culture, Part I: Jewish Messianism in the Early Modern World*, New York: Springer, 2001, 139–187.

'Murmuring Secrets: Eroticism and Esotericism in Medieval Kabbalah', in Woulter J. Hanegraaff and Jeffrey J. Kripal (eds.), *Hidden Intercourse: Eros and Sexuality in the History of Western Esotericism*. Leiden: Brill, 2008, 65–109.

'New Jerusalem Glowing: Songs and Poems of Leonard Cohen in a Kabbalistic Key', *Kabbalah: Journal for the Study of Jewish Mystical Texts* 15 (2006), 103–153.

'Not Yet Now: Speaking of the End and the End of Speaking', in Hava Tirosh-Samuelson and Aaron Hughes (eds.), *Elliot R. Wolfson: Poetic Thinking*. Leiden: Brill, 2015, 127–193.

Open Secret: Postmessianic Messianism and the Mystical Revision of Menahem Mendel Schneerson. New York: Columbia University Press, 2009.

'Patriarchy and the Motherhood of God in Zoharic Kabbalah and Meister Eckhart', in Ra'anan S. Boustan et al. (eds.), *Envisioning Judaism: Studies in Honor of Peter Schäfer on the Occasion of His Seventieth Birthday*. Tübingen: Mohr Siebeck, 2013, 1049–1088.

'Review of Moshe Halbertal, Concealment and Revelation: Esotericism in Jewish Thought and Its Philosophical Implications', *Journal of Religion in Europe* 2 (2009), 314–318.

'From Sealed Book to Open Text: Time, Memory and Narrativity in Kabbalistic Hermeneutics', in Steven Kepnes (ed.), *Interpreting Judaism in a Postmodern Age*. New York: New York University Press, 145–178.

'Structure, Innovation, and Diremptive Temporality: The Use of Models to Study Continuity and Discontinuity in Kabbalistic Tradition', *Journal for the Study of Religions and Ideologies* 18 (2007), 143–167.

Through a Speculum That Shines: Vision and Imagination in Medieval Jewish Mysticism. Princeton University Press, 1994.

Venturing Beyond: Law and Morality in Kabbalistic Mysticism. Oxford University Press, 2006.

'Weeping, Death, and Spiritual Ascent in Sixteenth Century Jewish Mysticism', in John J. Collins and Michael Fishbane (eds.), *Death, Ecstasy, and Otherworldly Journeys*. Albany: SUNY Press, 1995, 209–247.

'Woman – The Feminine as Other in Theosophic Kabbalah: Some Philosophical Observations on the Divine Androgyne', in Laurence J. Silberstein and Robert L. Cohn (eds.), *The Other in Jewish Thought and Identity*. New York University Press, 1994, 166–204.

Yaakov, Efraim, *God Came from Yemen: The History of the Kabbalah in Yemen*, Meir Bar-Asher (ed.). Jerusalem: Ben Zvi Institute, 2016. [Hebrew]

Yassif, Eli, *The Hebrew Folktale: History, Genre, Meaning*, J. Teitelbaum (trans.). Bloomington: Indiana University Press, 1999.

Yates, Frances, *Giordano Bruno and the Hermetic Tradition*. London: Routledge, 1964.

Yayama, Kumiku, 'The Singing of *Baqqashot* of the Aleppo Jewish Tradition: The Modal System and the Vocal Style', 2 vols., unpublished Ph.D. dissertation, Hebrew University of Jerusalem, 2003, vol. I.

Yosha, Nissim, *Captivated by Messianic Agonies: Theology, Philosophy and Messianism in the Thought of Abraham Miguel Cardozo*. Jerusalem: Ben Zvi Institute, 2015. [Hebrew]

Myth and Metaphor: Abraham Cohen Herrera's Philosophic Interpretation of Lurianic Kabbalah. Jerusalem: Magnes Press, 1994. [Hebrew]

Zadoff, Noam, *From Berlin to Jerusalem and Back*. Waltham, MA: Brandeis University Press, 2017.

Zimmer, Eric, *The Fiery Embers of the Scholars: The Trials and Tribulations of German Rabbis in the Sixteenth and Seventeenth Centuries*. Bialik Institute: Jerusalem, 1999. [Hebrew]

Index

Made in the USA
Middletown, DE
20 October 2023

41124857R00198